C000299166

'CLOTHING FOR THE SOUL DIVINE': BURIALS AT THE TOMB OF ST NINIAN

Archaeology Report no 3

'CLOTHING FOR THE SOUL DIVINE': BURIALS AT THE TOMB OF ST NINIAN

Excavations at Whithorn Priory, 1957–67

Archaeology Report no 3

CHRISTOPHER LOWE

with specialist contributions by

Carol Christiansen, Gordon Cook, Magnar Dalland, Kirsty Dingwall, Julie Franklin, Virginia Glenn, David Henderson, Janet Montgomery, Gundula Müldner and Richard Oram

illustrations by

Caroline Norrman, Marion O'Neil, Thomas Small and Craig Williams

Edinburgh 2009

Cover photo by David Henrie, Historic Scotland; with inset of the Whithorn crozier © National Museums Scotland.
Licensor www.scran.ac.uk

Published in 2009 by Historic Scotland

Historic Scotland
Longmore House, Salisbury Place
Edinburgh, EH9 1SH
Tel 0131 668 8600
Email: hs.inspectorate@scotland.gsi.gov.uk
Website: www.historic-scotland.gov.uk

British Library Cataloguing-in-Publication Data
A catalogue record for this book is available from the British Library.

ISBN 978 1 84917 017 8

Design, typesetting and production by Lawrie Law, Alison Rae and Headland Archaeology Ltd
Manufactured in Malta by Gutenberg Press Ltd

Contents

Foreword

This report documents the results of one of the most important excavation projects of the medieval period in Scotland, made all the more important by the fact that for decades it was thought to be unpublishable. The timing of publication is especially auspicious, in the year following the centenary anniversary of State care at Whithorn.

The excavations were led by Roy Ritchie between 1957 and 1967, when he was an Assistant Inspector of Ancient Monuments for the predecessor body of Historic Scotland. Although part of the excavated assemblage – the renowned crozier, silver-gilt altar plate and bishops' rings – became an important part of the collections of the National Museums of Scotland, the essential analysis and publication of the wider results faltered. The excavation records became dispersed, and as a consequence the greater part of the finds assemblage, notably the human remains, went into safe storage and were largely forgotten.

A fortunate set of circumstances combined when Peter Yeoman was the area Inspector with a heightened focus on Whithorn, brought about by the project to redisplay the collection of early Christian carved stones. At the same time, Dr Virginia Glenn confirmed the location of the finds assemblage. Peter Yeoman realised, as others had before, the tremendous importance of Ritchie's work as the only modern investigations of this key part of the monument – the choir of the later medieval cathedral priory church. As Headland's excellent report demonstrates, these excavations allow a better understanding of the development of the east end of the church, coupled with the full pathological examination of the only group of high-status clerics ever discovered in Scotland.

These fascinating results give an insight into the archaeology of the church, and into the lives and deaths of some of its bishops, canons and patrons. Balanced with the results of the excavations within the early precinct of the 1980s and 1990s, we now have a more rounded appreciation of the core of the monastic complex, albeit of the later medieval period only. But the story will not end here; Historic Scotland remains committed to unravelling more of the complex development of Scotland's Cradle of Christianity, working alongside our valued partners in the Whithorn Trust, as we enter our second century of caring for Whithorn Priory.

Peter Bromley
Director of Properties in Care
Historic Scotland

Acknowledgements

It was only in 2005 that it became possible to complete the project that Roy Ritchie had started in 1957. As a result of the assistance and efforts of Historic Scotland in locating both the finds assemblage and parts of the excavation documentary record, as complete a story as possible of what has been one of Scotland's 'lost excavations' can now be told for the first time.

In 1957, Ritchie was an Inspector of Ancient Monuments in the Ministry of Public Buildings and Works, one of the predecessor bodies to today's Historic Scotland (HS). Although Ritchie had compiled and completed parts of the archive necessary to enable publication, unfortunately he was never able to achieve this in his lifetime. At his death in 2006, his family was kind enough to hand over a large volume of material, of which Whithorn formed only one part, to the National Museums Scotland (NMS). Dr David Clarke of NMS worked in partnership with HS to catalogue this material, with the portion relevant to HS-funded projects being passed back to HS. The finds assemblage had already been assigned to NMS and, indeed, appears to have been deposited there directly during the excavation and then reported to Treasure Trove in 1968. The ecclesiastical objects, including the crozier, were conserved and displayed; the rest were placed in store, no doubt awaiting Ritchie's final analysis. At the same time, Ritchie had also passed the site drawings to NMS. The various components of the archive were reassembled by Peter Yeoman of HS. Headland Archaeology successfully tendered for the first phase of works in 2005, involving assessment of the archive, as well as the post-excavation analysis and publication project which followed in 2006, culminating in this monograph.

Particular thanks are due to HS for funding this project, to NMS for facilitating study of the material in Chambers Street, and to the Bishops' Graves Project Management Group, led by Peter Yeoman. Meetings of the Management Group were attended by Peter Yeoman, Adrian Cox, Jane Flint, Doreen Grove, Chris Tabraham and Richard Welander (from HS); David Caldwell, Jane Clark, Virginia Glenn, Jackie Moran and Jim Tate (from NMS); as well as members of the Headland Project Team who were brought in as required. Thanks are also due to Peter Yeoman and Chris Tabraham for refereeing this volume.

My thanks too to all the various specialists for their contributions to this project. Particular thanks must go to Kirsty Dingwall, who acted as research assistant on this project, for getting to grips with the archive in its entirety so that she could field the most obscure of my and others' enquiries. Thanks too to Craig Williams for his fine technical drawing of the Whithorn Crozier and to Mike Middleton, then Headland's Graphics Manager, for devising the methodology for its illustration (then used by Marion O'Neil for her drawings of the crozier). Although numerous photographs of the crozier have been previously published, we now have for the first time a comprehensive illustrative record of the crozier, both in terms of its iconographic content and its appearance.

Also, my thanks to Magnar Dalland for taking on the Bayesian statistical analyses of the radiocarbon dates; to Dr Scott Timpany, Headland's Environmental Department Manager for co-ordinating the isotope work and undertaking the wood identifications; and to Andrea Smith for co-ordinating the final graphics work and typesetting, and to Caroline Norrman for the typesetting itself. Finally, my thanks to Alison Rae and Lawrie Law for seeing this through the publication process. As ever, any remaining errors, inconsistencies or idiosyncrasies will almost certainly be mine.

Chris Lowe
15 April 2009
Edinburgh

Acknowledgements (VG)

I should like to thank the following for their expert help and opinion: Marion Campbell and Lesley Miller, Victoria & Albert Museum, London; John Cherry, British Museum; Geoff Egan, Museum of London; Victoria Harrison, Collections Manager, York Minster; Geoffrey Barrow, University of Edinburgh; Beatrice Paolozzi Strozzi, Museo Nazionale del Bargello, Florence; Claudia Bolgia, University of Edinburgh.

Acknowledgements (CC)

Grateful appreciation to Dr Jim Tate and Lore Troalen of the Department of Conservation and Analytical Research, National Museums Scotland, for use of laboratory facilities, carrying out SEM analysis, and micro-photography. All images supplied with this report are copyright the Department of Conservation and Analytical Research, NMS.

Acknowledgements (JF)

My thanks to David Caldwell, Jackie Moran and Chris Tabraham for their help during this project; to Nicholas Holmes and Colin Wallace for their work, respectively, on the coins and the sherd of samian pottery; to Fraser Hunter for his comments on the prehistoric pottery; and to George Haggarty, particularly for his advice on the French wares.

Acknowledgements (KD)

Special thanks to Michelle Andersson of Historic Scotland's Image Library for all her help in sourcing the original photographs from the excavation and providing digital versions at a moment's notice. Thanks also to Margaret Wilson of National Museums Scotland for her help in sourcing photographs of the Whithorn material; finally to Leslie Smith FSA of the Monumental Brass Society for bringing the Greenhill paper to our attention and for providing advice and comment on the indented slabs.

List of contributors

DR CAROL CHRISTIANSEN	Shetland Museum & Archives, Hays Dock, Lerwick, Shetland, ZE1 0WP
PROFESSOR GORDON COOK	SUERC Radiocarbon Dating Laboratory, Rankine Avenue, Scottish Enterprise Technology Park, East Kilbride G75 0QF
MAGNAR DALLAND	Headland Archaeology Ltd, 13 Jane Street, Edinburgh EH6 5HE
KIRSTY DINGWALL	Headland Archaeology Ltd, 13 Jane Street, Edinburgh EH6 5HE
JULIE FRANKLIN	Headland Archaeology Ltd, 13 Jane Street, Edinburgh EH6 5HE
DR VIRGINIA GLENN	Department of Scotland and Europe, National Museums Scotland, Chambers Street, Edinburgh, EH1 1JF
DAVID HENDERSON	Flat 19, 1 Chapel Lane, Leith, Edinburgh EH6 6ST
DR CHRISTOPHER LOWE	Headland Archaeology Ltd, 13 Jane Street, Edinburgh EH6 5HE
DR JANET MONTGOMERY	Division of Archaeological, Geographical & Environmental Sciences School of Life Sciences, University of Bradford, Bradford BD7 1DP
DR GUNDULA MÜLDNER	Department of Archaeology, University of Reading, Whiteknights, PO Box 227, Reading RG6 6AB
CAROLINE NORRMAN	Headland Archaeology Ltd, 13 Jane Street, Edinburgh EH6 5HE
MARION O'NEIL	National Museum Scotland, Chambers Street, Edinburgh EH1 1JF
PROFESSOR RICHARD ORAM	Department of History, University of Stirling, Stirling, FK9 4LA
THOMAS SMALL	Headland Archaeology Ltd, 13 Jane Street, Edinburgh EH6 5HE
CRAIG WILLIAMS	British Museum, Great Russell Street, London WC1B 3DG

List of figures

List of plates

List of tables

Chapter 1

The Background to the Project

CHRISTOPHER LOWE

1.1 INTRODUCTION

Whithorn Priory, near the south end of the Machars peninsula in south-west Galloway (Figure 1.1), is the site of the earliest recorded Christian church in what is now Scotland. The antiquity of this claim has traditionally relied on the testimony of Bede. In his *Historia Ecclesiastica* (HE iii, 4), completed before 731, he refers to the place which was known as *Candida Casa*, as 'the White House, because Ninian built a church of stone there, using a method unusual among the Britons' (Colgrave & Mynors 1979, 223). Although the chronology is not precise, it is clear that Bede was referring back to a period, prior to 565, that he recognised as 'long ago'. A 5th-century floruit for Ninian is usually assumed. Meanwhile, contemporary evidence for the presence here in the 5th century of an Early Christian community is provided by the inscription on the '*Latinus* Stone', with its introductory exclamation *Te Dominum laudamus.* Indeed, it was this link with the past and particularly the link with the cult of Ninian that made Whithorn one of the premier places of pilgrimage in the country in the later medieval period (Yeoman 1999, 39–41).

As we shall see, fragments of this story resonate with some of the things that Roy Ritchie found during the course of his excavations. Evidence for the circulation of pilgrims between the presbytery of the later medieval cathedral church and the crypt below is marked by his rediscovery of the north ambulatory staircase and his likely identification of a second matching stair to the south. The early part of Whithorn's chronology, what might be termed the *Candida Casa* phase, however, is noticeably absent despite the proximity of Ritchie's trench to the low stone foundations that Galloway had found in the 1890s below and to the east of the 13th-century priory church, and which Radford and others have described as part of the Ninianic or early settlement (Radford 1949, 119; Radford 1956, 181; Cruden 1963; Cruden 1986, 90, Fig. 7). Indeed, attempts have been made to accommodate the unpublished results of Ritchie's work within this early chronology (Chapter 1.3 below). This, however, is largely a red herring and the real significance of Ritchie's work lies squarely with the graves themselves and the late medieval church beneath whose floor they were buried.

Ritchie's work at Whithorn Priory in the late 1950s and 1960s is the only 'modern' excavation campaign to focus on the high-status burials near the high altar of a major Scottish medieval church. Remains of earlier graves, as well as structures that we can now recognise as parts of the extended medieval church, were also found. As we shall see, among the uppermost level of graves are those that belong to a number of bishops of Whithorn, some of whom we can possibly name. Also present are other ecclesiastics, as well as (we shall suggest) a number of lay patrons, some of whom, again, we can tentatively identify. Many of these graves were richly furnished. Some (but not all) of the decorated metalwork from these graves – including croziers, chalices, patens and finger-rings – has recently been published in a National Museums of Scotland Monograph (Glenn 2003). The full assemblage of artefacts from the excavation is now published here for the first time. This publication also resolves, once and for all, the nature and date of the earliest graves that were identified at the base of the trench.

1.2 PREVIOUS INTERVENTIONS

(Figure 1.2)

Archaeological interventions in and around the priory at Whithorn have been undertaken since the late 19th century. The results of these excavations, in terms of what is known of the form of the priory and its development, are discussed in more detail in Chapter 8.2. Much of the early work at the site was undertaken at the behest of the Third Marquis of Bute (d 1897). It is clear from Julia Muir Watt's recent research in the Bute Muniments that there is a largely undocumented phase of work on the site, dating from at least 1885 and associated with Sir Herbert Maxwell (Muir Watt 2001, 134); the greater part of the Bute-sponsored work, however, was conducted by a local architect, William Galloway. Galloway's investigation, from 1886 until his death in 1897, was largely focused on the eastern end of the priory.

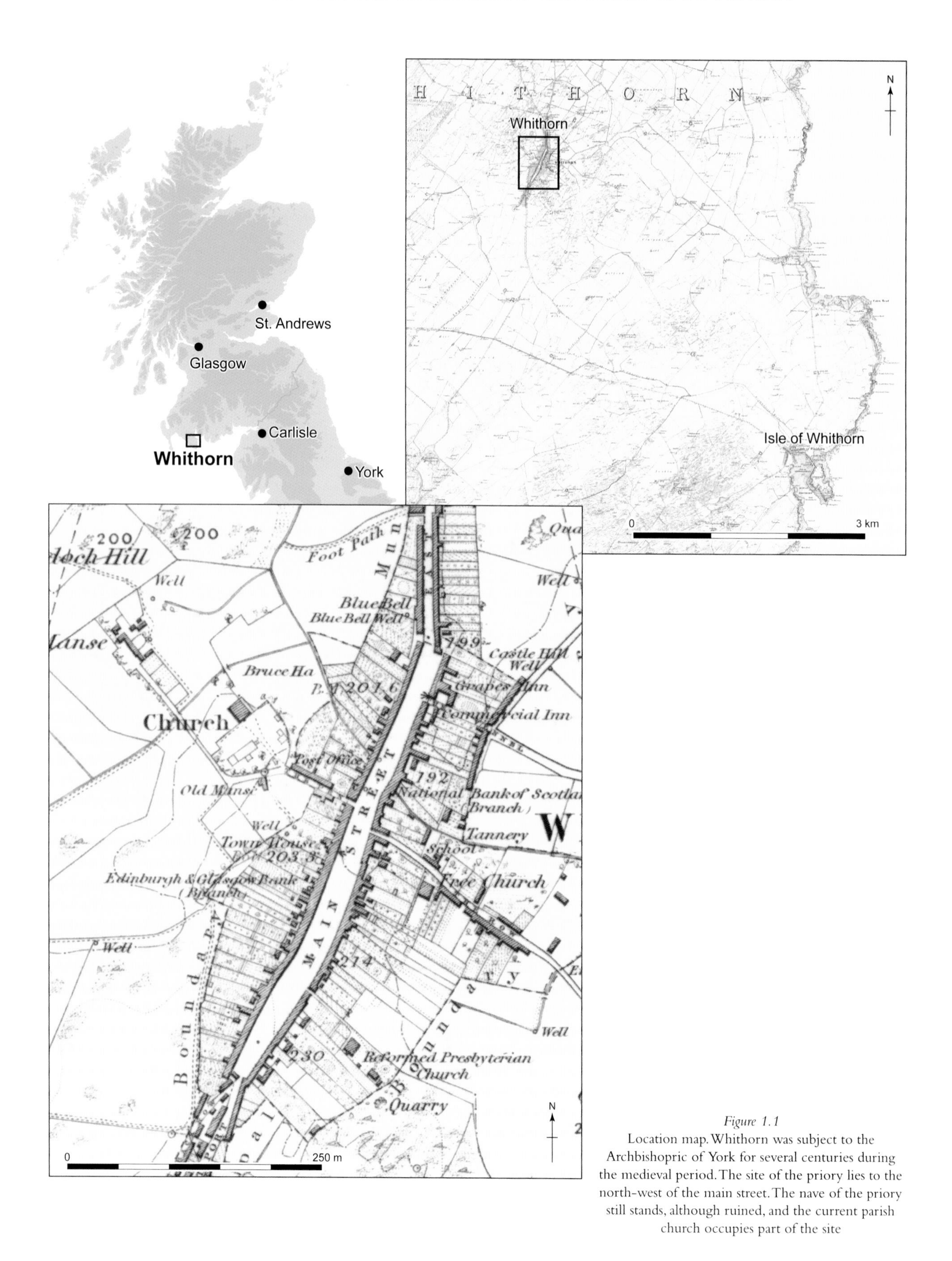

Figure 1.1
Location map. Whithorn was subject to the Archbishopric of York for several centuries during the medieval period. The site of the priory lies to the north-west of the main street. The nave of the priory still stands, although ruined, and the current parish church occupies part of the site

TIMELINE

4th century AD	Whithorn was already established as a centre of trade and power for the local British population, within the sphere of Roman Carlisle.
431	the traditional date ascribed to the death and burial here of St Ninian.
***c* 450**	the oldest surviving Christian monument in Scotland erected on the hilltop by Latinus and his un-named daughter. Aspects of this inscription demonstrate that Roman culture still had a strong appeal to the upper echelons of Galloway society in the 5th century.
589	death of Finnian of Moville (the Briton Uinniau), great scholar and founder of monasteries associated with Whithorn, who may have come from the area.
7th century	the 'Peter' stone was erected probably beside a chapel just outside Whithorn.
***c* 700**	Galloway fell under the control of the Anglian kingdom of Northumbria. Whithorn became the head of one of the four diocese of Northumbria.
731	Bede writes in his Ecclesiastical History, that Ninian was a bishop and holy man who built a famous church at Whithorn, known as *Candida Casa* ('shining white place').
8th century	the Anglians embraced and embellished the cult of Ninian, promoting the importance of the shrine by circulating literature, describing the numerous miracles, written by Whithorn monks during the 8th century. One of these works, a poem entitled Miracula Niniae Episcopi, provides a unique contemporary insight into the appearance of the place, describing a (presumably empty) rock-cut grave, as well as Ninian's stone reliquary sarcophagus which rested beside the altar of his main church.
10th–11th centuries	Whithorn School of stone carving, producing large numbers of monolithic stone crosses with round heads and interlace decoration.
***c* 1128**	Fergus of Galloway appointed Gille-aldan as bishop. This was followed by the construction of a large cruciform cathedral church built on the site of the principal older church. At this time the sepulchral church housing Ninian's tomb probably remained as a separate building on the eastern slope of the hilltop.
***c* 1160**	Vita Niniani (Life of St Ninian) written by Ailred of Rievaulx.
***c* 1177**	a house of Premonstratensian canons was established.
***c* 1200**	cathedral extended to the east, possibly incorporating the sepulchral chapel as a crypt. This enlargement was required to accommodate the liturgical needs of the canons recently introduced to the cathedral priory. Their needs necessitated the construction of a cloister; topography determined that this had to be to the north of the church.
1329	miraculous cures attracted King Robert I (1306–29) to endure a long and painful journey to Whithorn, just 3 months before his death.
***c* 1500**	A large chapel with undercroft was added to the south of the choir during a major rebuilding and restoration programme. This chapel provided space for altars, and created a grander setting in which pilgrims could observe the activity around the main shrine. The Stewart kings adopted and revered the cult of St Ninian. By the reign of James IV (1488–1513) the cult of St Ninian was at the height of its popularity, and the subject of national devotion to rival that of St Andrew.
1511	burgh refounded as a royal burgh by James IV.
1560	the shrine was destroyed at the Reformation, and the cathedral was stripped of its wealth and estates.
Late 16th century	the church was in ruins. But within a few years repairs had been effected to the nave, probably by Bishop Gavin Hamilton, who was consecrated in 1610. A bell tower was built at the west end. From then on, the east limb was abandoned and robbed of stone.
17th century	economic and ecclesiastical control shifted to Wigtown. In 1690 Presbyterianism was finally stabled in the Church of Scotland, and the church at Whithorn became a simple parish church. A pulpit was placed in the middle of the north wall, and timber galleries were built.
Early 18th century	the west tower fell, causing the rebuilding of the west gable.
1822	the present parish church was built over the east claustral range.
1886-89	Whithorn was visited by General Pitt-Rivers, the first Inspector of Ancient Monuments, who sketched some of the stones.
1886–1897	1890s – excavation and restoration works by William Galloway funded by third Marquis of Bute.
1891	sculpted stones taken into State care.
1908	cottages in Bruce Street leased by HM Office of Works from the Dumfries Estate, converted and extended to display the crosses and other carved stones. Priory ruins taken into State care.

The record is slight but what is clear is that Galloway's work here involved a considerable amount of rebuilding and 'restoration'. This would ultimately have an impact on what Ritchie saw during the course of his work, particularly insofar as he was able to distinguish between what was *in situ* and what had been altered or reconstructed; there are issues, for example, with the rear of the barrel vault and the north intramural stair (Sections 3.2.2 and 3.2.5). Galloway's work not only led to the discovery of the *Latinus* Stone, but also to the low foundations of a building whose walls protruded below and to the east of the medieval crypt. This structure was tentatively identified as a 'Lady Chapel' and was thus labelled on Galloway's plan of the site (MacGibbon & Ross 1896, Figure 877).

The site was taken into state care in 1908 when the Heritors of the Parish of Whithorn transferred the ruins into the guardianship of the Office of Works, a predecessor body to the Ministry of Public Building and Works and today's Historic Scotland. The site was scheduled in 1935. The first modern excavation at the priory came with Ralegh Radford's excavations over the period 1949–51 and 1953. Work within and below the nave of the cathedral church clearly indicated that this part of the site had been extensively levelled (Radford 1956, 143–5). Meanwhile, at the east end of the church, Radford reinvestigated the foundations of Galloway's 'Lady Chapel'. The walls were found to have been constructed of clay-bonded rubble, on the outer face of which were preserved patches of a 'coarse cream mortar of poor quality' (Radford 1949, 118). In his initial report, this structure, Radford declared, could only be 'the remains of the church of St Martin built by St Ninian or one of his immediate successors, the church in which his body lay through the earlier centuries' (Radford 1949, 119). This, in other words, was the stone church – *Candida Casa* – reported by Bede (Radford & Donaldson 1953, 32–3). In his final report, however, Radford (1956, 181) was to conclude that this building

> was one of the smaller oratories and that the great church lay elsewhere, probably on the summit, where early remains would have been planed off by the twelfth-century builders. The small oratory may well have been the burial place of St Ninian ...

And it is this revised interpretation that accords best with the model proposed by Peter Hill (1997) as a result of his excavations here over the period 1984–1991. The use of clay-bonded stone foundations resembles the plinth of the clay-walled mortuary chapel that was built in the early 8th century immediately to the east of the (presumed) subsidiary church that Hill identified in the area to the south of the medieval cathedral (Hill 1997, 164–70). The Galloway/Radford building, therefore, has been interpreted as part of the range of Northumbrian buildings, as an axial chapel lying to the east of the (putative) principal church (Hill 1997, 10, 40–4).

After Radford came Ritchie, whose work over the period 1957–67 is the subject of this monograph. Then in the 1970s a new phase of archaeological activity was ushered in, ahead of potential development plans for the fields immediately outwith the church and graveyard. This spurred on a new phase of archaeological investigation and in 1972 Christopher Tabraham excavated a series of small trenches in the market garden and Glebe Field to the west of Bruce Street. Deposits up to 1.5m in depth and showing extensive stratification and complexity were present, with evidence of walls, burials and cultivation soils, dating from the 7th century through to 1500. As a result of these discoveries, the limits of the Scheduled Ancient Monument were extended to include these areas. Further work undertaken by Tabraham in 1975 largely focused on the area to the north of the ruined nave and west of the current parish church. Evidence of the cloister to the north of the priory church was recorded, along with associated deposits running down the slope to the north (Tabraham 1979).

Further test excavations in the Glebe Field, by Peter Hill, followed in 1984, and were subsumed within the larger project which followed the establishment of the Whithorn Trust in 1986. Hill's excavation in the Glebe Field and market garden revealed multiple phases of activity and changes in the ecclesiastical focus of the site and its associated settlement (Hill 1997). In addition to the structural evidence for the sequence of churches and associated religious buildings in the area to the south of the ruined nave of the priory, Hill's work also took him into the Museum Garden, to the south of the area where Ritchie had excavated in the 1950s and 1960s. Among the primary features here were identified the fugitive remains of a series of possible structures and surfaces. From a spread of burnt debris were recovered two mid-9th-century *stycas*. A populous graveyard subsequently extended over this early horizon (Hill 1997, 277–86).

In the years following Hill's work, some small-scale work has continued to be undertaken, generally as a result of funding for further research from the Whithorn Trust and Historic Scotland. This work has been focused on looking at the wider environs of the monastic settlement, in particular in the fields to the north and west of the church, with the aim of defining the outer limits of the monastic settlement. Fieldwork in 2001 established that whilst there was little evidence for activity in the peripheral areas to the north–west and west of the church, there were, however, well-preserved features and deposits in the area to the north of the medieval priory, in the Manse Field (Morrison 2001). Subsequent excavation here has identified

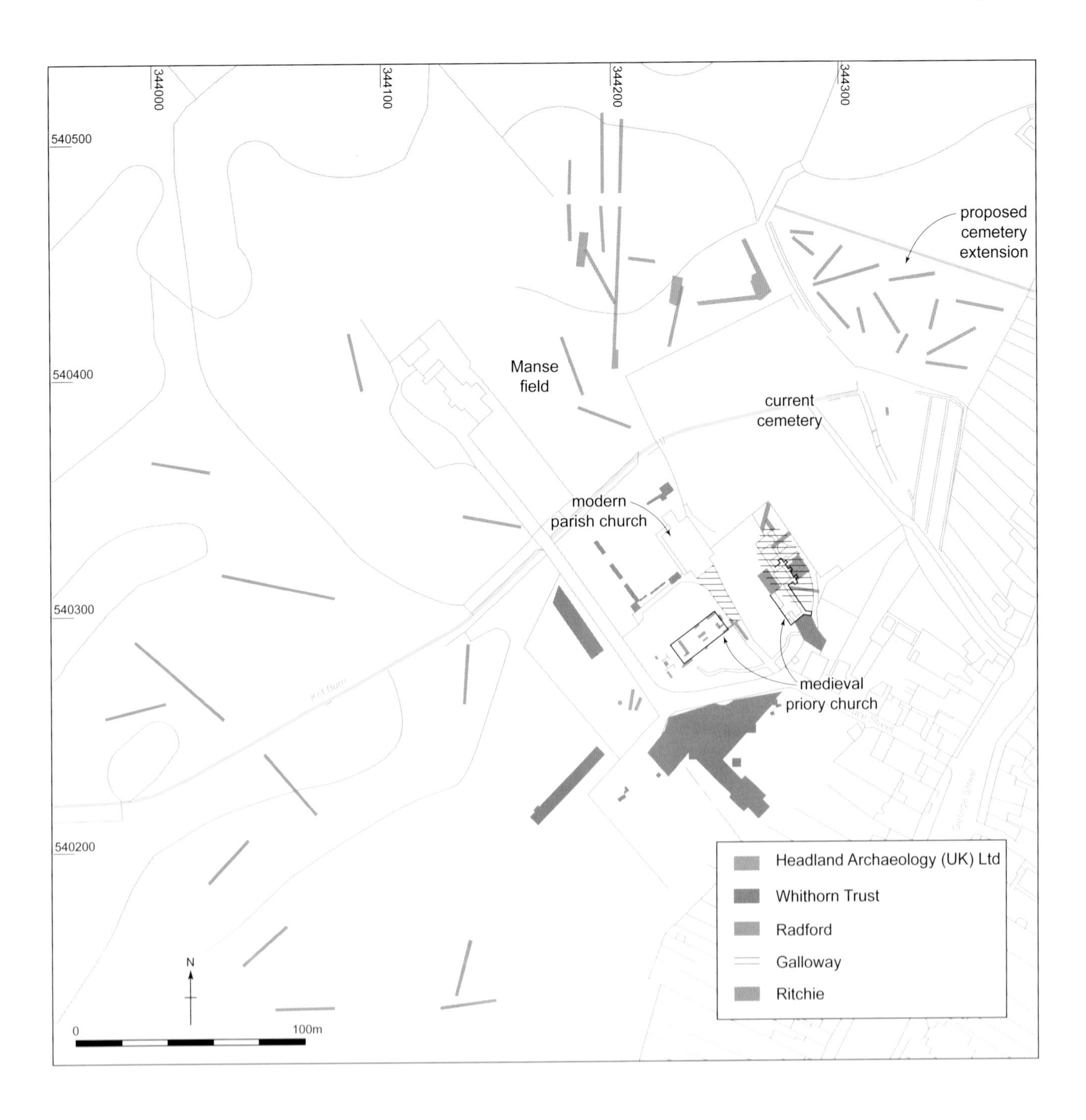

Figure 1.2
Previous work at Whithorn Priory. Early work was largely concentrated around the core of the priory, however in recent years investigations have taken place in the surrounding farmland

the remains of a sunken-featured building (possibly a smithy) which has been radiocarbon-dated to the late first millennium (Table 1.1), as well as other, later deposits and structures (Morrison 2003).

Most recently, trial trenching in advance of the creation of a second extension to the parish cemetery, in a field to the north–east of the medieval priory, has established that there is little indication here of either Early Christian or medieval activity (Dingwall 2008). Clearly, this area must be peripheral to the monastic site. Gradually, then, a picture of the wider area around the ecclesiastical core of the site is beginning to emerge.

1.3 DISCOVERY

The discovery of the first graves in October 1957 came about quite by accident, as the result of trenching by the local MoPBW (Ministry of Public Building and Works) work squad who were endeavouring to waterproof the vaults below and adjacent to the east end of the medieval priory cathedral (Figure 1.3). The very presence here of medieval graves, however, came as something of a surprise, given the general understanding at the time that this area had been dug over and remodelled as part of the 'restoration' works carried out by a local architect, William Galloway, on behalf of the 3rd Marquis of Bute at the end of the 19th century.

In a 1963 newspaper article about Ritchie's excavation (until now the only published account of that work), Stewart Cruden, then Principal Inspector of Ancient Monuments, remarked that although the chamber below the burials was complete, nonetheless the vault 'has been refashioned in medieval times and rebuilt by Lord Bute' (Cruden 1963). The same is also implied by Radford & Donaldson in the 1953 HMSO guidebook to the site which describes the vault of the crypt below the east end of the church as having been restored as high as the floor level of the church above (Radford & Donaldson 1953, 31). Meanwhile, correspondence in the Bute Muniments, dated 21 December 1885, refers to Galloway's comments that 'the vaulting [of the crypts] is demolished and the soil above poses difficulties' (Muir Watt 2001, 136). Indeed, patching of the roof across the north and north–west areas of the vault is still evident in the fabric today, although it is not clear if this relates to Galloway's work or later MoPBW repairs.

Further information about the condition of the western barrel vault at this time is contained in Ritchie's unpublished notes on the Galloway papers (Archive D9, p.5). Of particular relevance in the present context, because it appears to confirm that the north–west side of the western barrel vault has been extensively restored, is Ritchie's description of an annotated Galloway plan:

> The twin barrel vaults under the east end of the church appear on the early plan, but not as we know them today (ie 1967 or later). The area outside to the north is marked unexplored.
>
> Inside, a pencil line runs in a ragged manner from west to east approximately across the centre of the two chambers. To the south of the line a note tells that barrel vaulting remained at this point in each chamber. It has to be inferred that the vaulting was either defective or altogether absent in the northern parts. The western of the two chambers had red cross-hatching in its northern half with the words 'Debris and Masonry'. A question mark is inked in against the northern part of the west wall and the line of the wall face is shown dotted. To north and south of the question mark are lines suggesting the presence of a doorway or other in-go. At the least there seems to have been a partial void in the vertical masonry.
>
> The north wall is shown solid with its western face dotted and presumably largely hidden by the debris and masonry recorded on the plan. There is no sign of the corner springing for rib-vaulting which we see today.
>
> *(Archive D9, pp.5–6)*

Although transcriptions of several pages of Galloway's notes are contained in Ritchie's draft publication text (Archive D9, pp.15–63), unfortunately the relevant drawing has not been traced.

The fact that the finest and most ornately furnished series of medieval graves ever found in Scotland – and indeed the largest excavated group of such from any episcopal (or archiepiscopal) seat in Britain – lay just a few centimetres behind the roof of the vault could not have been anticipated when the first reports of the discovery landed on Cruden's desk in Edinburgh in October 1957; nor, it seems, was it quite appreciated how deep the surviving deposits would prove to be. In any event, neither Cruden nor Ritchie would have envisaged that it would be 1967 before the fieldwork was completed and the waterproofing work could proceed. Although the records

Table 1.1 Radiocarbon dates from sunken-featured building in the Manse Field

Context	*Dated element*	*Uncalibrated*	*Calibrated (2-sigma)*	*Laboratory Code*
Clay floor of sunken-featured building	Alder charcoal, single entity	1255 ± 40	AD 670 – 890	AA-48440 (GU-9889)
Clay floor of sunken-featured building	Alder charcoal, single entity	1295 ± 45	AD 650 – 870	AA-48441 (GU-9890)

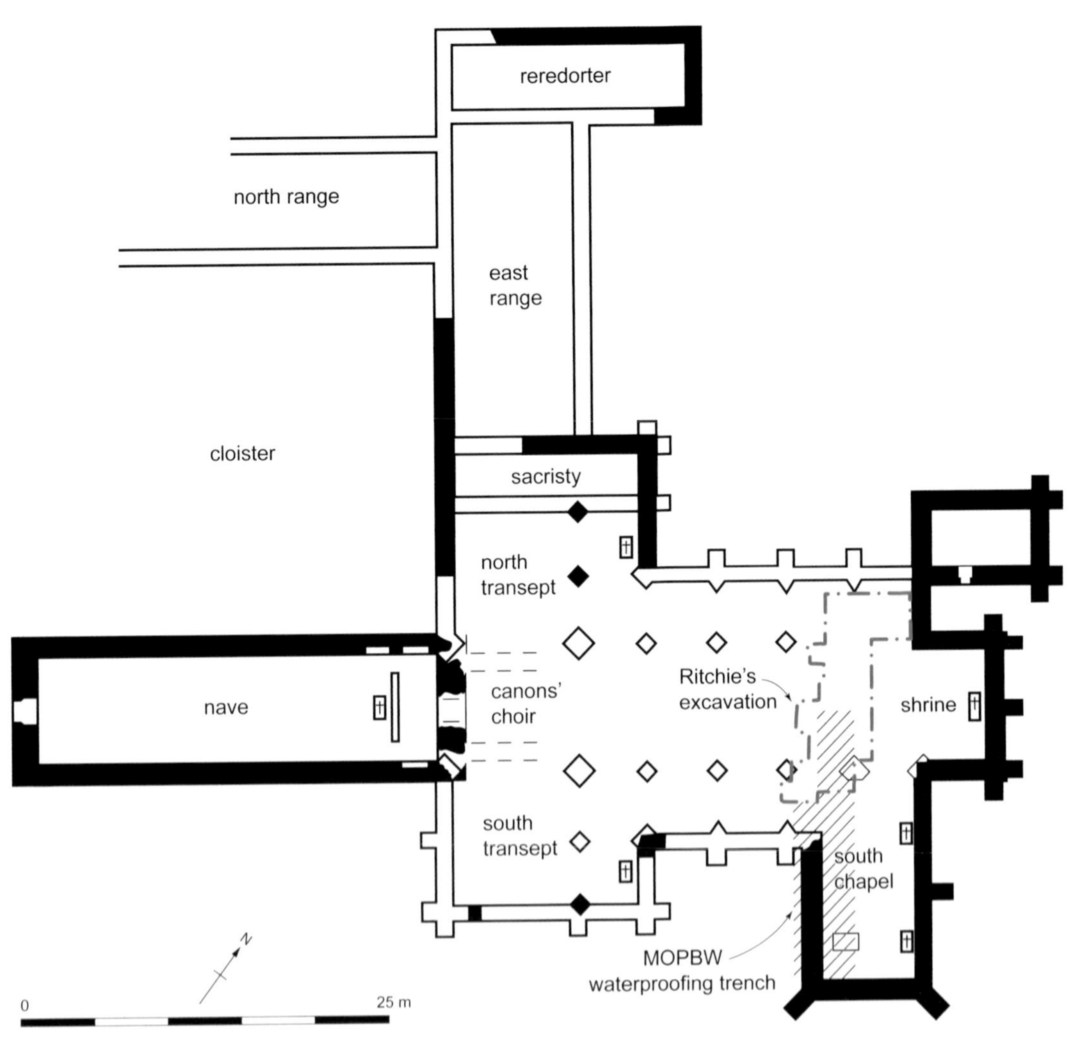

Figure 1.3
Plan of Whithorn Priory after Radford & Donaldson (1984) and developed from Galloway's original 19th century plan. In this reconstruction of the priory layout, the choir of the priory is flanked by aisles. Blocked in wall lines represent upstanding masonry (including elements reconstructed by Galloway) or fragments of foundations identified during the course of excavation and other groundworks; inferred wall lines are shown in outline The presence or absence of aisles at Whithorn has been the subject of much debate in recent decades

are incomplete, with the exception of 1958, 1959 and 1963 when there was no excavation on site, the project was undertaken as a series of (roughly) 4–12 week-long campaigns, with occasionally more than one excavation season per year (Dingwall, Chapter 2). Over the course of the decade, Ritchie excavated (effectively in four parts) a trench some 13m long, 2–4m wide and (in places) nearly4m deep. In this task he would have had the assistance of the labourers from the MoPBW squad. According to information in the drawing record, we know that a certain Fraser and Swan were also on site in 1960 and there are references in the correspondence file to the temporary employment in 1961 and 1962 of Dr and Mrs Cormack who were brought in to provide skilled help, along with Audrey Henshall, then of the National Museum of Antiquities, who was involved from 1957onwards; otherwise, this is all Ritchie's work. And what he found constitutes one of the major archaeological finds of medieval Scotland. With the passage of time, however, the significance of the medieval bishops' (and others') graves has somewhat been lost sight of; instead, published references to the site, by others, have largely focused on the basal features of the excavation.

A summary of Ritchie's early work on the site was published in the *Scotsman Weekend Magazine* of 4 May 1963 (Cruden 1963). This gives us our first record of 'cremated' bone at the site, as well as possibly some insight into how the overlying deposits on the site were being interpreted:

'Cremated bones are not likely to be Christian at this level, nor in the 12 feet of soil above it which represent a thousand years of history' (Cruden 1963).

A sketch section through the east end of the church noted the presence of 'Early Christian graves on rock' at the base of Ritchie's trench, to the west of the crypt, and the remains of *Candida Casa* (as labelled) to the east (Figure 1.4). Academic visitors to the excavation, such as Radford and Thomas, have subsequently incorporated their impressions of the excavations into their own published works. Radford (1967, 110), for example, envisaged a cemetery of oriented long cists around a small plastered oratory, among which lay an inscribed upright stone, the *Latinus Stone*. It is clear, however, as Derek Craig (1997, 614) has shown, that the *Latinus Stone* was found in the area to the north of the medieval cathedral, in the pathway leading up to the present parish church.

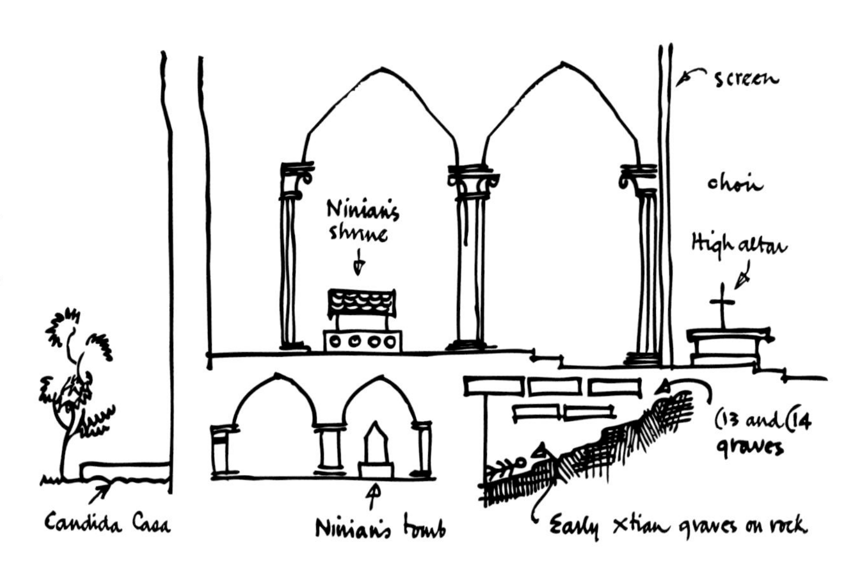

Figure 1.4
Stewart Cruden's sketch of the remains at the east end was published in *The Scotsman* article and was based on his understanding of the site following visits and reports from Ritchie

Charles Thomas (1971, 55 & 81: 1992, 19), on the other hand, has described the lowest levels of Ritchie's excavation in terms of a Roman-period cremation cemetery which had been disturbed by a series of 'oriented dug graves, with greatly crushed skeletons, which one can regard as probably being, not only of the period of Ninian, but also indeed as the *raison d'être* for the ecclesiastical foundation at this precise point in the burgh' (Thomas 1971, 55).

With the partial archive now to hand, together with the new radiocarbon dates (Chapter 7) from the burials themselves, we are now in a position to get some real clarity on the site stratigraphic sequence and to understand better the relationship between the primary graves at the base of the sequence and those that were buried inside the Premonstratensian cathedral-priory church that was extended eastwards around the year 1200 (Yeoman 1999, 36).

1.4 THE EXCAVATION ARCHIVE

KIRSTY DINGWALL AND CHRISTOPHER LOWE

The excavation archive that has allowed this publication to be written comprises a range of documentary records. It also includes, of course, the human remains themselves and the various objects that were found in the graves or (occasionally) recovered from the heavily turbated cemetery soil which extended across the upper levels of the excavated area. All this material was examined and catalogued as part of the pre-publication assessment for this project. It is clear, however, that there are gaps in the site record, and the written, drawn and photographic records of the site are not necessarily as coherent and 'cross-reference-able' as one might wish. There is a day-book, of sorts, entitled *Whithorn 2* (Archive, A29), covering the period 1961–1967 but it by no means gives us a complete narrative of the excavation; nor does it give us a complete and fixed number sequence for the earliest graves on the site. Examples of some of the 'double-numbering' of skeletons that has clearly occurred are explored elsewhere (Henderson, Chapter 4.1.2). No equivalent note-book, presumably *Whithorn 1*, has come to light for the earlier excavation seasons (1957 & 1960).

The primary documentary archive relating to the contemporary excavation record comprises a series of pencil-drawn plans and sections, inked-up versions of the same, as well as a series of annotated dyeline copies, and a notebook (Table 1.2: Archive items, A1–A41).

The photographic archive from the time is also of primary importance, as some of the features and structures identified are only known from a single (or series of) photograph(s), and many are best understood through the photographic evidence. Also primary, although not individually listed here, are the various notes written on or appended to the original finds bags (see, for example, the discussion of Saintonge pottery in Franklin, Chapter 6.11.2).

Just as important for the present study, there are also several different versions of a draft publication report that was written by Ritchie, some of it as early as 1962 (Table 1.2: Archive, D8 & D9). Although not technically 'primary'

Table 1.2 The primary documentary archive from the P R Ritchie excavations, 1957–67

HA number	*Description*	*Scale*	*Author / Date*
A/1	Sheet of imperial graph paper showing outline of 2 graves and nails. No location but possibly identifiable as Graves 10 & 11, with the South Choir wall.	-	-
A/2	Detailed plan of Tournai slab, reused as a gravestone.	2" to 1'	1960
A/3	Drawing of left humerus of Grave 1 with note '6 days after removal from grave. Cased in moist paper in interval, moderate cracking on drying out'.	1:1	Ritchie (04.12.1957)
A/4	Schematic plan (with triangulation points) showing location (from S to N) of Graves 8, 3, 1, 2, 7, 5 & 6: see also A5	-	Ritchie 1960
A/5	Schematic plan, with measurements, showing location of Grave 1: see also A/4	-	Fraser & Swan 1960
A/6	Long section through Graves 1 and 2.	1" to 1'	Ritchie (22.11.1960)
A/7	Plan of Graves 3, 4 and showing location in relation to Grave 1. Also elevation of end of crypt?	-	Fraser & Swan 1960
A/8	Plan of Graves 5 and 6, with skeletons. Nails and miscellaneous finds also indicated.	2" to 1'	1960
A/9	Plan of Grave 5, showing cover slabs.	2" to 1'	1960
A/10	Plan of Grave 5, showing skeleton and stone sides of cist	-	-
A/11	Plan of Grave 6, skeleton only, with location of coffin nails	-	-
A/12	Sections through Graves 5 and 6.	1" to 1'	-
A/13	Plan of Grave 7, outlined with nails. Location of 'gold sequins' and chalice also indicated (see also A/17).	2" to 1'	Ritchie 1960
A/14	Plan of Grave 12 & base of 'bench'. Locations of miscellaneous nails, coin & bronze tube - with relative levels - also shown.	2" to 1'	1961
A/15	Plan showing Graves 13, 14, & 15, along with another possible grave, various fragments of bone, miscellaneous nails and a bronze bead, with relative levels. The 'bronze bead' is otherwise unrecorded and is not present among the finds assemblage.	-	1961
A/16	Plan showing outline of cut(?) of Graves 5 and 6.	1" to 1'	-
A/17	Plan of Graves 5, 6 and 7. Also shows location of crozier, 'gold rosettes', chalice, paten and miscellaneous nails (see also A/13).	2" to 1'	Ritchie 1960
A/18	Plan of collection of bones (possible grave?) and nails, unknown location	-	1961
A/19	Section - mid section running EW behind choir (see also A/22).	1" to 1'	1960
A/20	Section - 'East Section', aligned NS - adjacent to graves in Lady Chapel. Graves 1, 2 and 3 labelled.	1" to 1'	Ritchie 12/1957
A/21	Section running NS. Section elements numbered 1–32 and also shows Burials 19 & 20 at base of section. Descriptions of Section elements 1–3 only are contained in the Ritchie day-book (A/29); entries for Section elements 4–32 are left blank.	1" to 1'	1962
A/22	Section running EW - located from E parapet wall. Intersects with Main NS 1957 section (see also A/19).	1" to 1'	1960 or later
A/23	Copy of plan locating graves and some structural detail; same lithograph base-plan as A/25 but with pencil drawing showing plan & section of 'Anglian grave cover'	-	-

HA number	*Description*	*Scale*	*Author / Date*
A/24	North–South elevation (sectional) across east end of church.	1" to 1'	MOPBW, Ancient Monuments Branch (26.07.1961)
A/25	Copy of plan locating graves, some skeletons and some structural details; Graves 12 and 12A numbered; others can be numbered with reference to A/26.	-	-
A/26	Copy of plan showing location of Graves 10–15, others (un-numbered) with skeletons. Also pencil notes concerning depths and form of grave-cuts.	-	-
A/27	Location of excavation area, related to existing walls. Also shown in relation to crypts.	-	MOPBW, Ancient Monuments Branch. August 1965 (amended 1966)
A/28	Inked up versions of Graves 5 and 6	-	-
A/29	Notebook entitled: 'Whithorn 2'. Day-book of sorts for excavation seasons 1961–1967		Ritchie, 1961 - 1967
A/30	Original survey drawings of excavations at Whithorn - N elevation (Sectional) and S elevation (Sectional). Upper part of elevations of north and south choir walls showing back of barrel vault. (HS124-314-55)	1" to 1'	MOPBW, Ancient Monuments (26.07.1961)
A/31	Version of A/27 with additions of detail in north and south stair. (HS125-314-58)	1/4" to 1'	MOPBW, Ancient Monuments Branch. August 1965 (amended 1966)
A/32	Measured sketch of N elevation for A/30. (HS125-314-72)	-	-
A/33	Measured sketch of N elevation for A/30. (HS125-314-73)	-	-
A/34	Measured sketch of S elevation for A/30. (HS125-314-74)	-	-
A/35	Measured sketch of S elevation for A/30. (HS125-314-75)	-	-
A/36	Plan of S excavation area, overlaid with profile of transverse wall (HS125-314-87)	-	Ritchie 18-20/12/1962
A/37	W-facing elevation of transverse wall - Section B-B (HS125-314-88)	-	Ritchie 18-20/12/1962
A/38	Opening in north wall of crypt showing excavated area on north side of wall (HS125-314-89).	-	02/06/1966
A/39	N-facing elevation of south choir wall, with transverse wall (HS125-314-90).	-	Ritchie 18-20/12/1962
A/40	Plan and elevation of south choir wall (HS125-314-91)	1" to 1'	8–9/12/1965
A/41	Plan and elevation of north choir wall and north stair (HS125-314-92)	1" to 1'	19–20/01/1965
D/8	Whithorn Priory Excavations: preliminary report Nov.1962' (three drafts [D8i, D8ii & D8iii] with various manuscript amendments); manuscript list of Whithorn photographs held in MPBW photo library, with reference numbers, descriptions & occasional sketches: all in folder labelled 'General scheme of work'.	-	Ritchie 1962 and later
D/9	Typescript – with B&W photos – entitled 'Excavations at Whithorn': contents comprise the following: (1) 19th century excavations at Whithorn Priory; (2) Summary of works carried out in 1953–67 by MoPBW; (3) Report on the excavations at Whithorn Priory, 1957–67	-	Ritchie – late 1960s / early 1970s

documents, they are clearly central to understanding what he found. These draft texts discuss many of the findings of the site: the series of graves, the precious metal finds, as well as some of the structures. None of these accounts, however, provides a full record of all the features (or finds) that Ritchie encountered.

The four draft reports, the first written in November 1962 (Archive, D8(i)), the rest in the late 1960s or even into the 1970s are all roughly similar, although the D8(iii) and D9 documents (the latest of the drafts) omit the draft section entitled 'The sequence of events on the site' which is found in the D8(i) and D8(ii) documents. With this exception, all four drafts follow the same broad layout:

- the circumstances of the discovery;
- the graves and their finds, divided into a 'late group' comprising Graves 1–8, 12 and 21; and an 'early group', consisting of Graves 9–11 and 13–15;
- structural remains at the east end of the church.

Included in the early drafts (Archive, D8(i) and (ii)) are occasional discussions of the potential dates of individual graves or features, as well as thoughts on where they come in the overall sequence of events. Only one of the graves (Grave 3), however, is firmly ascribed to a named individual, Bishop Henry who died in 1293 (Archive, D8(i), pp.7–8). An alternative interpretation is explored in Chapter 9.

Ritchie's publication drafts also set out some of the stratigraphic relationships between features, as well as indications of what assumptions have been made. Although some of these can now be shown to be incorrect and others may now look questionable, Ritchie's draft publication text has, nonetheless, been indispensable for coming to terms with those parts of the site where primary records were often incomplete, difficult to relate to modern known points, or non-existent. It has been invaluable in helping the present team to piece together not only the archaeology of the site, but also the circumstances of the discovery of most of the major finds from the excavation.

The other crucial part of the story, although not part of the Ritchie archive, has been the file held by Historic Scotland that records all correspondence relating to the site maintained by the Inspectorate of Ancient Monuments (SDD27/1582). This included numerous minutes from Ritchie to individuals in the MoPBW offices in Edinburgh, outlining recent discoveries, along with problems relating to the excavation and its progress. It proved invaluable in working out the sequence of work over the years, and in helping to understand the development of Ritchie's interpretation of the site as new discoveries were made.

Deciphering the information in the archive was not a straightforward task, and numerous problems were encountered on the way. These originated mainly from the heavy focus that was accorded to the graves and their associated finds, even where the structural remains were recorded. While we may have Ritchie's drawn plans and elevations of elements of the actual building, often these are difficult to interpret and Ritchie does not comment on them. Moreover (insofar as we can see on the basis of the current archive), after 1964 the level of recording of features and deposits becomes somewhat less extensive, doubtless in part due to the pressures on Ritchie to finish the excavation.

Ritchie's publication text, the photographic records and, to a lesser extent, the plans are all principally concerned with the finds from the graves. In his descriptions of the graves, it is the existence and location of any finds that is most fully discussed. There are sometimes indications of relationships between one grave and another, or even more rarely a note on what deposits lay above or below, but the account usually consists of a description of the skeletal remains and any associated finds.

The main discoveries of the excavation are undoubtedly the graves of the medieval bishops or other high-status individuals. It is also clear, however, that several structural features were encountered but these are only briefly mentioned and are little photographed, if at all. Indeed, this lack of detail with regard to the structural elements that were identified during the course of the excavation is one of the most frustrating aspects of the record.

The other major problem that has very much affected our ability to create a continuous stratigraphic sequence concerns the trench that was excavated by the labourers along the line of the back of the west vault prior to Ritchie's arrival on site (roughly shown as the western limit between the areas of minimum intervention and deeper excavation in Figure 2.1). This is a critical area of the site as it is the place where the relationship between the graves and the vault could have been tested. Ritchie indicates in his draft publication text what he thinks the relationship is, but this is one of the occasions where he would seem to be contradicted by the photographic evidence.

At some point during the 1962 season, there is a marked reduction in the level of recording of features, and more specifically the remaining graves. In a letter to Stewart Cruden, dated 18 September 1962, Ritchie remarks that 'further graves are merely to be noted unless there is special reason for expecting finds' (SDD27/1582, 19 September 1962). The reason for this appears to be related to the increasing pressure on Ritchie to complete the excavation, so that the originally planned waterproofing work could take place. There is an increasing amount of correspondence between Ritchie and the architects of the Ancient Monuments Division who were clearly very concerned about the unstable nature of the rear of the vault, once the overlying material had been removed. Specifically, Angus Graham, the architect in charge of the work, expressed his concerns about the exposed walls in May 1962 (SDD27/1582, 16 May 1962). Indeed, in his report for the previous year's work, Ritchie had noted that the wall of the existing barrel vault could collapse (SDD27/1582, 16 June 1961). The recommendation, therefore, was that the excavation be considerably speeded up, and the large open trench backfilled and the wooden covering removed as soon as possible.

The result is that from Graves 13–15 onwards, the records become increasingly 'thin'. There are some photographs of what we can identify as Graves 17–20 and 22–27, but these are just described in the records as 'early graves', with no indication of numbers or location. Two of the graves (Graves 19 and 20) appear in the drawing of the main north–south section but there is no other information about them in the record. This is also true of the structural elements in the lower parts of the excavation. There are several photographs of fragments of walls and what appear to be pits cut into soil and possibly bedrock, but no information to which they can be related. The final stages of the excavation, involving work around the locations of the northern and southern stairs, are recorded on plan and in elevation, but Ritchie's interpretations and thoughts on these remains have not come down to us.

These, then, were the sources that were available to us. This is the material that forms the basis of the narrative that follows in Chapter 2 and the stratigraphic analysis in Chapter 3.

Chapter 2

The Ritchie Excavations, 1957–67

KIRSTY DINGWALL

2.1 INTRODUCTION

The discovery of the graves in 1957 was one of those great accidents that occur from time to time in archaeology, and is a reminder of the role that chance plays in enriching our knowledge of the past. Given the understanding then of William Galloway's work in the 1880s and 1890s, and his enthusiasm with the spade which was equal only to his passion for restoration, it is not difficult to appreciate the surprise that this discovery undoubtedly created. It was assumed that any graves in this area would have been removed or extensively disturbed when the barrel vault in the west chamber of the crypt was reconstructed in the late 19th century. Graves in this area, particularly medieval graves, therefore, would have been the last thing on anyone's mind when one of the MoPBW labour squad came across the stone cist of Grave 1. When Mr Brown, the chargehand, removed the 'brass cup' therein with the aid of a stick, he set in motion a programme of occasional excavation which would not be completed until 1967 and, some 40 years later, the current programme of post-excavation analysis which has culminated in this publication.

2.2 NARRATIVE OUTLINE OF THE INVESTIGATION, 1957–67

Work on waterproofing the barrel-vaulted crypts below the east end of the church began in 1957. This was meant to be the culmination of a programme of work that had started in 1953 along the west side of the 15th-century chapel and its undercroft which adjoins the south side of the church.

The method of working involved lifting the existing 19th-century paving (part of William Galloway's restoration programme), removing the material that overlay the top (back) of the vault, and then laying down a protective layer to prevent ingress of water into the walls. The overlying deposits and paving were then replaced. This work was undertaken by the MoPBW direct labour squad based at Glenluce Abbey. No features of archaeological interest were reported during the work along the side of the south undercroft.

The work on and above the barrel-vaulted crypt and undercrofts below the east end of the church was undertaken by the same team of MoPBW labourers under the supervision of the chargehand, Mr Brown, and after his death, Mr Steel. As before, work proceeded by removing the paving and material over the top of the barrel vault, and then excavating a strip of ground along its outer (west) face with the intention, clearly, of taking this down to the base of the wall.

Excavation of the strip of ground to the west of the vault proceeded from south to north following the line of its outer face. In Ritchie's preliminary typescript, he notes that 'a number of human bones' (Archive D9, p68) were found prior to his arrival on site. The presence of human remains would not in itself have given great cause for concern, given the location of the work within an area of the parish graveyard that had been in use down to the late 19th century. Therefore it seems clear that the first substantive remains of archaeological interest identified were indeed those that brought Ritchie to the site in October 1957, namely the discovery of Grave 1. Plate 2.1 shows the main line of graves at a later date (1960), but the line of the workmen's trench is clear at the base of the picture where it truncates the two left-hand graves.

Grave 1 was located near the centre of the choir and roughly 1m below current ground level. It was initially recognised as two large flat stones lying side by side and when these were lifted by the workmen, a plaster-lined cavity was seen containing a human skeleton and, in the area of its chest, a 'brass cup'. At this point work was suspended, a report was made to the Superintendent of Works and the slabs replaced, the 'cup' having been removed from the cavity. The information was passed on to the Inspectorate of Ancient Monuments and Roy Ritchie was appointed to investigate the discovery. Ritchie travelled to Whithorn to inspect the finds and the stones, and found that the 'brass cup' was a gilt chalice, whilst the cavity was clearly part of a stone-lined grave. He also noted further flat stones immediately to the north, which he identified

Plate 2.1
Showing Graves 1–6 during excavation

as the cover slabs for a grave of similar type (Grave 2). As Ritchie's report to Stewart Cruden at the Inspectorate of Ancient Monuments (dated 21 October 1957) noted, these discoveries 'lay in the way of the Architects' work' (Archive D9, p.68). Clearly, there would be some delay to that exercise.

Work on the waterproofing of the vault was consequently put on hold whilst the necessary permissions were obtained, including those from the Whithorn Town Clerk and Provost. Their consent was required given the sensitive nature of archaeological excavation within the parish graveyard, along with the presence of relatively recent burials in the area. In the meantime, the two graves were covered over and preparations made in Edinburgh for the excavation of what was thought to be at least one, possibly two ecclesiastical burials. The presence of the chalice in the first grave and its location near the likely location of the high altar raised the possibility that here were the burials of senior medieval churchmen.

The investigation of the graves began on 30 October 1957 (Archive D9, p69), with Ritchie present on site. The graves were fully revealed (Plate 2.2), the cover slabs recorded and then removed, and recording of the grave's contents commenced. The truncated remains of two further graves (Graves 3 and 4) were also identified in the workmen's trench to the south of Grave 1. It was decided at this point to leave these burials *in situ* and concentrate on the two original discoveries. With further metal objects present in Graves 1 and 2, it was clear that further resources would be required. On Day 2 (31 October 1957), the site was again, therefore, briefly closed down. This allowed Ritchie to re-equip himself with

Plate 2.2
Facing west, Graves 1 and 2 as seen by Ritchie once they were first fully revealed. Note the broken slab on Grave 1 on the left where the chargehand was able to remove the 'brass cup'

'more equipment including small boxes, packing, and instruments for fine excavation ... (as well as) the services of the photographer and the A.M. (Ancient Monuments) Drawing Office' (Archive D9, pp.69–70).

Under Ritchie's supervision, work on the site resumed on 5 November 1957 and, as he puts it:

> secrecy [was] maintained until two chance onlookers on Wednesday, 6th November, realised the nature of the excavation. On arrival at the site next morning it was realised that the protective covering had been disturbed and replaced. Underneath, it was seen that the paten in Grave 1 had been lifted and replaced in the wrong position. The police were notified. Rumours started to circulate and there was a constant stream of visitors to the site which was now roped off. A watch was maintained on the crowd by the police.
>
> *(Archive D9, p.70)*

With 'rumours of desecration and removal of gold coins and the like' (Archive D9, p.70), a public display of the finds was hastily arranged and the local authorities formally notified; the excavation was also visited by local dignitaries. This phase of the fieldwork campaign, continuing through to the beginning of December, saw the complete excavation of Graves 1 and 2. With their contents removed, the site was then closed down and a protective cover of concrete beams, roofing felt and soil laid over the empty graves and the adjacent trench where the ends of Graves 3 and 4 (unexcavated) had been glimpsed. Following the flurry of activity at the site towards the end of 1957, excavation was not to resume until 1960, by which time the size and logistics of the future operations had been established.

In contrast to the reactive nature of the 1957 fieldwork, the 1960 campaign was an altogether more structured piece of excavation, initially at least. On the basis of the surviving documentation and records, it seems that the plan was to lift the stone lining of Graves 1 and 2 (the work in 1957 had merely removed their contents) and then to deal with Graves 3 and 4 to the south. Ritchie also sought to establish the stratigraphic relationship between the graves and the church by means of transverse and longitudinal sections across and along the building. The transverse section ran roughly in line with the head of the graves and revealed two further graves (Graves 5 and 6), in the area north of Grave 2. The longitudinal section lay roughly parallel to the north side of Grave 2 (Figure 2.1). It is as a result of this intended section that deposits to the north–west of Grave 2 were initially left *in situ*, with the longitudinal section extending a few metres to the west. The only alterations to this were with Graves 8 and 12 (see below), which were found to extend beyond the transverse section and small areas were therefore opened up to remove each one. This explains the gap in excavation between Grave 8 and Grave 12. In the event, the longitudinal section was not maintained and only the first few layers were recorded. The southern part of the transverse section is illustrated below (Figure 3.3).

Graves 3–6 were dealt with, recorded and the bones lifted. Further examples of altar plate and jewellery were found in Graves 3 and 4, and a coin and bead were recovered from

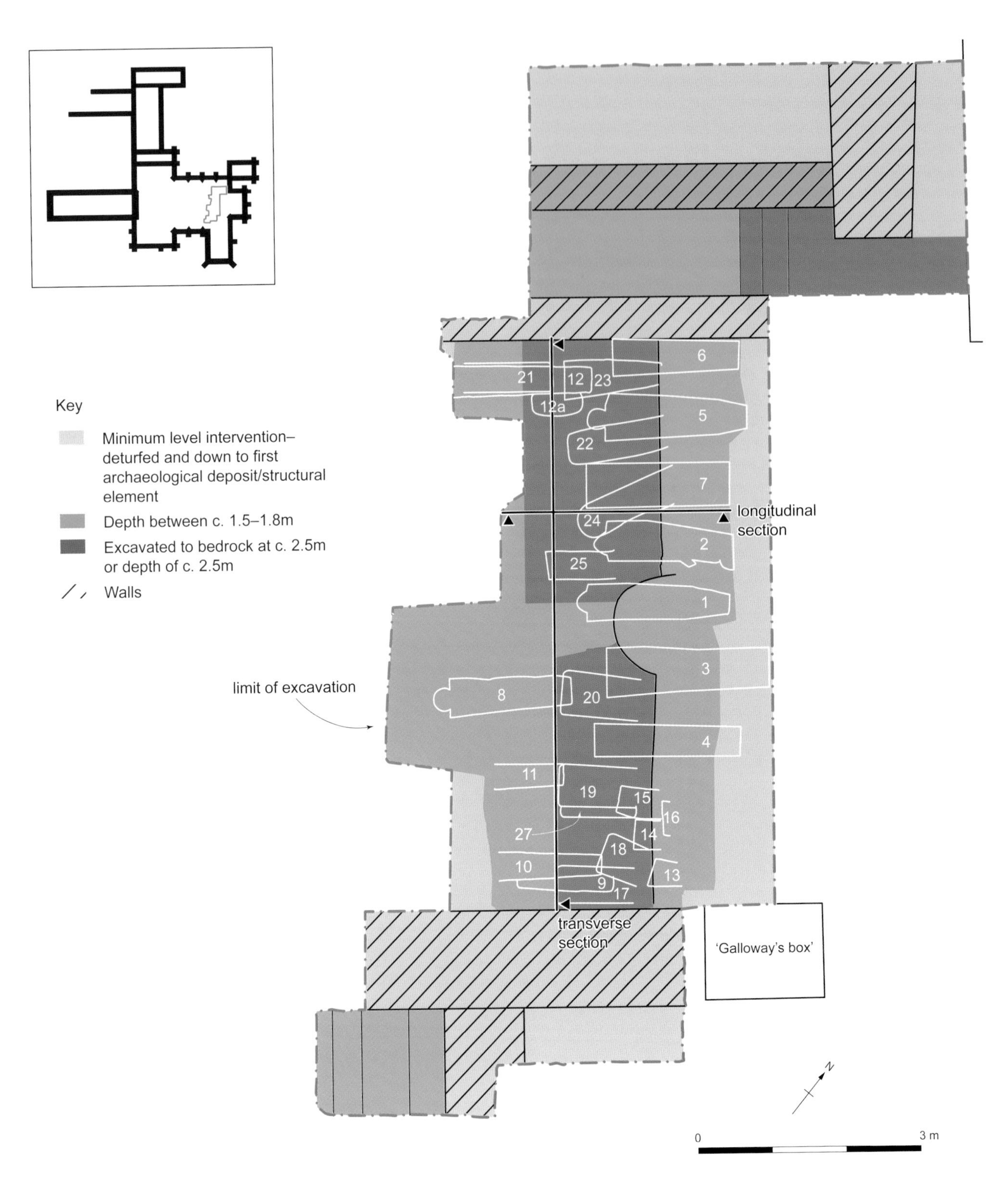

Figure 2.1
Plan of areas of excavation and depths; in some parts of the excavation, the depths are estimated or interpreted from photographic evidence. The southern part of the transverse section was drawn, while the longitudinal section was never fully recorded

Grave 5. The site was closed down on 31 August and all the indications are that this was to be the end of the excavation. The only outstanding issue revealed in the correspondence between Ritchie and Cruden is that decisions still needed to be taken about whether the stone linings of the graves should be preserved *in situ* or removed and preserved, and when this should be undertaken (SDD27/1582, 30 August 1960). It is clear, however, that all parties were of the opinion that the important archaeological remains had been dealt with and that no major further work was going to be needed. The project, however, was about to get a new lease of life – one that would lead to the discovery of what is undoubtedly the richest of all the medieval burials from Whithorn.

On 19 September 1960, a letter was sent from the site foreman, whose team had been backfilling the site, reporting the discovery of further items (SDD27/1582, 19 September 1960). Ritchie promptly returned to Whithorn to deal with these new discoveries. These comprised further pieces of altar plate, apparently within a grave that had not been previously identified. The area of this new grave (Grave 7) lay between Grave 2, the stone cist excavated in 1957, and Grave 5, another stone cist, which had been identified and excavated the previous month (August 1960).

Ritchie returned and attempted to define the limits of the grave. In the process of removing the finds and fill, he uncovered an enamelled gilt crozier, now known as the Whithorn Crozier. The precious metal finds were removed and the grave excavated, or at least partially excavated. There is some confusion as to whether the full extent of the grave was fully recognised at this stage, for while the presence of the plate and crozier do seem to have been noted, it was not until 1 May 1964 that the last of the silver-gilt spangles (small metal mounts, mostly flower-shaped and 4–8mm in diameter: Franklin, Chapter 6.4.3) were finally lifted. The excavation of this single grave thus spanned two different excavation seasons (September/October 1960 and April/May 1964), some three-and-a-half years apart, and the quality of the record of the grave is all the poorer for that.

Grave 7 lay at a slightly lower level than those previously found, raising the possibility that there could be further graves below the stone cists. It was decided that these would be removed to establish if this was the case. Work therefore resumed in November 1960. A further burial in a stone cist (Grave 8) was found at a similar level to Graves 1 and 2, albeit situated further to the west, and the remains of a stone wall aligned north–south were also identified below the stone cists. The north and south walls of the choir had also been revealed by this stage. Plate 2.3 shows the southern part of the area with the graves removed, and the stone wall and associated 'buttress' just visible in the foreground.

By the end of the 1960 season, it had become clear that the features and deposits being encountered had the potential to add considerably to the understanding of

Plate 2.3
View south across excavation area in 1960, showing the rear of the barrel vault on the left. Graves 1–8 have been removed from the foreground and the transverse wall begins to emerge. 'Galloway's box' is visible at the top centre of the image

high-status Scottish medieval ecclesiastical burials. There was also the added bonus that the excavations might throw considerable light on the structural development of the church itself. The decision was therefore taken that the waterproofing of the outside of the vaults would require excavation of a relatively large area, overall measuring roughly 7.5 long, 3m wide and 3.65m deep, down to the natural subsoil. In the event, the total area excavated exceeded even this estimation.

With the exception of 1963, when there were no works on site, the excavation continued on a seasonal basis from 1961 down to 1967, probably with the same team of Ritchie and the Cormacks each year, with additional references to the couple appearing in April 1961 and April 1962 (SDD27/1582, 23 April 1961; SDD27/1582, 13 April 1962). A certain Fraser and Swan appear on the drawing list for the 1960 season, and specialist advice on the textiles was provided by Audrey Henshall (Archive D9, p.69). Initially, work was focused on the south part of the site. The excavation area here was roughly 3.4m by 1.3m, its extent marked by the choir wall to the south, the existing north–south section to the west, and the newly discovered north–south wall to the east. The north side of the area was marked by the large semi-circular mass of masonry (subsequently described by Ritchie as a 'buttress'), forming part of the transverse wall (Figure 2.1). This area was excavated down to the natural subsoil and bedrock, and then the same process was undertaken in a trench to the north. The area there was formed by the choir wall to the north, the 'buttress' to the south, and the existing section and wall-lines respectively to the west and east. Again, the area was excavated down to bedrock. In addition, the north–south section across the site was also extended beyond the limits of the choir walls. The partially excavated stairway originally discovered by Galloway was identified in this north section, and Galloway's backfill and any collapsed debris was removed. A second stairway was also observed to the south (Figure 2.1), in the area to the west of the South Chapel. The fact that it appears to fall from east to west suggests that it must belong to a later phase of construction. Any contemporary south stair, it is assumed, will have been destroyed by the construction of the South Chapel in the later medieval period.

It is around this time (c 1965) that Ritchie must have removed the structure that he refers to as 'Galloway's box', an enigmatic stone construction (Figure 2.1, Plate 2.3) which lay roughly over the line of the south wall. While there is no record of Ritchie's interpretations of this feature, he undoubtedly recognised Galloway's hand in its construction. Our study suggests that it was rebuilt by Galloway over the site of a column base associated with the later South Chapel (Chapter 3.2.5).

Further burials were identified in both the north and south trenches as a large volume of overlying material was removed. The excavation at its full extent was 12' (3.65m) deep, from the original ground surface of the modern graveyard to bedrock found at the base of one of the trenches. Two basic levels of burials were identified during the course of the excavation: Graves 1 to 16 and 21 lay at or near the top of the sequence; around 6' (1.8m) below these was a second group (Graves 17–20, 22–25 and 27) cut into and immediately above the bedrock; 'Grave 26', meanwhile, relates to a collection of charnel that was found on top of the central 'buttress'. The numbering system for the graves, particularly those excavated in the latter part of the excavation, is explained in detail elsewhere (Henderson, Chapter 4.1.2).

A number of structural elements were also identified, primarily the wall aligned north to south that Ritchie called the transverse wall, and two linear stone features adjacent to the internal wall-face on either side of the choir, to north and south, which Ritchie referred to as 'benches'. There are also some fairly fragmentary and tantalising records relating to the possibility of burials and structures outwith the main excavation area. It is very difficult to know to what Ritchie is referring with these, but plans do indicate what appear to be a number of phases of walls in the area of the north stair. The overall sequence of the excavation, insofar as it can be cross-referenced to the surviving records and official correspondence, is summarised in Table 2.1.

2.3 RESULTS OF THE EXCAVATION

(Plates 2.4–2.15)

The principal results of the excavation are comprehensively set out in Ritchie's draft report (Archive D9, pp.73–126). The same format, comprising first the graves and then the structural and other remains, has been adopted here. The following section thus précis Ritchie's original report, together with his use of imperial measurements where this is useful (with their metric equivalents), and provides an overview of what was found. Our observations on the record are added in those cases where we feel that further comment is required. The stratigraphic relationships between these features and their phasing are explored in Chapter 3.

2.3.1 Burials

Grave 1 — Plate 2.4. Stone cist located on centre line of church. The cist was lined with mortar and the semi-circular head recess was formed on a single piece of carved stone. Covered with eight slabs *in situ*, their joints sealed with white mortar,

Table 2.1 The Whithorn excavations, 1957–67: a timeline of principal activities and events

1957	
14 October	Human bones first noted by work squad waterproofing vault but disregarded because of proximity of recent grave-yard
14x20 October	Two graves partially uncovered by work squad
by 21 October	Ritchie visits site, identifies and confirms graves (Graves 1 and 2)
30 October	Excavation of Graves 1 and 2 commences, with removal of important finds. Identification of Graves 3 and 4
31 October	Excavation closed down to get more equipment
5 November	Excavation resumed: Graves 1 and 2 fully excavated
early December	Graves covered with concrete beams, roofing felt and site backfilled
1960	
8 or 9 August	Ritchie returns, with assistance of Dr and Mrs E A Cormack, D Simpson of Edinburgh University, Fraser and Swan to excavate two sections across graves to establish relationship with church, and to deal with any further graves that appear
15 August	Article ('150 visit ancient graves') in *The Scotsman*, with photograph, describing visit to excavation on Saturday 13 August: five graves found, three (identifiable as Graves 3, 4 & 5) still contained skeletons in process of excavation
late August	Additional grave (Grave 6) identified. All burials excavated and removed from cists
31 August	Site closed down
19 September	During backfilling of site work by MoPBW squad further altar plate found in a previously unrecorded grave (Grave 7)
September/October	Ritchie returns to deal with Grave 7, removing the altar plate.
November	Permission sought from Architects' Office by Cruden to continue with the excavation
–	Excavation of Grave 7 continues; crozier identified and removed
–	Decision taken to remove stone cists and check for earlier burials below
December	Work continues, further stone cist (Grave 8) identified, excavated and removed
–	Transverse wall (wall running north–south next to barrel vault) identified under stone cists
–	Graves 9–12 identified
5 December	Decision taken that further excavation will be necessary and that the area will need to be cleared down to the natural subsoil
1961	
May	Work commenced on the south excavation area, probably dealing with Graves 9–11 and 13–15
–	South 'bench' identified
–	Work probably continues on Grave 12 next to the north wall, although it is not clear if it is removed at this time
June	Excavation closed down
July	Recording of Ralegh Radford's test-pits in the *Candida Casa* building at east end of priory by MBPW Drawing Office Recording of North and South elevations by MoPBW Drawing Office
1962	
April	Removal of Graves 9–11 and 13–15
April (?)	Excavation closed down
18 September	Work recommences on south excavation area
–	Decision taken that any further graves encountered will merely be noted, 'unless there is special reason for expecting finds'
–	Deep layers of deliberate infilling removed

–	Grave 16 identified and removed without record (?) – no record at all of this feature beyond noting that its west end truncated Graves 14 and 15
–	Graves 17–20, 27 identified and removed, photographs taken
–	Main north-south section drawn for the south excavation area
–	Mortar floor identified at base of section
30 October	Excavation reaches 'rock at 12' below the surface'; graves identified as extending below the transverse and south choir walls; burnt bone and charcoal in the cemetery soil interpreted as disturbance of pre-existing cremation: (Ritchie correspondence to Cruden, 30 Oct 1962)
15 November	Excavation closed down
8–20 December	Ritchie on site to record elevations and sections of south excavation area
1963	*No activity: Cruden's article on the excavation appears in The Scotsman Weekend Magazine, 4 May 1963. Refers to discovery of 'fragments of cremated bone, disturbed by Christian burials, on the rock'*
1964	
27 April or earlier	Work continues on part of south excavation area adjacent to 'buttress', probably taking deposits down to bedrock
28 April	Grave 7: '?crushed skull cleaned with UV [ultra-violet light]. Small frags of carbon around head'
28 April–01 May	Remaining material relating to Grave 7, including spangles, removed
–	Work begins on north excavation area, probably removing Grave 12 initially
06 May or later	Excavation closed down
1965	
August	Composite site plan of excavated area, undertaken by MPBW Drawing Office
07 September or earlier	Excavation recommences with south excavation area extended along line of main section, across south choir wall to reveal south stairway
–	Work continues in north excavation area, removing mortar layer roughly halfway down section
c 15 November	Work begins at end of season on area to north-east of north excavation area, outside north choir wall
–	North stair with Galloway's work revealed
8/9 December	Ritchie records elevation and plan of south stair
9 December or later	Excavation closed down
1966	
January	Work continues on north stairway, removing Galloway's infill
–	Bones found at bottom of stairway (?)
–	Blocking removed from door at north end of west crypt
1966	
January	Ritchie records elevation and plan of north stair
–	Grave 21 identified and removed (?)
–	Graves 22–26 identified and removed (?)
26 October or later	Excavation closed down

1967	
31 May or earlier	Clearing out of north stairway and north door of west crypt completed
	Final work within north excavation area
29 June	Cremated bone identified in 'area of strongly coloured black and red earth'. Located opposite central 'buttress'
–	Final work in south excavation area, associated with the transverse wall and 'buttress'
4 July	Recording levels in and around the church. Excavation closed down?
24 October	Working on electricity cable trench outside entrance to undercroft of South Chapel

Plate 2.4

Graves 1 and 2, facing west. The plaster lining of Grave 1 on the left can be seen to spread into the stones of Grave 3 at the far left of the picture preventing ingress of overlying soil. Contained silver-gilt chalice and paten, a gold, amethyst and sapphire ring, two copper-alloy buckles, a small fragment of textile made with gilt thread, and the remains of a wooden crozier head, carved with a foliaceous design and crocketed.

Extended adult inhumation, with arms along its sides. The wooden crozier head, covered with a white substance, lay beside the left shoulder; fragments of wood, identified as its shaft, were traced down the centre of the grave as a discontinuous line to the region of the waist. On the mid-line of the grave, roughly 12" (0.3m) from the head-recess, was a dark circular stain, 3" (75mm) in diameter, interpreted as the decomposed wooden base of the chalice. Next to this was the finger ring. The paten lay at the waist. Only the right side of the pelvis was preserved; against it were found two copper-alloy buckles, each with fragments of leather and textile adhering. From the area of the left shoulder a piece of gilt braid was also discovered.

Grave 2 Plate 2.4. Stone cist lined with brown mortar, and a carved ogival head recess. Covered with five(?) slabs, apparently *in situ*, although upon removal the cavity was found to have filled with soil. Contained pewter chalice and fragments of a possible paten, a silver-gilt ring set with a pierced amethyst, two copper-alloy buckles, a copper-alloy brooch and fragments of textile with gilt thread.

Extended adult inhumation, with arms folded across its chest. The small brooch lay inside the lower jaw and had presumably originally been positioned at the neck. One of the buckles was recovered from the upper chest area; the other beside the right hip. The stem, together with fragments of the bowl and base of the pewter chalice, lay beside the right arm; the paten, also in fragments, was found near the right hip, pinned vertically against the side of the cist by earth infilling of the grave. The silver-gilt ring was found on one of the fingers of the right hand.

In the region of the right arm were many small fragments of gilt thread and when the upper part of the arm was lifted it revealed a piece of gilt cloth. Other threads were seen amidst a black stain which extended from the neck to a point between the thighs. The stain, roughly 2" (50mm) wide, ran slightly to the right of the spine and at one point a substantial part adhered to the surface of a rib, demonstrating the layout of the gilt threads.

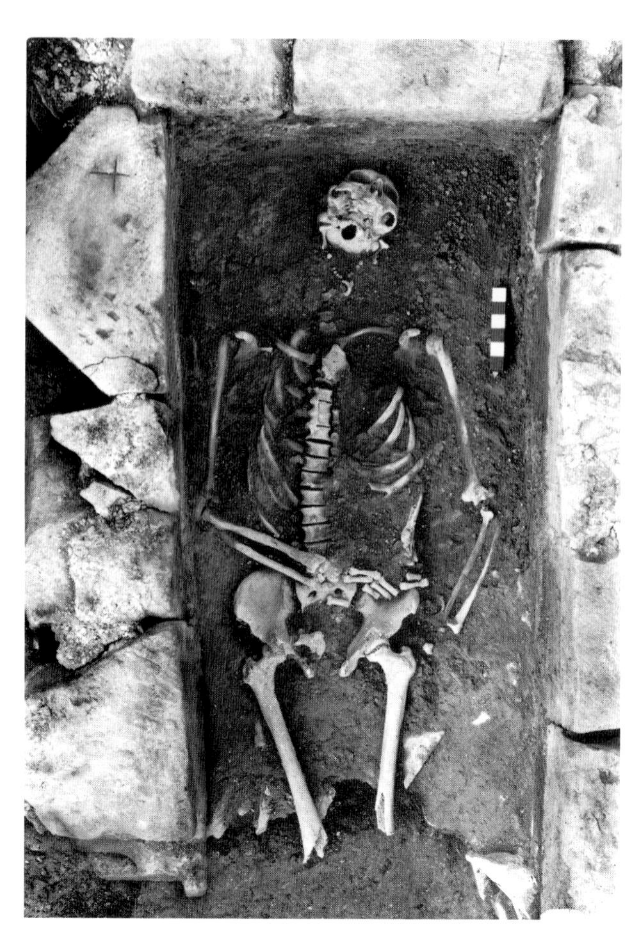

Plate 2.5
Grave 3 showing the large masonry used in its construction

Grave 3 Plate 2.5. Stone cist, bedded in yellow clay and partly built with reused architectural fragments, including the capital of an engaged shaft of late 12th-century date, and two slabs with a heavy chamfer on each of two corners, both marked with a small incised cross. No mortar lining, no head recess.

Cist walls only present on north, south and west as eastern end has been truncated. A vertical stain was present immediately next to the three remaining walls, possibly indicating the presence of a wooden lining. Cover slabs, although fractured, survived over the western part of the grave. Contained gold ring, set with rubies and emeralds, a copper-

Plate 2.6
Grave 4 with chalice and paten lying between thighs

alloy buckle and the highly decayed remains of a wooden crozier head, which does not now survive.

Extended adult inhumation, with right arm laid across its waist and the left arm along its side. Truncated roughly from the knees down. Fragmentary remains of wood covered with a white substance, interpreted as the head of a crozier, were found in the corner of the cist, beside the left shoulder. No trace of its shaft, however, could be determined. The gold ring was found on the tip of the third finger of the right hand. The copper-alloy buckle, again with leather adhering, lay beside the left hip.

In addition to the grave-goods listed here by Ritchie (the ring, the buckle and remains of a wooden crozier), the finds bags indicate that a small copper-alloy strap-mount (of 14th-century type: Franklin, Chapter 6.6) was also recovered from this grave. Given, however, that the grave almost certainly dates to the 13th century (Chapter 7, below), this object is probably intrusive.

Grave 4 Plate 2.6. Wooden coffin seen as stains in the soil along its north, south and west sides, the eastern end of the grave having been truncated. No grave covering was seen. Contained extended adult inhumation with hands crossed at the hips. Between the thighs was a pewter chalice and paten.

Grave 5 Plate 2.7. Stone cist, mortar-lined, with a semi-circular head recess formed of three stones, subsequently plastered over. Four cover slabs survived, two over the head area and two over the knees, and the cavity of the grave had filled with soil. The south-west side of the grave

Plate 2.7
Graves 5 and 6 at north of area. The diagonal 'stripe' of disturbance across the chest of Grave 5 is very noticeable

had been truncated and the stones of the cist removed in this area, almost certainly when a relatively modern burial in a wooden coffin was inserted above. Inside the cist was an extended adult inhumation, although the head and trunk area had been disturbed. The lower part of the right arm remained *in situ* and lay across the pelvis. A silver Edward I–II penny was found on the floor of the cist, close to the left leg. Below the right leg was a small bone bead.

No altar plate was found in the grave and the absence of such material is suspicious, given the similarity of construction to Graves 1 and 2. The known presence of disturbance at the head of the grave, to the extent that the side of the grave was removed, may explain this.

A photograph (Plate 2.7) of the remains *in situ* shows a distinct line of disturbance across the middle of the trunk, just above where the hands would be, and where the majority of the other liturgical plate was found. Our interpretation is that the grave was robbed 'sideways' by later grave-diggers who came down onto the stones at the side of Grave 5, removing them in the process and opening a void in the side of the grave. It is not difficult to imagine that on looking into the void they could have seen a 'shiny' cup and plate and, perhaps like the chargehand in 1957, have used a stick to pull the items across to the side of the grave. Other items, such as finger-rings, could have similarly been removed. The existence and nature of any such finds would be difficult to prove for certain, but that something was disturbed within the grave is indisputable.

Plate 2.8
Outline of Grave 7, facing west. No full images survive of Grave 7 *in situ*; here we see the hollow formed by its probable cut, to the left (south) of the head recess of Grave 5

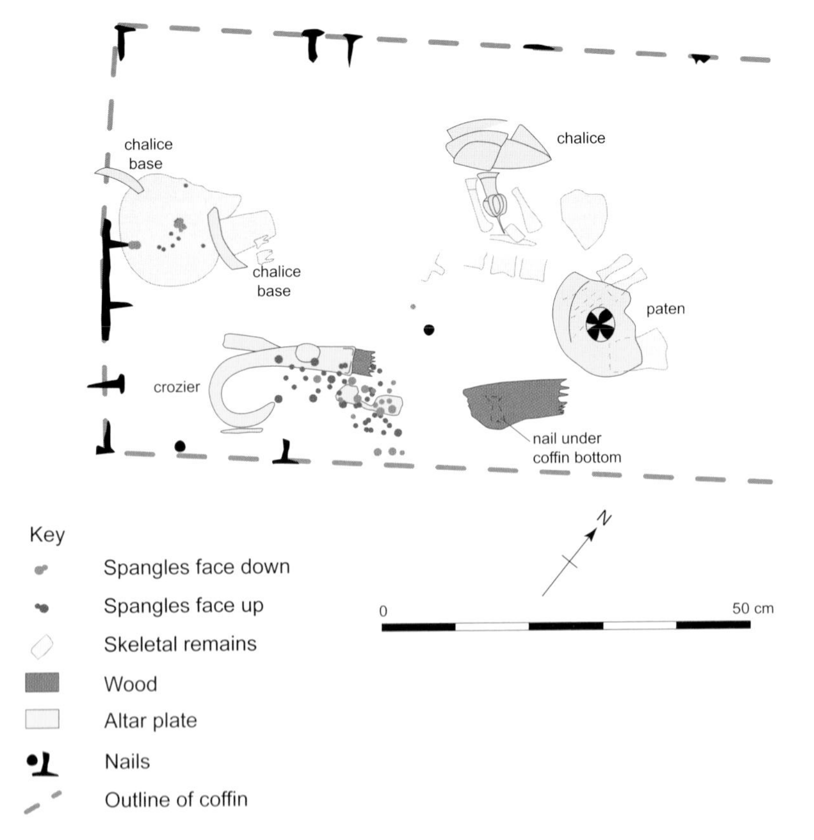

Figure 2.2

This plan of Grave 7 is a composite from a number of sources. Various elements of the grave (human remains, altar plate and nails) were planned by hand and appear in surviving archive material. The detail of the location of the spangles and some of the human remains appeared in sketches in Ritchie's daybook of the excavations (Archive A29)

Grave 6 Plate 2.7. Extended adult inhumation, with hands crossed over the pelvis. Only identified during removal of Grave 5 adjacent, the north wall of which overlies its right arm and leg. Traces of a wooden coffin were subsequently identified as stains in the soil along the south side of the grave, but nowhere else. Iron nails were also identified, at roughly 1' (0.3m) intervals along the north and south sides of the grave. No grave covering, however, was seen and no grave-goods were present. The absence of a skull led Ritchie to believe that the remains were headless; it seems more likely, however, that the grave has been truncated by later burials.

Grave 7 Plate 2.8. Figure 2.2. Accidentally discovered by workman during back-filling and located in the area between Graves 2 and 5 where modern disturbance was identified 7" (180mm) below the base of Grave 2. Iron nails were identified by the labourer along the north side of the grave; 'rather more than halfway along the grave he found a silver paten and chalice which he recognised and then stopped' (Archive D9, p.100).

Wooden coffin, evidenced only by presence of iron nails: 'the nails which fastened the headboard were found and the top of the coffin defined. Parts of the south side were also found but nothing at all of the north side' (Archive D9, p.100). The crushed silver chalice lay roughly on the mid-line of the grave, 2' (0.6m) from the headboard; the stem was intact, with finger bones around and under it. The silver paten lay face upwards, 6" (150mm) further east and closer to the south side of the grave; on top of it was a piece of wood and, underneath, fragments of finger bones. One foot (0.3m) to the west of the chalice and touching the south side of the coffin (and thus beside its occupant's right shoulder) was the enamelled copper-alloy gilt crozier head, its volute turned outwards.

Ritchie's description then turns to the discovery of the spangles, described by him as rosettes or sequins. It deserves to be quoted in full:

> Three inches (75mm) from the collar at the base of the stem, a gilt rosette or sequin lay on top of the stem. Another lay 3" (75mm) to the west of the volute, whilst a third lay on the mid-line of the grave. After the crozier head had been lifted, more sequins were found to form a pattern underneath the volute. Two layers were present, the upper layer face downwards, the lower layer face upwards. The sequins which lay with their faces upwards formed three distinct pattern groups. Nearest to the head of the grave was a square whose corners were defined by larger sequins and inside this a circle of five smaller sequins was centrally placed. Nearer to the foot of the grave were [sic] a larger and a smaller circle all composed of small sequins. The sequins which lay facing downwards did not fall into such easily recognizable patterns. Two groups of large sequins formed a rectangle and triangle respectively, with smaller sequins forming an arc of a circle between these two main groups.
>
> Eight inches (200mm) to the north of this it was possible, with the aid of ultra-violet radiation, to make out the outline of a skull which appeared to lie on its left-hand side, facing north. Under

Plate 2.9
Grave 7 during excavation showing the remains of the chalice and paten lying under 'rubble' type material

> the skull were various gilt sequins and also gold threads. With the exception of one square motif, it was not possible to work out any pattern from these finds. To the west of the skull numerous sequins were concentrated in a line and lay in alternating bands – face down, face up, face down. It seems likely that these represent the decoration from a mitre which had been placed at the head of the grave and that the sequins took up this disposition as the fabric of the mitre decomposed
>
> *(Archive D9, pp. 101–2).*

In addition to the grave-goods listed here by Ritchie (the silver chalice and paten, the enamelled copper-alloy gilt crozier, the spangles and fragments of textile), it is clear from the information on the finds bags that the grave also contained a copper-alloy pin shaft and a glass bead. Interestingly, information on the finds bag also indicates that two sherds of undecorated window glass were also recovered from or assigned to Grave 7 (Franklin, Chapter 6.9). No evidence, however, contrary to Glenn's note (2003, 17) on its provenance, has been found to suggest that the copper-alloy gilt pinnacle was also recovered from this grave. There is no reference to it in the Ritchie archive. The only documentary reference to it that has been traced is a note and list of finds which Ritchie sent to Cruden on 19 December 1960 (SDD27/1582). The gilt pinnacle – 'broken from some larger object' – is the last item in the list. It is preceded in the list by 'silver coin of Edward', presumably the coin from Grave 5, and 'crozier head, wood',

Plate 2.10
Grave 8, facing north, with possible stone flooring to west

presumably the one from Grave 1. Although it is clear that there are items from Grave 7 in this list, there is, however, nothing here to suggest that the pinnacle was one of these.

The grave was excavated over two seasons, some three-and-a-half years apart (Chapter 2.2). The precise circumstances of its excavation, however, are difficult to reconstruct. Nonetheless, it is clear that the full length of the grave was not recognised for some time after the initial discovery of the altar plate: a photograph (Plate 2.9) of the partially excavated grave shows that to the west of the chalice and paten there was a large amount of overlying rubble still *in situ*, which also contained fragments of window glass. This rubble, along with other elements of the grave, is an example of the different and slightly unusual nature of Grave 7 as a whole. Firstly, the grave lies at a lower level than either Graves 2 or 5 on either side of it, or any of the other graves in this line (Graves 1, 3, 4 or 6). It is also unusual in that it is in a wooden coffin. While other examples of wooden coffins containing altar plate are known (eg Graves 4 and 21), the more richly equipped burials appear to have been placed in stone cists and dressed for display. The presence of rubble is also unusual as this is the only example of such material being found within what are thought to be the limits of a grave. The rubble may have collapsed into the grave following the decay of the coffin, but this in itself is also fairly unusual – in general, all the graves seen are remarkably well-preserved for their age, regardless of whether they were in stone cists or wooden coffins, and the only infilling otherwise noted was where soil-trickle had gradually infiltrated the grave cavity.

Grave 8

Plate 2.10. Stone cist, plaster-lined with a semi-circular carved head recess, and reported to have been covered with seven cover slabs, their joints sealed with white mortar. No soil was present inside the cist and the absence of any disturbance is explicitly remarked upon. Inside the cist was an extended adult inhumation, with the arms laid by the sides. Ritchie noted that the right tibia was fractured and that beside the left leg were the remains of a child. No grave-goods were present inside the cist.

In spite of Ritchie's assurances to the contrary, this present study suggests that the chest area of the skeleton has been extensively disturbed and that charnel,

Plate 2.11
Grave 10 cut through an earlier *in situ* burial (Grave 9) lying immediately to the south

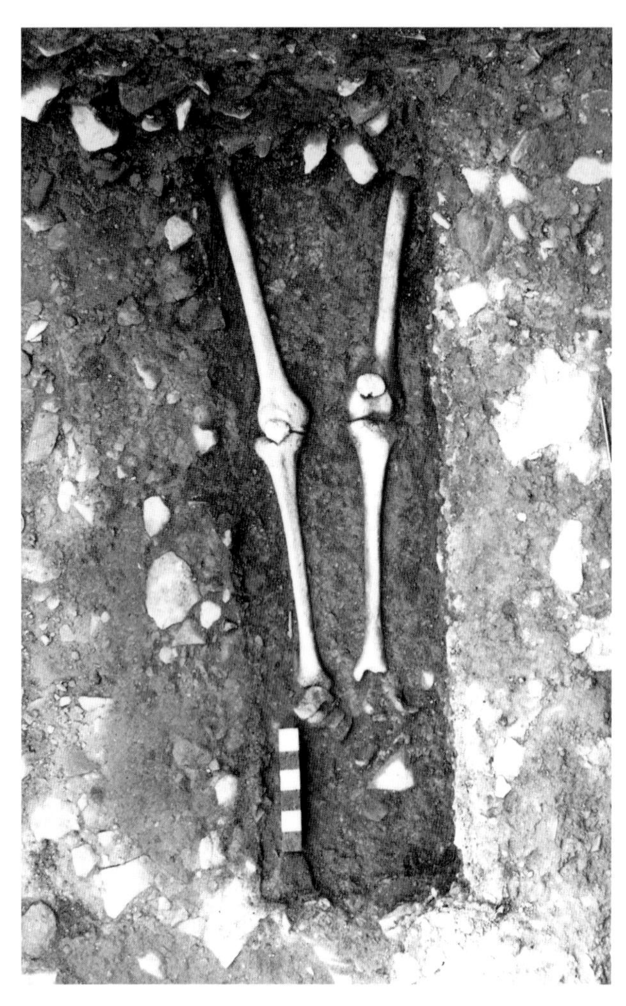

Plate 2.12
Grave 11 (like Graves 9 and 10) was only excavated below the waist

including the partial remains of a young child, were redeposited inside the cist at the time of its disturbance. The fractured leg, noted by Ritchie (Archive D9, p.107), is identified here as almost certainly the result of post-mortem breakage (Henderson, Chapter 4 below). There are also indications on the bones themselves, in the form of (lead or silver?) staining on the pelvis, that grave-goods, presumably robbed in antiquity, were also originally present in the grave (Henderson, Chapter 4.3). As in the case of Grave 5, photographic evidence (Plate 2.10) again reveals extensive disturbance around the upper part of the body where altar plate might be expected. The ribs appear out of place and there is a general jumble of bones around the lower chest and stomach area. It is impossible to confirm that this grave would have contained such material, but the evidence points to it being extremely likely.

Below Grave 8 was found one of the few pottery sherds that could be firmly located within the excavation – a body sherd of French origin. A note with the find indicated it was found in material below the cut for the stone cist (Chapter 6.11.2)

'Grave 9' Plate 2.11. A collection of non-articulated charnel found on the south side of (and cut by) Grave 10, including the right hip and upper leg of a female.

Grave 10 Plate 2.11. Wooden coffin, recognised as a stain in the soil on the two long sides and its east end, the west end extending into the baulk, outwith the area of excavation. Iron nails were also found at intervals along the sides of the coffin but no lid could be recognised.

Extended inhumation only revealed from upper waist down: 'bones of the fore-arms, hands, lumbar and pelvic region survived only as red-brown stains in dark brown soil. Fluorescence effects produced by UV radiation were used and these confirmed that the hands were crossed over the pubic region'(Archive D9, p. 120). No grave-goods were present within the excavated part of the grave.

Grave 11 Plate 2.12. Wooden coffin, seen as a stain in the soil on its north, south and east sides, the west end extending into the baulk, outwith the area of excavation. No coffin lid was recognised. Extended inhumation only revealed from the upper legs down, and no grave-goods were present within the excavated part of the grave. Information on the finds bags indicates that a painted sherd of window glass (No. 44) was also recovered from or attributed to Grave 11 (Franklin, Chapter 6.9).

Grave 12 Plate 2.13. Extended adult inhumation, with the hands placed palm downwards on the mid-line of the lower part of the abdomen. Sides of the wooden coffin were recognised as stains in the soil although no trace of the lid was identified. No grave-goods present.

Plate 2.13
Grave 12, facing west. To the right is the north stone 'bench'

'Grave 12A' Collection of semi-articulated and jumbled charnel found to the south of Grave 12. At least two skulls and a number of large limb bones present.

Grave 13 Plate 2.14. Wooden coffin, seen as a stain in the soil along the north, south and west sides, the east end having been truncated, possibly by insertion of the barrel vault, or by Galloway's workmen in the 19th century, or by the MoPBW squad in 1957. No grave covering seen. Extended inhumation of a youth, the surviving elements consisting of the area from the skull to the lower part of the chest. No grave-goods present within surviving part of grave.

Grave 14 Plate 2.14. Wooden coffin, represented only by a stain in the soil along the north, south and west sides, the east end having been truncated by Grave 16. Only fragments of an adult skull survive, and no grave-goods were present within the surviving part of the grave.

Grave 15 Plate 2.14. Wooden coffin, marked only by a soil stain and truncated on the east by Grave 16. Extended inhumation of a youth, the surviving elements consisting of the area from the skull to the lower part of the chest. No grave-goods present within surviving part of grave.

Grave 16 Grave number assigned to the wooden coffin that truncates Graves 14 and 15. No human remains or coffin remains survived, and the full extent of the feature identified by Ritchie appears to have consisted only of the west end of the coffin: 'the nails marking the outline of the headboard of another coffin were found to truncate both graves' (Archive D9, p.117). This may, itself, have been truncated in antiquity by the construction of the barrel vault, or by Galloway in the 19th century.

Graves 17–20: SEE BELOW.

Grave 21 Plate 2.15. Wooden coffin, seen as a soil-stain along its long sides and east end. At the foot-end of the coffin, forming a handle, was a large iron ring. Located below Grave 12.

The west end of the grave extends beyond western limit of excavation so that only the lower half of the skeleton, from the waist down, was excavated. No grave covering seen. Extended adult inhumation with hands crossed, palms downwards, over the front of the lower part of the abdomen.

The remains of a pewter chalice were recovered from the area beside the lumbar vertebrae and pelvis, suggesting that it had originally been placed upon the lower part of the chest. At the time of excavation Ritchie also believed that there was a pewter paten present, but analysis of the wear patterns on the two fragments shows that these are part of the same item, with the 'paten' being part of the base of the cup (Chapter 6.3.2).

No surviving descriptions have been traced among the Ritchie papers for Graves 17– 20 and 22–27. The descriptions presented here derive from the evidence of the drawings and the site photographic archive. All of this group predate the construction of the transverse wall.

Plate 2.14
Graves 13, 14 and 15 truncated below the chest region by the insertion of the barrel vault c 1500

Graves 17–20, 26 and 27
A series of graves was identified at the base of the trench in the South Excavation Area. The grave-cut was only identified at the level of the skeleton which survived only in a thin layer of soil above bedrock. No coffin-stains were identified and it seems likely that these were dug graves, with the burials in shrouds. None contained grave-goods. Grave 19 cuts Grave 27. 'Grave' 20 comprises a collection of charnel which overlies a possible *in situ* (and unexcavated) burial which itself lies entirely under the central 'buttress'. This possible burial was seen only in the form of a skull which lies adjacent to the rest of the charnel group but was pinned down by the rubble supporting the 'buttress'. Ritchie does not appear to have noted this as a separate group of material and certainly the skull was never lifted from the ground.

'Grave 26' (Temporarily 'double-numbered' by Ritchie as Grave 9 in his correspondence to Cruden: SDD27/1582, dated 27 November 1960) relates to a group of charnel on top of the central 'buttress', possibly redeposited at the time of the construction of the transverse wall.

Graves 22-25 Series of graves identified at base of trench in the North Excavation Area. Again, the grave-cut was only identified at the level of the skeleton although here the layer of soil over the bedrock was roughly 1' (0.3m) thick. As with the group nearby at the same level, these are likely to have been dug graves, with the burials in shrouds. None contained grave-goods.

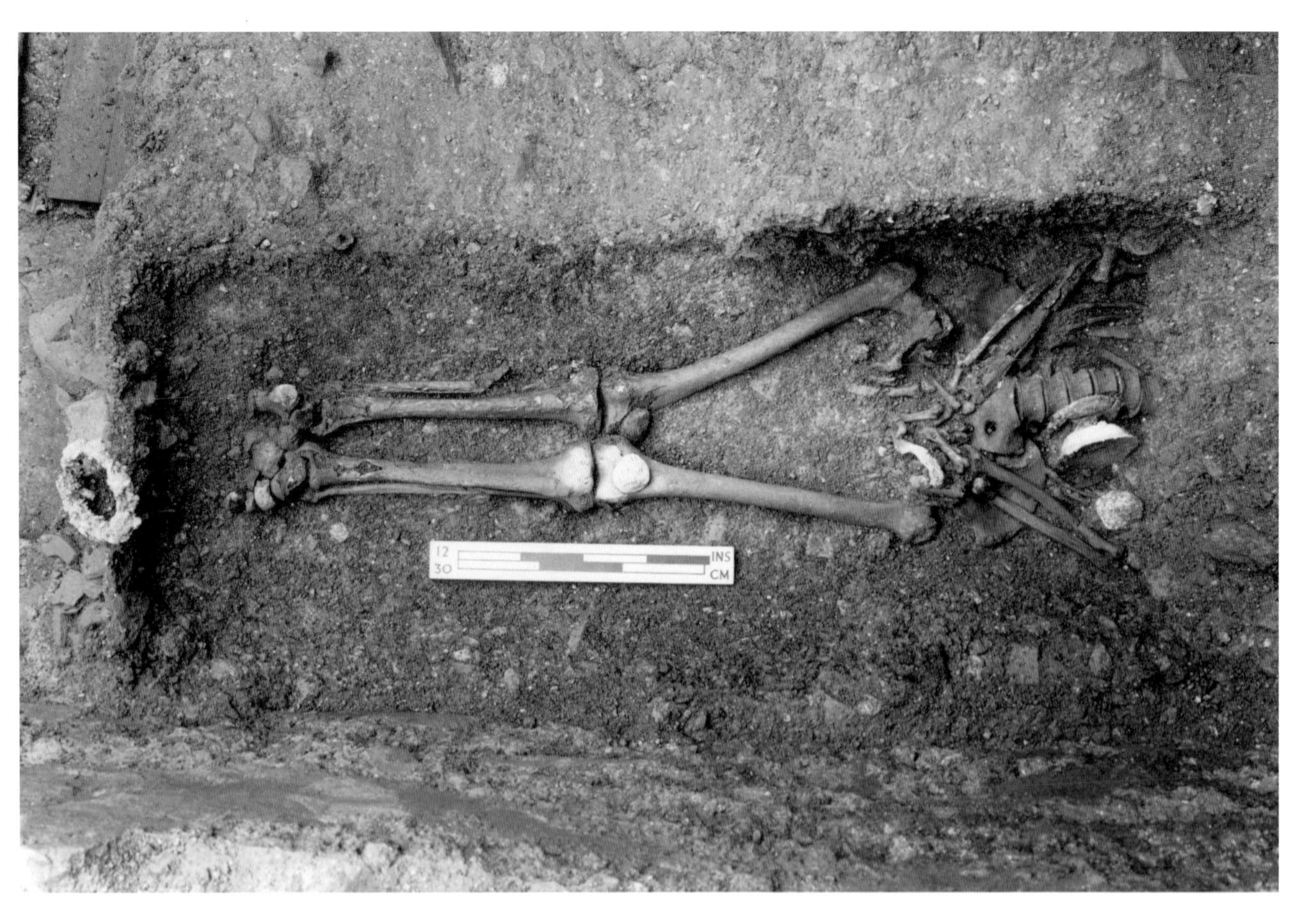

Plate 2.15
Grave 21 facing south, with the chalice over the lower chest area and the loop of the coffin fitting (Cat. no. 37) visible near the feet

Grave 28 No plan or photographic evidence has been traced for this grave but there is a brief mention of 'a burial embedded in lime' which was discovered 'at a high level' in the course of clearing out the north stair (Archive D9, p.71). It should be noted that fragments of three early crosses were found here by Ritchie, built into the fabric of the walls. These fragments now form Crosses 36, 38 and 39 in the Whithorn Museum collection (Derek Craig, pers comm).

2.3.2 Other features and structures

North wall of the choir

Stone wall at least 7' 10" wide (2.4m), aligned east to west, at north side of the excavation area. The outer face was not seen as it extended beyond the limit of excavation. Within the wall was an intramural stair, of which at least two steps were exposed, falling from west to east and leading down into the crypt. The northern part of the wall was at least 1' 11" (0.6m) wide, the steps were 3' 9" (1.15m) wide and the south wall was 2' 2" (0.65m) wide. Located more than 3.5m below current ground level, the northern part of the wall only survived to a height of 1' 9" (0.53m), while the southern part of the wall was at least 6' (1.8m) high. As a result of this current study, it is clear that some fairly major rebuilding or remodelling of the wall (largely the stair side of the southern part of the wall) had been undertaken by Galloway.

When the intramural stair was identified, it had been backfilled with rubble from Galloway's excavations. The same material also overlay a wall, erected (we suggest) by Galloway and partially obscuring the line of the steps. This is discussed in more detail below (Chapter 3.2.2).

South wall of the choir

Stone wall, 4' 1" (1.2m) wide, aligned east to west, at the south side of the excavation area. Seen on plan in several photographs; there is also a drawing of part of the wall, on plan, showing some of its masonry detail. Ritchie describes three different phases of construction, based on the pointing and mortar coating present on the interior face of the wall, but the existence of three separate phases seems unlikely. Some reconstruction of the upper portion of the wall is likely to have been undertaken by Galloway, and certainly his hand can be seen in the stone 'box'-like structure which was built over the foundations of the south wall. It is also likely that some rebuilding of the wall would have been necessary when the South Chapel was constructed, however the difference in pointing techniques may simply reflect whether that part of the wall was buried as a foundation or visible above ground. Clearly, the south wall of the choir is much narrower than the north wall and also lacks any intramural element. Possible reasons for this are discussed in more detail below (Chapter 3.2.5).

Transverse wall

Stone wall aligned north to south across eastern part of excavation area. Roughly parallel with west side of barrel vault, although Ritchie states that it is 4' 6" (1.35m) behind the inner face of the wall bearing the barrel vault on the north side, and 2' 10" (0.85m) on the south side. Semi-circular projection, up to 4' (1.2m) wide, formed of mortared rough masonry – described by Ritchie as a 'buttress' – lay about halfway along the length of the wall, at the mid-line of the building. Built into, and of one build with, the north and south choir walls at its lower levels, its function was to provide a platform for the made-ground to the west and provide a springing for the primary vault to the east. It was never intended to be a visible structure within the church. Truncated on east side by construction of the later barrel vault, and potentially by Galloway's reconstruction work.

In some of Ritchie's records of the wall, there appears to be a deliberate gap in the masonry of the wall on the south side of the 'buttress' and Ritchie marks it as 'straight jamb?'. Clearly the potential is that he thought that there was an intentional break in the wall, perhaps even a door in the line of the wall. This is discussed below (Chapter 3.2.2).

Stone 'benches'

Stone features, aligned east to west, adjacent to and clearly abutting the north and south interior wall-face of the choir. The north bench was 7' 2" (2.15m) long and at least 8" (0.2m) wide; the south 'bench' was about 5' (1.5m) long and 8" (0.2m) wide.

Possible floor surfaces

Number of stone slabs, 3¼"–4" (8–10mm) thick, observed in north–south section, possibly remnants of stone floor. Others were seen on plan adjacent to Grave 8.

Possible wall foundation

A layer of mortar and stones, interpreted by Ritchie as a possible wall foundation, aligned north to south across the building, was identified adjacent to and roughly 200mm above the level of Grave 8: 'a layer of mortar and stones which may represent the footing for a wall ran from north to south about 8" above the cover slabs at the head of Grave 8' (Archive D9, p.106).

Possible wall

A line of stones, adjacent to south choir wall, was observed to run off at an angle of 20 degrees (Archive D9, p.126). No photographs or plans of the feature, however, have been identified and its precise location (whether inside or outside the church) is not known.

Mortar layers

Two separate layers of mortar-rich deposit, roughly 4' (1.2m) apart, are noted in the drawn sections and photographs but are nowhere described or discussed in any detail. They could be floor surfaces but they are more likely, given the structural development of the building, to represent construction or demolition layers.

South stairway

Within the trench on the south side of the south choir wall, a large concentration of rubble was identified. Ritchie's drawn records indicate the presence of the remains of at least two dressed steps and potentially a third. There may also be a door check built into the south choir wall which would mark the entrance to the stairway. The stairway appears to fall from east to west.

Structures in north stairway

Other 'structures' described as being in the area of the north stairway were found when this part of the site was being cleared out. Their precise form is difficult to understand for while Ritchie recorded them on plan and photographed them, he provides no notes on what was original and what related to Galloway's work of the late 19th century. It is clear that Galloway rebuilt at least some of the walls in this part of the site, and must have built a wall along the inside the intramural passage which also closed off the entrance to the crypt.

A wall, 4' 7" wide and aligned north–south, overlies the line of the intramural stairs and must post-date them, as it effectively puts the stairs out of use. It is possible that this wall dates to the immediate post-Reformation period, although a much later chronology perhaps seems more likely. While it is difficult to tell from photographic evidence alone, it is highly likely that this wall was built by Galloway at the same time as he built the false wall along the south side of the intramural space. Possibly the cross-wall marks the extent of his clearance of the stair.

Beyond the base of the stair, a wall 8' 6" high and aligned north–south possibly marked the east end of this part of the church. It is not known how this wall relates to the remains that Galloway found and subsequently reconstructed as the 'Pantry'. This wall can still be recognised although it has now been built into the north side of the current stairway into the crypts.

Early bones

Collection of bones found under wall(?) adjacent to door into the west barrel vault, potentially early in date. Photographs exist but no further records.

2.3.3 Conclusions

These, then, are the headline results, the blow-by-blow account of the graves and other features that Roy Ritchie found over the course of his ten-year campaign. Ritchie certainly had his views on the relative lateness and earliness of the graves, whom at least one of them might be, and how the east end of the priory church developed over time. However, not all of these views are easily demonstrable or reproducible on the basis of the site record. The site stratigraphic sequence and phasing are explored in the next chapter.

Chapter 3

Stratigraphy and Phasing

KIRSTY DINGWALL

3.1 INTRODUCTION

Roy Ritchie's draft publication texts (Archive D8 & D9), with their variously defined groups of 'late' and 'early' graves and other structures, were the starting point for this investigation. It was only by understanding the basic outline of the excavation (essentially the narrative and the results sections presented in Chapter 2) that it became possible to recognise how the various parts of the record fitted together.

The intention had always been to try to examine the data as objectively as possible, as if this were a current excavation. However, because of the lack of useful primary archive material for some important parts of the site, it quickly became clear that Ritchie's interpretations and guidance would be vital in creating any sort of stratigraphic sequence. Despite the existence of at least three drawn sections across the excavation area, they were not particularly helpful in understanding the deposits, as very few individual context or deposit records are present in the surviving archive. In trying to resolve these issues it was seen to be most effective to take Ritchie's interpretations and test them, checking if the plans and, most importantly, the photographic evidence could be used to back them up. Where Ritchie's suggestions clearly make sense, they can be taken at face value, but where there were contradictions between his interpretation and the evidence of the photographs, then a return to first principles was required to distinguish between what was irrefutable, what was possible and what was clearly impossible.

It was only once the main structure of the sequence of the excavation and its broad phasing had been established that it was then possible to go back into the more detailed aspects of Ritchie's archive, such as the day-book. Here, what we attempted to do was to reconcile the records with the known features on the site; any records which could not be matched with known features were then assessed with a view to identifying whether further burials or other features were present, but not fully recorded. Some parts of the record, unfortunately, were impenetrable and some of the features that Ritchie describes are of uncertain function, uncertain location and uncertain association. The phasing scheme that follows is based on Ritchie's original sequence, albeit one that has been tested and amended in light of our analysis of the archive.

3.2 STRATIGRAPHY AND PHASING

3.2.1 The primary cemetery (Phase 1)

(Figure 3.1)

Phase 1 comprises a group of graves that appears to lie either on or near to the level of bedrock, at a depth of about 12' (3.65m) below the current ground level at the east end of the church. The group comprises eight articulated *in situ* burials (Graves 17–19, 22–5 and 27) plus a charnel group ('Grave' 20) which appears to overlie or abut a further, articulated burial which was neither excavated nor numbered (Chapter 2.3.1).

The key photographic evidence for these early graves is reproduced here as Plates 3.1, 3.2 and 3.3. It is difficult to establish their precise location although it is clear that the skull of Grave 19 and charnel associated with 'Grave' 20 were located at the base of the deep north–south section. To make matters worse, some of the skeletons in this group were lifted and stored together, without (so far as we can tell) any grave numbers having been assigned to them, or the grave numbers being incorrect within the existing sequence of numbers that Ritchie was using (see the confusion over Graves 20/25 and the multiple use of 21: Henderson, Chapter 4.1.2). Henderson's reconstruction of the various skeletons here and our numbering of them thus depends partly on their anatomical 'fit' and partly upon the photographic evidence itself.

The Phase 1 graves are located at the base of the two trenches excavated between 1961 and 1967, lying to the north and south of the semi-circular masonry 'buttress'. All are contained in simple dug graves and none was buried with any grave-goods. In the south trench were three extended inhumations (Plate 3.1). These have been numbered in the course of the present analysis as Graves 17, 18 and 19. All three skeletons were relatively intact,

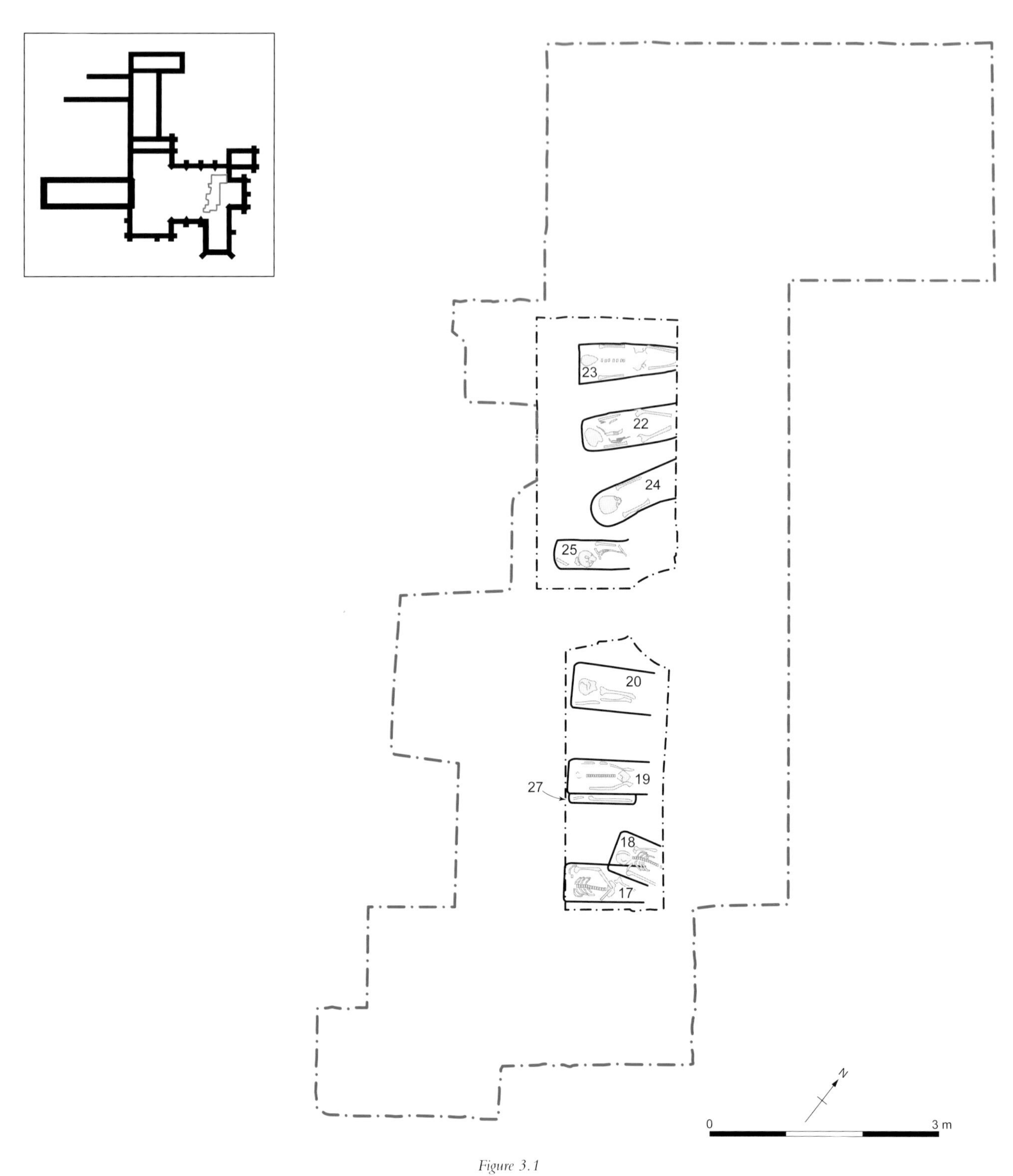

Figure 3.1
Primary Cemetery (Phase 1). The burials were encountered below several metres of deliberately dumped deposits associated with later construction work. The Phase 1 burials form part of a normal cemetery population that predates the eastern extension of the church

Plate 3.1
Graves 17, 18, 27 and 19 lay at the base of the excavation, sitting almost directly on bedrock

although the skulls of two of them (Graves 17 and 19) lie beyond or within the north–south section to the west, and the lower legs of all three lie beyond the edge of excavation to the east. Immediately to the south of Grave 19 was a group of bones (numbered here as Grave 27) that initial analysis of the archive suggested was charnel. It is clear, however, that it comprises an articulated leg which belonged to a burial that was truncated when Grave 19 was placed in the ground. In the north trench were a further four extended burials (Graves 22–5). These are known from photographs (Plate 3.2) that show the four burials lying roughly in a row north to south, and from a basic plan of the bodies that was added to an earlier dye-line plan of other graves, apparently completed during the excavation. The photographs suggest they were probably excavated during the latter part of 1966, well towards the end of the fieldwork. The plan and photographs give no indication of which graves they are, and the numbers given to them here (Graves 22–25) simply continue the number sequence. Only the human remains from Grave 23 were labelled. In the case of this group, all four skulls lie within the trench although the lower parts of the bodies again extend beyond the east edge of the excavation. Although clearly part of the same line of graves as Graves 17–19 to the south (which are aligned roughly NE–SW), it is noticeable, however, that there is a more north–north-easterly aspect to the north group, most notably in the alignment of Grave 24.

Between the north and south grave groups was 'Grave' 20 (Plate 3.3). Aside from the bones themselves, it is only known from the photographs and it is not fully understood.

Plate 3.2
Graves 25, 24, 22 and 23 with the overlying transverse wall visible along the bottom

The photographs appear to show a jumble of charnel, but analysis of the material lifted would suggest that this was associated with some element of articulated material. The layout and depth of the graves implies that the two groups are part of the same broad phase, despite there being no direct relationship between the two, due to the presence of the large masonry buttress at the centre of the site that was not removed during the excavation.

The section across the east ends of Graves 17–19 is one of the few hand-drawn sections that exists from the site (Figure 3.3 below), and it shows the skull of Grave 19 *in situ* and one of the limb bones from 'Grave' 20 extending into the section. The section drawing also provides information about the deposits into which the graves were cut. Adjacent to Graves 19 and 20, it is referred to as 'dark soil'; in the area around Graves 17 and 18 the basal layer is described as 'lighter in colour'. Neither of these descriptions gives much indication of the type of ground into which these graves were inserted; however, the absence of stones in the section would not be incompatible with a buried topsoil horizon. No section survives across the north trench and we have very little information about the nature of the primary soil horizon there, into which Graves 22–5 were inserted. Pencil notes on the dye-line plan suggest that the cut of these graves survived to a depth of at least 1' (0.3m).

Both sets of graves appear to have been cut down to bedrock. The images of Graves 17–20 show only a thin layer of deposit below them; in places, what appears to be a shattered bedrock can be seen between the graves. This material will be familiar to anyone who has dug in or around the church at Whithorn. A later photograph shows the skeletons removed, but the section on either side does not seem to be appreciably deeper. The drawing convention that is used in the section to depict the material into which Graves 19 and 20 have been cut would also be consistent with an attempt to indicate this kind of shattered bedrock, and one of Ritchie's elevations of the south choir

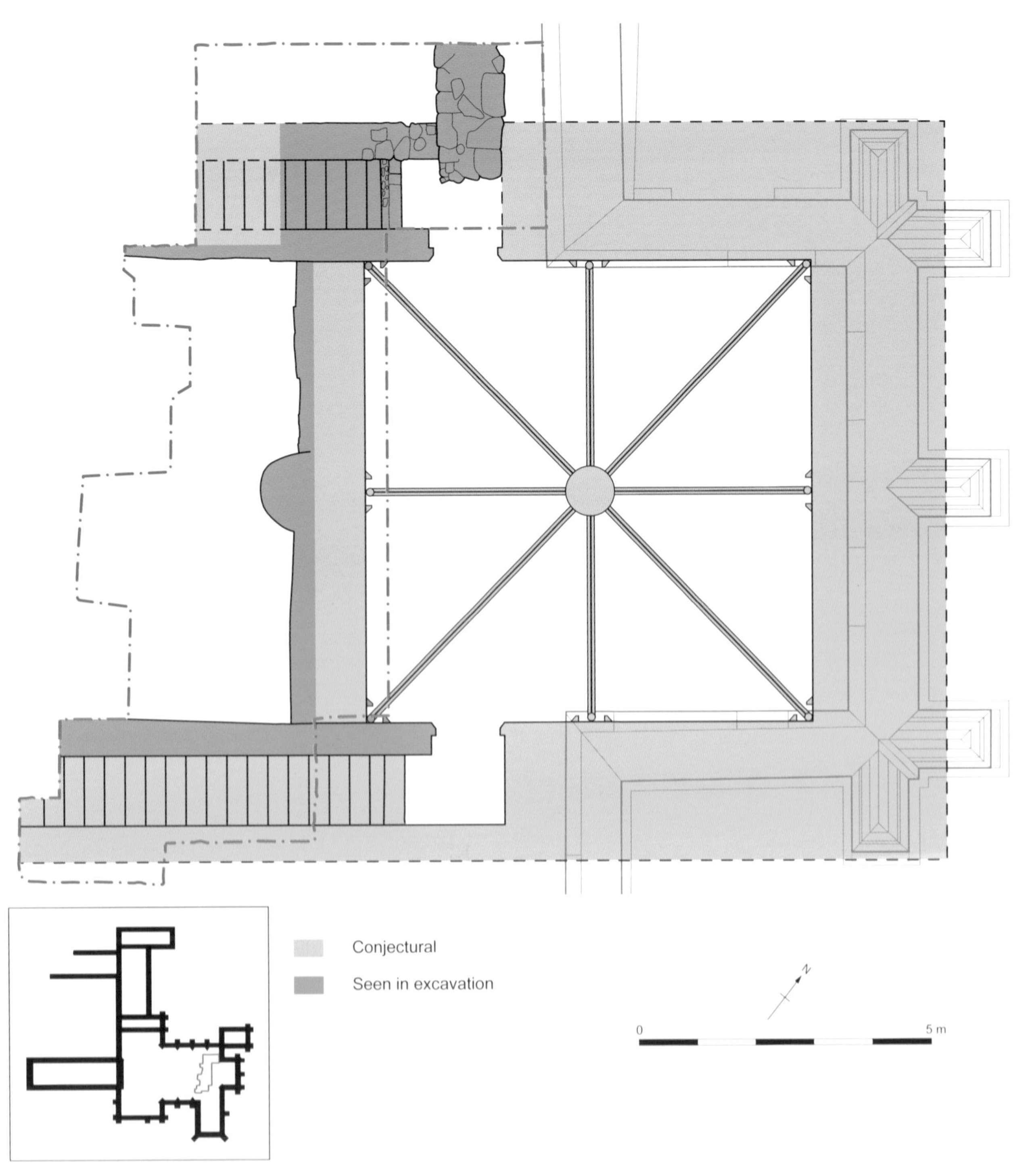

Figure 3.2

Extension of Romanesque Cathedral (Phase 2). Much of the original fabric of the extension is masked by Galloway's work of the 19th century and later repairs However, the transverse wall that Ritchie uncovered is thought to be part of this structure. The north stair was also part of this original construction, as was (presumably) an associated south stair; subsequent construction work, however, has effectively removed the south stair

Plate 3.3
The central buttress of the transverse wall, facing north, overlay a collection of charnel material termed 'Grave' 20

wall certainly notes rock at the base. Meanwhile, images of the north trench with the skeletons and deposits removed show a similar 'rocky' horizon.

Although it is not explicitly stated in the excavation record, it is clear that the graves must predate the transverse wall and buttress, as well as the north and south choir walls. Photographs looking directly down onto the graves show that their eastern ends run below the transverse wall, although it is difficult to say if they are specifically truncated by it (Plate 3.2). Another image also shows Grave 17 continuing below the foundations level of the south choir wall (Plate 3.4). Meanwhile, there is another photograph (Plate 3.5) which, although not positively located, appears to show the west face of the transverse wall, against which there is a deposit through which a number of U-shaped hollows (tentatively identified as Graves 22–5) have been cut. If this correlation can be sustained, then it would be evidence that the transverse wall physically truncates the graves, rather than merely sits on a soil that overlies them.

Radiocarbon dating of the Phase 1 burials was potentially problematic, at least in the sense of correlating the archaeological records with the physical skeletons. Samples from all the skeletons were sent for radiocarbon dating, and encouragingly consistent results were obtained (Chapter 7). The earliest graves in this group, such as the curiously aligned Grave 24 (cal AD 980 – 1160: SUERC-12521) and possibly Grave 27 (cal 1010 – 1160: SUERC-16070) to the south, whose dates might more likely fall into the 11th rather than the 12th century, could belong to the cemetery associated with the late Northumbrian minster of Peter Hill's Period III settlement (Hill 1997, 183–208; see Chapter 1.2). For the others the dates are more likely to fall into the 12th century and, as such, these are interpreted as elements of a normal graveyard population who were interred to the east of the original 12th century Romanesque church, prior to its extension in Phase 2. The latest grave in the group is Grave 18 (cal AD 1185 – 1285: SUERC-12519).

3.2.2 Extension of Romanesque cathedral, c 1200 (Phase 2)

(Figure 3.2)
Phase 2 appears to be related to the extension of the original 12th-century Romanesque cathedral, out beyond the edge of the natural slope and over the old graveyard of Phase 1. To allow for the change in ground level to the east, the extension incorporated a vaulted crypt, over which lay the choir and presbytery. The original vault was a ribbed structure, with a central column surrounded by four bays. Fragments of it and its springing are preserved behind

Plate 3.4
The foundations of the south choir wall overlay Grave 17

Plate 3.5
A series of possible grave cuts that have been tentatively identified as belonging to Graves 22–5. They appear to be cut by the transverse wall

this more visible part of the wall included some ashlar blocks, but without conclusive photographic evidence it is difficult to be sure.

The north wall of the choir is noticeably different in form and scale to the wall opposite, most notably insofar as it contains an intramural stair which leads down into the crypt below the east end of the church. While Ritchie photographed and planned its structural elements, he makes almost no comment on them, and certainly makes no specific mention of an intramural stair, although clearly he must have recognised its presence. Understanding of the wall and stair is further complicated by the extent to which the fabric of the building here was altered or restored by Galloway. Although Ritchie's plan and photographs survive, they make little sense without an understanding of what Galloway had already rebuilt.

the masonry of the later inserted barrel vault which was constructed sometime around 1500 (Yeoman 1999, 39).

In terms of structures and volume of deposits, and the physical effort that would have been required for their original formation as well as their later excavation, Phase 2 features dominate the archaeology of the site. Ironically, they are among the least well-recorded elements of the entire excavation. The principal structural elements comprise the north and south choir walls, the foundations of which formed the (original) north and south limits of Ritchie's excavation, and the transverse wall that lay between them.

The south choir wall is relatively well-recorded, with elevations of both its inner and outer face surviving. The full width of the wall is not explicitly recorded, although several different plans indicate that it must have been more than 4' wide. Ritchie discusses its construction in some detail, suggesting that there appear to be three different phases of building, based on the different types of pointing and mortar present on the inner face of the wall. Images of this wall certainly show some apparent differences in the build of the very upper parts in comparison to the lower, but this is far more likely to be the result of Galloway's rebuilding in the 19th century (Plate 3.6). The presence of 'Galloway's box' over the south wall is evidence of the level of rebuilding and this could be the reason for the difference in mortar-type rather than phases of construction. The general construction of the wall is of roughly squared and mortared masonry, set over a rubble foundation. The outer elevation of the wall may give hints that perhaps

Plate 3.6
South choir wall, interior wall-face: the upper part of the wall is likely to have been reconstructed by Galloway, and the edge of 'Galloway's box' can just been seen in the top left hand corner of the photograph

Plate 3.7
The north stair. Image A shows Galloway's walls lying directly over the line of steps, with the remains of the north part of the choir wall on the right hand side of the image. Image B shows the full width of the stair, once the east–west wall had been removed, although the north–south wall which may also have been constructed by Galloway remains.

It is known from documentary evidence that Galloway came across a door in the north wall of the vault. Upon discovering this, he removed or partially removed the debris that was blocking it, and revealed a stairway beyond the door, rising to the west (along the line of the northern stair that lies open and accessible today). Having exposed part of the stair, he then constructed a wall running east–west partly along the line of the southern part of the north wall or over it (Plate 3.7). It is not clear if this was intended to stabilise this part of the original wall or if it marked the limit of Galloway's investigations.

The doorway into the crypt was subsequently blocked up again by Galloway, and it is this blocking that Ritchie encountered and recorded in photographs (Plate 3.8; A). When Galloway's backfill was removed by Ritchie, the stairway was revealed once again, with well-defined cut steps leading down from west to east, where it met an arched door in the north wall of the vault. At the end of Ritchie's excavation, the stair was again backfilled. It was subsequently re-excavated by Andrew Nicholson in the 1990s (Plate 3.8; B).

Once the later remodelling by Galloway is removed from the picture, it becomes easier to see the overall form of the north choir wall. In total it was over 7' wide, including the stair, and the south side of it stood to a height of at least 6'. It appears that the north side, along with the steps, had been more extensively demolished at some stage, as these only stand a few feet high. The construction of the wall is broadly similar to the south choir wall, with roughly squared and mortared masonry set over a rubble foundation.

There was no surviving trace of an equivalent intramural stair on the south side of the choir, and the form of the south wall itself differed noticeably from that of the north. Possible explanations for this are discussed below (Chapter 3.2.5), but it is thought that originally there would also have been a stair in the southern wall, most likely an identical intramural construction. It is likely that later alterations associated with the construction of the South Chapel resulted in its removal.

The transverse wall was constructed of mortar and rough rubble, some of it dressed, and it was found to stand up to 3' 6" (1.05m) high (Plate 3.9). On the basis of the photographic evidence (Plate 3.10), it is clear that it is tied in to the north and south choir walls at both ends.

The full width of the wall, however, is not known as its eastern side has been removed in antiquity, probably as a result of the insertion of the barrel vault. At roughly its midpoint there is a large masonry projection, referred to by Ritchie as a 'buttress'. The buttress is semi-circular on plan, although again the eastern part of it has been cut away during the insertion of the barrel vault, and its original shape is not known. The buttress is about 4' (1.2m) wide

Plate 3.8
Doorway between the north stair and the crypt. The same view of the doorway to the crypt, taken over 40 years apart. The base of the metal staircase constructed by Historic Scotland in the 1990s can be seen in the image on the right

Plate 3.9
The central 'buttress' of the transverse wall, with the wall visible in the background

and survives to a height of about 2' 6" (0.75m). It appears to sit on a rubble foundation, marked by a collection of larger stones under the mortared core. The wall appears on several of the excavation plans, both original pencil versions and later dye-line and inked-up versions. These indicate that the wall lay parallel with the barrel vault. However, in his draft publication text, Ritchie implies that it lay at a slight angle to the barrel vault. At the north end, it is recorded as being situated 4' 6" (1.37m) behind the west face of the barrel vault, whereas at the south end, it is said to have been set back only 2' 10" (0.86m) (Archive D9, p.125), implying that the wall was skew and that it cannot have lain entirely perpendicular to the north and south choir walls.

The rough construction of the wall and buttress make it likely that this is merely a foundation level of a wall, and was never meant to be seen. Ritchie's interpretation of this feature changed over the course of the excavation. While he originally believed that it was the remains of the west end of an earlier, discrete building (probably a church) that were located to the east of the medieval church, he subsequently concluded that they were associated with the primary vaulting of the crypt below the extended east end of the church. The present analysis of the structural evidence follows this latter view.

There is an elevation of the south part of the transverse wall (Archive, A33) on which there is marked 'straight jamb?' in Ritchie's hand roughly halfway along (Figure 3.3). This is where the height of the wall falls abruptly away and presumably Ritchie wanted to record the possibility of a deliberate gap in the wall. Interestingly, there are also some notes referring to a possible slot in the rear of the 'buttress' in his notebook (Archive A29, after page dated 31/05/1967). The idea of a door or window jamb in the transverse wall certainly does not fit, as it has already been established that it was buried below ground amidst several tons of soil. The slot to the rear of the 'buttress' may indicate that both of these features relate to the ribbed vault, potentially being slots for supports for its construction. With the eye of faith, a possible similar slot might also be seen in the section of wall to the north of the 'buttress'.

The key observation is that the north and south choir walls continue to the east beyond the transverse wall and

Plate 3.10
The join between the transverse wall and the south choir wall indicates they were both constructed at the same time

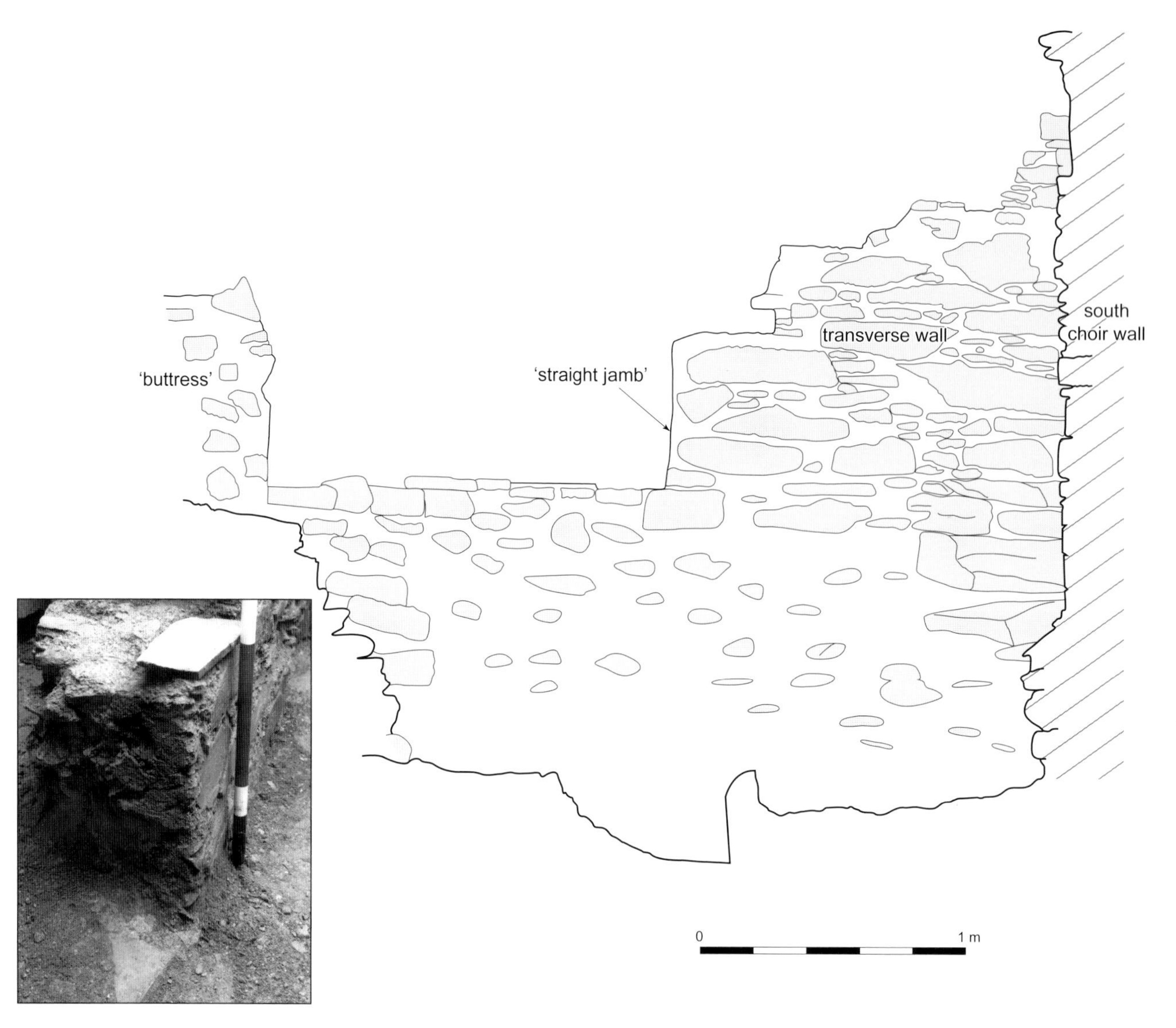

Figure 3.3
Ritchie clearly considered there to be a deliberate break in the construction of the transverse wall, and the mortar around this section of it (as we see in the photograph) certainly seems to confirm this. Despite this, there is no suggestion that this was an additional entrance into the crypt - the wall was buried underground and the gap is more likely to relate to construction techniques

that all three are tied into each other, making it impossible that the transverse wall could have ever belonged to an earlier, discrete building (Plate 3.10). In addition, photographs of the junction between the south choir wall and the transverse wall show disturbance in the south wall in the area to the east of the transverse wall (Plate 3.11). The disturbance appears to match neatly the line of the rubble fill which forms the backing of the barrel vault, suggesting that this occurred when the east side of the transverse wall was cut back to facilitate the insertion of the later barrel vault. Tellingly, the photographs also show that the transverse wall was at its full height when Ritchie recorded it – there is no indication, for example, that it originally extended higher up the south choir wall. The purpose of the wall, together with those in the choir, in other words, was as a retaining wall for the creation of a level platform as part of the new two-storey east end. Meanwhile, given the preservation of the ribs behind the later barrel vault, it is clear that the east side of the transverse wall also formed the base for the springing of the primary ribbed vault.

When the vault and transverse wall were constructed there would have been a need to infill the space between the original ground level to the east of the church and the

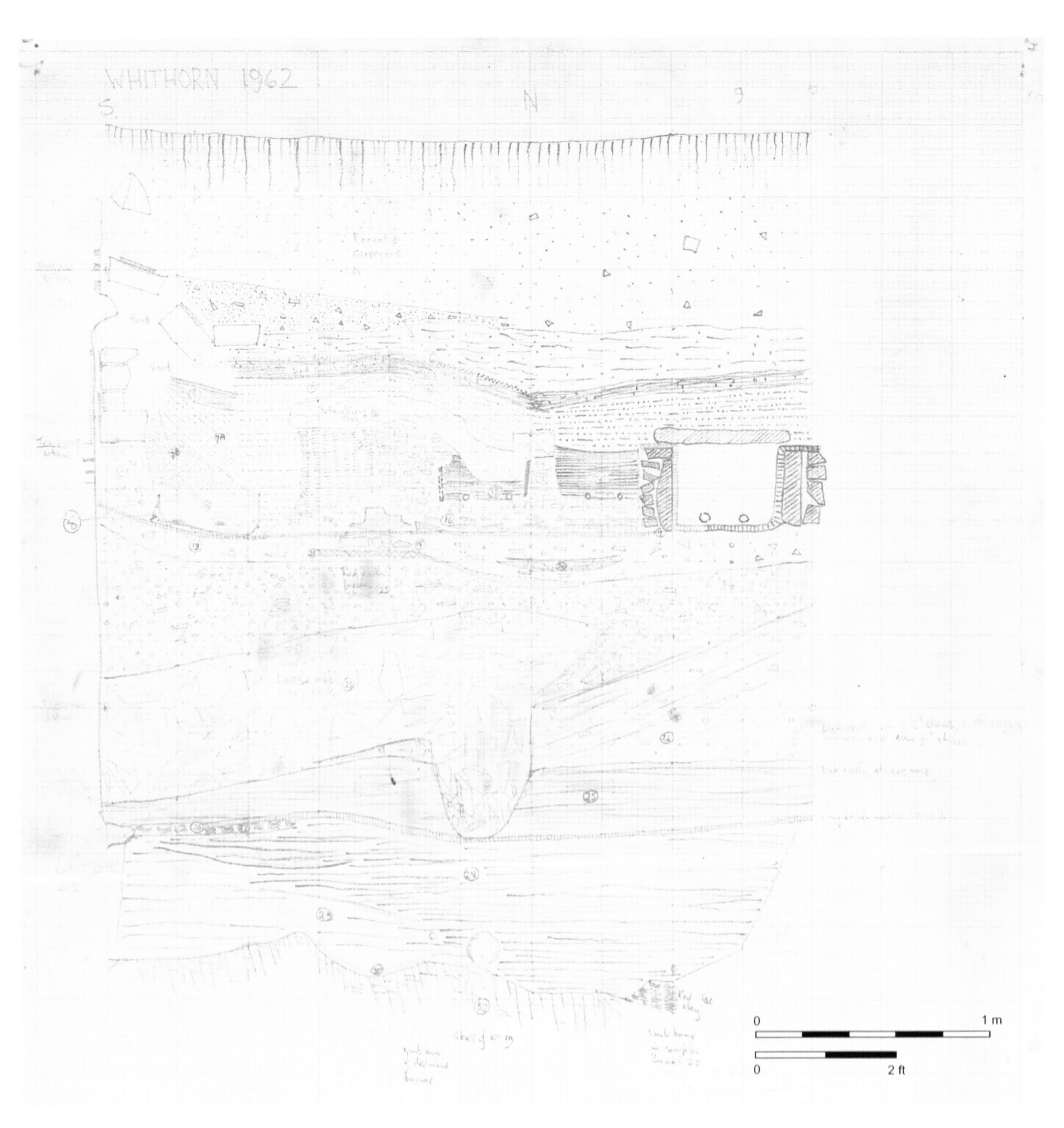

Figure 3.4

North–South (transverse) section, 12 feet deep. This is the most detailed record we have of the stratigraphy present within the main area of the excavation. It shows the upper series of graves, with extensive deposits present below

Plate 3.11
Transverse wall and south choir wall, facing south, with Galloway's 'box' at top left. The area to the rear of the transverse wall shows extensive disturbance due to the later insertion of the barrel vault. The lack of disturbance above the transverse wall suggests that this is the original height and that it has not been altered

top of the vault, to bring it up to the level of the surface within the rest of the building. This would have required a substantial amount of infilling, and evidence of this survives in the hand-drawn north–south section (Figure 3.4).

Above the level of the deposit into which the graves of Phase 1 were placed, there are three or possibly four deposits that appear to represent deliberate dumping of material. These extend from a depth of roughly 6' to 9' (1.8–2.7m) below the current ground surface and the base of these deposits is at about the same level as the base of the transverse and choir walls. The section shows the deposits tipping down from the middle of the area between the choir walls to the edges, which would fit with the settling of a large amount of dumped material. The extent of the dumped material can also be seen in Plate 3.12.

All of the evidence of the construction of the vault, the transverse wall, the choir walls, the stairways and the infilling supports the concept of a deliberately planned programme of building, occurring in one large phase, rather than as a series of expansions or repairs to an existing or gradually evolving building. The extension of the Romanesque church has conventionally been dated to around 1200, based primarily on the architectural style of the primary ribbed vault. The implications of this chronology, in light of the results of the radiocarbon-dating programme, are explored in Chapter 9.

The extension of the east end of the cathedral church had most likely been driven by a need for greater space for an expanding body of canons, coupled with an ambition by Bishop John to create a more magnificent setting for the high altar. It has been proposed that this allowed the church to enshrine at least part of an older church (Radford's *Candida Casa*: Chapter 1.2) lower down the hillside which was recognised as housing the tomb of St Ninian (Figure 3.5: Yeoman 1999, 36–7). A similar sequential development has been postulated for Glasgow Cathedral, where the saint's tomb was incorporated into an enlarged two-storey east end (Yeoman 1999, 20).

Plate 3.12
Infill deposits, facing south. The presence of several metres of material to the west of the transverse wall was deliberate and filled in the space between the choir walls and the transverse wall, making the structure above much more stable

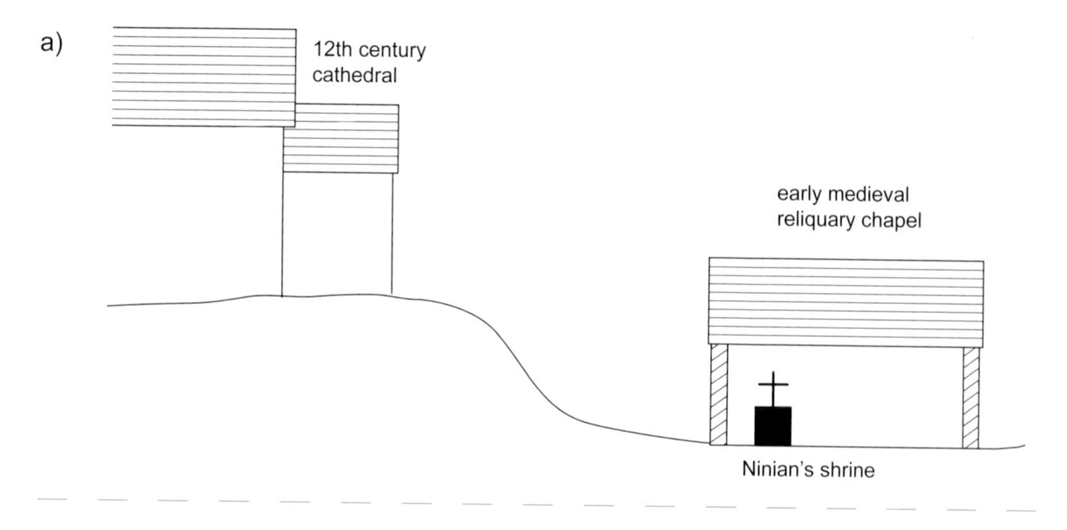

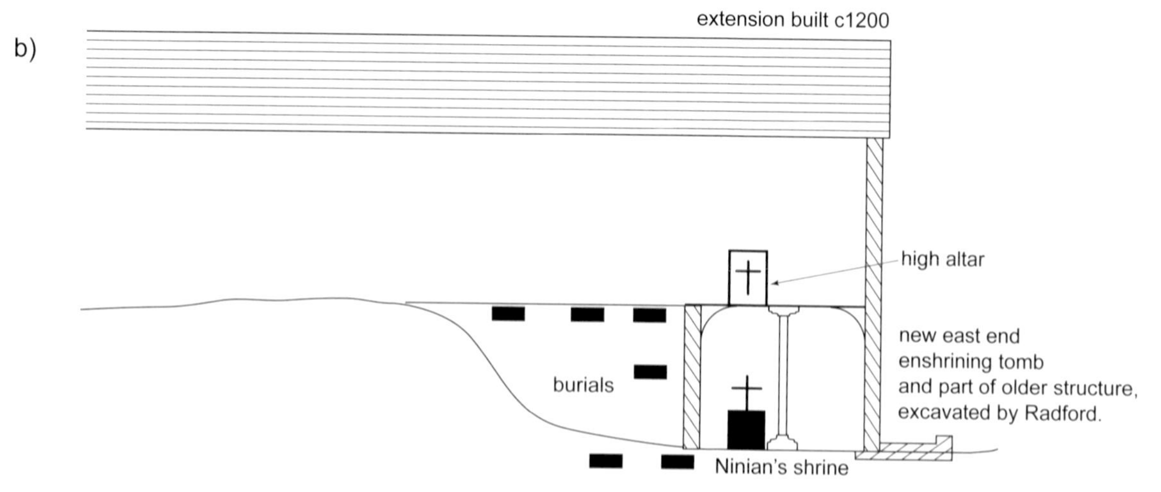

Figure 3.5
Schematic model indicating how the proposed early medieval reliquary chapel could have been incorporated into the extension to the cathedral of *c.* 1200 and the space used for burials

3.2.3 High-status burials and other additions (Phase 3)

(Figure 3.6)

Burials: Graves 1–8, 10–12, 14 and 21

Following the extension of the Premonstratensian church, in or around 1200, the new east end of the building began to be used as a location for burials. Indeed, our interpretation of the burial sequence is predicated on the basis that burial in proximity to the high altar and the crypt below would have been one of the beneficial outcomes of the building's extension at this time. The graves were inserted at floor level, from above, inside the church and spanned it in two rows. The more easterly row lay directly over the transverse wall of Phase 2. Among the Phase 3 graves are all the stone-built cists, most of the coffin burials, as well as all those that contained liturgical plate and other grave-goods. The chronology for this activity, and this is explored in detail in Chapter 9, extends from the early 13th century down to the third quarter of the 14th century.

No justification has been found to support any distinction between Ritchie's preliminary groups of 'late graves' (Graves 1–8, 12 and 21) and 'early graves' (Graves 9–11 and 13–15) that he set out in his publication draft (Archive D9). The radiocarbon-dating evidence (Chapter 7) indicates clearly that these are broadly contemporary, and that Graves 13 and 15, if anything, are slightly later (Phase 4), rather than earlier. Nor have we found any clear evidence to support Ritchie's assertion that the eastern ends of some of the graves directly overlaid and thus post-dated the construction of the barrel vault. Nor

Plate 3.13
The south 'bench' can be seen clearly abutting the south choir wall

have we found any clear evidence to substantiate the claim that others were truncated by the construction of the barrel vault, although the areas of disturbance across the east end of Graves 3 and 4 would not be inconsistent with this.

The problem, of course, is exacerbated by the fact that the 1957 waterproofing trench cut through and removed deposits, and possibly features, in the very part of the site where these relationships might have been addressed. In the draft publication report, Ritchie claims that 'the lower courses [of the stone cist of Grave 1] were bedded in yellow clay and at the east end lay directly on the rear of the stones forming the barrel vault of the western chamber of the crypt' (Archive D9, p.83), a fairly unequivocal statement. Despite this, there are no photographs to support this claim and those that do exist suggest that not only would it have been impossible for him to tell if this were the case, the evidence suggests strongly it is not. The barrel vault clearly lies to the east of the workmen's trench and the foot of Graves 1 and 2 lie about 2' (0.6m) to the west of the vault (see Chapter 2, Plate 2.1: the barrel vault is marked by the line of rubble at the bottom of the photograph).

Very little stratigraphic evidence can be recovered from Ritchie's work. Between the graves themselves, just five key relationships were recorded:

- that the cover stones of Grave 2 overlay the side-stones of Grave 1;
- that the mortar lining of Grave 1 laps over the edge stones of Grave 3 and thus postdates its construction;
- that Grave 8 also postdates Grave 3, given that it was cut into the yellow clay associated with its construction;
- that Grave 5 overlay Grave 6, with the wooden coffin of Grave 6 only being revealed once the stones of Grave 5 had been removed;
- that Grave 12 overlay Grave 21, again with the underlying grave only being revealed once the upper grave had been removed.

The longest stratigraphic chain identified here comprises Grave 2 over Grave 1 over Grave 3. Only Grave 3 is accorded a named individual (Bishop Henry who died in 1293) in Ritchie's draft publication text (Archive D8(i), pp.7–8); Grave 1 was therefore broadly dated by Ritchie to the period 1300 x 1325, and Grave 2 to 'later than 1325'. These relationships and a new chronology are revisited in Chapter 9 where we set out a possible model for the sequence in which the various graves were constructed and used.

Structural evidence

Aside from the graves themselves, there are also a number of extremely fragmentary and poorly understood structural features that appear to be broadly contemporary with this phase of use (or could be later). All overlie the dump deposits of Phase 2. Among this group of features are the so-called 'benches', roughly 0.2m wide, that lay adjacent to and along the north and south interior wall-face of the choir (Plate 3.13 and Plate 3.14).

Both were clearly secondary features that were butted against the wall-face. They could conceivably represent the bases of wall-tombs or alternatively they could be associated with the provision of a suspended timber floor at this end of the building; neither interpretation, however, is particularly satisfactory and their function is unknown.

There are also hints in the record of what might be the fragmentary remains of a stone floor. Some of these were recorded in the north–south section (Figure 3.4); others were exposed on plan immediately to the west of Grave 8 (Chapter 2, Plate 2.10). It is by no means clear, however, what the floor of the choir would have looked like. Interestingly, there are four very large slabs of what may be Tournai limestone, set against the parapet of William Galloway's restored east end. Subsequent fieldwork and analysis, undertaken as part of this project, has

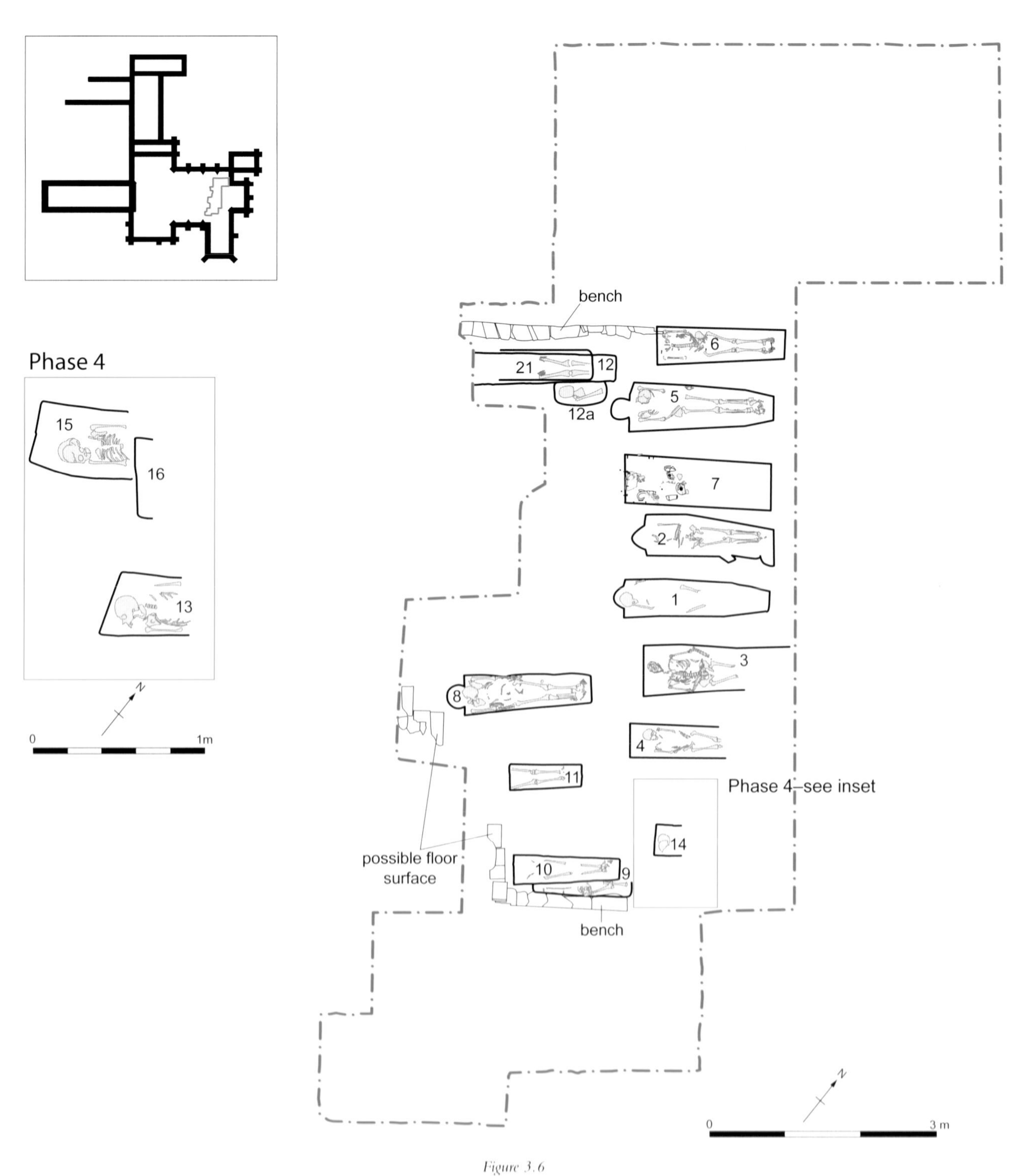

Figure 3.6
High-status burials and other additions (Phase 3), and later graves (Phase 4). The main group of bishops' graves belong to Phase 3, as do some of the structural details such as the 'benches'

Plate 3.14
The relationship of the north 'bench' and the north choir wall is less obvious

shown that these belong to two different slabs on which was originally mounted a monumental brass; indeed, one of them clearly shows the outline of an ecclesiastical figure with a mitre standing within an elaborate, niche-like setting (Dingwall, Chapter 6.12). This raises the possibility that the floor of the choir was made up of large slabs over the graves, with the area between and around the edges possibly formed of smaller slabs.

In the area adjacent to Grave 8, Ritchie also identified what he described as a possible wall-footing. Also possibly part of this phase is a wall that Ritchie found abutting the south choir wall: it was located 'immediately below the turf and extending downwards for 1' 8" was found the face of a wall which abutted the south side wall. Its junction was 12' west of the inner face of the west wall of the barrel vault and made an angle of about 20° with the side wall' (Archive D8(i), pp.12–13). It is not at all clear, however, what this refers to and no corresponding photographs have been traced; it could, for example, simply be the side wall of a grave that is not otherwise recorded. All of the Phase 3 structural features, aside from the graves themselves, are poorly preserved and poorly recorded (Figure 3.6).

3.2.4 Later graves (Phase 4)

(Figure 3.6)
On the basis of the radiocarbon dates, Graves 13 and 15 are the latest burials inside the church. It is also clear from Henderson's analysis (Chapter 4) that these are the remains of juveniles. As such, this appears to mark a departure from the burial population of Phase 3.

3.2.5 The barrel vault (Phase 5)

(Figure 3.7; Plate 3.15)
Phase 5 accommodates those changes to the east end of the church which would have witnessed the removal of the early 13th-century ribbed vault and seen its replacement with the two barrel vaults, set side by side, that we see today, along with the addition of the South Chapel.

In his working text, Ritchie is explicit in saying that the first seven graves identified lay with the foot end of each resting on the back of the barrel vault (Archive D9, p.73), implying therefore that these burials all post-dated

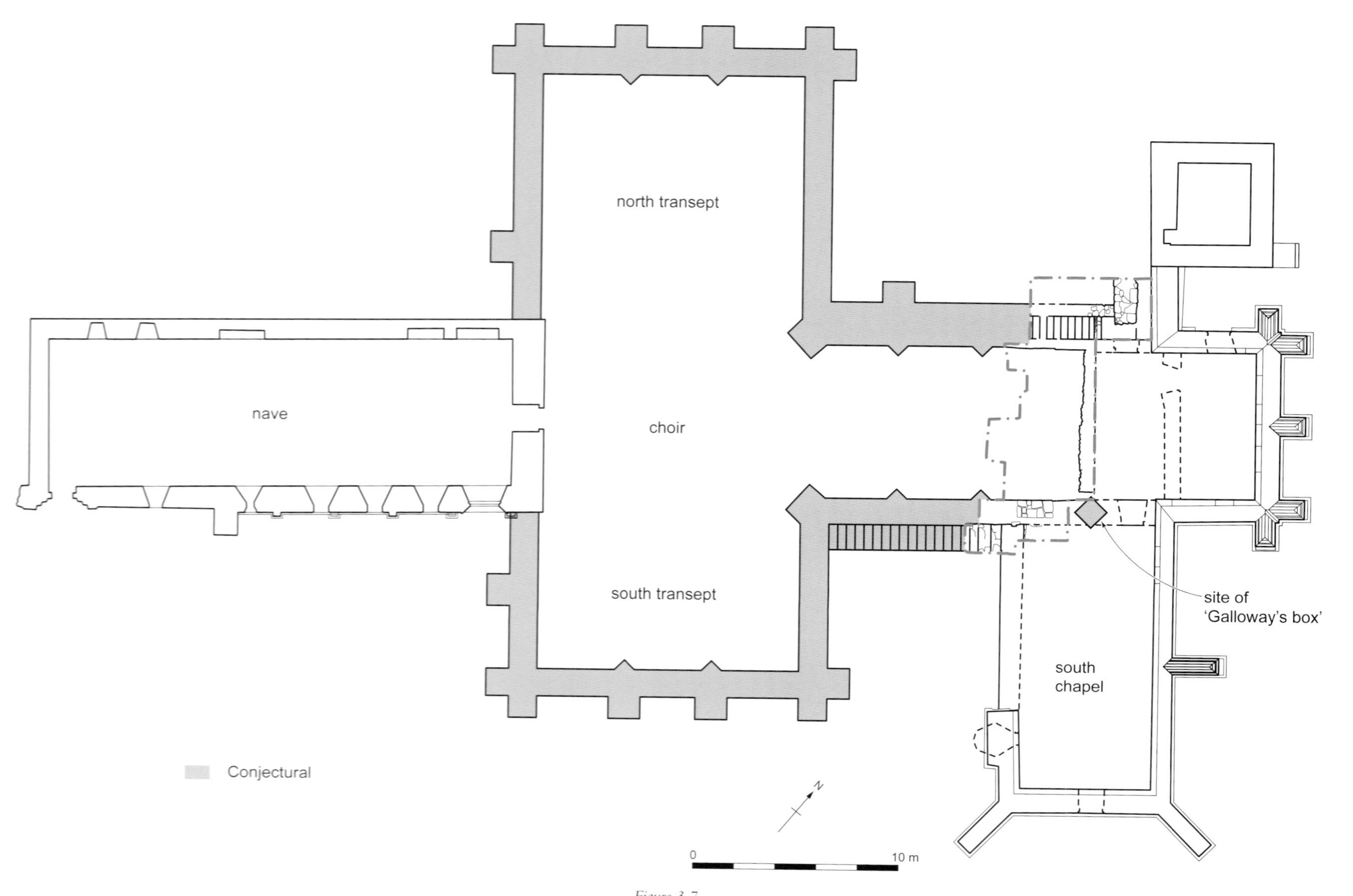

Figure 3.7
Whithorn Priory c 1500 with the remodelling of the east end. The barrel vaults were still accessed via the intramural north stair, but the south stair was replaced with a different version falling to the west, towards the south transept. With the new evidence gleaned in this study, it is now clear that the choir was never aisled, as had been previously suggested. Even with the replacement of the intramural stair, the walls at the east end must have been at least 2m thick. The new proposed layout combines this new information with the known structural elements from previous excavations

Plate 3.15
The eastern barrel vault, facing south, represents part of the remodelling of the crypt space in the late 15th or early 16th century

the construction of the barrel vault. It is generally accepted that the barrel vault was constructed in the late 15th or early 16th century, around the same time that the South Chapel was added, with its own barrel-vaulted undercroft below, and that the two spaces were joined by means of a new remodelled doorway (Radford & Donaldson 1953, 32). This is the broad chronology which is followed here.

Ritchie's alternative construct is worth exploring. The radiocarbon dates that we now have (Chapter 7) clearly demonstrate that Graves 1–7 variously date to the 13th and 14th centuries. If they overlay the barrel vault, then its construction would be pushed back to the 12th or 13th century. Not only is this unfeasibly early, but it would also imply given the dating of the primary Phase 1 graves at the base of the sequence, that the original ribbed vault was extremely short-lived. The construction and removal of the ribbed vault and its replacement with the construction of the barrel vault would thus be 'squeezed' into an extremely narrow time-frame.

This is highly unlikely. Taking into account all the available evidence, this seems to be one of the occasions where Ritchie's account should be disregarded, no matter how strongly he states it. The sequence of ribbed vault – burials – barrel vault is far more likely and this is not inconsistent with all the other evidence from the site, such as the dating of the artefacts (Chapter 6) and the radiocarbon dates (Chapter 7). It is still difficult to see how this could have been done without disturbing the *in situ* burials but clearly this was what happened. When the barrel vault was inserted, the only burials that appear to have been extensively disturbed by it were Graves 13–15 and possibly the very eastern ends of Graves 3 and 4. It is important to remember that most, if not all, of the graves would have been marked in some way, and their location

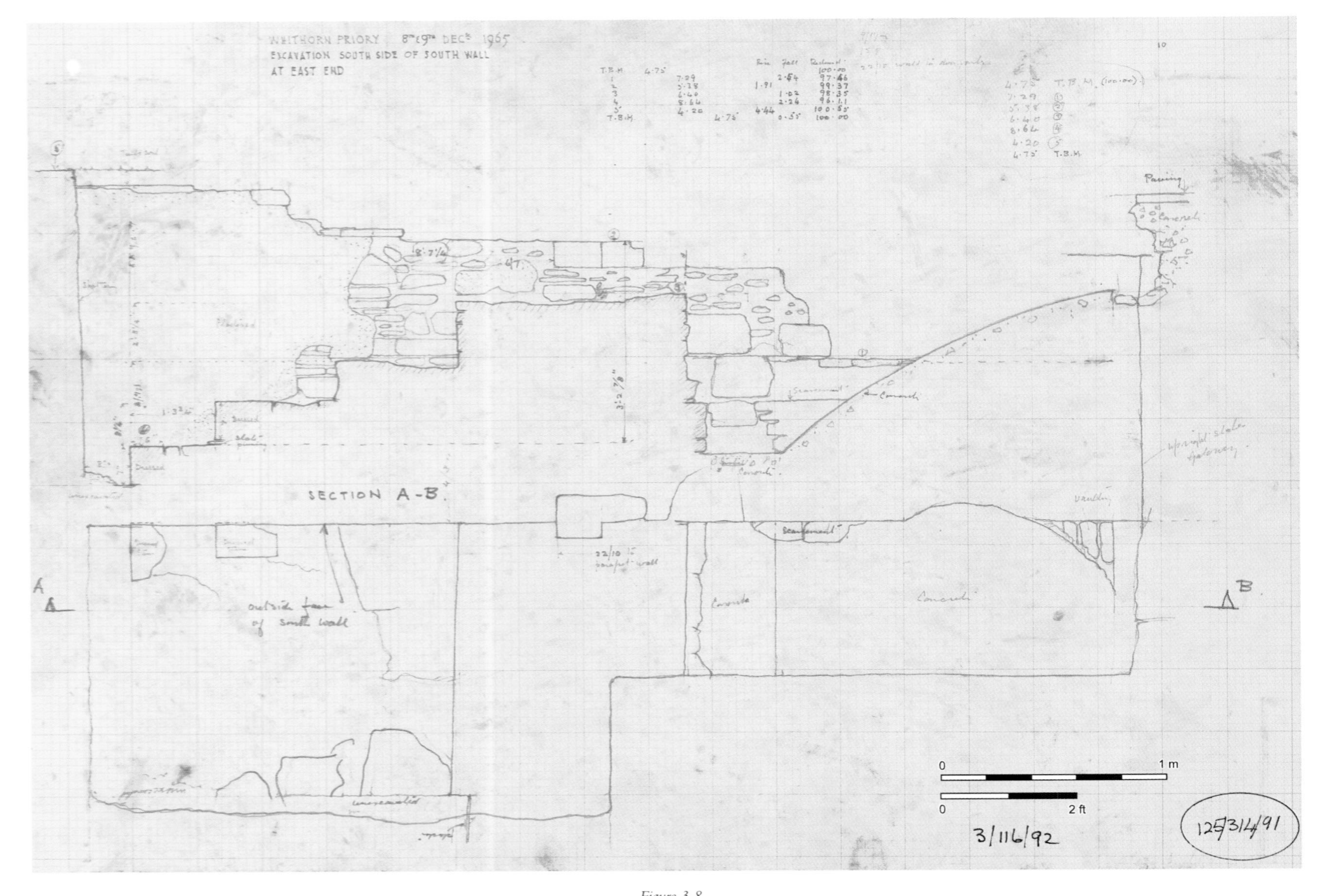

Figure 3.8
Ritchie's elevation and plan of the area of the south stair. The steps can be seen in the top left of the image, falling to the west

known. Presumably great care would have been taken not to disturb them, and the evidence suggests that disturbance did not extend across the full width of the transverse wall.

When a section was extended across the south choir wall, instead of identifying an intramural stair as seen in the north, a very different and more fragmentary series of remains was revealed. At the eastern end of the trench was the concrete covering over the undercroft below the South Chapel, which was the result of the original scheme of work to waterproof the vaults that eventually led to the excavation. Adjacent to this was a large mortared stone wall, aligned north–south, and apparently abutting the south choir wall. The wall was 3' 7" wide and, on the basis of the photographs, was of a similar construction to the south choir wall. An area measuring 1.75m by 1.4m was opened to the west of this wall and found to be largely filled with rubble. Abutting the south choir wall were the remains of at least two (or possibly three) steps, seen as dressed stones marking the edge of the step (Figure 3.8). The main part of the steps seemed to have been removed but it is clear from Ritchie's profile of the stones against the wall that he was sure they formed a stair, and that it fell from east to west, ie from ground level at the inside of the church down to a lower level further to the west, presumably somewhere around the supposed south transept. This may be tantalising new evidence of other previously unknown crypts on or around the summit where the nave of the cathedral stood.

The construction of the barrel vault and south chapel altered the way that pilgrims and clergy would have moved round the church. While the north stair is likely to still have been in use allowing access to the the new barrel vault, the exit on the south side would lead into the undercroft below the South Chapel, and out by the door at its south end. The circulatory route between the north intramural stair and the (assumed) south stair would no longer have functioned and undoubtedly this must reflect a change in the pilgrims' devotional activities. No doubt this would have involved new shrines in new parts of the church, such as the South Chapel. The feature that Ritchie called 'Galloway's box' may also relate to this reorganisation. The details of what Galloway uncovered in this location are not known, but it is presumed that some structural foundation was identified, resulting in the construction of the rectangular box. It would also seem that Ritchie recovered no further evidence of this foundation when he removed the box, but the location of it on the mid-point between the east and west walls of the South Chapel and lying directly on the south choir wall point to it being the location of a column base. This would support the roof of the South Chapel and allow access into it from the choir itself.

3.2.6 Post-Reformation to modern (Phase 6)

The final phase of archaeological activity on the site relates to the post-Reformation use of this area as part of the parish graveyard. Several modern graves in wooden coffins were encountered in the upper levels of the excavation. One of these, simply recorded by Ritchie as '19th century', returned a radiocarbon date of 140 ± 35 bp (SUERC-12526).

Chapter 4

The Human Remains

DAVID HENDERSON

4.1 INTRODUCTION

A large quantity of human bone was recovered during the course of Ritchie's excavations. The absolute minimum number of individuals (MNI) represented by the assemblage was 41 adults (represented by left femur shafts) and nine immature individuals (represented by right temporal bones). From assessing sex by examination of the greater sciatic notch of the pelvis, 21 males and 13 females were indicated in the adult material. The assemblage comprised skeletal material from all age groups from perinatal babies to the elderly (probably over 70 years old).

At least 18 of the individuals (including two 12-year-old juveniles) were *in situ* and articulated when excavated; it can be inferred from the contemporary field notes and labelling of the assemblage that some of the other burials may have been intact when encountered, but these (probably of 19th-century date) were not recorded and the excavated skeletons were not stored as discrete entities. Other material was unarticulated and had been previously disturbed by groundwork activities on site. This part of the assemblage is referred to below as charnel.

The material designated as cremations by Ritchie (Lab. No 24/01 'WH1962 cremation beside 18/-' and Lab. No 28/84 'Temp No 7' 'WH1967 Cremated bone from red patch & assoc. finds ie bronze and medieval pot from 1" underneath') are not cremations, but fully calcined faunal bone. The only identifiable items are part of a lamb's sacrum and a sheep's rib.

4.1.1 The material examined

It is worthwhile explaining the state of the assemblage as it was when first brought to be analysed. Due to the length of time since excavation and the paucity of contemporary field notes, much of the information relating to the excavation of the assemblage was unavailable. The finds, including the skeletal remains, when recovered from the NMS, were stored in over 67 boxes of various sizes (from cigarette packets to crates), many of which were unmarked Following completion of a research loan, Historic Scotland arranged for AOC Archaeology to assess the contents and to repackage and assign laboratory numbers (Lab. No.) based on the assigned number of the box from which they had been removed and any subdivisions (eg boxes, bags, layers of newspaper) within the box. Any further information from the original boxes or packaging was collected and related to the new Lab. No. of the find(s).

Using this information, usually starting from skeletal material for which some label relating to the grave number had survived, other material from the same box could be visually and anatomically analysed to see if it was from the same skeleton. In collaboration with Kirsty Dingwall, given her knowledge of the site record (particularly the photographs), other parts of the skeleton could sometimes be identified. Often, missing, unlabelled parts of a skeleton could be found packed in a single box (or layer within a box) and securely identified by reference to the photographic or drawn record, once this had been related to Ritchie's grave number by Dingwall. On some occasions the process worked in reverse, with labelled skeletal parts being related back to a drawing or photograph, which was then securely identifiable to a grave number. Although the author would consider the final grouping of the material into *in situ* skeletons to be secure, some slight doubts must remain, mostly where photographs are not sufficiently detailed due to angle or distance or having been taken of a partially excavated skeleton. A fuller description of the evidence relating each Lab. No. to the skeleton is available in the Project Archive.

4.1.2 Ritchie's grave numbers

In the extant notes of the fieldwork mention is made of 23 grave numbers. During the analysis of the skeletal assemblage and photographic archive, it quickly became apparent that some of these numbers had been assigned more than once, some related to charnel deposits and some related to empty graves. Not all *in situ* skeletons were assigned a grave number; conversely, skeletal material from the same area (whether an *in situ*, articulated skeleton, charnel in the backfill or merely 'loose') could be given the same grave number, if labelled at all.

For the purposes of this report, any *in situ* skeleton from a grave is given a skeleton number (SK), usually that of the grave number, unless this had been used more than once. Where non-articulated deposits of charnel had been assigned a grave number by Ritchie, these will be referred to as a Charnel Group with the original grave number (again, excepting duplicated numbers). Additional SK and Charnel Group numbers have been assigned to *in situ* skeletons and charnel where the original number is missing or duplicated, bringing the total of individual numbers in this report to 27.

There are also several groupings of 'modern' skeletal material. These were not recorded or stored individually by the excavation team and they have not been analysed beyond a counting of the skeletal parts and a visual scan for major pathological lesions. One fibula (Lab. No. 47/01) which was marked '19th century' returned a date of 140 ±35 bp (SUERC-12526). This was probably the individual from the grave visible in photographs as cutting Grave 5, confirming that some post-medieval and more recent inhumations were probably removed with little or no recording. A skull with no context information (Lab. no. 65/01) was found partially filled (post-decomposition) with what appears to be lime plaster. This may be part of burial described by Ritchie as 'in lime'.

The original grave numbers are listed below (Table 4.1), with comments on this author's subsequent reassignments. Because of the complexities that arise in the case of the several renumberings of SK20 and SK21, this information is set out in detail, outwith Table 4.1.

Grave 20 Contains SK20. Located north of Grave 19. Truncated to north and east by the construction trench of the central buttress. This grave number was later duplicated as the grave immediately to the north of the central buttress (Archive photograph A2644-8) probably during a later field season (possibly 1966) when the excavators had misremembered how far they had got in the consecutive numbering system. Some material from this grave retained 'grave 20/' labels in storage. The skeleton in this, more recently excavated 'Grave 20' is now SK25.

Grave 21 Four different skeletons were labelled with this designation at different times. In this report, SK21 refers to the individual from the 'Grave 21' immediately below Grave 12. The grave contained a pewter chalice and the excavated portion of the skeleton consisted of the area from feet to waist. It is unclear when the designation was assigned to this grave.

Chronologically, the first description 'Grave 21/' appears to have been given to items of unarticulated bone in the fill of the construction trench to the west of the central buttress. This material is now Charnel Group 26 (Archive photographs A1598-4 and A1599-3).

The second use of the description '21/' was for the inhumation to the north of what is now SK25 and south of Grave 22 (Archive photograph A2644-8) and which is now designated SK24.

A third group of bones marked as coming from Grave 21 was a cranium and mandible, later identified by photographic and anatomical evidence as having originated from SK17. The skull was not lifted with the rest of the skeleton, as it lay within the east-facing section of the trench, but may have been recovered after the section had been drawn and straightened, and the correct designation had been misremembered.

4.1.3 Preservation and disturbance

Preservation of bone was very mixed on site, seemingly this depended on the type of inhumation and the degree of disturbance after interment. In the case of Graves 1–5, 7 and 8, almost all show signs of having been disturbed before excavation by Ritchie. Whether this occurred in medieval times, or during grave-digging in the 19th century, is open to question. Grave 5, for example, shows a very disturbed area in the thorax and by the left hip which appears to coincide with a part of the stone lining having been removed by the grave for the 19th-century coffin visible just to the south (Dingwall, Chapter 2.3.1). Similarly in the case of Grave 8, the left tibia has been chopped in antiquity, and *post mortem*, probably by a spade and the chest area has been heavily disturbed (Dingwall, Chapter 2.3.1). It is also evident that this grave once contained artefacts: the hands were once clutching an object over the abdomen, which had deposited white, crystalline, corrosion products (lead salts?) onto the pelvis. That these salts were bactericidal is evidenced by the preserved skin adhering to the bone. There is also a stain on the right forearm which is large and annular in shape. No surviving artefacts, however, were present in the grave.

In the case of SK7, although artefacts have survived, almost no bone has; a few finger-bones are preserved (apparently because of the copper corrosion products from the object which was presumably originally clutched in the hand). Although a few lumbar vertebra bodies are depicted on a plan of the grave, there is no sign of them in

Table 4.1 The Grave Number Sequence (after Ritchie, with additions and amendments)

Grave/ Charnel Group	*Description*
Grave 1	Stone-lined grave containing SK1
Grave 2	Stone-lined grave containing SK2
Grave 3	Stone-lined grave containing SK3, truncated at the knees in antiquity
Grave 4	Stone-lined grave containing SK4, truncated at the knees in antiquity
Grave 5	Stone-lined grave containing SK5
Grave 6	Stone-lined (?) grave containing SK6
Grave 7	Grave containing SK7, scant remains, terrible preservation, possibly head to knees only
Grave 8	Stone-lined grave containing SK8
Charnel Group 9	Pile of non-articulated charnel to South of Grave 10. Now Charnel Group 9. Mostly an OA female
Grave 10	Contains SK10, excavated from feet to waist only
Grave 11	Contains SK11, excavated from feet to femurs only
Grave 12	Contains SK12, complete skeleton
Charnel Group 12A	Charnel to south of Grave 12 (?in backfill). Now Group 12A. Mostly a very tall YA male
Grave 13	Contains SK13, 12-year-old. Head to elbows only
Grave 14	Contains SK14, broken adult cranium only
Grave 15	Contains SK15, 12-year-old. Head to elbows only
Grave 16	No skeletal remains, located east of Graves 14 and 15
Grave 17	Contains SK17, head to knees only. Most southerly of the earliest row of burials
Grave 18	Contains SK18, head to waist only. Immediately north of Grave17
Grave 19	Contains SK19, head to mid-thigh only. All bone not identified in assemblage, but may have been too delicate to recover successfully
Grave 20	Contains SK20. To North of Grave 19 (complex renumbering – see Henderson, Chapter 4.1.2)
Grave 21	Contains SK21, immediately below Grave 12 (complex renumbering – see Henderson, Chapter 4.1.2)
Grave 22	Contains SK22, head to knees only. To the North of SK24
Grave 23	Contains SK23, head to knees only. To the North of SK22
SK 24	Located south of Grave 22: head to knees only (ex-duplicate Grave 21)
SK 25	Located south of Grave 24: head to knees only (ex-duplicate Grave 20), truncated by central 'buttress' to south and east
Charnel Group 26	Located west of the central 'buttress' in the backfill of its construction trench. May contain elements of SK20 and SK25. Also designation now contains charnel elements which overlay SK20
SK 27	The right leg of an *in situ* skeleton immediately to the south of (and truncated by) SK19. Included by Ritchie in 'Grave 19'

Table 4.2 Demographic information (Age Class: OJ = 12–18 years, SA = 18–25 years, YA = 25–35 years, MA = 35–45 years, OA = over 45 years AD = adult)

SK#	*Sex*	*Age*	*Estimated height*	*Portion present*	*Pathology*
1	Male	OA	–	Head to thighs	–
2	Male	YA	1.673 m ± 0.029	All except skull	–
3	Male	OA	1.758 m ± 0.041	Head to thighs	DISH, probably obese
4	Male	OA	1.664 m ± 0.033	Head to knees	Tooth abscesses, skull osteoma
5	Male	?YA	1.80 m ± 0.029	Complete	–
6	Female	OA	1.583 m ± 0.036	All except skull	–
7	?Male	AD	–	A few scraps	Arthritis of fingers
8	Male	MA	1.687 m ± 0.029	Complete	Cleft palate, fractured frontal
10	?Male	AD	–	Waist to feet	?Marrow/blood cancer
11	?Female	AD	1.591 m ± 0.036	Legs	–
12	Male	MA	1.836 m ± 0.033	Complete	–
13	–	OJ	–	Head to elbows	–
14	Female	MA	–	Head only	–
15	–	OJ	–	Head to elbows	–
17	Male	YA	1.74 m ± 0.033	Head to knees	–
18	Male	YA	1.82 m ± 0.041	Head to hips	Childhood anaemia
19	Female	OA	1.598 m ± 0.037	Head to knees	Osteoporosis
20	Male	YA	1.712 m ± 0.041	Skull and arm	?Anaemia
21	Male	MA	1.669 m ± 0.029	Feet to elbows	?Psoriatic arthritis
22	Male	OA	1.68 m ± 0.033	Head to knees	Osteomyelitis of cheekbone?
23	Male	OA	1.764 m ± 0.036	Head to knees	–
24	Male	MA	–	Head to waist	Gingivitis
25	Male	OA	–	Head and arm	–
27	?Female	AD	–	Right leg	–

the assemblage. They may have been too degraded to lift. Skeletons 1 and 2 also show signs of disturbance.

The earliest skeletons – the Phase 1 burials at the base of the excavated area – are generally quite poorly preserved.

4.2. METHODOLOGY

Tooth-wear analysis (as outlined by Brothwell 1981, 72) was used, where possible, to determine the age classes of the adult skeletons. Immature skeletons were aged by reference to the stage of dental development (Hillson1986, 190–1). Other methods were used to estimate a more exact skeletal age in adults. These were examination of the pubic symphyses (Brooks & Suchey 1990), the auricular surface of the ilium (Lovejoy *et al* 1985) and the sternal end of the fourth rib (Iscan *et al* 1984 and 1985).

Sex in adults was assessed by examining the form of the skull and the pelvis (WEA 1980), with more emphasis being given to pelvic form. Stature was reconstructed using the standard regression formulae from longbone lengths of Trotter and Gleser (in Bass 1987). Skeletal measurements were taken as per Cross and Bruce (1989) and indices were calculated using the formulae in Bass (1987). Non-metric traits were recorded from those in Brothwell (1981, 93–100). All bones were examined for pathological lesions and, where possible, these were classified according to cause.

4.3 RESULTS

4.3.1 Demography

Totalling the most common skeletal element for the entire assemblage, the minimum number of individuals (MNI) for the site is 41 adults and 8 immature (left femur midshaft). A further immature individual was evidenced by the presence of nine right temporal bones. This figure is certainly a large underestimate of the number of inhumations disturbed during the excavations and the number of individuals represented by unarticulated material which was excavated but unrecorded. Several of the earlier *in situ* interments were only partially excavated and so have not contributed their full number of skeletal elements to this analysis; the same will be true for the large unrecorded portion of the assemblage, especially as it is evident that some of the material in store has derived from areas outside the main excavations, where trenches were dug to investigate stratigraphic and architectural questions, rather than demographic enquiries.

For these reasons, only the *in situ* interments will be considered here, along with a few assemblages of charnel which can be securely dated by stratigraphy to the medieval period. Using these criteria, the secure medieval MNI (including both *in situ* and charnel) is 23 adults (right femur midshaft) along with two immature individuals (the 12-year-old juveniles, SK13 and SK15). This figure (obviously an underestimate, given 24 *in situ* skeletons, as well as individuals represented in charnel) is based purely on the most common skeletal element recovered. The MNI is used as it was impossible to be sure whether parts of disturbed interments were recovered from among the 'charnel' fraction of the assemblages and some parts of the skeletons had decayed or were left in the ground during excavation.

As would be expected given the presence of several ecclesiastical graves, there is a heavy bias towards male individuals. Based on the form of the 19 pelvises from secure medieval contexts (including from interments and charnel material), 15 were male and four female. Similarly of 21 frontal bones, 17 were males and four were females. It should be noted that SK7 was assigned an inferred gender, rather than an examined sex, based on the presence of episcopal trappings in the grave. The age, sex and stature distributions of the *in situ* assemblage are set out in Table 4.2

It is worth noting that the average male height is 1.733 m, a full 2.5cm more than the average for British medieval men (Roberts and Manchester 1995, 27) and over 3cm taller than broadly contemporary populations in Aberdeen and Linlithgow (Cross & Bruce 1989, 125) where no male reached the height of 1.80m (around 5' 10"). The average for the males in the high status, later graves was 1.736m, nearly 5cm greater than the average height in the general population buried at Whithorn at the time (1.69m: Cardy 1997, 522). The individual from Charnel Group 12A was also tall, over 6' in height. As indicated by the associated finds (Chapter 6) and by their very location

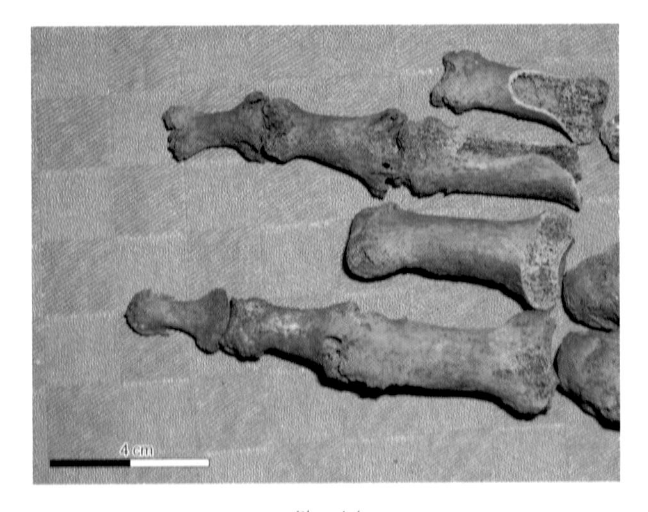

Plate 4.1
Right hand of SK 21, showing evidence of psoriatic arthritis

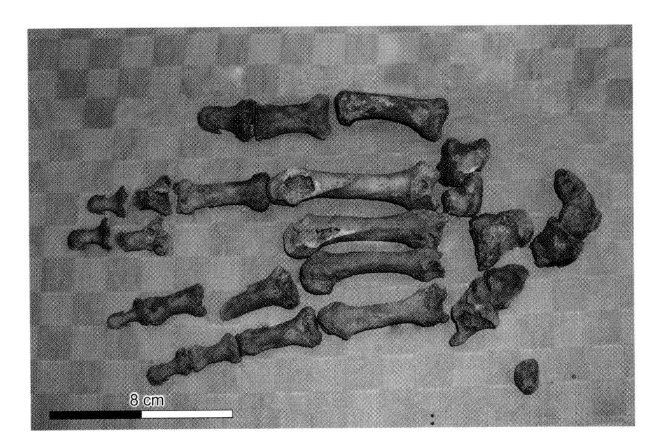

Plate 4.2
Left hand of SK 21, showing evidence of psoriatic arthritis

inside the church, it is clear that the population represented in the sample were of higher than average status, with good childhood nutrition allowing them to achieve their full potential for height. This is explored further in the isotope work in Chapter 5.

4.3.2 Metrical data

Thirteen male and two female crania from the *in situ* sample were measured to give craniometric indices. Because of the fragmentary nature of most of the material, too few data are available from the site to make statistical analysis worthwhile. It was noted that two of the crania (SK3 and SK4) it was possible to measure were broad-headed (brachycranic), a category not seen in the general population (Cardy 1997, 522), where all 18 measured crania were long- or medium-headed.

Lower limb shape may reflect lifestyle variations, where greater flattening of the upper parts of the femur and tibia (platymeria and platycnemia, respectively) may indicate a more active lifestyle or poorer nutrition. The figures for platymeria in the general medieval population at Whithorn were very high at 90% of individuals (Cardy 1997, 524) but much lower in the current study (8 of 14, or 57% overall, dropping to 6 of 11 in Graves 1–12 and 21), possibly indicating a more sedentary life for the higher-status individuals. A full list of the measurements taken is available in the Project Archive.

4.3.3 Pathology

Arthritic lesions

As would be expected with eight individuals in the Older Adult (OA) category out of 24 articulated skeletons, degenerative changes to joint surfaces were commonly recorded. In all, 12 individuals (five OA, three MA, one YA and three Adults) had extraspinal joint changes past Sager's Grade I (Brothwell 1981, 150, ie severe lipping, change in surface texture or eburnation of the joint). The most common sites for osteoarthritis were the wrist end of the right radius (5 of 10 examined), the knee joints (5 of 13 distal femurs and 3 of 8 proximal tibiae) and the right hip joint (4 of 11). The lesions to the right wrist are much more common than usual; for example, in Peter Hill's excavations at Whithorn, the wrist was only the fourth most common site of degenerative joint disease (Cardy 1997, 538), and it is tempting to speculate that its higher frequency among Ritchie's skeletons may be the result of scribal work. Other arthritic-type lesions were noted. SK21 had severe erosive and ankylosing (fusing) lesions of his hands, feet, ankles, wrists and elbows, fairly symmetrically distributed. There is a slight involvement of the sacro-iliac joints. It is possible that he may have suffered from rheumatoid arthritis, but the fused and distorted fingers with 'pencil and cup' deformity suggest that psoriatic arthritis may be a more likely diagnosis (Plate 4.1; Plate 4.2). This is a rare complication of the skin condition psoriasis, which is often thought to have been easily confused in the medieval mind with leprosy (skin lesions and mutilating deformities of the fingers and toes are similar).

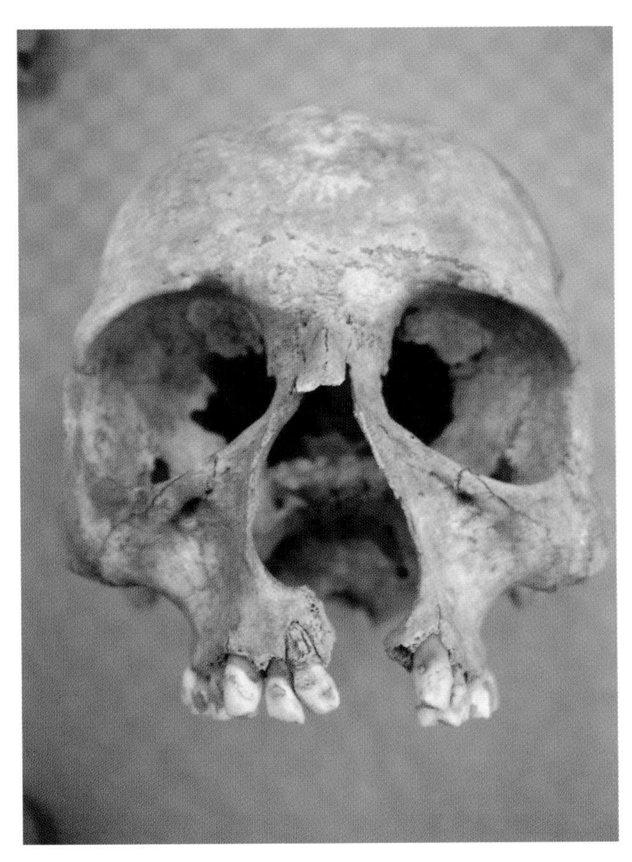

Plate 4.3
The cleft palate of SK 8 is thought to have been present from birth and would have resulted in a severe speech defect

Deficiency diseases
Cribra orbitalia was observed in SK18. This condition, of porosity in the roofs of the eye-sockets, is a consequence of certain iron-deficiency anaemias, caused, for example, by a heavy load of gut parasites or poor nutrition. The porosity of the parietal bones of the skull of SK20 may have had the same aetiology.

The older adult female SK19 showed signs of osteoporosis, in the form of a very thin, lightweight innominate bone. Her 4th and 5th cervical vertebrae had also fused, perhaps as a result of them collapsing also due to osteoporosis; not enough of the vertebrae, especially of the bodies, survived to confirm this diagnosis. Another case of osteoporosis was noted in the female OA cranium from Charnel Group 26 (overlying SK20) which was so thinned that the parietal bones had become sunken.

Developmental lesions
The middle adult male (SK8) from a high-status stone-lined grave with (now missing) grave-goods was born with a cleft palate; judging by the extent of the lesion, he would certainly have had a 'hare lip' also, suggesting that the defect was genetic in origin. (Roberts & Manchester 1995, 40–41). Given the paucity of published examples of this condition in the archaeological literature (the modern incidence is about 1:600 births) it is apparent that infants with cleft palate had difficulty in reaching adulthood. The defect of the bony palate and soft palate creates great difficulty in suckling, and even if weaning is achieved can make it easy for food particles to be aspirated into the lungs. In such an extensive lesion as the present case, there would also be a severe speech defect, potentially a significant disability to someone who appears to be a candidate for episcopal status.

Description of the non-united maxillae: The left side is developed from the third molar (M3) to the lateral incisor (I2), which appears to have a 'stunted' root. The right side has M3 to the central incisor (I1) and (?)half the alveolus of the left I1, lost *post mortem*. The right I1 is malformed (small/peg-shaped with a large enamel defect on the buccal surface and a stunted root). The left half of the pirifom aperture is deeper than the right, ie from nasion (at the top of the nose) to the base of the nasal aperture at nariale (approximately) is 52.2mm on the left; 50.4mm on the right. The edges of the 'hard palate' parts of the maxillae are very thin, but not extensively broken and with a large gap in the horizontal plane, so that the roof of the palate is some 8mm inferior on the left compared to the right. All teeth are in wear except the right I1, although there is a polished facet on the disto-buccal aspect (Plate 4.3).

Another developmental anomaly, on SK3, was spina bifida occulta, a failure of the spines of the sacral vertebrae to unite. This is a common finding, and is usually symptomless for the individual concerned. In this case the original open hiatus had become resealed by the ossification of ligament tissue in the gap, due to DISH (see below).

Trauma
There is very little evidence of trauma. SK8 had an old, healed depressed fracture of the frontal bone (in the centre, about at the level of the hairline), and a possible healed fracture of the left ulna.

In SK22, the poor preservation precluded an exact diagnosis of a lesion to the right side of the face; there was extensive periosteal bone formation, extending over the right zygomatic bone from the junction with the frontal bone and continuing down over the right side of the mandible to the alveolus of the first molar. The infection had also tracked back to the temporal bone, completely destroying the arch of the tempero-zygomatic process, presumably by osteomyelitis. Although there is infection around the root of the first molar, it appears that this is a consequence, rather than the source, of the lesion. It is most likely that some injury to the cheekbone became infected, causing the destruction of the underlying bone.

Infectious disease
No evidence was seen of transmissable diseases such as tuberculosis or leprosy. Apart from the infection due to injury, mentioned in *Trauma* (above) the only evidence of bacterial infection was in the form of abscesses in the jaws and one possible case of gingivitis (gum infection, usually due to poor oral hygiene) in SK24. In the seven OA dentitions recovered (>45 years old) every one had at least one dental abscess.

Systemic
Diffuse Idiopathic Skeletal Hyperostosis (DISH) is a condition of unknown aetiology, where an individual starts to overproduce bone, especially by the ossification of spinal ligaments and points where tendons are joined onto the bone (such as the Achilles tendon to the calcaneus at the heel or the triceps tendon to the ulna at the elbow). Blocks of adjacent vertebrae may fuse completely together, losing all mobility. The condition is commoner in old men than women, and may be linked to obesity and late onset diabetes. This is significant in the case of SK3, an OA male, where the position of the skeleton in the grave, with the arms bowed out from the sides, and the presence of a larger than usual amount of adipocere (a chalky or soapy white substance, the mineralised remains of the products of body fat decomposition) suggest that the individual may have been obese. It has been noted (Roberts & Cox 2003, 246; Rogers & Waldron 1995, 48) that the prevalence of DISH is significantly higher in skeletons from 'high-status' areas

of monastic sites, probably reflecting a more sedentary lifestyle and access to richer foodstuffs.

Neoplastic

One of the individuals represented in Charnel Group 12A was very tall and robust. This was also the individual with one of the largest mandibles the author has encountered, possibly due to acromagally. This is a condition of continued growth of parts of the skeleton after the end of puberty, caused by a benign tumour of the pituitary gland, producing excess growth hormone. A very thick cranium identified in the charnel deposits (Lab. No 06/-, 'from Cutting 2') may also have been the result of this condition (Roberts & Manchester 1995, 181).

The skull of SK4 had a 'button', or 'ivory' osteoma on the frontal bone. This is a very common, completely harmless bony growth, usually found on the outside of the skull.

An unknown substance was packaged with SK10, possibly from the region of the right radius or ulna or within the abdomen (the excavation photographs are very unclear in the crucial area). Of unmistakably organic origin, the bulk of the item is of a hard, but finely granular, brown substance. The original shape seems to have been oblong, about 120mm long, perhaps up to 50mm wide and about 15mm thick, with a smooth but slightly lobular surface. This ground is infiltrated by vascular lumens, filled with a lamellar substance of a whitish, slightly translucent and waxy appearance. Chemical analysis of this substance may help to elucidate its origins; at the moment the author's thoughts are leaning towards some kind of tumour, perhaps of plasma cell origin, some of which secrete excessive amounts of waxy globulin proteins (Aufderheide & Rodriguez-Martin 1998 351 ff) or perhaps a lipid granulomatosis (Ortner & Putschar 1981, 359).

Chapter 5

Isotope Analysis of Bone Collagen and Tooth Enamel

JANET MONTGOMERY, GUNDULA MÜLDNER AND GORDON COOK,
WITH SPECIALIST ANALYSES BY ANDREW GLEDHILL AND ROBERT ELLAM

5.1 SUMMARY

This report presents the results of carbon and nitrogen stable isotope analysis of human bone collagen of 14 individuals, and enamel strontium, oxygen and carbon isotope measurements from 13 individuals from Ritchie's excavations at Whithorn. No medieval animal bone reference data from southwest Scotland were available therefore detailed interpretations as well as comparisons with other sites have to be preliminary. Nevertheless, the carbon and nitrogen isotope data from Whithorn are very similar to those obtained from later medieval populations in northern England. By analogy with these, they are interpreted to indicate a diet which was mainly based on terrestrial C_3 foods with varying contributions of marine fish, which had special significance in the Middle Ages on account of the fasting regulations imposed by the Church.

The most important result of this investigation is the observation that the diet of the Phase 3 burials differed significantly from that of the burials of Phase 1. The later (Phase 3) population undoubtedly includes several former bishops of Whithorn, as well as other high-ranking ecclesiastical and secular figures (see Chapter 9); the earlier graves, however, are those belonging to lower-status individuals in the parish cemetery whose graves were built over and buried below the early 13th-century extension of the cathedral priory church. The Phase 3 group of clerics and other significant individuals consumed significantly more marine fish, which is consistent with historical evidence on medieval upper-class diet. The only cleric who did not appear to have consumed such a diet was Skeleton 8, who suffered from a severe cleft palate.

This is the first time that stable isotope data can demonstrate that a well-defined social group – the bishops of Whithorn and their immediate circle, including local benefactors – consumed a very distinctive diet in comparison with their contemporaries. These results make Whithorn Priory an important site for the investigation of medieval diet by stable isotope analysis. Further analyses may have the potential to address key questions relating to the relationship between dietary variation and social stratification in the Middle Ages.

Strontium and oxygen analysis to investigate mobility and origins indicated that one bishop (Skeleton 1) and one female (skeleton 19) have very different origins from the rest of the individuals and are not from the Whithorn area. In addition, the data separate the remaining individuals into two groups: the first group contains only clerics (Skeletons 2–5) and the second contains all the remaining low-status burials, plus the individual with the cleft palate (Skeleton 8). The clerics are consistent with origins in non-coastal regions either further to the east or possibly in north–east Ireland, whilst the second group is consistent with a childhood spent on the western seaboard of Scotland at Whithorn.

Interestingly, this split between high- and low-status burials is also reflected in the carbon and nitrogen data suggesting that, at Whithorn, geographic mobility and diet were correlated with status.

5.2 CARBON AND NITROGEN STABLE ISOTOPE ANALYSIS FOR DIETARY RECONSTRUCTION

5.2.1 Introduction

Carbon and nitrogen stable isotope analysis of bone collagen is currently one of the best established bone chemistry applications for reconstructing diet in archaeological populations. Isotopes are atoms of the same element with small but measurable differences in their atomic mass due to differing numbers of neutrons. Their abundance varies systematically in nature and also between certain types of food. As the body breaks down food to synthesise and renew body tissues, these differences are preserved, although somewhat altered, in the isotopic composition of consumers' tissues, including their bones. By extracting the collagen, which is the main bone protein and usually the best preserved constituent of archaeological bone, and analysing its isotopic composition (Figure 5.1), it is therefore possible to reconstruct the major components of the diet of an individual over the time of tissue formation – usually a long-term average that can reflect the last ten

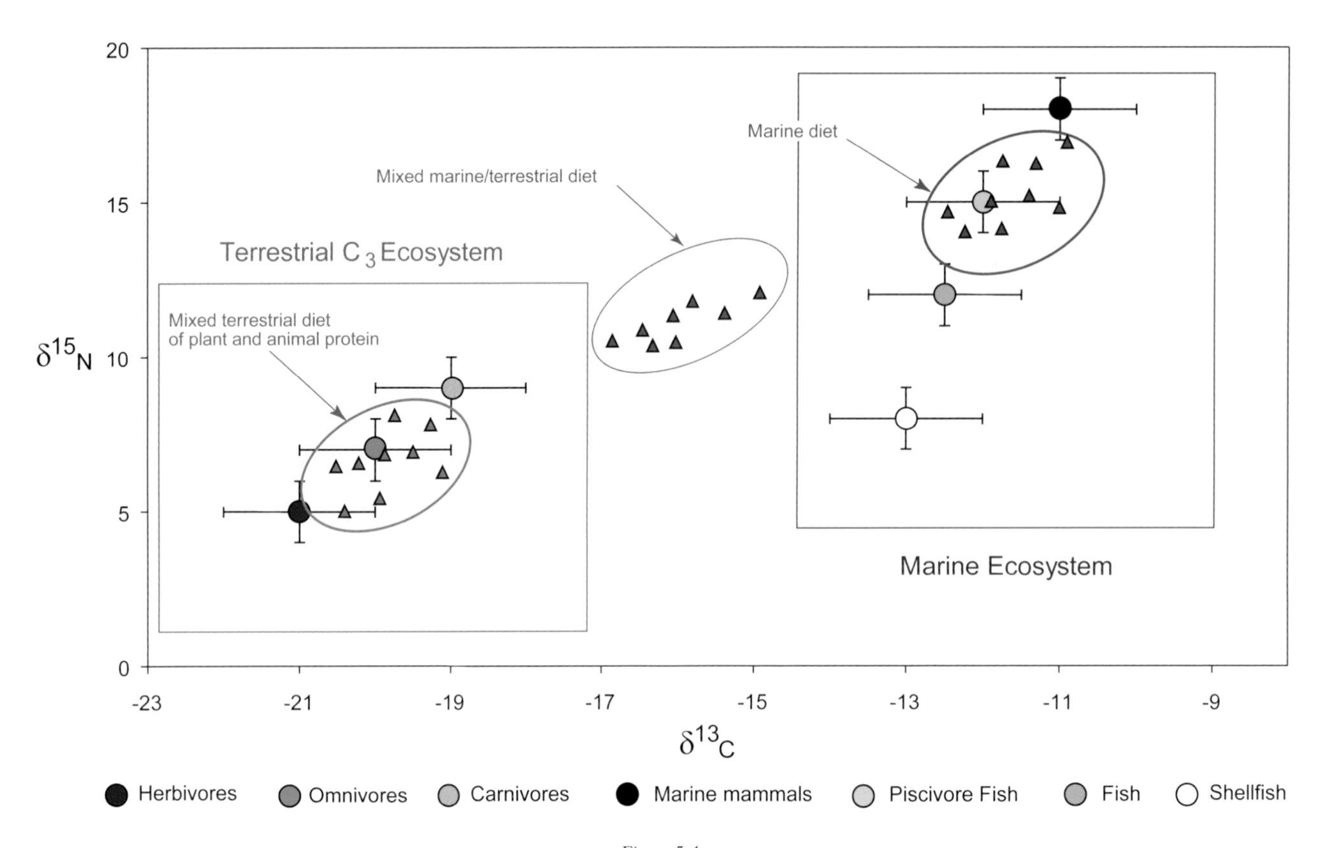

Figure 5.1

Stable isotope scatterplot illustrating the principle of stable isotope analysis for dietary reconstruction. (Round symbols show typical $\delta^{13}C$ and $\delta^{15}N$ ratios for different types of food ($\pm 1\sigma$). Triangular symbols represent typical bone collagen stable isotope values for human samples, whose diet is inferred by their position on the graph in relation to potential food sources. (Modified from Müldner & Richards 2006)

to 30 years of an adult's life (see Schwarcz & Schoeninger 1991; Katzenberg 2000; Sealy 2001; Hedges *et al* 2007).

Carbon stable isotope ratios ($\delta^{13}C$) are particularly suited to track the consumption of plants of different photosynthetic pathways (C_3 and C_4) through the food web, or, in areas like northwest Europe where C_4-plants (such as maize, sorghum or millet) never played a significant role in human subsistence, to distinguish between terrestrial (C_3) and marine-based foods. Nitrogen stable isotope ratios ($\delta^{15}N$) increase by 3–5‰ with each trophic level (Bocherens & Drucker 2003) and are therefore useful to assess the importance of plant versus animal protein in the diet. They can also help detect the consumption of aquatic resources, which are usually more enriched in ^{15}N than terrestrial foods (Schoeninger *et al* 1983).

With the exception of very low-protein diets, collagen is synthesised primarily from dietary protein, and its stable isotope composition reflects the main protein sources rather than diet as a whole (Ambrose & Norr 1993; Tieszen & Fagre 1993). Consequently, low-protein foods, such as most fruit and vegetables, can be effectively invisible in the collagen isotope signal, while foods with a relatively high-protein content such as lean meat may be somewhat over-represented. However, in low-protein diets (eg < 5% protein) energy sources can contribute a significant (ie > 50%) of the carbon in collagen (Ambrose & Norr 1993). Also, since there are no isotopic differences between different types of protein from the same animal, collagen stable isotope analysis cannot distinguish between the consumption of herbivore meat and dairy products (O'Connell *et al* 2001).

The systematic variation of stable carbon and nitrogen isotope ratios between different ecosystems and trophic levels is very well-established and broad ranges of typical δ-values for C_3-, C_4- and marine feeding organisms can be easily defined (eg Schoeninger & DeNiro 1984; Kelly 2000; see Figure 5.1). Nevertheless, it is becoming increasingly apparent in recent years that these values can vary significantly, not only between different locations but also over time (van Klinken *et al* 2000; Richards & Hedges 2003; Hedges & Reynard 2006). For correct interpretation of human isotope data it is therefore necessary to determine local environmental background values. This is usually achieved by stable isotope analysis of animal remains, ideally from the same site and time period as the human samples.

Table 5.1 Carbon and nitrogen isotope data

Skeleton / Charnel Group	*Name*	*Wt (mg)*	*%Element*	*δ15N‰ Delta Air*	*Mean*	*%Element*	*δ13C‰ Delta PDB*	*Mean*	*C/N*	*Mean*	*Collagen yield %*
18	WPX18/25a	1.04	16.32	11.33	11.32	44.42	-20.58	-20.58	3.18	3.20	5.30
	WPX18/25b	1.03	15.88	11.31	–	43.81	-20.59	–	3.22	–	–
8	WPX22/93a	1.05	16.92	11.48	11.47	45.64	-19.92	-20.04	3.15	3.18	9.80
	WPX22/93b	1.16	16.48	11.45	–	45.39	-20.15	–	3.21	–	–
4	WPX31/15a	1.1	16.34	13.30	13.31	43.82	-18.94	-18.87	3.13	3.16	7.50
	WPX31/15b	1.11	16.09	13.33	–	43.97	-18.80	–	3.19	–	–
1	WPX41/12a	0.95	16.17	13.24	13.24	44.21	-19.37	-19.36	3.19	3.20	9.60
	WPX41/12b	1.04	16.12	13.24	–	44.45	-19.36	–	3.22	–	–
19	WPX42/05a	1.15	16.32	11.09	11.06	44.14	-21.10	-21.11	3.16	3.27	5.20
	WPX42/05b	1.05	15.61	11.03	–	45.25	-21.11	–	3.38	–	–
24	WPX43/02a	1.02	16.15	10.46	10.48	43.89	-21.05	-20.96	3.17	3.20	5.80
	WPX43/02b	1.18	16.14	10.51	–	44.58	-20.87	–	3.22	–	–
5	WPX44/07a	0.98	16.32	12.23	12.26	44.00	-19.36	-19.27	3.15	3.20	7.80
	WPX44/07b	0.99	15.69	12.30	–	43.70	-19.18	–	3.25	–	–
7	WPX48/03a	1.05	16.10	13.45	13.47	43.99	-19.05	-19.07	3.19	3.23	8.90
	WPX48/03b	0.99	15.65	13.49	–	44.02	-19.09	–	3.28	–	–
2	WPX5/-a	0.98	16.33	12.01	12.00	43.55	-19.30	-19.19	3.11	3.16	7.30
	WPX5/-b	1.05	16.15	11.99	–	44.37	19.08	–	3.21	–	–
3	WPX52/01/6a	1.05	16.82	13.47	13.49	45.27	-19.40	-19.31	3.14	3.18	8.10
	WPX52/01/6b	1.06	16.00	13.52	–	44.26	-19.22	–	3.23	–	–
6	WPX56/15a	1.12	16.64	11.92	11.92	44.61	-19.59	-19.65	3.13	3.15	6.10
	WPX56/15b	1.03	16.14	11.92	–	43.94	-19.70	–	3.18	–	–
15	WPX57/22a	1.06	16.48	12.07	12.01	44.07	-19.48	-19.45	3.12	3.15	5.60
	WPX57/22b	1.06	16.23	11.95	–	44.29	-19.42	–	3.18	–	–
9	WPX58/23a	1.14	16.66	11.28	11.21	44.10	-20.05	-20.19	3.09	3.11	8.10
	WPX58/23b	1.08	15.88	11.13	–	42.76	-20.32	–	3.14	–	–
23	WPX68/23a	1.07	14.83	10.94	11.01	41.14	-21.20	-21.14	3.24	3.26	3.50
	WPX68/23b	1.15	14.53	11.08	–	40.81	-21.07	–	3.28	–	–

International Standards analysed in the period of this work

	δ15N *Measured value*	*Accepted value*	*δ13C* *Measured value*	*Accepted value*
IAEA600	1.07 ± 0.06	1.0 ± 0.2	-27.66 ± 0.12	-27.5 ± 0.2
N2	20.57	20.3 ± 0.2	–	–
PEF1	–	–	-31.7	-31.8 ± 0.2

5.2.2 Sample preparation

Bone samples of typically 100–200 mg were prepared using a modified Longin Method (Brown *et al* 1988). Briefly, the bone was cleaned of adhering soil and the outer surfaces were removed by air abrasion. The samples were then demineralised over several days in 0.5 M HCl at *c* 5°C, after which the acid solution was discarded and the residue rinsed to neutrality with ultrapure de-ionised H_2O. The samples were placed in sealed tubes and HCl was added to form a pH 3 solution. The demineralised bone was then gelatinised for 48 hours at 70°C, before the acid-insoluble residues were removed with the aid of a 5–8μm Ezee® filter. The remaining solution was concentrated in Amicon® Ultra-4 filter devices fitted with PL-30 Ultracel® membranes (Millipore). The supernatant, purified 'collagen' (>30 kD) was freeze-dried, then weighed into tin capsules for isotopic analysis. $\delta^{13}C$ and $\delta^{15}N$ ratios were determined by continuous-flow isotope ratio mass spectrometry (CF-IRMS) using a Roboprep® elemental analyser coupled to a Europa 20–20 light stable isotope ratio mass spectrometer in the Department of Archaeological Sciences, University of Bradford. Analytical error, calculated from repeat measurements of international standards of known isotopic composition, was ±0.2‰ (1σ) for both elements. Results for samples and standards are tabulated in Table 5.1.

5.2.3 Results and discussion

In the absence of animal bone stable isotope data from Whithorn to provide typical isotope values of food available at the priory, a detailed interpretation of the human dietary signatures is not possible (see Chapter 5.2). Any comparison with other sites and populations therefore has to be preliminary. As there is no published faunal data-set from Holocene Southern Scotland, the Whithorn human data will be compared with later medieval animal bone stable isotope data from Northern England (North Yorkshire and the City of York) as the closest available parallel (Müldner & Richards 2005; Müldner & Richards 2007a).

Table 5.2 Sample summary for carbon and nitrogen isotope data

Skeleton No.	*Sample No.*	*Skeletal element*	*Sex/gender*	*Status*	*Mean δ13C‰,*	*Mean δ15N‰,*
1	WPX41/12a	left patella	male	high	-19.36	13.24
2	WPX5/-a	right fibula	male	high	-19.19	12.00
3	WPX52//01/6a	right clavicle	male	high	-19.31	13.49
5	WPX44/07a	right patella	male	high	-19.27	12.26
6	WPX56/15a	right tibia	female	high	-19.65	11.92
8	WPX22/93a	left patella	male	high	-20.04	11.47
9	WPX58/23a	right tibia	female	–	-20.19	11.21
15	WPX57/22a	left humerus	juvenale	high	-19.45	12.01
18	WPX18/25a	left humerus	male	–	-20.58	11.32
19	WPX42/05a	left femur	female	–	21.11	11.06
23	WPX68/23a	left humerus	male	–	-21.14	11.1
24	WPX43/02a	left femur	male	–	-20.96	10.48
				mean	-19.87	12.02
				±1σ	0.80	1.01

see Table 5.1 for analytical errors

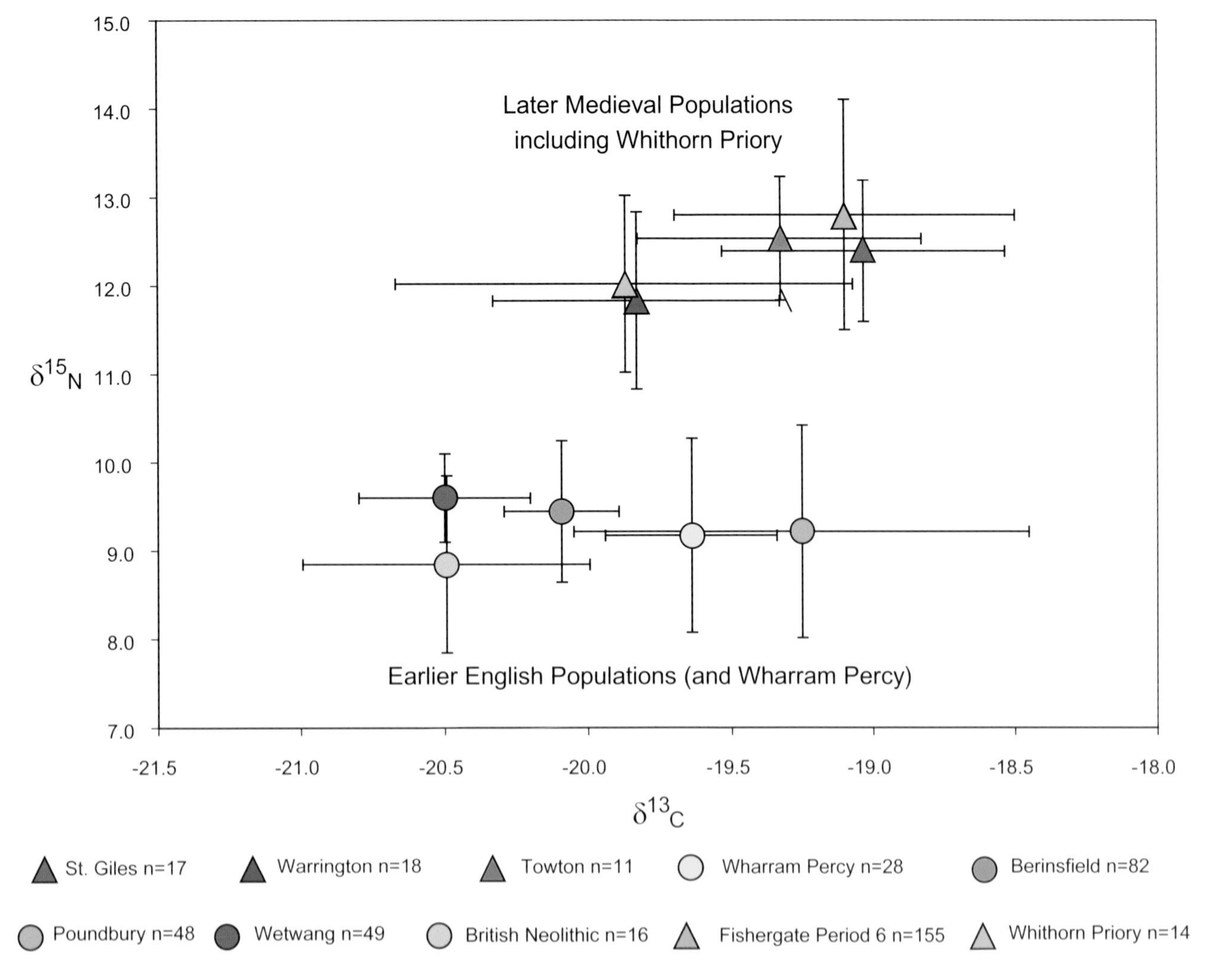

Figure 5.2

Stable isotope values (means $\pm 1\sigma$) for English populations from the Neolithic (Richards 2000), Iron Age Wetwang, N. Yorks. (Jay & Richards 2006); Romano-British Poundbury, Dorset (Richards *et al* 1998); Anglo-Saxon Berinsfield, Oxon. (Privat *et al* 2002) and 10th- to 16th-century Wharram Percy, N. Yorks. (Richards *et al* 2002) in comparison with later medieval (late 12th- to early 16th-century) sites from Northern England: St Giles and Towton, N. Yorks., Warrington, Cheshire (all Müldner & Richards 2005) and the Gilbertine Priory of Fishergate, city of York (Müldner & Richards 2007b). Note that all later medieval datasets (except for Wharram Percy) are significantly different from earlier populations, because of their higher δ^{15}N ratios. (Figure modified from Müldner & Richards 2005)

Dietary interpretation of the stable isotope data and comparison with other sites

Collagen quality indicators of all samples from Whithorn Priory were within the accepted range and indicate that the collagen was well enough preserved to yield reliable palaeodietary data (DeNiro 1985; van Klinken 1999).

δ^{13}C ratios of the 14 individuals range over 2.2‰, from -21.1‰ to -18.9‰, with a mean of -19.9 ± 0.8‰ (1σ). δ^{15}N ratios range over 3.0‰, from 10.5‰ to 13.5‰, with a mean of 12.0 ± 1.0‰ (Table 5.2).

These data indicate that human diet at the site was mostly based on terrestrial (C_3) foods with regular contributions of marine protein to the diet of at least some individuals (with δ^{13}C ratios > *c* -19.5‰, see discussion below). δ^{15}N ratios of *c* 10‰ and above are relatively high for what might be expected for a mixed diet of plant and animal protein (meat and dairy) that was typical for the medieval period (see Dyer 1998b). Where such high δ^{15}N ratios are associated with δ^{13}C values that suggest no measurable consumption of marine foods (individuals with δ^{13}C ratios < *c* -20.0‰), they could suggest a diet very high in animal protein (see Hedges & Reynard 2006).

In the absence of baseline data for typical herbivore stable isotope values from the Whithorn area, this point

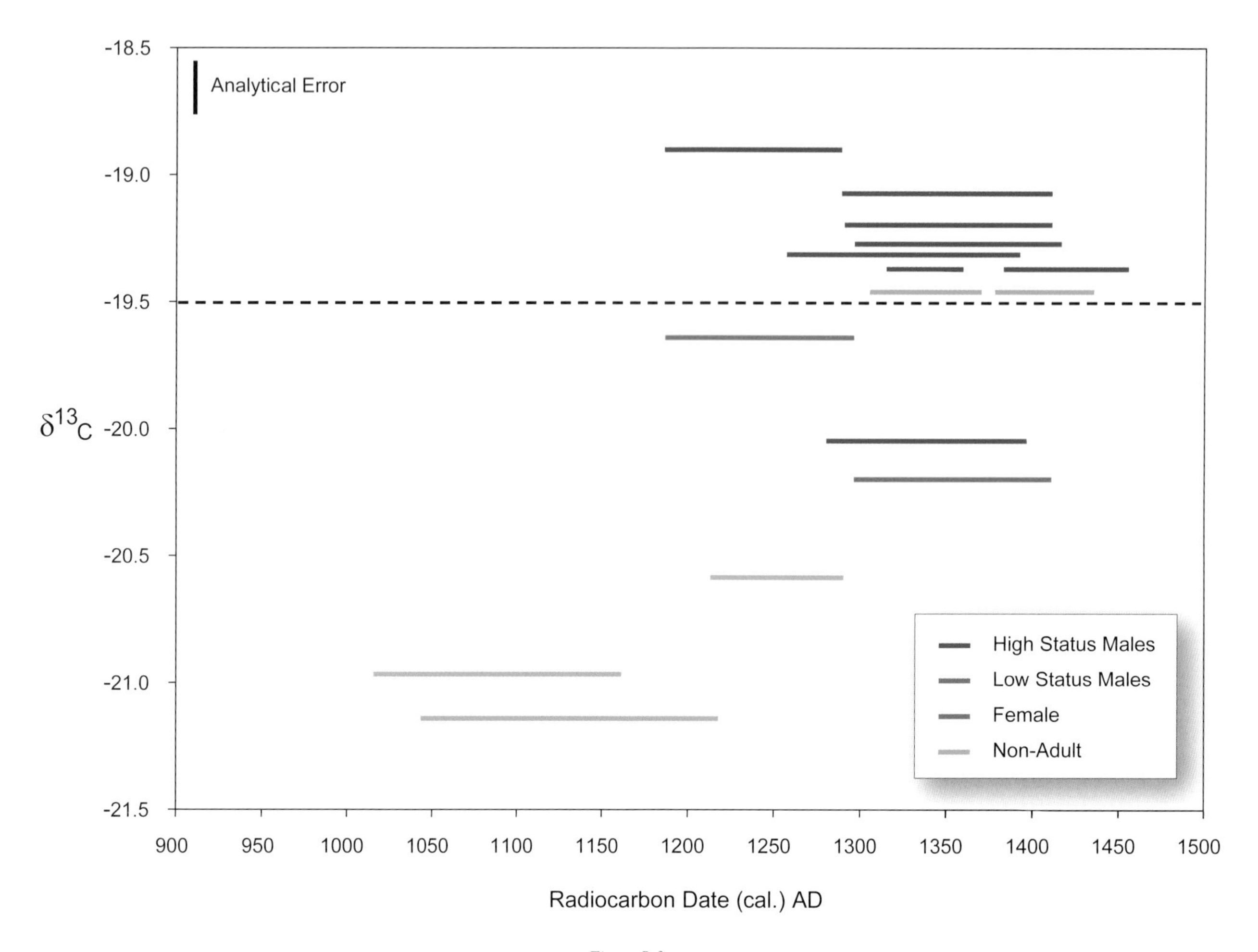

Figure 5.3
Calibrated radiocarbon dates at the 2σ level against δ^{13}C of 12 individuals from Whithorn Priory. The dotted line indicates a somewhat arbitrary 'thresholdvalue' of -19.5‰. Based on animal bone stable isotope data from Northern England, it may be reasonably assumed that individuals plotting above this line consumed marine protein on a regular basis. Prior to calibration, the radiocarbon ages were corrected for the contribution of marine resources to the diet using a linear relationship between a 100% terrestrial diet δ^{13}C end member of -21.5‰ and a 100% marine diet end member of -12.5‰ and the sample δ^{13}C value to estimate the percentage contribution. Calibration was undertaken using Calib 5 and a ΔR value of -14 ± 70

cannot really be evaluated for the human data set, as it is at least possible that δ^{15}N ratios of plant foods available at the site were higher than those reconstructed for the Northern English sites. Nevertheless, the Whithorn human data, although they appear to be significantly different from those of earlier British populations from the Neolithic onwards, are very similar to carbon and nitrogen stable isotope values reported from medieval populations in Northern England (Müldner & Richards 2005; Müldner & Richards 2007a; see Figure 5.2).

The stable isotope signal observed in these medieval populations is complex, as may be expected in a society with a sophisticated system of food production, distribution and trade, and not easy to resolve. Nevertheless, detailed analysis of diachronic changes in diet at the city of York (Müldner & Richards 2007a) have recently suggested that the ^{15}N-enriched human isotope values are the result of the consumption of various foods, and especially pork from animals fed on animal protein, which are characterised by high δ^{15}N, yet 'terrestrial' δ^{13}C ratios. These ^{15}N enriched foods were present in York in all time periods, but, as Figure 5.2 suggests, were not universally consumed in England prior to the later Middle Ages.

The main new item that was added to the diet in the medieval period, however, was marine fish. This was consumed in varying amounts by most individuals, on account of, it is argued, the medieval fasting regulations that proscribed meat on almost half the days of the year (see further discussion below). Combined with a basic diet of terrestrial plant (mainly cereals) and herbivore (cattle, sheep) protein all these foods together produce the 'unusual' human isotope signal that appears to be typical of most later medieval populations (Müldner & Richards 2006; Müldner & Richards 2007a). This interpretation is also consistent with historical and zooarchaeological evidence for diet at the time (Woolgar *et al* 2006).

Diachronic change in diet at Whithorn

One of the most significant changes in medieval subsistence was the introduction of significant amounts of marine fish to the diet, in the wake of the intensification of deep sea fishing and large scale long-distance fish trade. This development, which was most likely fuelled by the increasing demand for fish in the growing towns, not least due to the medieval fasting regulations, was traditionally dated to the 12th and 13th centuries. However, a large survey of the English fishbone evidence has recently shown that off-shore marine species were increasingly abundant in coastal and inland settlements from around AD 1000 (Barrett *et al* 2004; Serjeantson & Woolgar 2006). Similarly, stable carbon and nitrogen isotope evidence from York show a transition to a more marine based diet in the mid-11th to early 12th centuries (Müldner & Richards 2007a).

The fact that the individuals from Whithorn Priory submitted for stable isotope analysis have also been radiocarbon dated, potentially allows for an examination of diachronic changes in diet at the site. The carbon stable isotope ratio ($\delta^{13}C$) is the main indicator for the contribution of marine foods to terrestrial C_3-based diets (Chisholm *et al* 1982). If, based on animal bone reference data from Northern England, we assume that $\delta^{13}C$ ratios < *c* -19.5‰ indicate a measurable contribution of marine protein to the human diet (see Müldner & Richards, 2007a), we can observe that most individuals above this 'threshold value' date to the mid-13th century and later (Figure 5.3).

Social differences in diet

The most remarkable aspect of the Whithorn Priory data set is the obvious dietary differences that are expressed between individuals of different social groups, in particular between the higher-status burials of Phase 3 (including several individuals who can be identified as former bishops of Whithorn) and the burials of Phase 1 for which a lower social status can be inferred.

With one exception (Skeleton 8), all individuals identified as bishops or other high-status individuals display the most ^{13}C and ^{15}N-enriched δ-values in the population, indicating that they consumed significantly more marine protein than the lower-status individuals, for whom a marine contribution to the diet is not measurable (at least if the Northern English baseline values are assumed) (Figure 5.4). A group of two ecclesiastics (Skeletons 1 & 3) appear different from the rest in that their $\delta^{15}N$ ratios are about 1‰ higher, suggesting that they consumed higher trophic level marine organisms or, perhaps, higher-protein diets than the others (see Müldner & Richards 2007a). Church superiors often kept a separate table (see Harvey 1993) and dietary differences between these two and the other high-status individuals could be explained by personal taste or different financial means, but also with different life-histories, particularly with respect to the number of years spent in high office; Grave 1 in particular contained an individual of some considerable age. Bone stable isotope data reflect a long-term average of diet, over several years to several decades before an individual's death. Therefore, if the accession to priestly or episcopal office was accompanied by dietary change, the previous diet would still be reflected in the individual's bone stable isotope signal for years to come. One possible way of testing this hypothesis is to conduct stable carbon and nitrogen isotope analysis of tooth dentine, which is renewed very slowly and therefore preserves the dietary signal from an individual's childhood (see Sealy *et al* 1995). Comparison of the stable isotope ratio of bone collagen with that of dentine of selected individuals would therefore enable us to detect whether this person's diet changed significantly since adolescence.

The suggestion that high-ranking clerics and lay benefactors should have consumed significantly more marine foods and, possibly, higher-protein diets than individuals of lower status is not at all surprising. It is well documented that medieval upper-class diets contained uncommonly large amounts of meat and fish as items of conspicuous consumption (Dyer 1998b; Woolgar 2001). Fish had a special religious significance as a fasting food and was usually eaten every Friday and Saturday, during the seasons of Lent and Advent as well as on the eves of important feasts (Woolgar 2000; Woolgar 2006). The lower classes, who could not afford the same expenditure on food, generally consumed less animal products (and protein as a whole). Especially in the centuries before the Black Death (*c* 1350 AD), they were also more likely to substitute meat with dairy products rather than fish on fast days (Dyer 1998a).

In the context of the Whithorn individuals, it would be interesting to see if there was any evidence to indicate whether the lower-ranking males were also members of the clergy, inmates of the priory or lay benefactors. Stable carbon isotope data from the Gilbertine Priory at Fishergate in York had initially suggested that members of the order, who were buried in a monastic cemetery to the east of the presbytery, consumed significantly more marine foods than lay people from the nave of the church (Mays 1997). Recent analysis of a larger number of samples has shown,

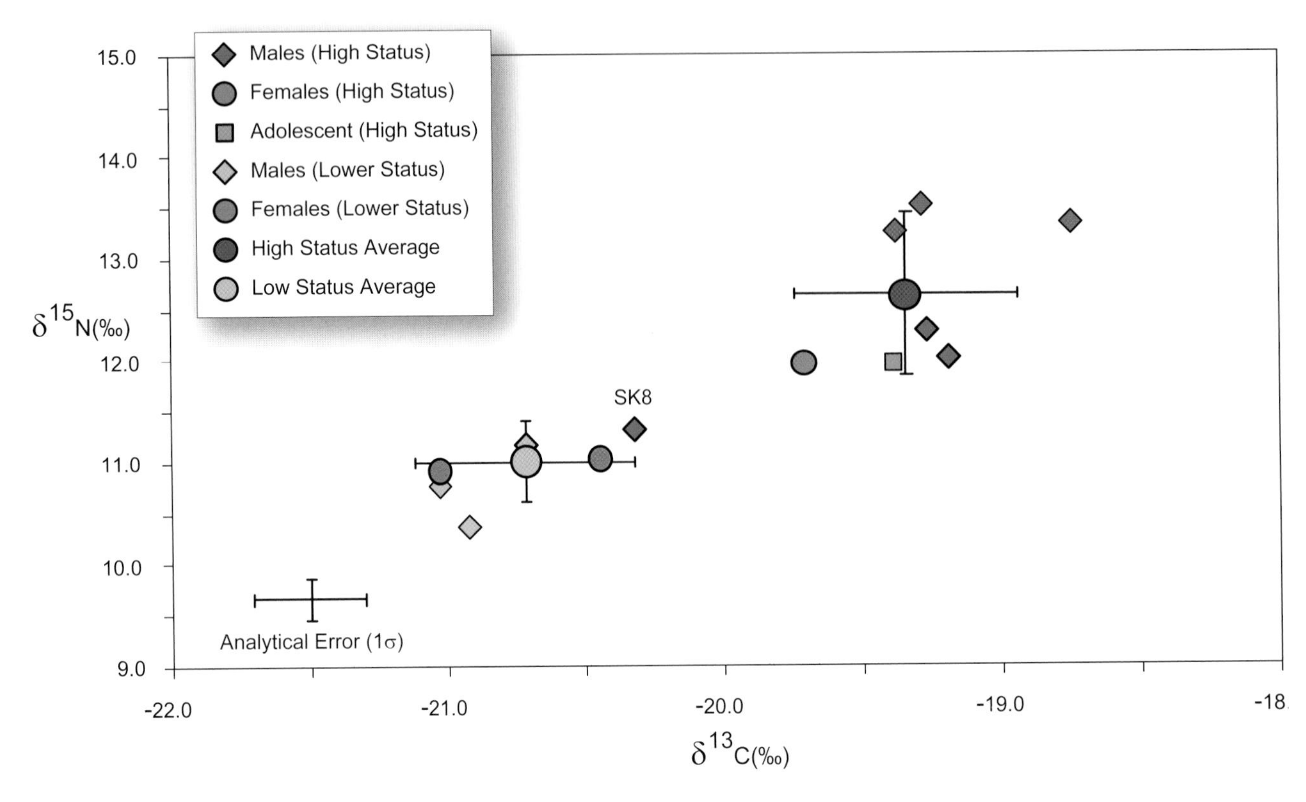

Figure 5.4
Stable carbon and nitrogen isotope ratios for individuals from Whithorn Priory and mean values (±1σ) for high and low status individuals. Note that with one exception (Skeleton 8), all individuals identified as bishops are exhibiting δ-values which are enriched in the heavy isotopes, indicating that they consumed significantly more marine foods than the lower status ones

however, that these results reflected dietary differences between males and females at Fishergate. Nevertheless, it was suggested that the stable isotope data of the Fishergate males may be skewed towards more marine values because of the presence of monastic individuals which could not be distinguished from male lay benefactors on grounds of their burial location (Müldner & Richards 2007b). If more detailed information on the identity of the lower-status males (monastic or lay people) was available for the Whithorn data-set, it could be used to test this hypothesis or, alternatively, to explore dietary differences between clerics of different rank.

Given the small sample size, it is not possible to evaluate potential differences between males and females (and their possible implications for differences between lay and monastic diet as set out above). Only three females were included in the data set and the values for them reflect their status rather than gender differences. Two of them (Skeleton 9 and19) are isotopically very similar to the low-status males, while the third (Skeleton 6) is similar to the bishops with lower δ^{15}N ratios. Assuming that the woman was buried at the priory as a wealthy lay benefactor, similarities in diet between her and the bishops would support the suggestion that the diet of high-status lay people, well-to-do monastic orders and the upper clergy were not significantly different by the later Middle Ages (Harvey 1993; Woolgar 1992–3; see Müldner & Richards 2007b).

Little can be said about the one sub-adult (Skeleton 15) in the Whithorn sample. At least in isotopic terms, the diet of this individual appears remarkably similar to that of some of the clerics as well as the above-mentioned female burial (Skeleton 6). This could suggest the child of an upper-class family and/or a boy who, at a young age, had been designated for a career in the Church.

The stable isotope data from Whithorn Priory therefore suggests that the consumption of marine fish was an indicator of status among high-ranking clerics and other upper-class individuals, a hypothesis which is clearly supported by the historical record (see Harvey 1993; Dyer 1998b). Considering their high status and also Whithorn Priory's location less than 5km from the sea, it is intriguing to compare the Whithorn data set with stable isotope data obtained for humans buried at the Gilbertine Priory at Fishergate in York (Müldner & Richards 2007b; Figure 5.5).

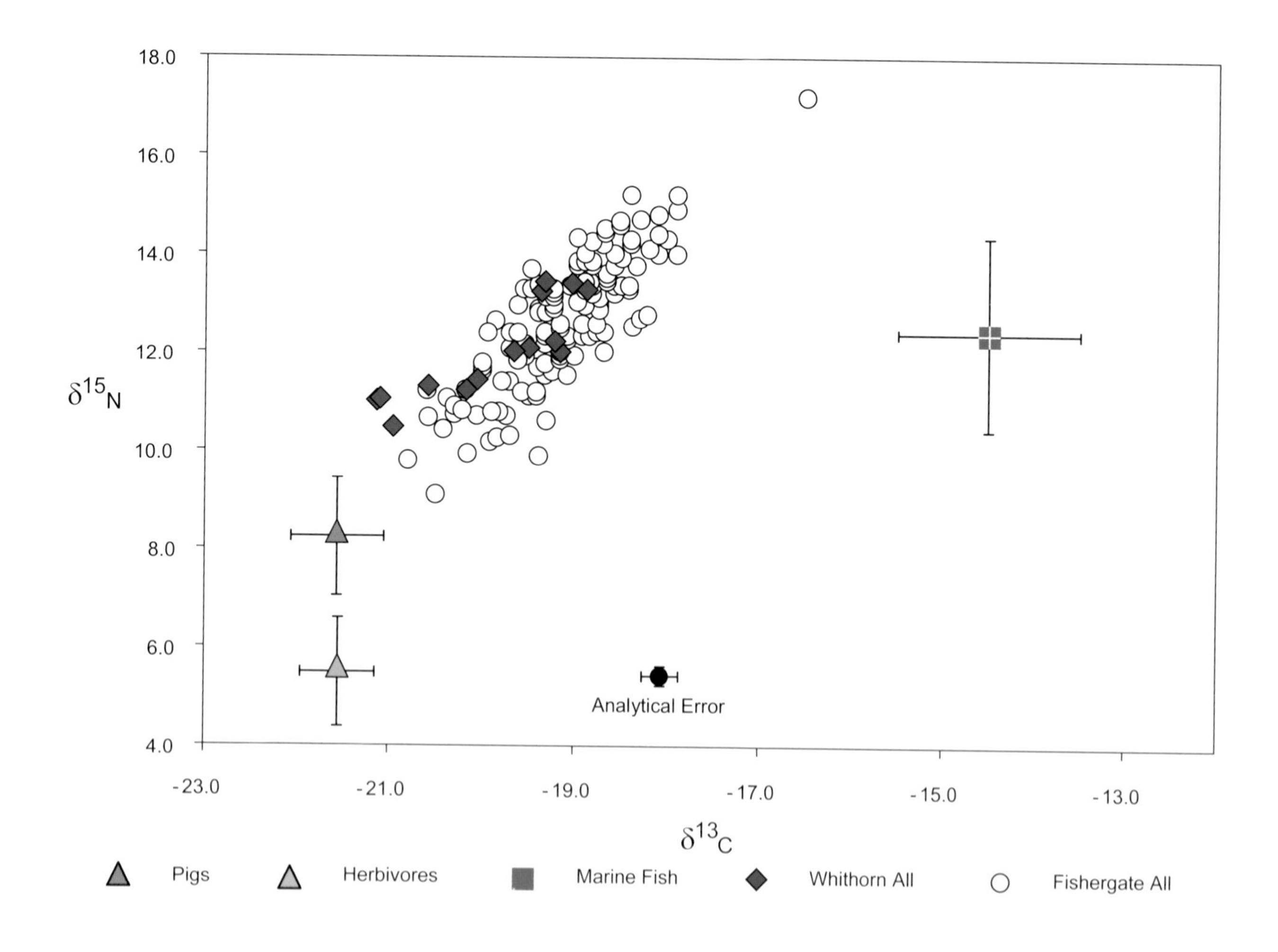

Figure 5.5

Stable carbon and nitrogen isotope ratios for individuals from Whithorn Priory in comparison with humans from the Gilbertine Priory at Fishergate (13th- to 16th-century) and later medieval animal bone samples from York (Müldner & Richards 2007a; Müldner & Richards 2007b). Note that the data suggest that the higher-status individuals at Whithorn (including some of its bishops) consumed significantly less marine protein than a large number of individuals from Fishergate

Even though Fishergate Priory is always described as a relatively modest establishment and neither its inmates nor its lay benefactors were ever particularly wealthy (see Kemp & Graves 1996), there appears to be a large number of individuals (almost exclusively males, see Müldner & Richards 2007b) who consumed significantly more marine protein on a regular basis than even the most exalted individuals at Whithorn. Although this observation, like most others in this report, will need to be verified by the comparison of animal bone data from York and Whithorn (in order to make sure that a direct comparison of the two human data sets is appropriate), it nevertheless suggests that stable isotope analysis of bone collagen has considerable potential to contribute further to research into medieval diet and society.

5.3 STRONTIUM AND OXYGEN ISOTOPE ANALYSIS TO INVESTIGATE ORIGINS

5.3.1 Introduction

Isotope analysis of archaeological human remains can provide evidence of their geographical origins (eg see White *et al* 1998; Bentley 2006; Evans *et al* 2006). Chemical elements from ingested food and water are incorporated into teeth and bones, and because the isotope ratios of some elements vary geographically, and on the assumption that ancient people sourced the bulk of their diet locally, these differences can be used to draw conclusions about whether individuals were of local or non-local origin. This report presents strontium and oxygen isotope data from tooth enamel, a skeletal tissue

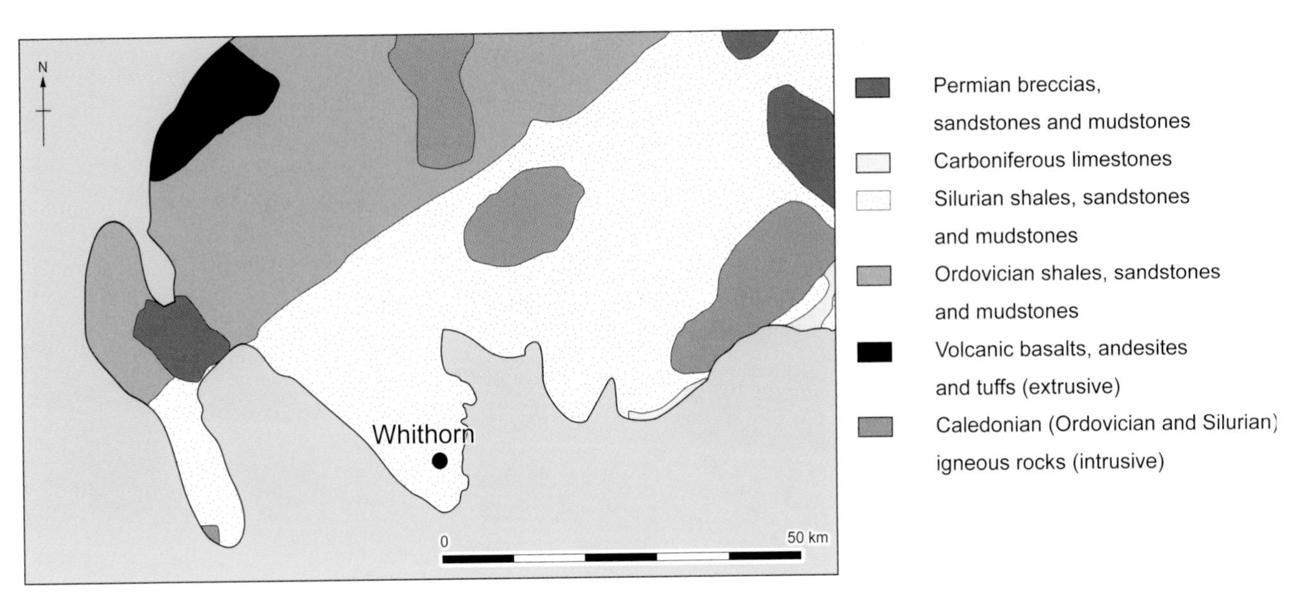

Figure 5.6
Schematic and simplified geology map of Dumfries and Galloway showing the location of Whithorn Priory and major lithological units

which is highly resistant to alteration during life or burial (Ericson 1993; Wang & Cerling 1994; Trickett *et al* 2003; Montgomery *et al* 2007), and represents childhood origins and diet. Strontium derives from rocks and its isotope ratios are indicative of the geology of the home region (Bentley 2006) whilst oxygen varies geographically with latitude, altitude and distance from the sea, and provides an indication of the climatic regime prevailing in the home region (Fricke *et al* 1995).

The isotope data presented here from the 13 humans and one pig from Whithorn Priory (13 teeth) are the first such data from archaeological human or animals from southwest Scotland. Consequently, there is currently no established isotopic baseline for the indigenous population at Whithorn in any period, and no directly comparative data against which to interpret the results obtained.

Geology of the region

Whithorn is located on the Machars, a peninsular area in Dumfries and Galloway, southwest Scotland. This region of the Southern Uplands is predominantly composed of Lower Palaeozoic sedimentary and igneous rocks (British Geological Survey 2001) which support fertile arable land. The solid surface geology of the Machar peninsular is Silurian sedimentary shales and muddy sandstones ('greywackes') (Figure 5.6) that formed on the ocean floor, overlain in parts by boulder clay and peat drift (British Geological Survey 1977). To the north of the peninsula, older sedimentary rocks of Ordovician age are found. To the west around Stranraer, at the entrance to the Rhins and east in the Dumfries region, Permian breccias, sandstone sand mudstones crop out. To the north and east beyond Newton Stewart and around Dalbeattie, there are outcrops of igneous granites of Caledonian (Ordovician to Devonian) age. On the northern coast of the Solway Firth are areas of Carboniferous limestone at Abbey Head and Southerness Point.

5.3.2 Sample preparation

Thirteen permanent teeth from 13 humans, plus one pig molar, from Whithorn Priory were submitted for enamel strontium ($^{87}Sr/^{86}Sr$), oxygen ($\delta^{18}O$) and carbon ($\delta^{13}C$) isotope measurements. The individual teeth are detailed in Table 5.3. As this table shows, the enamel of these teeth mineralised at various times during childhood but the majority would represent an isotope value from before nine years of age. Nonetheless, the age at which a specific tooth mineralises in individuals varies considerably and the formation of the third molar (or wisdom tooth) submitted for Skeleton 23 is particularly variable (Hillson 1986; Hillson 1996).

Preservation of enamel, determined macroscopically and during mechanical removal from the tooth, was not particularly good. All the human teeth were graded okay to poor, with the single exception of Sample 20 (the most recent sample that dates from the 19th century) where the enamel was graded as good. However, in most cases a sample of hard, translucent and unstained enamel with no visible caries or opacities was obtained for analysis.

Core enamel and, for four teeth, crown dentine were removed from the tooth samples and mechanically cleaned using tungsten carbide dental tools following the procedure given in Montgomery (2002). For strontium, all further preparation and analysis was carried out at SUERC. Strontium was separated from acid-digested enamel samples using conventional cation exchange methods and loaded onto single Ta filaments for mass spectrometry. The total procedural blank was < 500 pg. The samples were analysed on a VG Sector 54–30 mass spectrometer operated in dynamic (3 cycle) multi-collection mode. Instrumental mass fractionation was corrected to $^{86}Sr/^{88}Sr = 0.1196$ using an exponential fractionation law. Data were collected as 12 blocks of 10 ratios. NIST SRM-987 gave $^{87}Sr/^{86}Sr = 0.710255 \pm 0.000022$ (n = 15) during the course of this work.

In addition to the strontium isotope analyses, a portion of cleaned core enamel from the tooth crowns was also used in the determination of oxygen isotope ratios in biogenic carbonate ($\delta^{18}O_{carb}$) contained within the enamel mineral structure. The enamel samples were dissolved in '103%' phosphoric acid within sealed evacuated Pyrex tubes at a temperature of 25°C. The tubes were left overnight to allow complete dissolution of the material. For each sample, carbon dioxide evolved from the dissolution was isolated and purified (using cryogenic separation procedures) on a glass vacuum line and analysed by mass spectrometry. The relative abundances of masses 44, 45 and 46 in the gases were obtained using a VG SIRA Series dual inlet Isotope Ratio Mass Spectrometer. Their relative intensities are compared with those of a working standard reference gas of known isotopic composition. In practice this is achieved by automatic valve switching and data collection whereby reference gas and sample gas are alternately bled into the mass spectrometer, switching ten times over a period of several minutes, thus obtaining a mean delta value for the sample with respect to the reference gas. The reference gas is calibrated with respect to the international standard using reference materials of known isotope composition (NBS-19, IAEA-CO1 and IAEA CO-8) and from the latter, the delta values of the samples with respect to the international standard are calculated.

Table 5.3 Teeth samples analysed from Whithorn Priory

Skeleton No.	*Sample*	*Tooth*	*Crown mineralisation complete by approximately*	*Tooth preservation scores*	
				Root[1]	*Enamel*[2]
1	15	P_1R	7 years	5	4
2	16	P^1L	7 years	5	5
3	17	C_1R	7 years	5	4
4	19	P_2L	8 years	5	4
5	18	P_1L	7 years	5	4
Victorian	20	P^2L	8.5 years	5	3
8	21	P_1R	7 years	5	5
Charnel Group 9	22	P_2L	8 years	5	4
15	23	P^2L	8.5 years	4	4
17	26	I^2L	6 years	5	4
18	24	P_2R	8 years	5	4
19	25	P_1L	7 years	5	4
23	27	M_1R	16 years	5	4
Pig	28	mandibular molar	?	5	3

1Scored using the table given in Montgomery (2002) adapted from Buikstra & Ubelaker (1994): 4 = root ¼ formed, 5 = roots complete apices closed or closing.
2Scored using the table in Montgomery (2002): 2 = preservation excellent, 3 = preservation good; 4 = preservation okay; 5 = preservation poor

5.3.3 Results and discussion

The isotope data and associated errors are presented in Table 5.4 and plotted using the Skeleton numbers listed in the first column of Tables 5.1 to 5.4.

Strontium isotope results

The strontium results are shown in Figure 5.7. All the enamel samples with the exception of Skeleton 1 fall between the values of 0.7107 obtained for the pig molar, and 0.7092 which is the value of seawater and rain in coastal regions of western Britain (Capo *et al*, 1998). Skeleton 1 has a much higher (radiogenic) ratio and is a clear outlier from the main group. The mean human enamel $^{87}Sr/^{86}Sr$ is 0.7101 $\pm$ 0.0006 (1σ, n = 13).

All four dentine samples have lower $^{87}Sr/^{86}Sr$ than the corresponding enamel sample from the same tooth. In a modern tooth, the enamel and dentine have very similar strontium isotope ratios (Montgomery 2002). However, the observed convergence of the dentine (but not the enamel which is resistant to diagenetic contamination) towards a common value is frequently observed in archaeological studies (Montgomery *et al* 2007) and indicates the incorporation of varying quantities of mobile strontium from the burial environment into the dentine samples. Consequently, it can be assumed that the value of the diagenetic strontium in the burial soil is $\leq$ 0.7094 which is the lowest dentine ratio obtained (Skeleton 9) and is indicated by the brown dashed line in Figure 5.7.

The rocks that crop out in the vicinity of Whithorn Priory are Silurian sedimentary shales and sandstones (Figure 5.6) and it would be predicted that biosphere strontium here would reflect the significant age of these rocks (Åberg 1995; Capo *et al* 1998). However, there is, as yet, no published data to confirm this from human or animal populations inhabiting such lithologies. Mineral waters hosted by Silurian and Ordovician rocks in Wales have strontium ratios ranging from 0.7117 to 0.7139 (Montgomery *et al* 2006). Similarly, Welsh river water composition from the Plynlimon area that drains Ordovician rocks gives values up to 0.714 (Shand *et al* 2001). These are indicators of both dietary water sources and of the strontium that can be mobilised from these types of rocks into river and soil waters, and hence into plants and animals. Only Skeleton 1 is consistent with these values and indicative of origins in regions of Palaeozoic silicate rocks. All the remaining enamel and dentine isotope ratios from Whithorn are considerably lower and therefore inconsistent with Silurian and Ordovician hosted waters.

However, it is not necessarily the case that only Skeleton 1 is from the Whithorn area, indeed, the reverse may be true. For example, there are several studies which indicate that coastal, island communities in localities with high annual rainfall such as Anglesey, Lewis, North Uist, Skye, Orkney and Shetland have strontium isotope ratios that reflect their maritime biosphere rather than the underlying geology. Despite the variable and often ancient rocks in these places, humans and animals have a small range of isotope values between 0.7092 and 0.7100 (Montgomery *et al* 2003; Montgomery *et al* 2007; Montgomery & Evans unpublished data). The strontium isotope ratio of seawater has been ~0.7092 throughout the Holocene (Veizer 1989; Capo *et al* 1998). In other words, their biosphere and as a consequence, their dietary strontium isotope values are dominated not by the surface rocks but by marine strontium from a variety of possible sources such as rain, sea-splash and spray, sea-fish, marine mammals, seaweed as fertiliser, fodder or food, and crops grown on soil rich in shell-sand. The trajectory of the dentine samples towards the value of marine strontium would strongly support this also being the case at Whithorn. All the human samples at Whithorn with strontium ratios in excess of 0.7100 are high-status males (Skeletons 1 to 5). If the coastal community at Whithorn has a marine-dominated biosphere, this would suggest that the individuals with values below 0.7100 are of local origin and those with ratios exceeding 0.7100 are not (Figure 5.7).

Given that most strontium values in human teeth will tend to be an average obtained from two or more sources, it is likely that the majority of the results obtained from Whithorn reflect varying consumption of foods containing marine/rainwater and terrestrial strontium. Skeleton 19 has a strontium isotope ratio of 0.7092, and thus may represent a 100% marine-derived diet, although rocks will exist that can provide such a value. However, if marine in origin, the carbon and nitrogen data would suggest it does not result from a diet of marine fish and mammal meat (Figure 5.4), although it should be remembered that the strontium data derive from childhood, in this case before the age of seven, whilst the carbon and nitrogen data from bone collagen are a long-term average from later life. Crops grown on shell-sand or land subject to deposition of sea-salt and the use of seaweed could all explain a marine strontium signature in an individual with no evidence for the consumption of marine protein.

In contrast, Skeleton 1 shows little influence of coastal strontium in his diet before the age of seven and his strontium ratio is indicative of origins in a region of Cambrian or Lower Palaeozoic rocks, such as Devonian sandstones and Silurian or Ordovician sedimentary rocks and inconsistent with origins in regions of basalts, limestone, chalk, and younger Permo-Triassic and Jurassic sedimentary rocks (Bentley 2006; Evans *et al* 2006; Evans & Tatham

Table 5.4 Strontium, carbon and oxygen isotope data for the Whithorn teeth

Skeleton No.	*Sample No.*	*Status*	*Sex*	*Tissue*	$^{87}Sr/^{86}Sr$ [1]	$\delta^{13} C_{VPDB}$‰ [2]	$\delta^{18}O_{VSMOW}$‰ [3] *carbonate measured*	$\delta^{18}O_{VSMOW}$‰ [4] *phosphate calculated*	$\delta^{18}O_{VSMOW}$‰ [5] *meteoric water calculated*
1	15	High	Male	Enamel	0.711798	-13.9	27.9	18.1	-6.6
2	16	High	Male	Enamel	0.710431	-11.1	27.0	17.2	-8.0
3	17	High	Male	Enamel	0.710299	-14.0	27.6	17.9	-7.0
4	19	High	Male	Enamel	0.710377	-15.8	27.8	18.0	-6.8
				Dentine	0.709873				
5	18	High	Male	Enamel	0.710369	-15.7	27.5	17.8	-7.2
Victorian	20		Male	Enamel	0.709980	-15.9	27.9	18.1	-6.7
8	21	High	Male	Enamel	0.709928	-14.2	28.3	18.5	-6.1
Charnel Group 9	22		Female	Enamel	0.709585	-13.5	28.9	19.1	-5.1
				Dentine	0.709376				
15	23		Juvenile	Enamel	0.709916	-15.1	28.5	18.8	-5.6
				Dentine	0.709497				
17	26		Male	Enamel	0.709733	-13.7	28.8	19.0	-5.3
18	24		Male	Enamel	0.710051	-13.9	28.5	18.7	-5.8
				Dentine	0.709930				
19	25		Female	Enamel	0.709202	-10.7	31.3	21.4	-1.4
23	27		Male	Enamel	0.709708	-11.0	28.8	19.0	-5.3
pig	28		n/k	Enamel	0.710660	-13.3	26.1	16.4	-9.4
				Min.	0.709202	-15.9	26.1	16.4	-8.0
				Max.	0.711798	-10.7	31.3	21.4	-1.4
				Mean	0.710040	-13.6	28.3	18.4	-6.2
				1 σ	0.000586	1.9	1.5	1.1	1.8

[1] *Analytical precision is +/- 0.00002 (2σ)*
[2] *Analytical precision is better than +/- 0.1 ‰ (2σ)*
[3] *Analytical precision is better than +/- 0.2 ‰ (2σ)*
[4] *$\delta^{18}O_{VSMOW}$ ‰ phosphate calculated from Iacumin et al (1996)*
[5] *$\delta^{18}O_{VSMOW}$ ‰ meteoric water calculated from the calculated $\delta^{18}O_{phos}$ values following Longinelli (1984)*

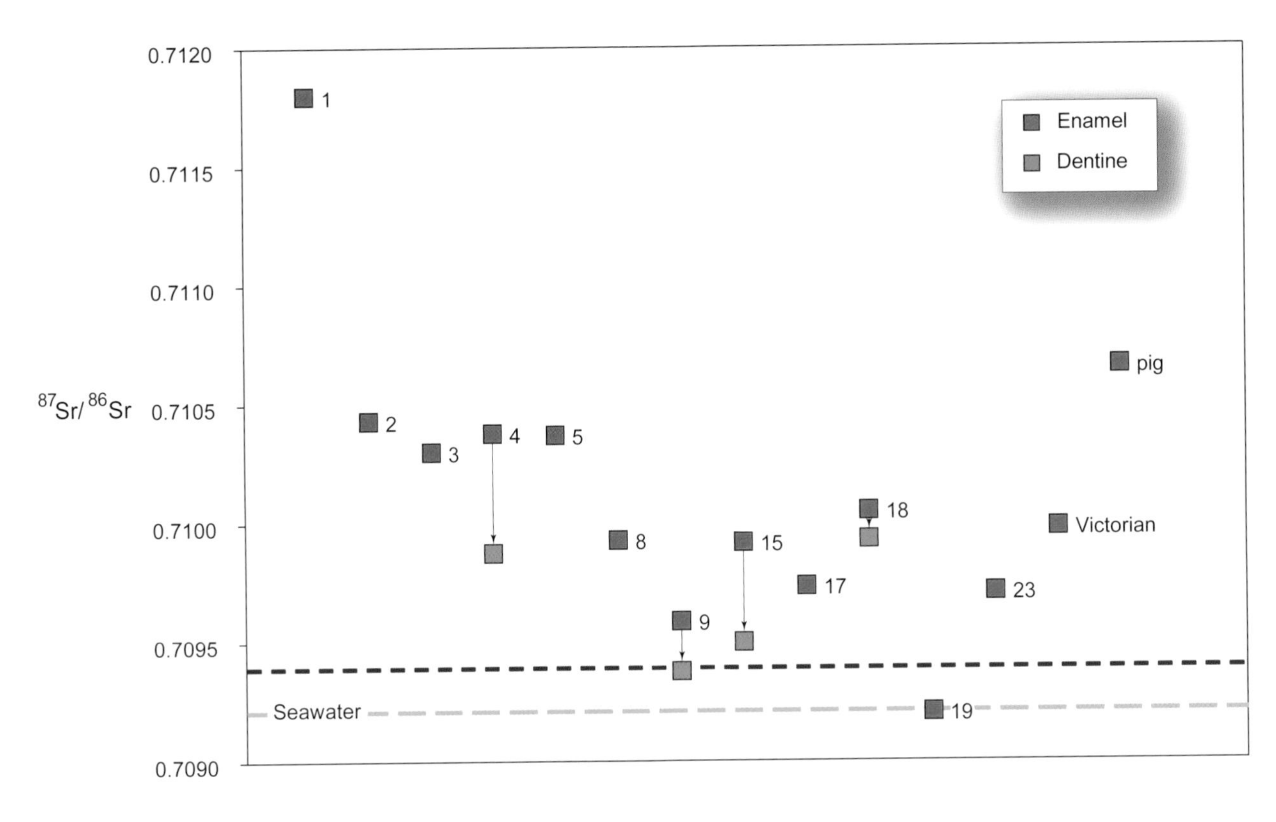

Figure 5.7

^{87}Sr/^{86}Sr for enamel and dentine samples. Analytical precision is ± 0.00002 2σ and is contained within the symbols. The majority of human enamel samples (red) fall between the pig and seawater. Skeleton 1 is a clear outlier. All four dentine samples (green) have lower ^{87}Sr/^{86}Sr ratio than their corresponding enamel sample which indicates that mobile diagenetic strontium in the burial soil is ≤ 0.7094 (brown dashed line)

2004; Montgomery 2002; Montgomery *et al* 2006, Montgomery *et al* 2007).

Isotope analysis is an exclusive technique and it is possible that, whilst the isotope ratios obtained are consistent with local biosphere values, they may equally likely be consistent with many other places in Scotland, the British Isles and much farther afield. It is, therefore, desirable to use other isotope systems that may be able to narrow down the possible places of origin.

Oxygen isotope results

Oxygen isotope data for Whithorn Priory are presented in Figure 5.8 plotted against the strontium results. All the humans have $\delta^{18}O_{carb}$ ratios between 27‰ and 29‰ with the exception of Skeleton 19, which has a ratio of 31.3 ‰. The mean human enamel value is 28.4 ± 1.1‰ (1σ, n = 13) and 28.1 ± 0.6‰ (1σ, n = 12) if the outlier Skeleton 19 is excluded from the calculation.

The oxygen isotope ratio of tooth enamel is an indicator of climatic and geographic variables (such as air temperature, latitude, altitude and distance from the sea) because it is primarily derived from the oxygen isotope ratio of drinking water, which in turn, reflects that of precipitation (Dansgaard 1964; Longinelli 1984; White *et al* 1998). Oxygen isotope values of precipitation vary in a systematic manner across Britain as illustrated in Figure 5.9. However, this map has been compiled from mean modern day groundwater values (the source of which is rainwater) (Darling & Talbot 2003; Darling *et al* 2003; Darling 2004). In order to use this map as an indicator of origin, an assumption has to be made that the climatic regime and hydrological conditions were the same in the period under investigation, in this case the 12th to 14th centuries AD, as today. Moreover, inhabitants of Whithorn could have obtained drinking water from several sources such as rainwater, surface water (eg stream water) or groundwater (eg well water) which may have different oxygen isotope values; they may have drunk from a combination of all three, and relative amounts may have varied seasonally or over the years due to choice or necessity. No water sources from Whithorn Priory or the wider region have been analysed in this study. It is possible, therefore, that local human values for various reasons may not always conform precisely to these contoured ranges.

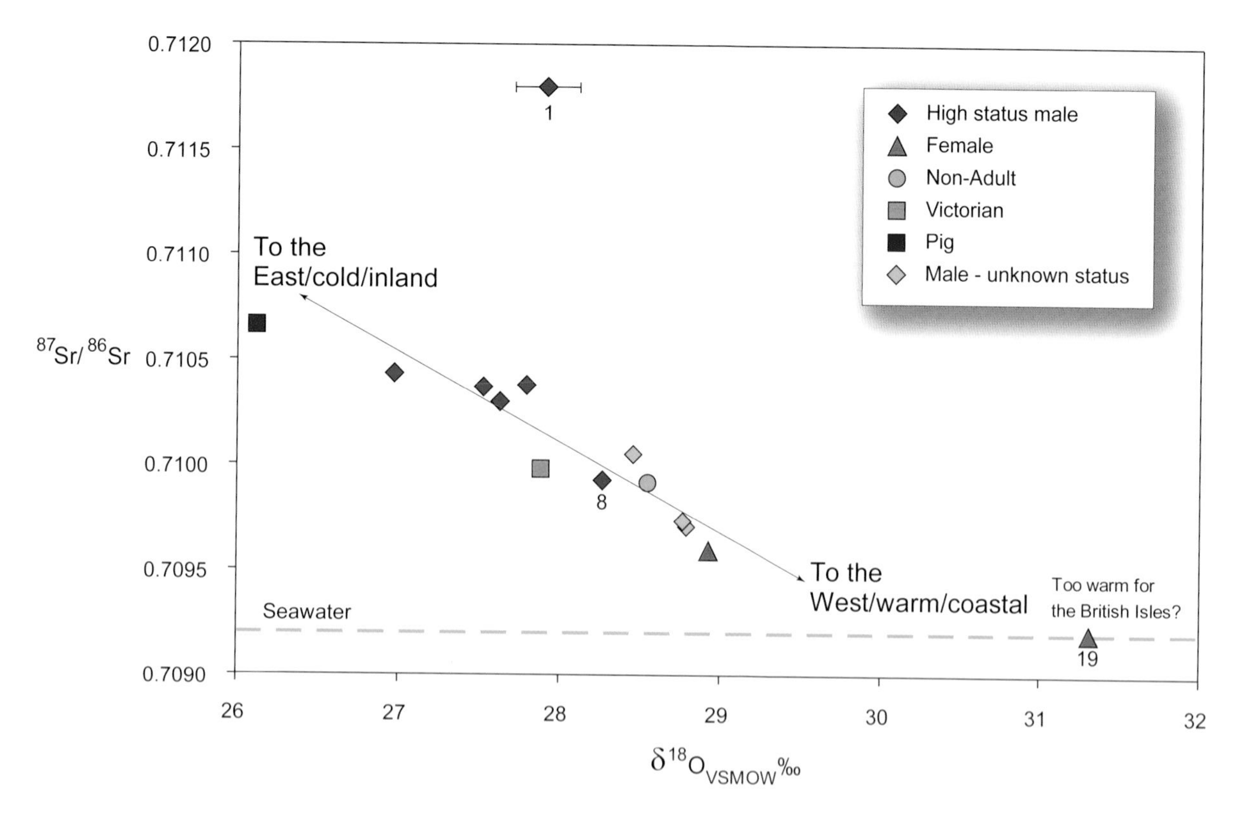

Figure 5.8
Enamel oxygen ($\delta^{18}O_{carb}$) and strontium isotope results for the Whithorn samples. The linear correlation between the two variables of the main human group is r2 = 0.856 (n = 11). 2σ analytical errors for the data set are illustrated on Skeleton 1

In order to be able to relate the measured enamel data to such maps, the results need to be calibrated using equations established for humans for either carbonate or phosphate (after conversion from carbonate ratios). Several are available (eg Longinelli 1984; Luz *et al* 1984; Levinson *et al* 1987) and all give slightly different results. The results from Whithorn are, therefore, interpreted below with these caveats which may introduce a significant margin of error; a more precise interpretation awaits a fuller investigation of both $\delta^{18}O_{carb}$ variations in humans across Britain and refined calibration equations.

To date, the majority of oxygen isotope data for archaeological humans from Britain has been obtained from enamel phosphate ($\delta^{18}O_{phos}$). There is very little published $\delta^{18}O_{carb}$ data from humans and, therefore, no established baseline against which to interpret the data from Whithorn. Individuals from sites in Eastern England (the green zones in Figure 5.9), who appear from their strontium ratios to be of local origin, have measured $\delta^{18}O_{carb}$ values ranging from ~25–27‰ and $\delta^{18}O_{phos}$ ~16–18‰ (Montgomery & Grimes unpublished data). For humans, there is an offset of ~10‰ between the oxygen isotope values of phosphate and carbonate (Iacumin *et al* 1996), and this conversion equation produces a calculated $\delta^{18}O_{phos}$ range of 17.2–21.4‰ for the Whithorn humans.

Whithorn lies within the -6 to -7‰ contour (the yellow zone in Figure 5.9) but it is in close proximity to the Isle of Man where the $\delta^{18}O$ of meteoric water is -5 to -6‰ (the orange zone in Figure 5.9). All four low-status males (Skeletons 17, 18, 19 & 23), the juvenile (Skeleton 15) and the cleric with the cleft palate (Skeleton 8), have $\delta^{18}O_{mw}$ values between -5 to -6‰. If measurement error, calibration uncertainties, unknown variables and the proximity to the Irish Sea are taken into account, it is highly likely that the $\delta^{18}O$ values of this largely low-status group are consistent with origins at Whithorn. The fact that the juvenile and cleric may also be local is perhaps unsurprising. The remaining clerics (Skeletons 1–5) have $\delta^{18}O$ values ranging from -6.6 to -8.0‰, which are mostly consistent with the light green zones in Figure 5.9 and indicate origins to the east or possibly NE Ireland.

Skeleton 19 has an oxygen isotope ratio that would appear, on the limited data available, to be inconsistent with origins in Britain and indicates origins somewhere considerably warmer and at a lower latitude than Whithorn. For example, Skeleton 19 ($\delta^{18}O_{carb}$ = 31.3‰) falls within

Figure 5.9

Map of modern day $\delta^{18}O$‰ values of ground water (and hence possible drinking water) in Ireland and the United Kingdom. Copyright of the British Geological Survey/NERC. Compiled by C Chenery from the isotopic data in Darling *et al* 2003a; Darling *et al* 2003b; Darling 2004

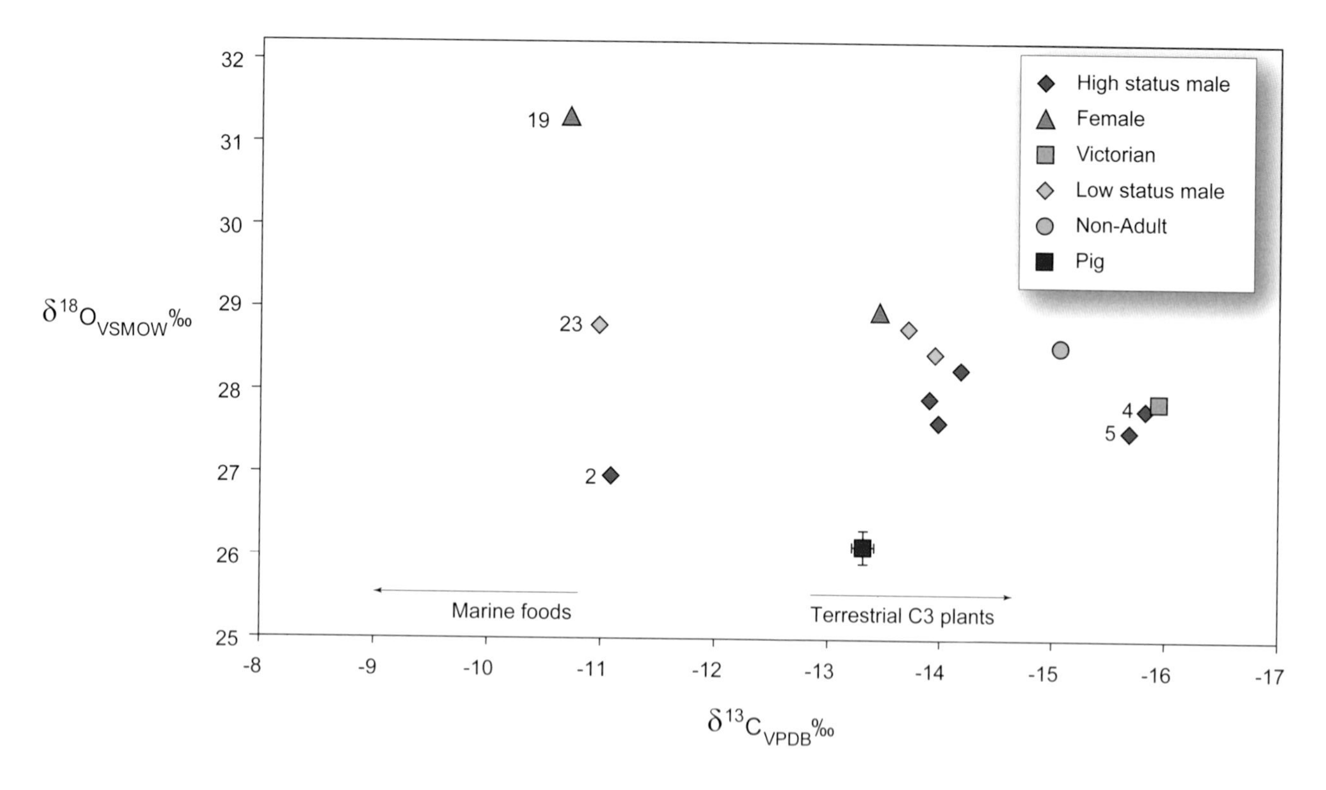

Figure 5.10
Enamel carbon ($\delta^{13}C$) and oxygen ($\delta^{18}O_{carb}$) isotope results for the Whithorn samples. 2σ analytical errors for the data set are illustrated on the pig sample

the range of values obtained from humans excavated in the Nile Valley, Egypt who have a $\delta^{18}O_{carb}$ range of 30.2 to 32.5‰ (Iacumin *et al* 1996). An alternative explanation for this highly unusual value is a childhood drinking water source that was subjected to considerable evaporation, for example, an inland loch in a region of strong, persistent wind, as was found by Darling *et al* (2003) in freshwater samples from the Shetland Isles. Unfortunately, there is currently no comparable evidence from inhabitants of places such as Shetland to show that this is a significant factor, but because very few individuals have yet been analysed, it is not possible to rule out this explanation at this time.

It is clear from Figure 5.8 that Skeleton 1 (a bishop), and Skeleton 19 (female) are outliers from the main group of samples due to their strontium (Skeleton 1) or oxygen (Skeleton 19) results. However, what is perhaps most striking is the strong correlation ($r^2 = 0.856$) between the strontium and oxygen isotope values for the remaining humans. As the strontium isotope values approach those of seawater, the oxygen isotope values indicate a progressively less negative water source, which is ordinarily explained by decreasing latitude, altitude or increasing proximity to the coast. In the British Isles, where the climate is dominated by the Gulf Stream and prevailing westerly winds, an east–west gradient exists (Figure 5.9). Such a correlation could, therefore, be explained by the clerics having origins further inland to the East with a decreased, or no, exposure to marine strontium (but possibly on the same type/age of rock), and the lower-status individuals, the juvenile and Skeleton 8 having origins on the western seaboard in a region dominated by marine strontium, ie Whithorn. Further work would help to confirm that an $^{87}Sr/^{86}Sr$ range of 0.7092–0.7100 is characteristic of inhabitants of Whithorn, as it is of inhabitants of the Western and Northern Isles (Montgomery *et al* 2007). This strong correlation provides additional evidence that, although the clerics (and the pig) have the higher strontium isotope ratios that could be considered more characteristic of the Silurian rocks of the Machars, they are unlikely to have originated there. Moreover, three clerics (Skeleton 3, 4 & 5), and possibly Skeleton 2, have remarkably similar values for both oxygen and strontium, strongly suggesting they had similar non-coastal, childhood origins. The remaining cleric, Skeleton 8, is different and clusters with the low-status, local group. Interestingly, Skeleton 8's affiliation with the local, low-status group is also seen in the carbon and nitrogen data presented in Figure 5.4.

Enamel carbon isotope results

Carbon isotope ratios of tooth enamel provide information about the energy sources consumed during childhood (Lee-Thorp *et al* 1989). The mean human enamel value obtained from the Whithorn individuals is -13.7 ±1.8‰ (1σ, n = 13) with a range of -10.7 to -15.9‰. However, as can be seen in Figure 5.10, with the exception of three individuals (Skeletons 2, 19 & 23), most have $\delta^{13}C$ values between -13‰ and -16‰. These $\delta^{13}C$ values are indicative of consumption of a predominantly C_3 terrestrial food source during childhood (Lee-Thorp *et al* 1989). Skeletons 2, 19 and 23 have $\delta^{13}C$ values of approximately -11‰ and this indicates a mixed diet of marine and terrestrial energy sources during childhood.

5.4 CONCLUSIONS

Although analyses were conducted on a small number of human samples only, the stable carbon and nitrogen isotope data from Whithorn Cathedral Priory has proved to be a key data set for the investigation of social differences in medieval diet by bone chemistry analysis. It is one of only a few medieval sites investigated to date where intra-population differences in diet could be convincingly demonstrated and the first where a well-defined social group, comprising some of its former bishops and other churchmen as well as other significant high-status individuals, can be shown to have consumed a very distinctive diet in comparison to their contemporaries.

The majority of low-status burials and the cleric with the cleft palate have strontium and oxygen ratios that are consistent with origins on the western seaboard of Britain and, more particularly, the Machar peninsula. One female burial appears to have originated from somewhere considerably warmer and at a lower latitude than Britain. All the remaining clerics have values that suggest they did not grow up on the western seaboard and are consistent with origins away from the coast, possibly to the east or in north–east Ireland. It is particularly striking that the strontium, oxygen, carbon and nitrogen data separate the Whithorn individuals into the same two groups, suggesting that lower status and a poorer diet restrict geographic mobility whilst higher status and a better diet correlates with greater geographic mobility in later life.

The site has great potential for further investigations, and it is hoped that at least a number of animal bones from later medieval Whithorn can be analysed in the near future in order to establish an environmental baseline and to substantiate the interpretations made in this report. If more human samples were available to enlarge the human data set and to further explore the dietary relationships between different individuals at Whithorn Priory and other medieval sites in Scotland and England, they could also potentially greatly enhance our understanding of dietary variation and its relationship with social, economical and political change in medieval Britain.

Chapter 6

The Artefacts

JULIE FRANKLIN, WITH VIRGINIA GLENN, CAROL CHRISTIANSEN AND KIRSTY DINGWALL.
ADDITIONAL NOTES BY NICHOLAS HOLMES AND COLIN WALLACE

6.1 SUMMARY

The finds from the excavation were rich and varied. Most came from the Phase 3 graves (13th- and 14th-century) that were inserted below the floor at the east end of the church. Among these are several bishops who were buried in stone cists or wooden coffins, some with their vestments and regalia. No artefacts were recovered from the Phase 1 graves, which date to the 11th and 12th century and belong with the earlier graveyard that was subsequently built over in the early 13th century. The fabric of the church was represented by window glass and floor tiles. A small amount of pottery was also found from graveyard and other contexts, including a sherd of Roman Samian ware, and later imported wares from France and Devon.

6.2 INTRODUCTION

The report brings together all the finds recovered from Ritchie's excavations. The archive appears to be complete; at least there were no finds recorded in contemporary notes and photographs which could not be located. In fact there were a few extra finds from other excavations which had somehow become mixed with the Whithorn assemblage, most notably some mosaic floor tiles from Newbattle Abbey. There were also four sherds of pottery from Tabraham's Whithorn excavations in 1972 (Tabraham 1979) and another which seemed to derive from Radford's work there from 1949 to 1953 (Radford 1956). This previously unpublished Whithorn material is therefore included here.

Context information is sometimes a little sketchy. Most of the finds from the graves were labelled with a grave number, and with the help of site notes and photographs it has been possible, for the most part, to recreate accurately the grave assemblages, including where each find was found in relation to the body. Other contexts are a little more vague, but some packaging included context descriptions, location sketches and excavation dates, which could then be related to the site notebook, sections, plans and photographs. There are still many finds which are essentially unstratified – most of the iron assemblage, for example, and much of the pottery. But as finds from graveyard soils are of little value in terms of stratigraphic analysis at the best of times, there is probably remarkably little important information which has been lost.

The Ritchie archive, when it was recovered, was stored in 1960s grocery boxes, cigarette packets and the like. For all this, the finds do not seem to have suffered too badly in the decades since they were excavated. Much of the metalwork is in surprisingly good condition. Each box was sorted though and repackaged by material. Each find was given a number (Lab. No.), in the form AB/CD: AB being the original box number in which it was found; CD being a number unique to that find. Some of the finds had already been accessioned into the National Museums of Scotland; indeed, several are on display and have already been published by Virginia Glenn in her work on the museum's collections of Romanesque and Gothic decorative metalwork and ivory carvings (Glenn 2003). Accession numbers are given for these, with the prefix 'NMS'.

As part of the current project, some of the metalwork was subjected to XRF analysis by Jim Tate and Lore Troalen of the National Museums of Scotland. Details of the composition of the metal are given with each find and the full report can be consulted in the Project Archive.

The finds have been ordered according to object types, rather than strictly by material, thus bringing together similar objects such as the chalices and finger rings, which are made of different metals. The report begins with the coins and the more precious metal artefacts, and proceeds to the plainer small finds, the structural fittings and pottery. The finds from the burials are then pulled together and discussed grave by grave in Chapter 6.9.

Each find catalogue entry gives the lab or accession number, with any relevant context information available, including year of excavation, grave number and location within the grave relative to the body. When describing finds' locations relative to bodies, the terms 'left' and 'right' are from the wearer's perspective, not the observer's. All measurements are in millimetres, unless otherwise stated.

Plate 6.1
In situ view of the Whithorn Crozier (Cat. no. 6), Grave 7. The crozier appears heavily corroded, while the excavator carefully removes spangles from the surrounding material

6.3 COINS

NICHOLAS HOLMES AND JULIE FRANKLIN

1. Edward I penny, type 4d (*c* 1286–7). NMS Reg. No. K2000.63, small find 1, at junction between dark earth and underlying sand, over Grave 11, 36" below surface, 1961.
2. Edward I–II penny, class 10 of 3a Canterbury (1307–9). NMS Reg. No. K2000.64, on floor of Grave 5, between left lower leg and wall of grave, 1960.
3. James I billon penny, probably contemporary counterfeit (*c* 1424–37). NMS Reg. No. K2000.65, in recent graveyard soil, over top of Grave 12, near foot, 1961.
4. James IV half-groat, type IIIa (*c* 1496–1513). NMS Reg. No. K2000.66, loose find made prior to start of excavation work, during trimming of grass, 1957.
5. James VI two pence. First post-Union issue (1614). Lab. No. 24/03, unlabelled, from box marked 'Whithorn 1962, Nave, E Gable, S Tomb Recess'. XRF: highly corroded copper.

Only one coin was firmly located in a grave: No. 2, from Grave 5. Others are closely related to graves but, because they are from the general graveyard soil, cannot be used as firm dating evidence for those graves.

Coin No. 5 was covered in mineralised textile on one side, suggesting it may have been placed in a grave, inside the shroud cloth. The circumstances of this discovery and Ritchie's involvement in investigations in the nave in 1962 are not known.

6.4 THE LATER MEDIEVAL ECCLESIASTICAL METALWORK AND RELATED ITEMS

VIRGINIA GLENN

6.4.1 Introduction

The grave-goods from six of the graves were of outstanding importance, adding considerably to our meagre knowledge of medieval church plate in Scotland. Sixteenth- and 17th-century iconoclasm and continuous strife with England have otherwise left us with fewer than 20 examples of ecclesiastical metalwork in use in the country before 1500 (McRoberts 1959, *passim*), making the Whithorn finds a particularly valuable addition to the *corpus*.

The medieval inventories of Glasgow and Aberdeen cathedrals, for example, list large collections of gold and silver vessels, rich vestments and books (Dowden 1899, 280–329). Some of these objects may have been imported or gifts from foreign institutions or individuals, but Scotland itself had an established tradition of fine metalworking from at least the 12th century (Finlay 1991, 28–32). However, although the surviving evidence for comparable Scottish vessels in the 13th and 14th centuries is virtually non-existent, the more elaborate of the Whithorn artefacts suggest English, rather than local, manufacture. The similarities between them and metalwork uncovered at York, in particular, are entirely predictable. Whithorn recognised the metropolitan authority of the archbishops of York from 1128 until 1355 and the bishops of Galloway generally went there to be consecrated (Donaldson 1949, 129–34; Watt & Murray 2003, 168–171).

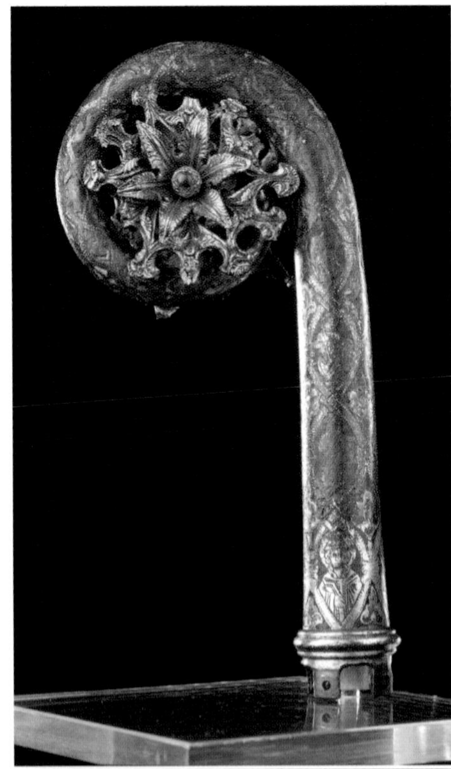

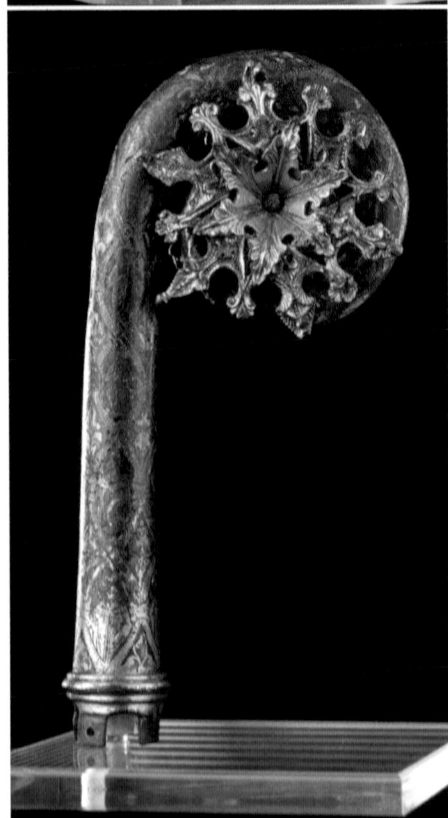

Plate 6.2
The Whithorn Crozier (Cat. no. 6), reproduced by courtesy of the Trustees of the National Museum of Scotland

It happens that one of the more important groups of 13th- and 14th-century liturgical objects preserved in England, with a number of items which can be securely attributed to the tombs of two known individuals and therefore approximately dated, survives in York Minster. It is also fortuitous that the York tombs were opened in modern times, under controlled conditions, overseen and recorded by H G Ramm, resident archaeologist of York Minster in 1967–9, and examined by leading curators, historians and conservation scientists of the day. Other comparative burials in English cathedrals from which grave-goods survive, mostly discovered in quite random circumstances, are listed in Appendix 1.

Given Whithorn's formal relationship with the diocese of York (Oram, Chapter 8) and its geographical position, the probably English origin of some of the material is not altogether surprising. The sea voyage to Furness, for example, would have been fairly sheltered and the journey onwards to York about the same as that from Whithorn to the cathedral at Glasgow and considerably shorter than the route to St Andrews. It is very unlikely that any silversmithing, other than the production of a few primitive dress ornaments, would have been carried out in this remote area of Galloway itself in the 13th or 14th centuries. The nearest discoveries of even crude silver jewellery from the period, so far, have been in Dumfries (Glenn 2003, 55).

6.4.2 Croziers and pinnacle

6. Enamelled copper-alloy gilt crozier

Dating:	Art historical dating: *c* 1175 Radiocarbon date: (wooden shaft): cal AD 1185–1285 (SUERC-13243)
Location:	Grave 7, to right of head, above right shoulder
Dimensions:	diam 92mm (across crook), height 162mm, depth 30mm
References:	Glenn 2003, 29–33, no C1; NMS 1992.1833
Illustration:	Figure 6.1, Figure 6.2 (between pp 92 and 93), Plate 6.1, Plate 6.2, Plate 6.5

The Whithorn Crozier belongs to an outstanding school of champlevé enamels produced in England during the second half of the 12th century. These objects were strongly influenced by Northern French or Mosan metalwork and possibly sometimes carried out by immigrant artists from the Meuse region (Stratford 1984, 265, nos 278– 280). The figure styles and the taste for luxuriant blossoms as decoration also relate closely to sculpture and manuscript illumination from South West England. Three of the most imposing examples are the famous Morgan, Balfour and Warwick Ciboria (Gauthier 1972, 157–162, 361–363, nos 113–5). They have white, blue and green enamelled scenes

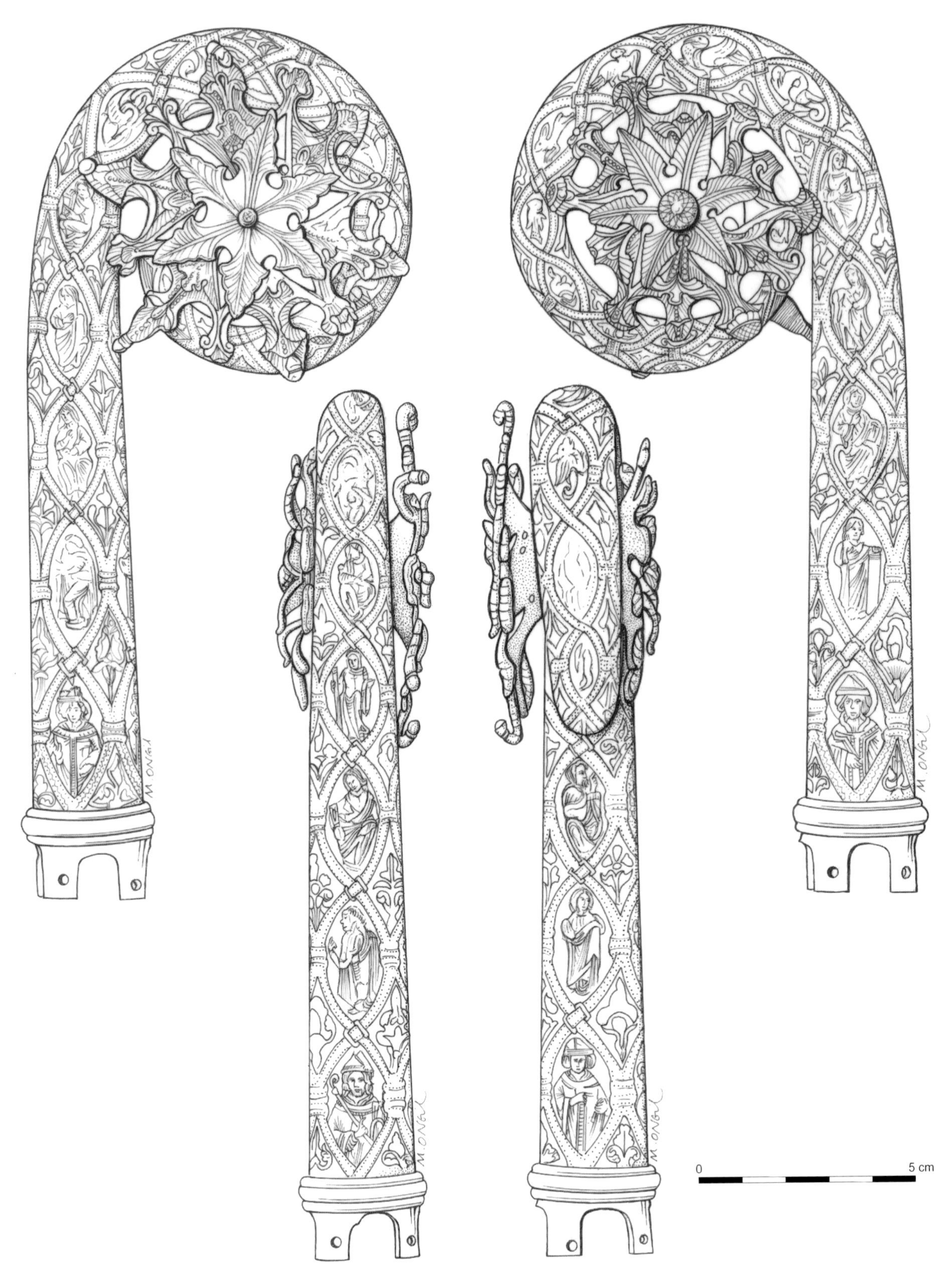

Figure 6.1
The Whithorn Crozier (Cat. no. 6)

from the Old and New Testaments in roundels covering the bowls and lids (the lid is missing from the Warwick example), framed by gilded ribbons engraved with inscriptions taken from verses originally painted in the chapter house at Worcester Cathedral, thus placing them firmly in the context of English art of 1160–1175. Filling the spaces between the roundels are fantastic blossoms with long trailing tendrils.

This technique and method of laying out the decoration was also adopted for enamelled croziers. A magnificent example of about 1175 in the Bargello in Florence has a large oval knop with vigorous scenes from the life of David similarly framed by gilt scrolls with inscriptions and surrounded by flamboyant curling leaf forms (Plate 6.3). On the shaft above, pointed ovals formed by interweaving ribands frame figures of the Vices and Virtues in two zones above the knop and grotesques in four further zones stretching into the crook (Campbell 1979, 364–8). Between each oval is an enamelled blossom, more rigid and upright than those on the knop. The Bargello crozier has lost the end of its original crook, which has been replaced by a plain gilt tube with a dragon's head terminal. It is quite probable that it originally had large gilt flower heads like the Whithorn Crozier, as the inner surfaces of the crook are rough and damaged and may have been intended to be hidden.

The Whithorn Crozier represents a later development of this scheme, with the ovals becoming more pointed and regular, neatly belted together between the figures, which themselves show a naturalism characteristic of the emerging early Gothic style. The crozier is copper-alloy, gilded and enamelled, but has suffered widespread surface corrosion rendering some of the enamel decoration indecipherable. The gilded blossoms on either side of the crook are very brittle, with three leaves missing from one side and lacking the central berry from the other.

A single hollow tapering tube forms the staff and the spiral volute of the crozier head, with a lavish gilt blossom sprouting from each side. The blossoms are similar, but not identical. One has a central peg in the form of a tall oval berry with cross-hatched engraving, which pierces the centre of a flower with six pointed curving petals with slanting veins. Behind is a circle of openwork leaves, originally sprouting 12 semicircular fronds. The other blossom has a flower of six pointed petals with serrated edges and a central vein. The leaves behind are long and pointed, six large alternating with six smaller fronds; the whole is cast and engraved with a pattern of scrolling foliage. A very comparable composition of a symmetrical concentric flower form with curling waisted fronds and a central berry was carved on a keystone for Keynsham Abbey, Somerset, about 1170–80 (Zarnecki *et al* 1984, cat no 163a, 194).

A similar blossom fills the crook of a copper-gilt crozier, without enamel, found in a grave at St David's Cathedral,

Plate 6.3
The Bargello Crozier: copper alloy, gilt, enamel, probably English, *c.*1170. Florence, reproduced by courtesy of the Museo Nazionale del Bargello, Carrand Collection, no.662.

Pembrokeshire (Plate 6.4). It is arranged flattened against the crook, but shares the leaf shapes and the berry form of the ovary (Hope 1907, 488, pl. LIII A; Glenn 2003, 33; Lord 2003, 108, pl.157).

Interestingly, this was found near the tomb of Bishop Iowerth (1215–29), who reigned considerably later than the 1150–80 date ascribed to the crozier itself (Stratford 1984, 258, no 270 a & b). A slightly earlier 12th-century copper-gilt crozier, found in the same cathedral in 1865–6, came from a tomb believed to be that of Bishop Richard of Carew (1256–80) (Hope 1907, 488–9, pl. LIII B). Obviously the inclusion of an out-of-date base metal crozier in an important burial was not peculiar to Whithorn.

The Whithorn shaft is engraved and enamelled in four vertical bands of pointed ovals. The ovals are framed by a pattern of interwoven and loosely knotted ribands in plain gilt with pricked borders and a fine zigzag line engraved up the centre. The interstices are filled with enamelled

Plate 6.4
The St Davids Crozier: copper-alloy, English, c 1150-80, burial attributed to Bishop Iowerth (1215-29), reproduced by courtesy of the Dean and Chapter of St David's Cathedral, Pembrokeshire

flowers. Most of the colours – white, yellow, light and dark green, turquoise, light and dark blue, lilac and red – are in opaque enamel, but the backgrounds to some of the figures are translucent. Due to wear and corrosion, the decoration is most legible towards the bottom of the shaft.

The 14 tiers, each of four ovals, are possibly part of some formal iconographic scheme, centred on the spine of the shaft behind the crook. This is possibly detectable in the diagrammatic rendering in Figure 6.2 where the oval numbered as Tier T1/4 has the most prominent bishop with a crozier. Tier T3/4 and Tier T5/4 are all flanked by figures turning inwards towards them. In Tiers T2 and T4 the figure compositions are more random. Above that level, the decoration is of grotesques, a hare and fish. The key to the significance of the figures presumably lay in the knop of the crozier, which is now lost.

The Whithorn knop was attached in exactly the same way as the Florence one, with four pierced tangs and would have been similarly hollow, making it vulnerable to any sharp knock or dent, which would have caused the brittle enamel to come away from the malleable copper-alloy to which it was applied.

Tier 1
All four half-length figures face forward and do not seem related to each other.

1. A bishop(?) reserved in gilt, the drawing of his outline, features and vestments in red enamel. The background is mottled violet and blue. His face and mitre are indistinct. He wears an amice with scooping folds and decoration is indicated on his apparels.
2. A mitred abbot(?) delineated in the same technique as T1/1, with a deep red and dark blue ground. His beardless face and bushy hair are naturalistically drawn with a few flowing strokes. He wears a monastic habit with a cowl and holds a stole(?) in his right hand, which emerges from a wide sleeve falling in loose folds over his arm and showing the tight cuff of his undergarment. The left hand is indicated very summarily, but seems to be holding the folds of his habit.
3. A bishop saint with large gilt halo, the figure drawn in the same technique as before against a deep red ground. He has bushy bobbed hair and his long face may be bearded, but is damaged. His mitre is low and triangular with a horizontal band at the brim, his alb has a square neck over a softly folded amice and apparels curving round his shoulders and falling in two vertical strips in front. He holds a book in his right hand.
4. A bishop in the same technique against a dark red and brown ground. He has a short, rather shaggy beard and bushy wavy hair, and wears a low triangular mitre with a horizontal band at the brim. His alb has a round neck outlined by an apparel over a softly folded alb. Diagonally across his body is a simple spiral-headed crozier held in his right hand with his forefinger raised in blessing. A book(?) is roughly indicated in his left hand.

Tier 2
The poses of these full-length figures suggest that they are linked in some kind of narrative.

1. The upper half of this oval is almost indecipherable. The lower part shows a figure in semi-profile, with clinging folds over its legs, which are in vigorous motion.
2. Even more damaged than T2/1, there is a bareheaded standing figure in frontal pose with bobbed hair. Its arms are raised to hold an object at shoulder level.
3. The gilt is worn away, but the red champlevé drawing and a burgundy red ground with green flecks remain.

The figure is a standing female with long hair holding a book(?) at her left shoulder.

4. Also very worn, but traces of red drawing remain against a green and red ground. The standing figure is in semi-profile, raises its right hand up to its shoulder and holds a long scroll (or stole) in its left. The garments fall in looping folds.

Tier 3

The four figures form a balanced composition, but the iconography is completely inscrutable.

1. A seated female figure with long wavy hair, her head turned three-quarter face, looks down to her right hand raised on her breast and her left hand which holds a round object below her right elbow. Her costume has agitated criss-cross fold patterns. The ground is burgundy red with green flecks.
2. A three-quarter-length male figure, with his head in profile to the right, turns his body to that side. He has receding bobbed hair and a shaggy beard and holds a book(?) up to his left shoulder. The ground is very dark blue and green.
3. A seated female figure with long wavy hair shares the pose of T3/1, but reversed to the left. They also have the same ground colours.
4. Almost indecipherable, a figure with a beardless face is shown against an opaque burgundy ground.

Tier 4

These four female figures probably form a coherent group, but their significance is unclear.

1. A standing female figure with a veil over her hair, bowing her head to the right and holding a book(?) above her left shoulder, is shown against a ground which is burgundy on one side and green on the other.
2. (Partly under the crook.) A three-quarter-length figure of a young person looking downward to the left is shown against a burgundy ground with some opaque white.
3. A female figure with long wavy hair kneels with her body in profile to her right and looks down to her left. She raises an object in both hands to her right. The ground is dark green with some burgundy.
4. A female figure, in distinct secular dress wearing a head-dress and veil and a long bodice with centre fastening, stands with both hands raised in prayer against a dark green ground.

Tier 5

T5/1 and T5/3 turn towards T5/4 which is at the focal point of the curve of the crozier. Together they may represent the Virgin and Child flanked by musicians.

1. A seated female figure turns three-quarters to her right using her left hand to play a portable organ(?) on her knees, which is supported by her right hand at the top. The ground is mottled burgundy and green.
2. Difficult to see but a sea shell is shown in Figure 6.2.
3. The oval is very worn, but a seated female figure, with knees apart and feet together, wearing a coif on her head which is inclined to her left, rests her right elbow on her knee, with her hand raised and pointing to (or plucking) a large rectangular object balanced on her knee.
4. This very worn and corroded figure is seated and inclined to its right, holding an object in both hands or supporting a child reaching up to its face. There is possibly a halo.

Plate 6.5
The Whithorn Crozier (Cat. no. 6). The figure is one of the bishops within Tier 1. The surviving enamel of one of the flowers can be seen to his left and right. Reproduced by courtesy of the Trustees of the National Museums of Scotland

Tiers 6, 7 and 8

Partly hidden by the crook and the blossom and in poor condition, the identifiable decoration is of grotesque creatures with serpent heads, wings and feet.

Tier 9

One clear oval of an energetic galloping hare with long ears and a tail, against a green ground.

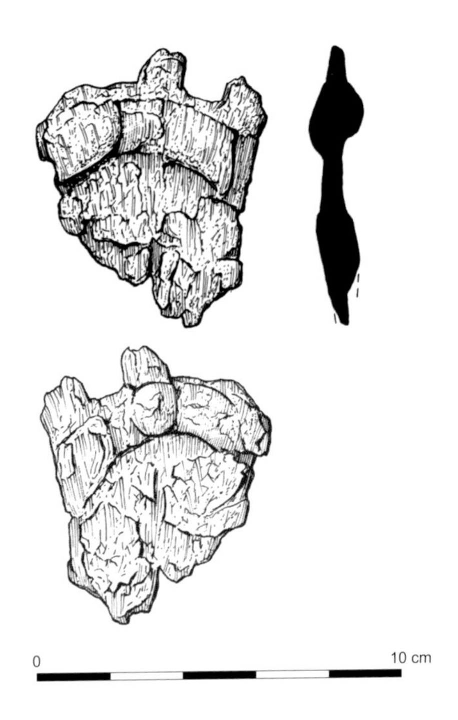

Figure 6.3
Wooden crozier head (Cat. no. 7), Grave 1. Unfortunately the surviving fragment of the wooden crozier head retains little evidence of the leafy design seen during the excavation

Tiers 10–14
These are virtually indecipherable except for fishes on T10/1, T10/3, T14/3 and T14/4.

Wooden Shaft

JULIE FRANKLIN

The remains of the wooden shaft to this crozier were rediscovered during the course of the present post-excavation project (Lab. No. 04/06). A small rounded piece of wood, 4cm long, with green copper staining was found in an unlabelled finds bag in a box of miscellaneous Whithorn finds. However, the pattern of green staining at one end was found to match exactly the tabs at the base of the crozier and, as a virtual refitting at NMS clearly demonstrated, there is no doubt as to the origins of this piece. It is clearly visible in photographs of the crozier under excavation. Identified as possibly hazel (Dr Scott Timpany, pers comm), the fragment was radiocarbon-dated as part of this project. The resultant date – cal AD 1185–1285 (SUERC-13243) – is not inconsistent with the art historical dating of the crozier itself; indeed, the present shaft may, of course, have replaced an earlier one.

7. Wooden crozier head

Dating:	mid- to late 13th century(?)
Location:	Grave 1, above left shoulder
Dimensions:	(incomplete) height 63mm, width 74mm, breadth 15mm
References:	NMS 1992.1864
Illustration:	Figure 6.3, Plate 6.6

The wooden crozier head, which has disintegrated further since the grave was discovered, consisted of a thick circular crook filled with fleshy leaf(?) forms and ornamented on the outer edge with large crockets. The condition makes close dating entirely speculative.

8. Copper-alloy gilt pinnacle

JULIE FRANKLIN

Dating:	mid-14th century
Location:	uncertain provenance
Dimensions:	height 30mm, width 7mm breadth 7mm
References:	Glenn 2003, 17, no A9; NMS K.2001.3.
Illustration:	Figure 6.4; Glenn 2003, 17, Plate A9

Although assigned to Grave 7 in Glenn's earlier work (Glenn 2003), no supporting data have been identified during the course of this project. It is not referred to in the Ritchie Archive and its only appearance in the SDD files is in a list of finds (SDD27/1582), compiled by Ritchie and dated 19 December 1960 (Dingwall, Chapter 2.3.1). The fact that Ritchie does not refer to it in his discussion of Grave 7 strongly suggests that it was a stray find from the churned over cemetery soil.

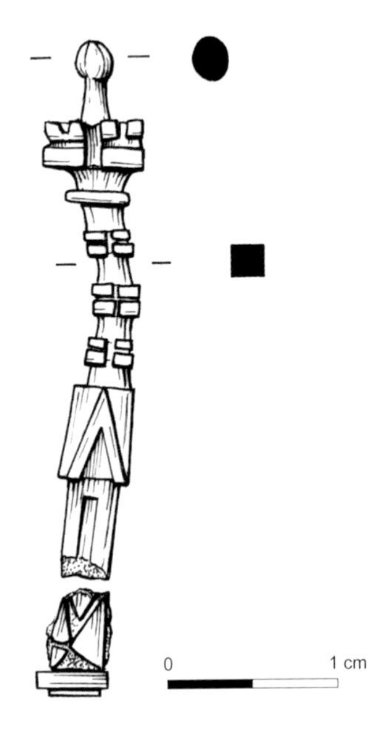

Figure 6.4
Pinnacle (Cat. no. 8), uncertain provenance. Previously believed to have come from Grave 7, the present study, however, suggests that it is more likely a stray find from the graveyard soil

Plate 6.6
The wooden crozier head (Cat. no. 7) from Grave 1 lies just above the left shoulder of the skeleton. The faint outline of the leafy decoration is also visible. Gold finger ring (Cat. no. 17) can be seen on the skeleton's chest

This fitment has been broken off an object such as a pax, a morse or possibly a girdle. It is a miniature decorative architectural pinnacle with a ball finial, above a square collar and curved moulding on top of a crocketted spire, rising from a square section pinnacle with a gable on each face. The general architectural style places it in the mid-14th century.

A girdle pendant found at Liège, dated by one author to 1380, has figures of St Catherine and St Barbara and retains a pinnacle of very similar form and almost exactly the same size. Girdles decorated with metalwork studs and pendants were worn by both men and women (Lightbown 1992, 339, fig 193), so ownership by a senior cleric would not be ruled out.

6.4.3 Chalices and patens

9. Silver-gilt chalice with repaired wooden stem

Dating:	early 13th century
Location:	Grave 1
Dimensions:	diam 121mm, height 111mm (to bottom of tang)
References:	Glenn 2003, 24–5, no B5; NMS H.1992.1838
Illustration:	Figure 6.5

10. Silver-gilt paten

Dating:	first half of the 13th century
Location:	Grave 1, right side of chest
Dimensions:	diam 135mm, depth 20mm

Plate 6.7
The chalices and paten(s) from Graves 1 and 2 lay on the upper part of both skeletons, indicating the grave-goods were originally placed on the chest of the incumbents

References: Glenn 2003, 24–5, no B5; NMS H.1992.1837
Illustration: Figure 6.5, Plate 6.7, Plate 6.8

The Grave 1 chalice and paten are somewhat damaged. Only the hemispherical bowl of the chalice remains, now attached to a square section base metal tang (No. 9a). When found, this was encased in the remains of a wooden stem (No. 9b). The paten, meanwhile has lost about a quarter of its rim. Both are silver, with much of the original gilding intact. The paten has a wide sloping rim with a moulded edge, bevelled into the dished centre, which is filled by a quatrefoil framed by a further bevel. There is a central engraved motif, the *Manus Dei*, within two circles either side of a wavy line punctuated by dashes.

The chalice cannot be very precisely dated as the diagnostic features of foot and knop have been lost. However, the shallow round bowl with everted lip is very similar to those on the chalices of de Gray at York and also Grosseteste (died 1253) and Gravesend at Lincoln (died 1279) (Hope & Fallow 1886, 142–3).

The paten design is classified as 'Type A' by Hope and Fallow in their analysis of 77 English medieval patens, a category they date from '*c* 1180 to *c* 1260'. These have a simple quatrefoil depression in the centre, while 'Type B' have foiled or octofoiled depressions and are ascribed to the second half of the 13th century; the *Manus Dei* being the preferred central motif from 1200 to 1350 (Hope & Fallow 1886, 152).

11. Silver chalice

Dating: mid-14th century
Location: Grave 7, mid-waist, finger bones around and under
Dimensions: diam 130mm, height 180mm (based on the reconstruction drawing)
References: Glenn 2003, 26, no. B6; NMS K.2001.1
Illustration: Figure 6.6, Plate 6.9, Plate 6.10

12. Silver paten

Dating: mid-14th century
Location: Grave 7, right side of waist
Dimensions: (incomplete) diam 135mm (based on the reconstruction drawing)
References: Glenn 2003, 26, no. B6; NMS K.2001.2
Illustration: Figure 6.6, Plate 6.9, Plate 6.10

The Grave 7 chalice and paten are both severely damaged and corroded. Altogether the chalice was broken into numerous fragments, the largest being the intact stem, which is still attached to part of the foot. A section of the bowl with a

Plate 6.8
The silver-gilt paten from Grave 1 (Cat. no. 10) with the *Manus Dei* engraved in the centre. Reproduced by courtesy of the Trustees of the National Museums of Scotland

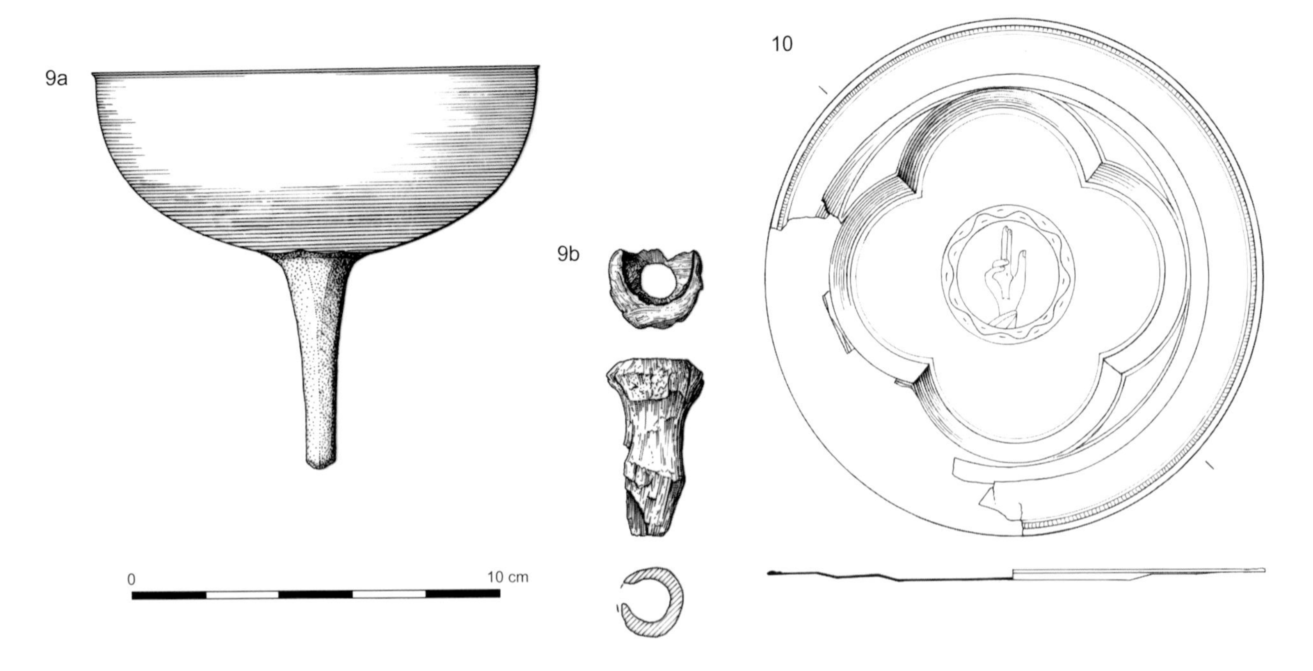

Figure 6.5
Silver-gilt chalice (Cat. no. 9a); wooden chalice stem (Cat. no. 9b); silver-gilt paten (Cat. no. 10); all Grave 1

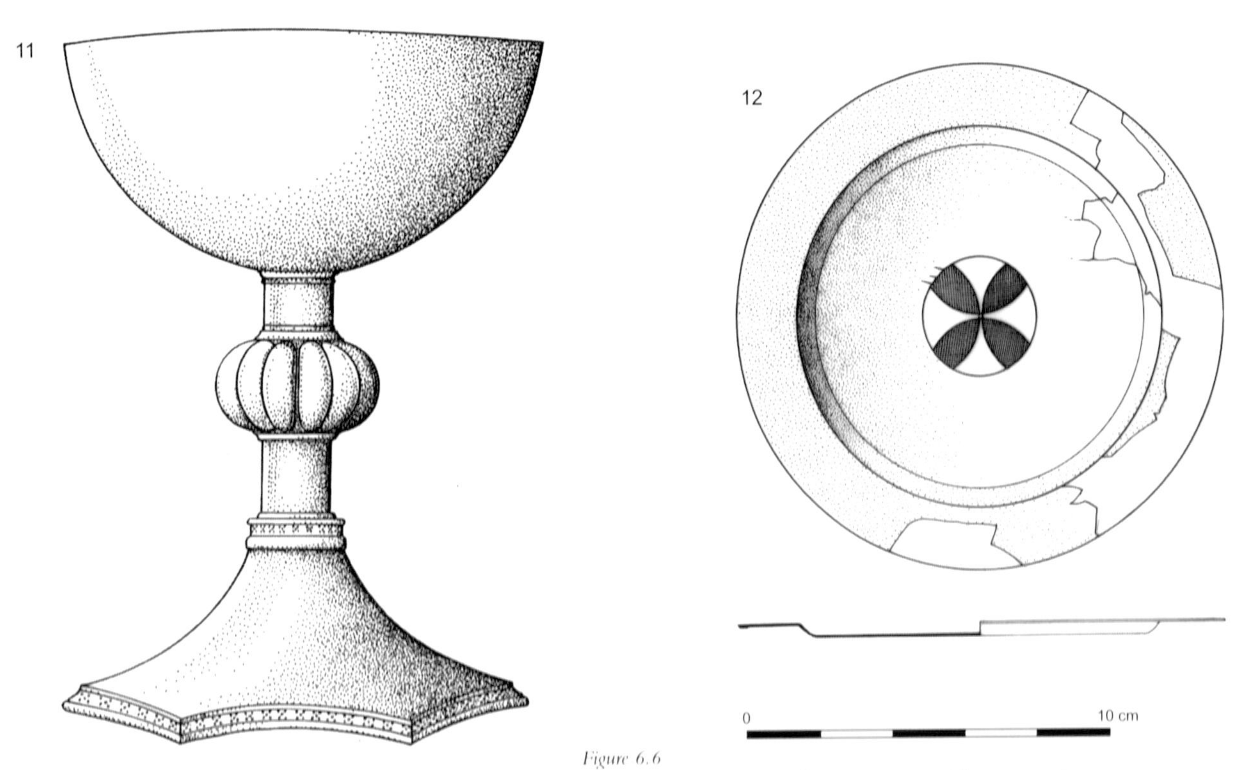

Figure 6.6
Silver chalice (Cat. no. 11); silver paten (Cat. no. 12), both Grave 7. The chalice illustration is a partial reconstruction

portion of the rim has been reconstructed. The paten is in 13 fragments, with the central area intact, but cracked.

Originally, the plain bowl of the chalice was slightly shallower than a hemisphere and joined to the cylindrical stem by a moulded collar. Two similar collars are above and below the knop, which is midway down the stem. The knop is a flattened sphere, with 12 vertical rounded segmental ridges. Joining the stem to the foot is another collar, moulded and stepped, with a frieze of small pierced quincunx ornaments. The concave flaring foot has a stepped and moulded hexagonal edge, each side being a concave arc, decorated to match the frieze above.

Plate 6.9
In situ view of the chalice (Cat. no.11) and paten (Cat. no.12) from Grave 7

The circular paten originally had a moulded edge, sloping slightly to the central depression, which is incised with a circle containing four radiating cup shapes filled with criss-cross matting.

Some deductions about the date of the chalice can again be made from other surviving English church plate. The bowl shape (insofar as it can be ascertained) and the lobed knop are close to the chalice of Archbishop William de Melton of York (1317–40), found in his grave in the late 18th century (Hope & Fallow 1886, 144; Fallow & McColl 1915, 3, pl III; Alexander & Binski 1987, 237, no 112). However, the foot of the Whithorn chalice was something of a departure, like the foot of a chalice from Hamstall Ridware, in Staffordshire, which has a similar incurving hexagonal design with a beaded moulding around the lower edge. These 'mullet' chalice bases seem generally to have replaced the round chalice foot about 1350 (Hope & Fallow 1886, 145–6; Alexander & Binski 1987, 237–8, no 113).

Plate 6.10
Post-conservation view of the fragmented chalice & paten from Grave 7 (Cat. nos 11 and 12). Reproduced by courtesy of the Trustees of the National Museums of Scotland

13. Pewter chalice

Dating:	mid-13th century
Location:	Grave 2, right side of chest/shoulder
Dimensions:	(from reconstruction) height of remaining stem fragment: 85mm
References:	NMS H.1992.1839
Illustration:	Figure 6.7, Plate 6.11

The Grave 2 chalice stem has a baluster knop consisting of three rings, the centre ring larger than those above and below. The stem flares at the top where it ends in a shallow depression to hold the cup. It is broken off below. More of the cup was present when the grave was excavated and is

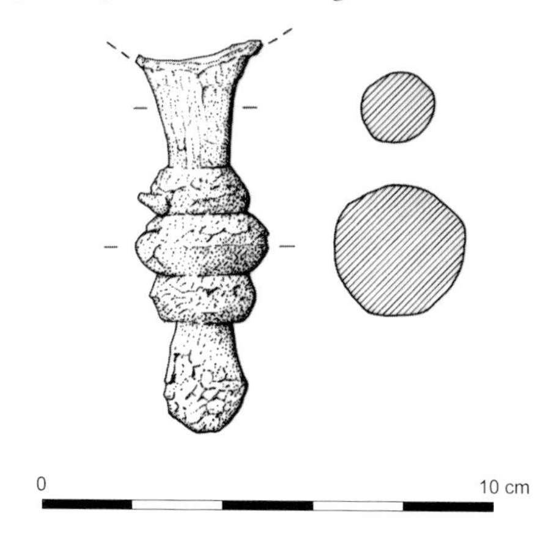

Figure 6.7
Pewter chalice stem (Cat. no. 13), Grave 2. A fragment of the bowl is noticeable in photographs of the grave during excavation (Plate 6.11 opposite). However and only the stem now survives

Plate 6.11
In situ image of the pewter chalice in Grave 2 (Cat. no. 13), showing a more complete bowl

clearly visible in excavation photographs, but this has since crumbled away. It is also possible there was originally a pewter paten in the grave which has met a similar fate. The forms are simple and the workmanship fairly crude. Very possibly, this is part of a vessel made specifically for burial.

14. Pewter chalice

Dating: 13th century
Location: Grave 4, between thighs
Dimensions: diam 92mm (from reconstruction of cup); height 120mm approx (stem and cup)
XRF: pewter, lead with 20–30% tin
References: Lab. No. 59/06
Illustration: Figure 6.8, Plate 6.12

15. Pewter paten

Dating: 13th century
Location: Grave 4, between thighs
Dimensions: diam 130mm (when complete)
XRF: pewter, lead with 30–40% tin
References: Lab. No. 04/01
Illustration: Figure 6.8, Plate 6.12

The Grave 4 chalice and paten are both badly damaged; the chalice very bent, corroded and missing part of the cup and the entire foot, the paten with most of the rim and part of the centre broken off. The cup was rounded, the stem cylindrical, flaring slightly to the cup and in a more pronounced curve to the foot. The knop is a depressed sphere with a horizontal moulding midway. The paten has a plain rim with an engraved line at the outer edge, which curves to a shallow dished area with a central engraved motif of a square cross with notched terminals, inside a circle.

16. Pewter chalice

Dating: 13th century
Location: Grave 21, left side of waist

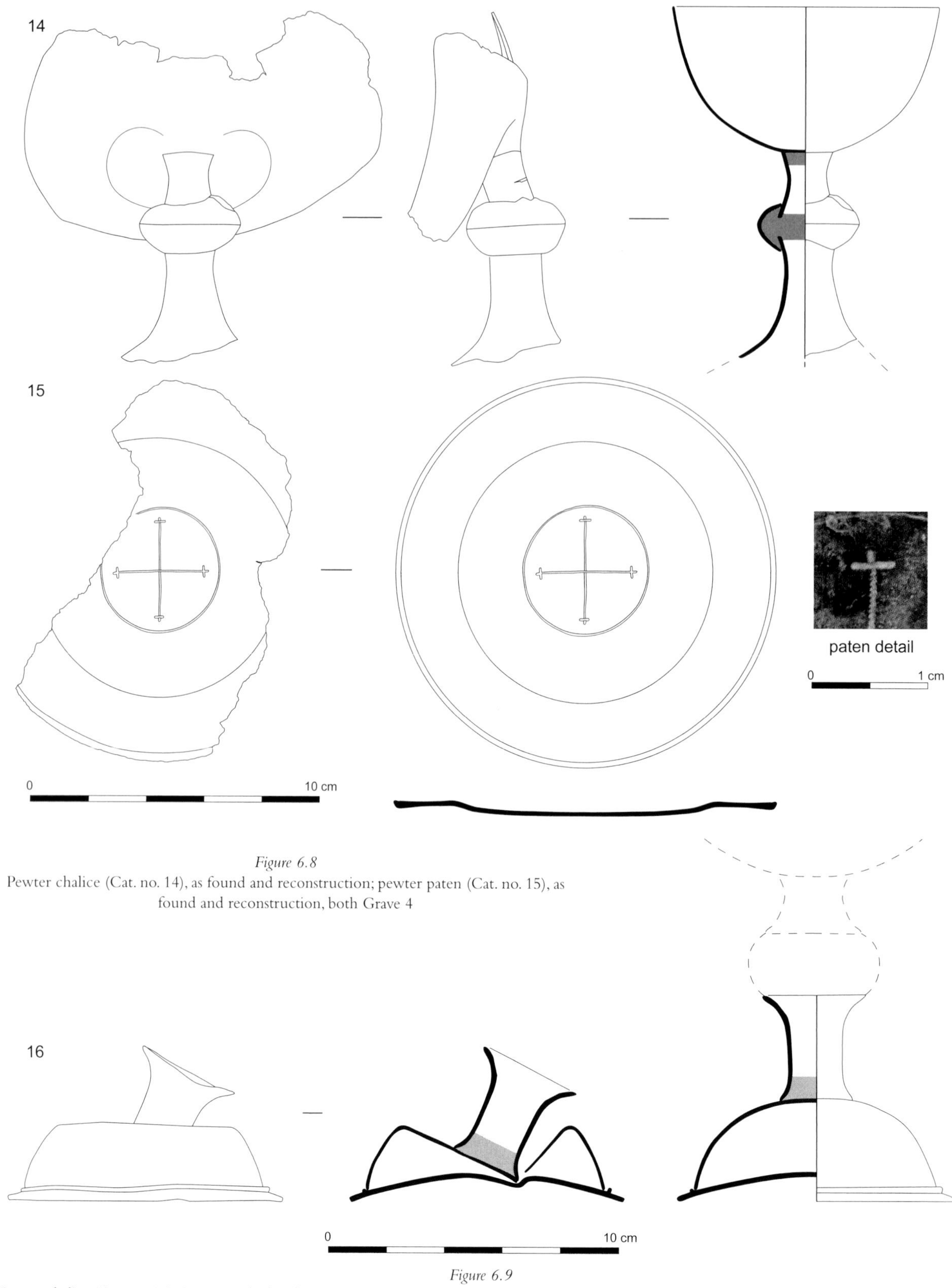

Figure 6.8
Pewter chalice (Cat. no. 14), as found and reconstruction; pewter paten (Cat. no. 15), as found and reconstruction, both Grave 4

Figure 6.9
Pewter chalice (Cat. no. 16), Grave 21. The bowl and disc were found close to the spine of the skeleton. While initially these were interpreted as a chalice and paten, the corrosion on the surface of the disc indicates it had been attached to the bowl at some stage. The two fragments together nowform a single chalice foot, as in this reconstruction

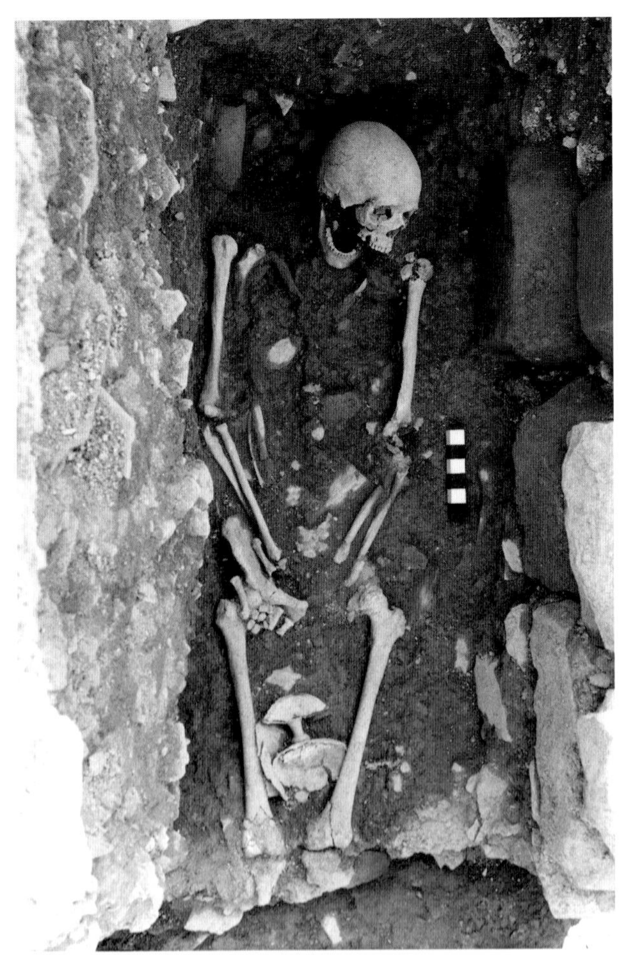

Plate 6.12
The pewter chalice and paten from Grave 4 (Cat. nos 14 and 15) lay between the thighs of the skeleton

Dimensions:	diam of base 96mm, height 69mm (of reconstructed extant remains)
XRF:	pewter, lead with 10–20% tin
References:	Lab. No. 59/02
Illustration:	Figure 6.9

A plain shallow bowl-shaped element attached to a cylindrical stem, flaring slightly where it meets the bowl and more widely at its open end, forms one surviving fragment. The other is a plain slightly dished disk with a shallow flange on the perimeter of the depressed area. The differential corrosion in the central area of the convex side of the disc indicates it was, at one time attached to the bowl-shaped piece, sealing it over. The conjunction of the dented area shows they were attached when this damage occurred. The bowl and disc have been interpreted as representing the base of the chalice, though this is a most unusual construction In medieval vessels of this type, the foot was normally a hollow cone. The present arrangement may represent a clumsy repair of an existing chalice which had been in use in the church, to prepare it for use as part of the bishop's grave-goods.

The widening of the stem suggests that the open end originally connected with the knop (a clear comparison is the more complete chalice surviving from Grave 4). In that case the bowl would originally have been the cup of the chalice.

6.4.4 Finger rings

17. Gold finger ring

Dating:	*c* 1250
Location:	Grave 1
Dimensions:	diam (hoop) 23mm, height 20mm, depth (with bezel) 29mm
References:	Glenn 2003, 48, no. D1; NMS H.1992.1835
Illustration:	Figure 6.10, Plate 6.6, Plate 6.13

The ring, in excellent condition apart from minor cracks and losses inside, is gold set with eight sapphires in collets, surrounding a large table-cut amethyst. The thin flat hoop, which narrows at the back, has a central beaded ridge and trapezoid shoulders notched in the middle. The diameter of the hoop is just sufficient for it to have been worn over a fine silk glove.

The date of the ring must be close to that of Walter de Gray, who died in 1255, which it strongly resembles (Cherry 1981, 58–9, 64–5, no. 127). If Grave 1 belonged to Henry of Galloway (Lowe, Chapter 9), he could have acquired it about the time of his consecration in 1253. Both are obviously formal ceremonial jewels.

18. Gold finger ring

Dating:	mid- to late 13th century
Location:	Grave 3
Dimensions:	diam 20mm (hoop), height 16mm (bezel), depth 26mm (with bezel)
XRF:	gold, alloyed with silver and copper
References:	Lab. No. 52/14
Illustration:	Figure 6.11

The ring is in fair condition and complete, although the bezel is detached. It has two small emeralds in plain settings, one attached to each end of the hoop, next to the bezel. The round hoop is flat in section. The bezel consists of an irregular ruby in a high, slightly moulded setting, with two very small rubies in plain cylindrical settings attached to top and bottom; a small personal ornament, rather than a piece of ecclesiastical regalia.

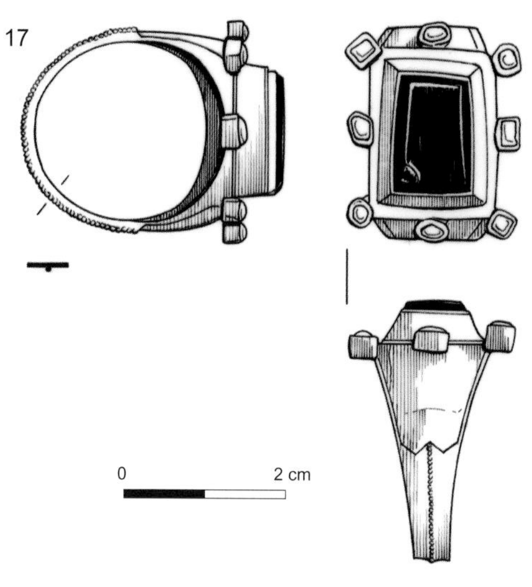

Figure 6.10
Gold finger ring (Cat. no. 17), Grave 1

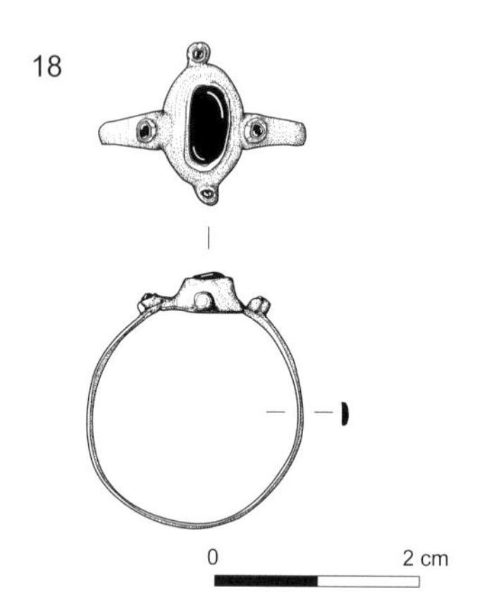

Figure 6.11
Gold finger ring (Cat. no. 18), Grave 3

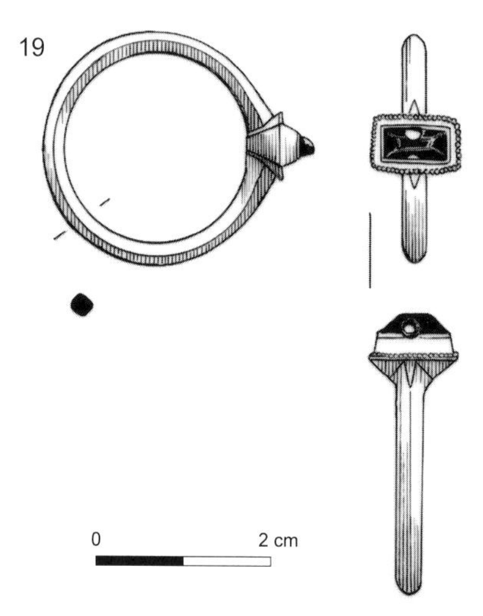

Figure 6.12
Silver-gilt finger ring (Cat. no. 19), Grave 2

Plate 6.13
Gold finger ring (Cat. no. 17), Grave 1. Reproduced by courtesy of the Trustees of the National Museum of Scotland

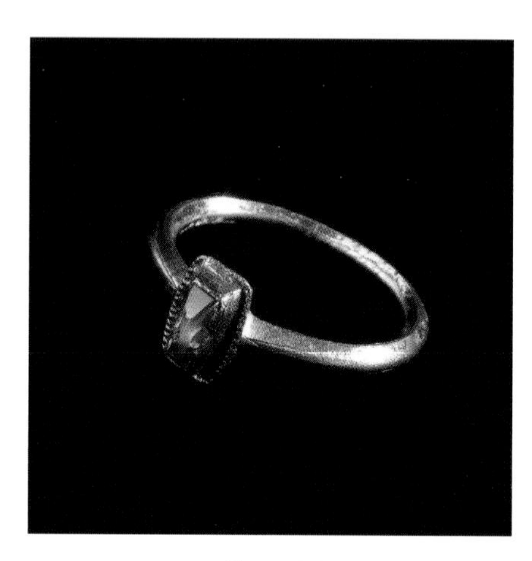

Plate 6.14
Silver-gilt finger ring (Cat. no. 19), Grave 2. Reproduced by courtesy of the Trustees of the National Museum of Scotland

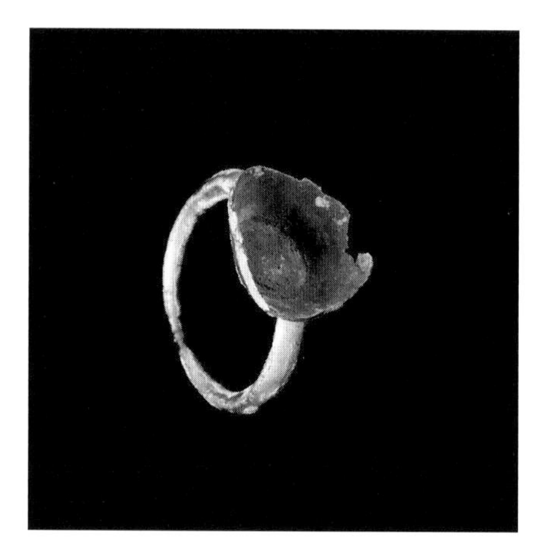

Plate 6.15
Silver finger ring (Cat. no. 20), unstratified. It is presumed that this was excavated from one of the graves, but there is no record of which one, and it is possible it was merely found within the soil surrounding the graves . Reproduced by courtesy of the Trustees of the National Museum of Scotland

19. Silver-gilt finger ring

Dating:	13th century
Location:	Grave 2
Dimensions:	diam (hoop) 25mm, height 11mm, depth (with bezel) 31mm
References:	Glenn 2003, 48 no. D2; NMS H.1992.1836
Illustration:	Figure 6.12, Plate 6.14

The ring, in good condition except for some corrosion to the silver and wear to the gilding, is set with an irregular amethyst cabochon. The hoop, lozenge in section, is slightly stirrup-shaped with an oblong bezel, consisting of a high, plain setting for the gemstone rising from a beaded border. The amethyst has been drilled horizontally, a not unusual practice in the 13th and 14th centuries, when stones pierced for another purpose were sometimes set into rings. This is probably a piece of personal jewellery, without religious significance.

20. Silver finger ring

Dating:	14th century
Location:	unknown provenance
Dimensions:	diam (hoop) 25mm, height 14mm, depth (with bezel) 27mm
References:	Glenn 2003, 49 no. D3
Illustration:	Plate 6.15

The ring is in poor condition, corroded, with the top edge of the setting partly broken and the gem missing. The large round hoop is lozenge-shaped in section. It broadens slightly to join the sides of a deep, plain, flaring triangular setting with rounded corners. Part of one small claw to hold a gem in place remains in the middle of one side. This ring is assumed to have been excavated from one of the graves, but it is not known which one.

6.5 TEXTILES, SILVER-GILT SPANGLES AND GLASS BEAD

CAROL CHRISTIANSEN WITH CONTRIBUTIONS BY JULIE FRANKLIN AND VIRGINIA GLENN, METALS ANALYSIS AND IMAGES BY LORE TROALEN

6.5.1 Summary

Textile remains were found in Graves 1, 2, 3, 7 and 21. The textile components can be grouped into two categories: tablet-woven braids and simple tabby fabrics. The braids survive as fragments of silver-gilt threads and as small fragments of tablet-woven silk with silver-gilt-wrapped threads attached. It is likely the tablet-woven silks and gilt threads originally were part of decorative bands on ecclesiastical garments. The tabby fabrics survive primarily on the surfaces of the buckles, probably the remains of clothing rather than shrouds (Franklin, Chapter 6.6). Textile fragments are referred to by Lab. No. (Franklin, Chapter 6.2). Locations of the fragments, relative to the body, are given where known. A complete catalogue appears in Appendix 2.

6.5.2 Methods

A total of 51 laboratory sample numbers, previously identified as containing or possibly containing textile fragments, were examined. Of this number, eight samples contained no evidence of textile structures or decorative elements. One sample was a section of twine, but with no obvious relation to a textile.

All of the woven fragments are very small, the largest measuring 7 x 13mm. Most samples are in a very poor state of preservation and very friable. Examination was carried out without prior conservation due to the fragile nature of the samples. Soil and small stones adhered to the surfaces of some of the samples, making full examination of structural elements difficult. Some fragments were still attached to a layer of soil, obscuring the reverse side and underlying textile structures.

Further microscopy was carried out using SEM on several samples to determine the nature and quality of the metal thread wrap.

6.5.3 The graves

Grave 1

There were four tablet-woven silk braids, one of which had a geometric, multiple diamond pattern visible on the surface, (Plate 6.17) and two samples of gilt thread fragments. Only two of these could be located to the body; one on the left scapula, the other under the pelvis. There were three tabby fabrics, associated with and preserved by the copper buckles, with a further tabby textile impression associated with a finger bone. These are probably the remains of outer clothing. The fabrics are in a poor state of preservation. Some structural elements are missing or too degraded for thorough analysis.

Grave 2

There were 16 fragments in all. The majority of fragments are gilt thread wraps without cores, similar to those in Graves 1 and 7. Five pieces containing more structural elements have survived. Most were from the upper body area, head, neck, ribs, right arm and one from the pelvis. One, from the neck area, has traces of a possible geometric pattern, similar to that from Grave 1. There were two pieces

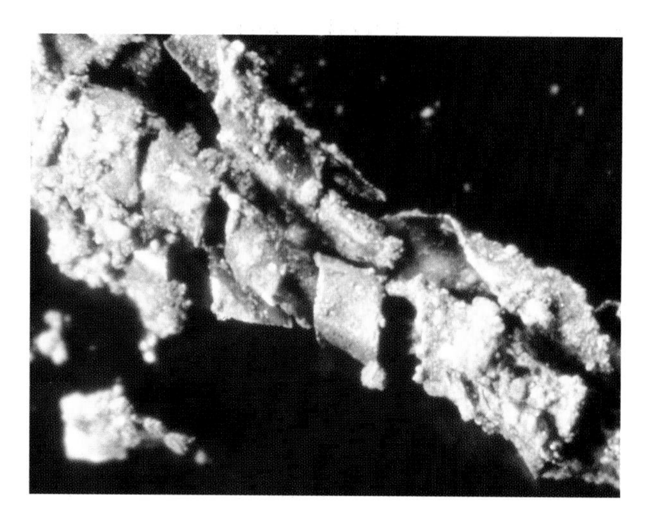

Plate 6.16
Spiral silver-gilt thread wrap (x40 magnification), Grave 1

of tabby, again preserved on the copper buckles and probably the remains of outer clothing.

Grave 3
Grave 3 contains a single textile: a small tabby fragment found on a buckle. It resembles similar fabrics found on buckles in Graves 1 and 2 and again probably represents outer clothing.

Grave 7
The textiles from Grave 7 contain numerous fragments of silver-gilt threads associated with the silver-gilt spangles and glass bead (see below) in the head and right shoulder area. A single fine tabby fragment was preserved on the chest under the silver chalice, where it is probably the remains of shroud cloth.

Grave 21
Several fragments of tabby weave were found in the area of the pelvis, probably preserved by the antibiotic properties of the pewter plate in the area. The largest is a stack of several layers of similar fabric. The evidence suggests this is shroud cloth rather than clothing.

6.5.4 Discussion

The tablet-woven braids
Graves 1, 2 and 7 contained remains of several braid fragments and numerous loose threads. The fabrics are tablet-woven, combined with a supplemental weft wrapped in silver-gilt, tied down by selected warp threads (Collingwood 2002, 239–56).

Tablet-woven ground
The ground fabrics of the textiles were woven using small tablets, usually squares made of bone, wood or leather. Each tablet is perforated with holes, usually four, although sometimes only two holes are used at one time (01/12, Grave 2). Warp threads are passed through the holes and each tablet is threaded in one of two directions, commonly denoted as S or Z. Weaving commences as the tablets are turned and a shed is formed through which the ground weft is passed. Patterns can be created by threading different coloured warp threads through the holes, and by turning the cards in different directions or by varying degrees. For fabrics where a secondary weft covers most or all of the ground fabric, deliberate thread patterning would have been minimal except where warp threads were visible on the surface of the fabric, such as edgings and tie down threads. A single selvedge (01/09, Grave 1, left shoulder), visible as an edge to the braid, and warp threads forming a narrow vertical stripe or ridge (14/04c, Grave 1) within the braid, indicate that warp threads were incorporated as decorative elements in some of the textiles.

Gilt threads
The gilt threads of the Whithorn samples were made by wrapping narrow strips (*lamellae*) of silver-gilt foil around a core yarn in an S twist. In the majority of the Whithorn samples, the cores no longer survive and all that remains is a narrow strip of twisted, gold-coloured *lamella* (Plate 6.16). In some of the larger fragments, the wraps still lie in parallel as they would have on the face of the ground fabric.

Analysis was made of the metal content of the *lamellae* from three different gilt threads: 01/12, Grave 1; 03/32, Grave 7; and 14/04a, Grave 1. All three *lamellae* were made of silver-gilt. The use of silver-gilt for wrapping core yarns

Plate 6.17
Decorative diamond patterning (x7 magnification), Grave 1

appears to be a slightly later practice than wrapping core yarns in pure gold (Crowfoot 1956, 435).

Lamellae widths were measured on two samples (03/32, Grave 7 and 14/04a, Grave 1), and ranged between 225 and 325 microns. This compares favourably with measurements taken of *lamellae* from other gold- or silver-gilt-wrapped threads (Crowfoot 1956, 442; Hoke & Petrascheck-Heim 1977, 51).

Tie down threads

It is usual for the gilt threads to be woven in at the same time the ground fabric is woven. This is clear in the Whithorn textiles by the placement of the gilt threads in relation to the one remaining selvedge and in the use of tie down threads. Tie down threads are selected warp threads that anchor the long floats of the supplemental gilt weft to the tablet-woven ground fabric. Because they are visible on the surface of the fabric, the selection and spacing of tie down threads often is a planned part of the overall design of the textile, as patterns can be created over the gold face of the fabric. Often the designs are lozenges, keys, or other geometric designs. Those textiles that contain tie down threads possibly incorporated geometric patterning in this way (01/20a & b, Grave 2?).

Two other fragments, in which only the parallel gold wraps survive, contain slight traces of patterning on their surfaces. Sample 01/24b, Grave 2, right upper arm, contains linear patterning. Sample 14/04b, Grave 1 contains a multiple diamond patterning, possibly lines forming large diamonds containing smaller diamonds (Plate 6.17).

Medieval tablet-woven braids

Tablet weaving has been practised in Britain since at least the Iron Age (Henshall 1950, 148–51). It was used to make straps and narrow bands, and starting borders or selvedges for fabrics woven on the warp-weighted loom, especially in Scandinavia (Hald 1980, 225–7). Both uses of tablet weaving, a separate band and a band with fringe, similar to the warping technique used in starting borders, are found in the construction of the Orkney hood (Henshall 1952, 9–12).

Incorporating metal threads into tablet weaving is recorded in Britain from the 7th century. In early Anglo-Saxon graves, gold was flattened and formed into long, thin strips, which were laid flat over the tablet-woven ground fabric and anchored with selected warp threads to form geometric patterns (Crowfoot & Hawkes 1967, 56). A similar weaving technique, but using thin strips of gold or silver wrapped around a core yarn, usually of silk, is a later development, appearing in northern Europe by the 10th century (Ræder Knudsen 2005, 40–3).

Tablet-woven gold- and silver-wrapped braids, similar in construction to those from Whithorn Priory, have been found in 10th to early 12th century Viking levels in Dublin (Pritchard 1988, 150). The late 10th-century grave of St Cuthbert contained a number of tablet-woven braids incorporating geometric patterns and using gold- and silver-gilt-wrapped cores (Crowfoot 1956, 433-52).

Orphreys and edgings of ecclesiastical vestments were typical applications for decorative tablet-woven bands during the medieval period. Richly patterned gold or silver-gilt silk braids have been found in a number of ecclesiastical graves. Vestments from the grave of William de Blois (d. 1236), Bishop of Worcester, were bordered in gold 'lace' and the orphrey was a gold band in a geometric pattern. Similarly, the remains of Bishop Walter de Cantilupe (d. 1266), his successor, were clothed in garments with various gold 'lace' edgings, one in a lattice pattern (Hope 1893). The grave of Walter de Gray, Archbishop of York (d. 1255) contained the remains of an elaborate 8cm wide tablet-woven braid, featuring gold or gilt wefts and a complex lozenge-based geometric design (Patterson 1987).

In Scotland, a decorative tablet-woven band was found within the tomb of Robert the Bruce (d. 1329), which resembles the construction techniques of the braids from Whithorn. In addition, the overall pattern was a series of diamonds (Henshall *et al* 1956, 30–3), similar to the patterning of No. 14/04b, Grave 1. A decorative tablet-woven band used as a seal tag for a forged Scottish document, prepared sometime before 1457, is similar to the Bruce band, both in design and technique (Henshall 1965, 159–61). A silver or silver-gilt decorative tablet-woven band was recovered from Kirk Close, Perth, possibly 14th century (Bennett 1987, 166). Two other tablet-woven braids from the later medieval period were found in bishops' graves from Fortrose and Glasgow, but their construction differs from those found at Whithorn (Henshall *et al* 1956, 32–5).

As demand for decorative tablet-woven bands increased during the 12th and 13th centuries, specialised workshops for manufacturing these complex fabrics developed, especially in London (Crowfoot *et al* 2001, 130). But tablet-woven braids could also have more humble origins. A German nun, writing in 1517, produced an 82-page pattern book for weaving tablet-woven bands, many incorporating geometric patterns, as an aid to her fellow sisters in the manufacture of such specialised fabrics (Ræder Knudsen 2004, 124–6).

The silk braids from graves at Whithorn Priory resemble similar decorative bands from other ecclesiastical graves of the period. The presence of silk indicates an imported fibre, although not necessarily foreign manufacture of the

Plate 6.18
In situ view of spangles during the excavation of Grave 7

textiles. The missing wefts and cores suggest that some of these yarns possibly were made of linen. The use of silver-gilt rather than pure gold is typical for similar fabrics of this period. The fragmentary nature of the samples makes it impossible to tell how much silk and silver-gilt was required to make the bands and, therefore, how opulent the garments may have been. The tablet-woven braids from Whithorn certainly were rich fabrics, but not made wholly of the most exclusive materials.

Tabby fabrics
The various tabby fragments from the graves at Whithorn Priory are similar. Where spin direction can be determined, it is usually Z in both systems. Fibre analysis was tested on several samples but the fibres were too degraded to make an accurate determination. The fabrics are often balanced weaves, and as a group they have similar thread counts in both systems. Five of the tabby fragments, from Graves 1, 2 and 3 were found attached to the underside of buckles and this suggests they represent outer clothing. In Graves 7 and 21, by contrast, it seems more likely they represent shroud cloth (Franklin, Chapter 6.8.3). Similar fine linen or silk 'winding-sheets', several layers thick (as No. 60/34, Grave 21, pelvis), were found around the remains of St Cuthbert (Battiscombe 1956, 8).

6.5.5 Silver-gilt spangles and glass bead

(Figure 6.13; Plate 6.18)
JULIE FRANKLIN

The 110 spangles and the glass bead were all found in Grave 7. About half of these (57 examples, Types 1–4) were excavated during the main Grave 7 excavation in 1960, found under and over the right scapula, while Ritchie was excavating the crozier between the head and the right shoulder. The remainder (53 examples, Types 2–3 and the glass bead) were recovered in 1964, when he returned to the grave, this time with a more considered recording strategy. The spangles were photographed *in situ* and a sketch plan made, apparently with the help of a pin and piece of tracing paper. Some were found in the head area with associated skull fragments, others in the area which had been under the crozier. Some were associated with gilt braid threads (Christiansen, Chapter 6.5.4) and hence must have adorned an expensive piece of fabric.

There are four different types: three in the shape of flowers, with relief detail down the centre of each curling petal; and simple discs with depressed borders. They are made of very thin sheet silver, 0.3mm thick, gilded only on the front. Each example of a type is identical to the next, with no badly trimmed edges or off-centre piercings and were probably stamped out of a sheet of pre-gilded silver, using a moulded punch. There are no traces of metal rivets, so they must have been sewn in place.

The use of metal mounts to decorate leather or textile is well-documented in the archaeological record of the medieval period (eg Egan & Pritchard 1991, 162–246). Excavated examples are generally more robust, made of copper-alloy, pewter or tinned iron, and secured by metal rivets. They were used on girdles, purses, shoes, and straps for horse harness and armour, from the 13th to the 15th century, though the vast majority are concentrated in the second half of the 14th century. Sexfoils are the most common type of all, with many examples decorated to resemble flowers (Egan & Pritchard 1991, 186). Some of

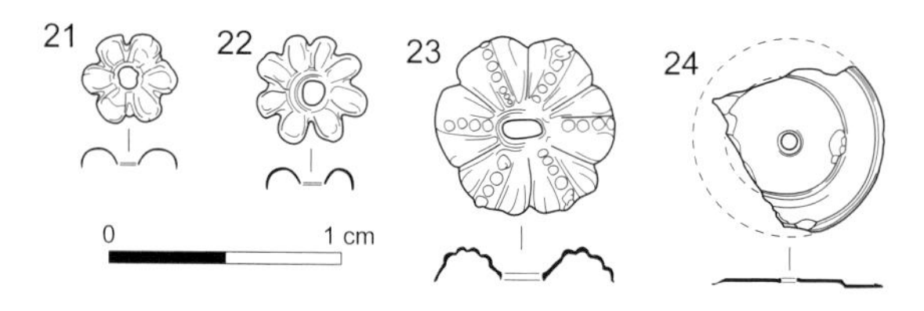

Figure 6.13
Spangles, Grave 7: Type 1 (Cat. no. 21); Type 2 (Cat. no. 22); Type 3 (Cat. no. 23); Type 4 (Cat. no. 24)

the shapes commonly found in copper-alloy are remarkably similar to the more delicate examples from Whithorn (cf Egan & Pritchard 1991, 178, fig.114: 926 to Whithorn Type 4; Egan & Pritchard 1991, 191, figs.119–21 to Whithorn Types 1–3). The use of finer mounts in more precious metals on lighter fabrics are rarer finds, for obvious reasons, but some examples are known (Glenn, Chapter 6.5.6).

The glass bead was in very poor condition, appearing brown and crystallised and appears to have been picked up accidentally with the spangles. There is no reference to it in the Ritchie Archive or among the finds labels. This area of the grave was clearly excavated with some care, but it is still possible there may originally have been far more, either corroded away completely, or left broken and mud-coloured in the spoil. Its original colour cannot be determined, but it would have sparkled.

Most excavated examples of medieval glass beads are large and brightly coloured, and small plain beads are probably under represented in the archaeological record. A collection of 145 slightly larger (5mm diam) pale amber-coloured glass beads were found in a 13th- and 14th-century midden in Perth (Thoms 1982, 449), while 13th- and 15th-century examples have been found in London (Egan & Pritchard 1991, 315, fig. 209: 1586–7). Little is known of medieval glass bead making, but assuming it was related to the window glass industry, at this date they would have been imported, probably from England or Northern Europe (Kidd 1979).

The combined effect of the different spangles, the gold braid and the glass beads would have been striking. The best clue as to how the spangles were used comes from Ritchie's notes. He could not discern an overall pattern, but at the time of excavating the skull area he records: 'the spangles were concentrated in a line W of the skull and lay face down, face up, face down' (Archive A29). Later in his publication draft, he words this as 'alternating bands' (Archive D9, p.101). Unfortunately he did not make a sketch plan of this line but it seems to refer to a band running horizontally(?) just above the head. The alternating pattern may be due to the way two layers of braid have rotted away. Others were found under the skull, which seems to have rolled to the left before it was crushed.

It is unclear whether the concentration around the crozier represents another matching spangled article or was part of the same. Though some spangles might have been spread about by animal disturbance within the grave, concentrations both under the skull and under the crozier imply an object or objects deliberately placed there. Beneath the crozier head, Ritchie records 'two layers were present, the upper layer face downwards, the lower layer face upwards' (Archive D9, p.101). This distribution was photographed (Plate 6.18) and sketched but the pattern seems rather random, showing larger Type 3 spangles (spaced *c* 2cm apart), interspersed by smaller Type 2 flowers (spaced *c* 1cm apart).

Ritchie concluded they were part of a mitre and this still seems a likely interpretation, probably placed on the head of the deceased. Decorated lappets (the bands that hang down from the back of a mitre) might explain the second concentration under the crozier. Alternatives might be a pillow, a collar or other item of clothing with decorative braiding, possibly folded under the crozier, or a similar glove.

6.5.6 Spangles as medieval dress ornaments

VIRGINIA GLENN

The position of the textile fragments and spangles as sketched during excavation suggests the deceased was wearing at least a mitre, possibly of *Opus Anglicanum* with silver thread worked in characteristic underside couching, and possibly also a similar glove. This would certainly be in keeping with ambitions to follow fashions in an English centre like York. The profusion of silver-gilt spangles (currently the largest group to have been discovered on a single British site) must have formed the ornament of richly embellished items. With the exception of William of

Table 6.1 Spangles and glass bead

Cat. no.	*Description*	*Spangle type*	*Diameter*	*Minimum number*	*Lab nos*
21	Small sexfoil flowers	Type 1	4mm	8	03/09, 03/10, 03/11, 03/12, 03/13, 03/18, 03/30, 03/37
22	Medium octofoil flowers	Type 2	5mm	76	Grave 7, head area and between head and right shoulder, 1960 & 1964
23	Large sexfoil flowers	Type 3	8mm	22	
24	Large discs	Type 4	8mm	4	
25	Glass bead	–	1.5mm	1	03/37, Grave 7, head area, 1964

Plate 6.19
Extant fragments of the mitre of of William de Wykeham: mitre fragments, cloth-of-gold, pearls, silver gilt ornaments, imitation turquoises and pastes, Englishlate 14th/early 15th century, Oxford, The Warden and Fellows of New College. Reconstruction arranged by W H St John Hope in 1906. From Archaeologia volume LX, 1907. Reproduced by courtesy of the Society of Antiquaries of London

Wykeham, Bishop of Winchester (1366–1404), no 13th- or 14th-century British prelate has left us remains of a mitre with substantial numbers of precious ornaments attached to it (Hope 1907, 472–81, pls XLVII, XLVIII, XLIX, Figs 1&2; King 1987, 471, no. 606).

Other surviving medieval mitres are much earlier and plainer, and decorated simply with silk embroidery (Christie 1938, 59, no. 19, pls XII A&B; King 1963, 15, no. 13, pl I), but an inventory records an example with *flosculis argentibus deaurata* at St Paul's in London in 1295 (Christie 1938, 21). They could also be expensive. Joseph the goldsmith was paid 14 marks for a mitre given to Peter de Aqua Blanca, Bishop of Hereford, in 1240 by the king (*CLR*, 501–2). Adam de Basinges, in 1239–40, charged 22 marks for an embroidered chasuble and seven marks for a mitre to be a gift to the Archbishop of Armagh (Issues of the Exchequer 14, 15, 16).

Although probably at least half a century later in date than anything in Grave 7 and the property of a much more opulently equipped bishop than one would ever expect to find at Whithorn, Wykeham's mitre (Plate 6.19) does give us some idea of what the decoration might have included, and Hope deduced roughly how it might have been applied. In addition to four magnificent silver-gilt crocketed crestings, it was decorated with gems, pearls, enamelled and jewelled 'tablets', silver-gilt flowers and 'stellar ornaments'. He concluded that these were arranged in a band along the lower edge and in a vertical strip up the centre. Our Whithorn bishop did not rise to the cresting or tablets, any pearls may not have survived burial, but he did have silver-gilt flowers in profusion. Also, it is possible that the 'trails of very small pearls' on Wykeham's mitre might have been replaced at Whithorn with trails of very small glass beads, as represented by the single surviving example (No. 25).

Similar cast silver-gilt ornaments in the form of flowers occur in European hoards, notably the *Trésor de Colmar* now in Paris (Taburet et Dhénin 1984, *passim*; Taburet-Delahaye 1989, 225, 231, no. 109, 233, no. 113, 238–9, no. 120, 240, no. 123). Found in 1863 in the wall of a house in the medieval Jewish quarter of the city of Colmar, the *trésor* was probably hidden during the persecutions which followed the Great Plague of 1348–9. This theory is borne out by the evidence of the coins in the hoard and the inclusion of a Jewish wedding ring (Taburet-Delahaye 1989, 229–230, no 108). Therefore, comparable dating could be applied to the Whithorn flowers.

Plate 6.20
Marginal illustration of a Scottish figure wearing a mitre: Herdmanstone Breviary, folio 138v Reproduced by courtesy of the National Library of Scotland, Advocates 18.2.13A. Scottish, mid-14th century.

The Colmar ornaments are attached to woven silk ribbons by little rivets on the reverse. The ribbons may have been intended to ornament a girdle or possibly a lady's headband. The flowers alternate with female heads and measure 9mm x 9mm, only a fraction larger than the largest of the Whithorn spangles. On the basis of the coiffures of the female heads, Taburet-Delahaye dates all these ornaments to the first half of the 14th century and ascribes them, with a question mark, to the southern Rhineland. The flowers have five petals, with a tiny pointed sepal between each one. The petals are bordered by a ridged line and surround a domed granulated centre.

As Taburet-Delahaye points out, rosettes are extremely frequent motifs in jewellery design, and comparison with the Colmar hoard does not necessarily imply a Continental source for the Whithorn spangles, but it does show what their original appearance would have been and at least one way in which they might have been used. Wykeham also had six-petalled star-shaped silver-gilt flowers alternating with large gem stones and pearls, in the vertical panel on the centre front of his mitre. The 'spanglers' were a specialist sub-group of the goldsmiths, formally defined as such in London by 1441, but obviously practising at least two centuries before (Reddaway & Walker 1975, 259; Campbell 1991, 148, note 211; Jefferson 2003, 508, b 104). Early records of York goldsmiths are very patchy, and spanglers are not mentioned as a separate group, but it is very likely that what seem to have been popular goods were also being made there in some quantity.

These fragmentary remains from Whithorn give us some precious clues as to the taste and appearance of the higher clergy in Scotland in the 13th and 14th centuries. Lacking stained glass or effigies in good condition, we are otherwise driven to rely on a few manuscript images and formal portraits on clerical seals. The 14th-century sketches in the margins of the Herdmanstone Breviary (Plate 6.20) at least show us the form of mitre and cope in use about the period of Bishop Wedale (1326–1355).

Seal impressions are often too indistinct to provide details of costume or ecclesiastical accoutrements, but we are very fortunate that the seal matrix of one Scottish bishop, Henry le Chen of Aberdeen (1282–1328), which shows no signs of wear has survived in an excellent state of preservation (Plate 6.21). As it does not appear on any of his extant documents and was found in a field in Northamptonshire soon after the Second World War, possibly it was lost before it could be used. It may have been made in London, a centre of fine seal engraving, and mislaid while the bishop was visiting family connections in Huntingdon on his way north (Glenn 2003, 133). Normally, seal matrices for an individual's official or personal use were destroyed on their death to prevent fraud or forgery.

Plate 6.21
Seal matrix of Henry le Chen, Bishop of Aberdeen (1282 – 1328), Scottish(?) or London. NMS H NM 209. Reproduced by courtesy of Virginia Glenn

The matrix shows very clearly the details of the bishop's vestments and ecclesiastical regalia. He wears a rather lower mitre than the Breviary figure, similarly triangular and pointed in the middle, gloves under a large ring on his right hand, a morse in the form of a rosette fastening his vestments at the throat and has flower ornaments in deep relief on the hem of his dalmatic. Henry carries an elaborate crozier with leafy crockets. This is an idealised portrait of a late 13th century Scottish bishop in his most formal attire and must convey some impression of how the Whithorn prelates would also have wanted to appear.

6.6 BUCKLES AND BROOCHES

JULIE FRANKLIN

The five ring buckles from Grave 1, 2 and 3 were all remarkably similar in size and form, including two pairs of

Plate 6.22
In situ view of buckle (Cat. no. 26) beneath the hip of Skeleton 3

identical buckles from Graves 1 and 2. They are a common form of buckle from the mid-13th to mid-15th centuries (Egan & Pritchard 1991, 57; Whitehead 1996, 16; Nicholson 1997, 370, fig. 10.56). The uniformity in this collection is marked. All but one are 46–7mm in diameter; the only differences are in the form of the pin and composition of the metal. In the catalogue below, they are listed in grave date order, with Grave 3 being the earliest, Grave 1 the latest.

The pair of buckles from Grave 2 are without pins. Given the substantial nature of the other buckle pins, it seems unlikely a copper-alloy pin would have corroded away completely, or that both would have fallen off and been lost in such an undisturbed context. It is more likely that the pins were made of iron (cf Egan & Pritchard 1991, 57, fig. 36:38), and have suffered accelerated corrosion due to their contact with the copper. An iron object from the grave, previously catalogued as the shank of a coffin nail (Lab. No. 01/04), was found to have mineralised textile rather than wood adhering to it. It has no sign of a loop at the end, but the coarse weave of the textile matches the pattern on the buckle frames exactly, and it is likely this is the remains of one of the pins. The composition of all the buckle pins was found to be different to the frame. The surviving pins all contained more zinc and, in some cases, more tin and less lead. This would have the effect of making the pin, the part under the most strain, stiffer than the frame. The use of iron in the Grave 2 buckles would have the same effect.

Plain rings such as these are classified as buckles, while rings with a constriction in the frame for the pin are called brooches (Egan & Pritchard 1991, 57). However, they could be used interchangeably, and where use can be determined, 'brooches' have been used as buckles and vice versa (Egan & Pritchard 1991, 248). Evidence from other graves and contemporary representations show that brooches were commonly used at the neck to secure two halves of an under garment or cloak together (Egan & Pritchard 1991, 247: Ward Perkins 1940, 274). The blunt end of the pin would not allow this to be pushed through textile, and prepared slits, holes or loops would be needed. Buckles were used to secure waist belts, sword belts and attach armour fittings (Clay 1981, 133–8, No. 24 & 65; Egan & Pritchard 1991, 56, fig. 34; Ward Perkins 1940, 274). All have textile (Christiansen, Chapter 6.5.4), preserved by mineralisation adhering to the underside, indicating it was from clothing rather than shroud cloth. Some also have mineralised leather around the junction of pin and ring.

In Grave 2, No. 29, the smallest example, has probably been used to secure an under garment at the neck, while the larger No. 27 on the chest, may have been for a mantle. The others are probably for girdles, secured at the hip. Each of the three men has one of these, and the man in Grave 1 appears to have two. This second buckle (No. 31) seems superfluous, but is probably not in its original location. The bones have been a little scattered and the buckle pin has rusted in an open position. It suggests animal disturbance. Mice bones were found in the vicinity of the grave, though there is no direct evidence of gnawing on the bones or of the grave having been disturbed in antiquity. The fact that in Graves 1 and 2 the two buckles are matching pairs, suggests that both were bought at the same time, whether as part of the bishop's vestments, or specially for the burial.

It would seem, then, that the individuals buried in these three cists were all fully clothed. Those buried in wooden coffins (Graves 4, 7 and 21) all have significant grave-goods, but no dress accessories (with the possible exception of a

Plate 6.23
In situ view of buckles (Cat. nos 27 and 29) on chest and neck of Skeleton 2

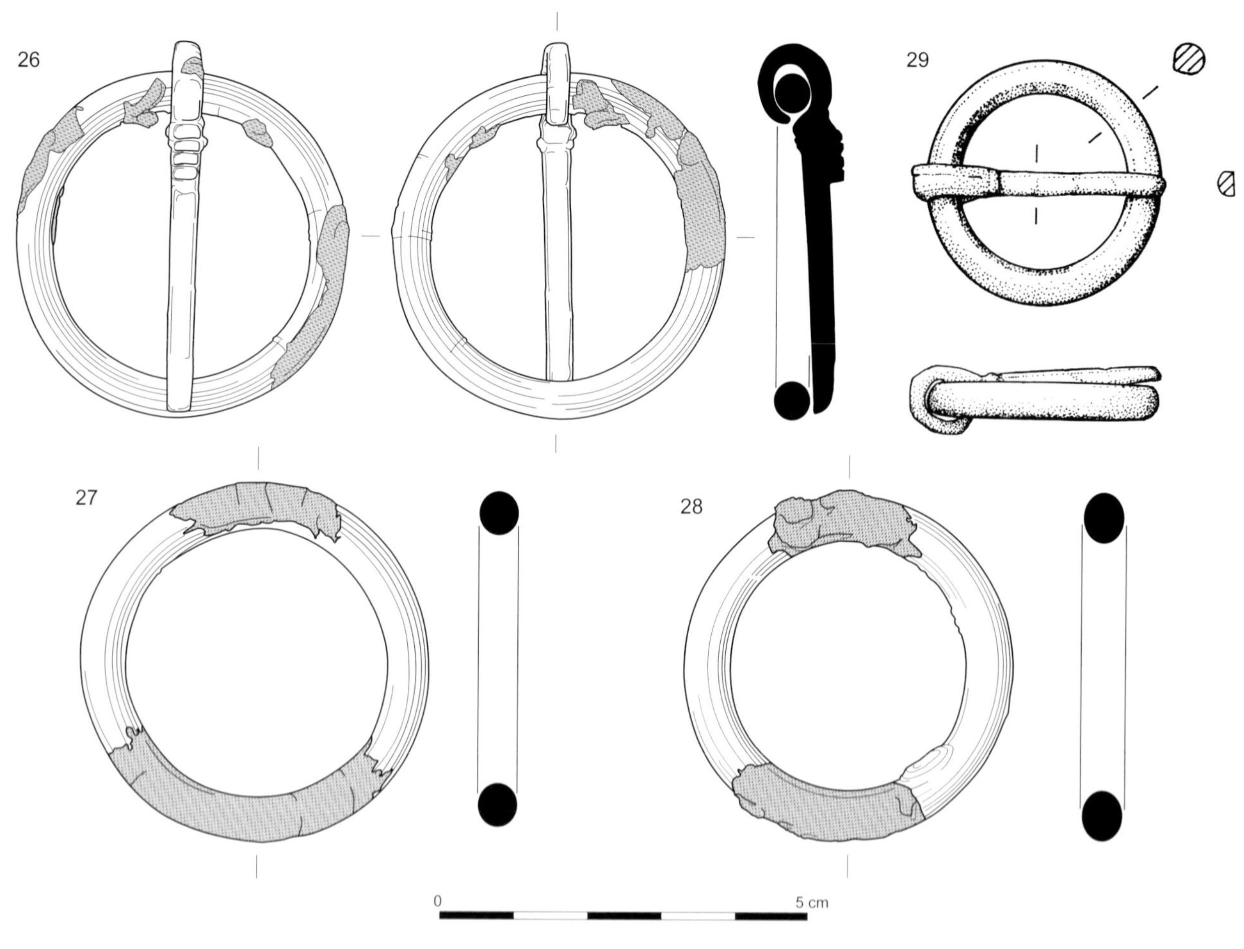

Figure 6.14
Copper-alloy buckles: Grave 3 (Cat. no. 26); Grave 2 (Cat. nos 27–29)

mitre in Grave 7), implying they were clothed only in a shroud. There is no particular chronological reason for this difference, but as the body is visible during a cist burial, there was clearly a preference for them to be clothed as they were in life. The remaining two cist burials, Graves 5 and 8, contain no evidence for clothing either. One may have had a shroud (see No. 35, below) but in both cases there are reasons to believe that the graves have been robbed (Dingwall, Chapter 2.3.1).

26. Buckle. Large plain ring, cast pin with ridged grip at base. Mineralised textile on opposing sides of the ring, next to pelvis and arm, perpendicular to pin. Diam 46mm. XRF: Leaded bronze ring, gunmetal pin, pin richer in tin and zinc. Lab. No. 52/17, 1960, Grave 3, upside down on left hip, pin pointing inwards, immediately to left of upper pelvis. Figure 6.14, Plate 6.22.

27. Buckle/brooch. Large plain ring, no pin. Mineralised textile on two opposing sides of ring, possibly leather on one. Diam 47mm. XRF: Gunmetal. Lab. No. 01/02, Grave 2, on chest between lower arms and sternum. Figure 6.14, Plate 6.23.

28. Buckle. Large plain ring, no pin. Mineralised textile on two opposing sides of ring. Diam 46mm. XRF: Gunmetal. Lab. No. 01/03, Grave 2, right hip, beside right pelvis (evidence of label only, not in photo). Figure 6.14.

29. Buckle/brooch. Small plain ring, cast pin. Diam 32mm. NMS 1992.1834, Grave 2, neck, inside mandible. Figure 6.14, Plate 6.23.

30. Buckle. Large plain ring buckle, cast pin. Remains of leather found within ring, mineralised leather remains

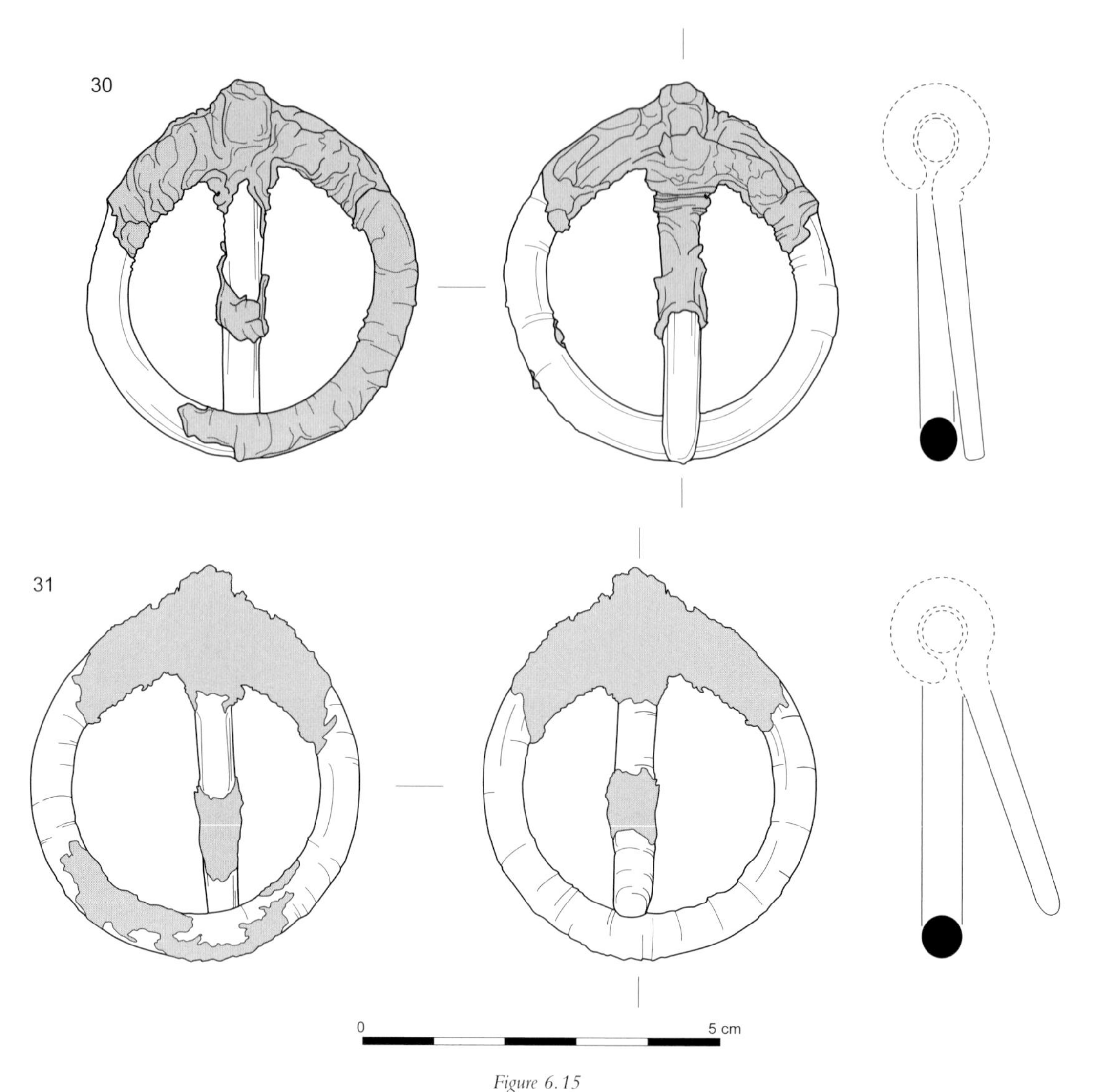

Figure 6.15
Copper-alloy buckle: Grave 1 (Cat. nos 30–31). The presence of buckles in Graves 1, 2 and 3 suggests that the individuals were clothed, whereas those in Graves 4, 7 and 21 appear to have been buried in shrouds

around junction of pin and ring with textile and leather (possibly flesh?) adhering to underside of lower half of ring. Diam 47mm. XRF: Leaded bronze/gunmetal ring, gunmetal pin, pin lower in lead and richer in zinc than the ring. Lab. No. 09/03, Grave 1, right hip, on right pelvis, pin pointing inwards. Figure 6.15.

31. Buckle. Large plain ring buckle, cast pin. Mineralised leather around junction of pin and ring, textile adhering to underside of ring under pin tip and pin junction. Diam 47mm. XRF: Gunmetal, pin richer in zinc. Lab. No. 09/04, Grave 1, crotch, under lower centre of pelvis, *c* 100mm to left of No. 30, pin pointing upwards. Figure 6.15.

6.7 OTHER SMALL FINDS

JULIE FRANKLIN

The first two finds (Nos. 32 & 33) are from the early graveyard soil, associated with the Phase 1 burials of the 11th and 12th century, pre-dating the extension of the east end of the church over the excavation area. Neither appears to be from a specific grave fill, a fact that Ritchie would probably have recorded.

The penannular bracelet (No. 32) is simply made and is difficult to date. It is now bent into a tight curve, and would only fit a child, though opened out a little would have fitted a small adult. No. 33 is some kind of strap attachment. The thin narrow plate, clearly not designed to withstand

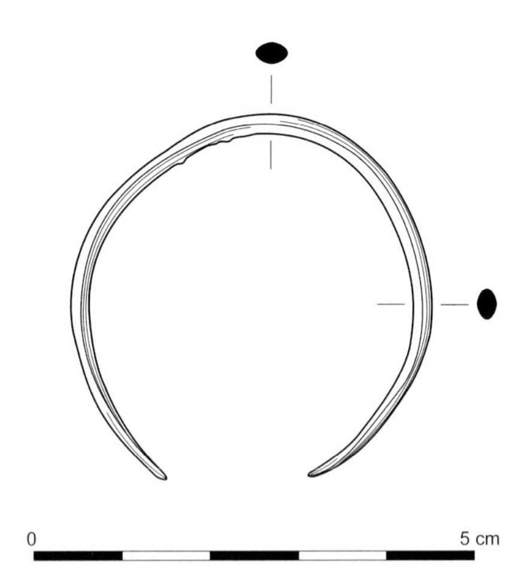

Figure 6.16
Copper-alloy bracelet (Cat. no. 32)

much strain, was probably riveted to a strap but has been torn off. A less decorative example from the 6th- to 8th-century Anglo-Saxon cemetery of Finglesham, Kent, was found outside the right knee of an adult male and was interpreted as a possible item of sword harness (Hawkes & Grainger 2006, 151, grave 204, No. 5). Closer to home, an example with a bone frame came from a grave in a 9th- to 11th-century cemetery in Dunbar (Franklin 2001, 305, illus 11:2). Similar items in later medieval contexts are interpreted as pendant loops for hanging a purse or other personal item from a belt (Egan & Pritchard 1991, 221, fig.138:1189–93).

Bar mounts are used as strap decoration from the 12th century onwards. A remarkably similar example to No. 34 was found in London, dating to the second half of the 14th century (Egan & Pritchard 1991, 214, fig. 134:1160–1). They are rarely used singly, straps are often decorated

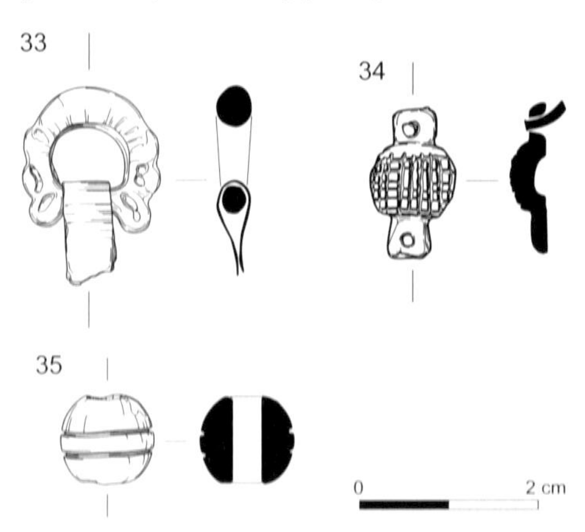

Figure 6.17
Copper-alloy objects (Cat. nos 33–34); bone (Cat. no. 35)

with a number of mounts and the fact its exact location within the Grave 3 cist was not recorded suggests it was not directly related to the body, but possibly residual in the upper fill. A strap loop with an identical central lobe was found during Hill's excavations at Whithorn, from a layer overlying the Period V (1250–1600) graveyard in the Glebe Field to the south of the Priory (Nicholson 1997, 371, fig. 10.57:11).

The bone bead, No. 35, was possibly part of a set of rosary beads. Two different-sized beads were generally used, smaller beads arranged in tens (or decades) divided by larger *paternoster* beads. Only one bead was found in the grave, though other beads may have been made of wood, or simply formed by knots in the cord. However, a single bone bead of similar size and shape was found in a remarkably similar context in St Giles Cathedral, Edinburgh (Franklin & Collard 2006, 56), in a 13th- or 14th- century (female) burial, between the knees. This may in fact suggest it was some kind of toggle or other dress accessory, related to clothing or shroud.

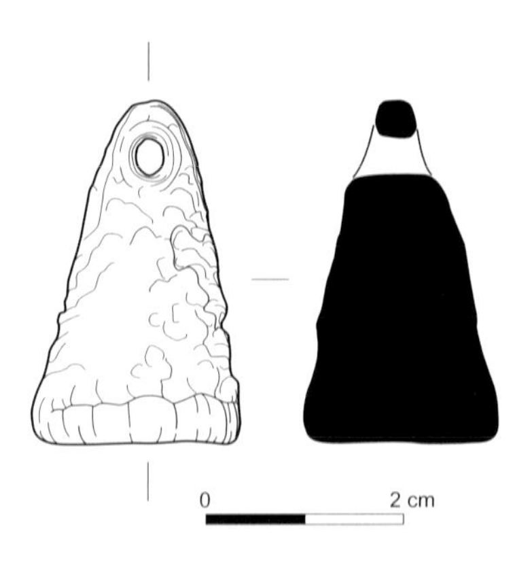

Figure 6.18
Lead (Cat. no. 36)

The weight, No. 36, is well-made of regular shape, with a pendant hole, possibly for fixing to some kind of apparatus. Its context could not be located. The flat base and pointed top means it could have stood on a scale pan, though could not have been stacked. Similar-sized, though cruder weights from London are suggested as either for handicrafts or commercial use (Egan 2005, 163).

32. Copper-alloy penannular bracelet. Plain, lentoid section, pointed terminals. Length (straightened) 113mm, diam (current) 41mm. XRF: Gunmetal, rich in lead and zinc. Lab. No. 04/14, September 1966 (probably from the early graveyard soil, possibly North Excavation Area). Figure 6.16.

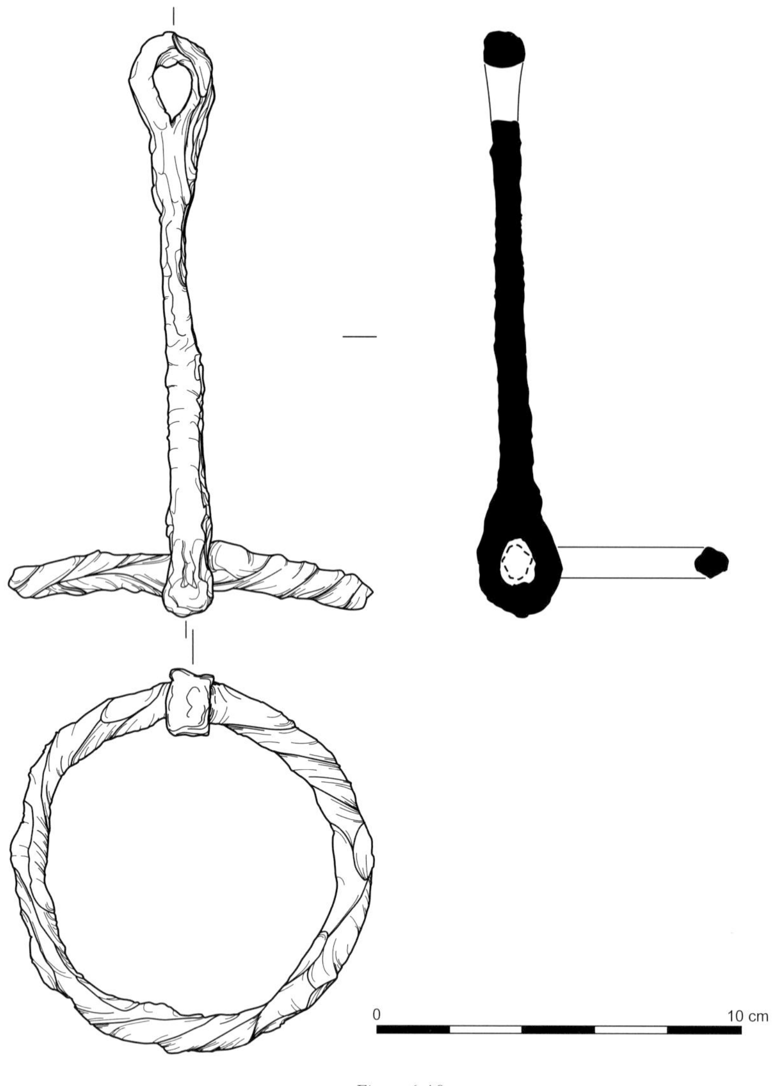

Figure 6.19
Iron coffin handle (Cat. no. 37)

33. Copper-alloy strap attachment. Small ornate D-shaped frame with narrow folded sheet plate, broken at end, no rivet holes remaining. Frame length 15mm, width 15mm. XRF: Gunmetal, rich in zinc. Lab. No. 01/01, 1962, lower black layer, S quadrant, within choir (early graveyard soil). Figure 6.17.

34. Copper-alloy bar mount with central lobe. Cross-hatched decoration on lobe, one rivet surviving. Length 16mm, width 10mm. XRF: Gunmetal, rich in lead and zinc. Lab. No. 52/18, 1960, Grave 3 (label only, no photographic evidence of location within grave). Figure 6.17.

35. Bone bead. Round bead, lathe turned, with two incised lines around middle. More worn on one side than other. Well-polished, abraded around perforation. Length 9mm, diam 10mm. Lab. No. 03/14, 1960, Grave 5, under right knee (upper tibia). Figure 6.17.

36. Lead weight. Small cast conical weight with pierced hole at pointed end. Height 34mm, diam 21mm, weight 65g. XRF: Pure lead (99%). Lab. No. 28/91, 1965, 'At bottom of green bed, Temp No. 18'. Figure 6.18.

6.8 COFFIN FITTINGS AND SHROUD FASTENINGS

JULIE FRANKLIN

6.8.1 Iron coffin nails and fittings

The iron finds are almost exclusively coffin nails, about half of which were assigned to particular grave fills. Many have traces of mineralised wood adhering to the shank, where the coffins have decayed *in situ*. The nails range from medium-sized flat-headed woodworking nails suitable for fixing corners, to small tacks, suitable for fixing down a lid. None of the nails has exactly recorded locations so no inferences can be made about coffin construction, but where a number of nails, particularly those with wood adhering to the shanks, are found in a grave, they can be taken as evidence for the presence of a coffin. Boyd states that at least a dozen nails were needed to make a coffin (Boyd 1989, 118). With the exception of Graves 12 and 14, this evidence for coffins is backed up by excavation notes of wooden remains *in situ*. The coffined burials contained between 10 and 45 nails.

Other types of coffin fitting include small iron straps from Graves 5, 6 and 21, possibly the remains of corner brackets (cf 8th/9th-century Whithorn coffins: Nicholson 1997, 414, fig. 10.93). A more ostentatious fitting comes from the foot end of Grave 21. Excavation photographs clearly show a large iron ring protruding from the ground in the centre of the foot end of the coffin (Plate 6.24). This almost certainly equates to No. 37, though the find was unlabelled. The ring is decoratively wrought with a twist in the metal, the rod must have been attached vertically to the centre of the foot end, probably by the means of a large staple, found in association. The loop

Plate 6.24
In situ view of coffin handle (Cat. no. 37)at foot of Grave 21

handle was found fused at an angle pointing into the grave and must therefore have been free-moving above the lid of the coffin. The upper end of this grave was unexcavated so there may have been a matching handle at the other end.

Further coffin furniture was found in a crate of Whithorn finds (Old Box Number 64), including a curved drop handle and part of a thin white metal (?tin) backing plate, but these are clearly from the post-medieval graveyard, probably very late (cf Cox 1998, 294, No. 7–10).

37. Coffin handle. Large wrought iron ring, of twisted square section. Attached to looped end of a rod. The other end of the rod has a similar loop, at a perpendicular angle. Diam of ring 98mm, length of rod 155mm. Lab. No. 59/07, Grave 21. Figure 6.19; Plate 6.24.

6.8.2 Copper-alloy shroud fastenings

Shrouds can be wound and stitched without the need for metal fastenings, but increasingly, in later medieval and early post-medieval graves, wire pins and laces were used to secure shrouds, with tags used to bind the ends of laces to prevent fraying and ease threading (Stones 1989, 159; Franklin & Collard 2006). Some 144 lace tags were found during Hill's excavations, almost all from 14th-century and later graves (Nicholson 1997, 375). The wire pin assemblage numbered 384 and though found in earlier contexts, the first large group is found in graves dating to between the late 14th and early 15th century (Nicholson 1997, 361). The pin and lace tag come from graves that date to the late 13th and 14th centuries.

Table 6.2 Summary of evidence for coffins and shrouds by phase. Wood identifications by Scott Timpany

Grave	*Stone cist*	*Shroud*	*Wooden coffin*	*Coffin nails and fittings*	*Wood id.*	*Grave-goods*	*Phase*
16	–	–	–	–	–	–	1
17	–	–	–	–	–	–	1
18	–	–	–	–	–	–	1
19	–	–	–	–	–	–	1
20	–	–	–	–	–	–	1
22	–	–	–	–	–	–	1
23	–	–	–	–	–	–	1
24	–	–	–	–	–	–	1
25	–	–	–	–	–	–	1
1	X	no	–	2 nails	–	X	3
2	X	no	–	8 nails (5 wooded)	cf Pinus	X	3
3	X	no	wooden lining	5 nails (1 wooded)	–	X	3
4	–	–	X	22 nails (most wooded)	Pinus	X	3
5	X	?toggle	–	6 nails (4 wooded) + strips	–	robbed?	3
6	–	–	X	27 nails (all wooded) + strips	cf Pinus	–	3
7	–	pin	X	13 nails (all wooded)	Pinus	X	3
8	X	–	–	12 nails (3 wooded)	–	robbed?	3
9	–	–	disturbed	–	–	–	3
10	–	–	X	33 nails (all wooded)	cf Pinus	–	3
11	–	–	X	10 nails (all wooded)	cf Pinus	–	3
12	–	lace tag	X	30 nails (most wooded)	cf Pinus	–	3
12A	–	–	disturbed	–	–	–	3
14	–	–	X	14 nails (most wooded)	Pinus	–	3
21	–	cloth	X	45 nails (most wooded) + strips & ring handle	cf Pinus	X	3
13	–	–	?	3 nails (2 wooded)	cf Pinus	–	4
15	–	–	X	10 nails (most wooded)	cf Pinus	–	4

38. Pin shank. Length 46mm. Lab. No. 03/22, 1964, Grave 7, possibly from left side

39. Lace tag. Simple rolled sheet tube, edge to edge seam, open ended. Length 14mm. Lab. No. 11/19, 1961, Grave 12.

6.8.3 Discussion of coffins and shrouds

The evidence for methods of burial is summarised in Table 6.2. None of the early burials (Graves 16–20, 22–25) appears to have had a coffin. These were originally buried outside the church, pre-dating the extension of the east end in *c* 1200 and hence are likely to be people of lower social standing than those buried later.

It seems likely that all the later burials within the extended east end were furnished with either coffins or stone cists, but never both. Only in Grave 3 were there wooden remains found inside a cist, but in this case, it would appear to be a wooden lining rather than a portable coffin. It is the only cist with no head recess and Ritchie notes 'against each wall a thin dark vertical stain was revealed as the infilled soil was removed' (Archive D9, p.83).

Only in Grave 13 are observations of wooden remains during excavation and photographic evidence not backed up by the finds, but these nails may well be among the many unlabelled examples. Graves 9 and 12A are the only later graves to contain no evidence at all for coffins, but both are truncated charnel, cut by Graves 10 and 12, respectively, both of which, apparently, contained enough nails for two. The mineralised wooden remains on the nails were examined to identify the species of wood used. All samples examined were of pine (Table 6.2).

The only evidence for shrouds comes from Graves 7, 12, 21 and possibly Grave 5 (see No. 35, 38, & 39 above, and Christiansen, Chapter 6.5.4), all towards the later part of the sequence, but it seems likely there were more. At this early date, they are more likely to have been simply stitched in place. Only in Graves 1, 2 and 3, where the occupants are fully dressed, would there seem to be positive evidence for no shroud.

6.9 THE GRAVE ASSEMBLAGES

VIRGINIA GLENN AND JULIE FRANKLIN

6.9.1 Dating

The objects are considered in the groups as found, in an attempt to establish *termini post* and *ante quem* for each grave. It must be remembered that contemporary or even near-contemporary precious metal objects were not normally used for burials. No less an individual than Hubert Walter, Archbishop of Canterbury (1198–1205), senior statesman under Henry II, Richard I and John, was buried in a splendid Purbeck marble tomb in his own cathedral, with accoutrements including a silver-gilt chalice and paten, generally considered to be no later than the mid-12th century (Stratford 1984, 294–5, no. 324d & e).

Many base metal objects were specially made for funerary purposes and enshrined in the written Constitutions and Rites of cathedrals such as Worcester and Durham. The former, written in 1230, specified that any church should have two chalices, one of silver, for use at mass and one of pewter, not consecrated, to be buried with the priest, while the latter said that on the death of a bishop or prior he was to be buried with a little chalice of silver, other metal or wax (Hope & Fallow 1886, 138–9). Numerous lead or pewter examples have survived in English medieval clerical tombs (Oman 1962, 196–8; Homer 1991, 78–9, note 93: see also Gammack 1883). One of the few medieval wax chalices to be found in Britain was in Kirkwall Cathedral, but it is later than the Whithorn material, being ascribed to Bishop Thomas Tulloch (1422–55) (Mooney 1925, 244, figs 4 & 5). Some of the rings found in episcopal burials, however, were possibly the personal property of the defunct, although in the case of bishops, they were not generally their consecration rings (Cherry 1981, 58–9; Cherry 1991, 205–9).

The graves containing (or considered to have originally contained) grave-goods are as follows: Graves 1–5, 7, 8 and 21.

Grave 1

- Stone cist, undisturbed (Chapter 6.6 for discussion of presence of mice), fully excavated
- Wooden crozier (No. 7), silver-gilt chalice (No. 9) and paten (No. 10), ornate 'pontifical' gold ring (No. 17), buckles (No. 30–31, for belt and mantle?) with mineralised cloth remains, tablet-woven silk textile
- Dating: *terminus post quem* mid-13th century (chalice, paten, finger ring and buckles)

The ring and the crozier indicate that the body was that of a bishop. Grave 1 is situated on the central axis of the church, which along with its contents suggests that its occupant was a figure of considerable importance.

There are strong similarities between the ring, the paten and the chalice bowl and the comparable items found in the grave of Walter de Gray, Archbishop of York (1216–55) (Oman 1971, 126–7, pls LIII–LIV).

Walter's gold ring, described by one writer as 'the only example of a "pontifical" ring found in an English bishop's or archbishop's grave' (Cherry 1987, 482, no. 635), has a large cabochon sapphire in an octagonal bezel surrounded by eight small emeralds and rubies in collets, as opposed to the Whithorn rectangular table-cut gem. It is just 2mm wider in diameter than the Whithorn ring and has very similar features, although the hoop is plain and not beaded, the sapphire is in a claw setting and the underside of the setting is octagonal with a triangular projection between each collet (Cherry 1981, 64–5, no. 127). When removed from the tomb, the York ring was quite damaged and missing a large section of its hoop (Ramm 1971, pl LIVc). The setting, particularly the reverse, now looks very sharp and symmetrical to the point of being rather mechanical and the hoop is entire with barely discernible joins. The 'delicate treatment' carried out by Mrs H Lane as described by A E A Werner (Ramm 1971, 137, 149) can hardly have been entirely responsible for this transformation.

The chalice bowls of both de Gray and Whithorn Grave 1 have a more or less identical profile, but this is fairly standard for a mid-13th-century date. The de Gray paten with its sexfoil central depression is unusual, but in the centre both have the *Manus Dei*.

Walter de Gray's tomb also contained a crozier, in this case made from walrus ivory (Wormald 1971, 125, pls XLIX–LII) and substantial textile remains. The crozier is a plain crook filled with a light delicate plant scroll, which Wormald compares with early 13th-century manuscript illumination. A metal band rather crudely set with stones has been added, perhaps to consolidate the object prior to the burial. The Whithorn Grave 1 crozier was quite dissimilar, probably a later design in a more developed Gothic style. The York textiles may provide a clue to the original appearance of the tablet-woven silk braids with a geometric, multiple diamond pattern at Whithorn (Plate 6.17).

Lowe's interpretation of the burial sequence, explored in Chapter 9, suggests that this is the grave of Bishop Henry (1253–1293). If so, it would be broadly contemporary with the similarly richly furnished graves of Walter de Gray, Archbishop of York (1216–1255) and Richard de Gravesend, Bishop of Lincoln (1258–1279) (Appendix 1). Formerly abbot of Holyrood, Henry was supported by the Comyn councillors of the young Alexander III and remained in his see during a long episcopate in spite of many contemporary political upheavals (Watt & Murray 2003, 169–70; Oram, Chapter 8). Henry had particularly close relations with York and made frequent visits there on church business, even regularly deputising for the archbishop himself which would have made him well aware of taste and customs at the Minster (Donaldson 1949, 130, 140). According to the *Melrose Chronicle*, Bishop Henry was actually consecrated by Walter de Gray, but although elected during the latter's episcopate, modern scholars incline to the opinion that his consecration in fact took place after the death of the Archbishop of York (Watt & Murray 2003, 169–70; see also Chapter 8.1.2).

Grave 2

- Stone cist, undisturbed, fully excavated
- Pewter chalice (No. 13), possibly also a paten, fairly simple gilt ring (No. 19), buckles (Nos. 27–29, for undershirt, belt and mantle?) with mineralised cloth remains, tablet-woven silk textile
- Dating: *terminus post quem* mid-13th century (chalice and buckles)

Although accorded a central position in the church, this interment (unless 'cleanly' robbed in antiquity) is apparently that of a less exalted priest.

Grave 3

- Stone cist with wooden lining, undisturbed, fully excavated
- Possible wooden crozier, a small finger ring (No. 18), buckle (No. 26, for belt?) with mineralised cloth remains
- Copper-alloy strap mount (No. 34, mid- to late 14th century): intrusive
- Dating: *terminus post quem* mid to late 13th century (finger ring and buckles)

Although including a possible wooden crozier denoting another bishop, the grave-goods here were quite modest with no chalice or paten and only a small finger ring. The strap mount is later than the assumed date of the grave but is almost certainly intrusive.

Grave 4

- Wooden coffin, truncated from knees down, fully excavated
- Pewter chalice (No. 14) and paten (No. 15)
- Dating: *terminus post quem* 13th century (chalice and paten)

The only liturgical items surviving in this grave were the chalice and paten, suggesting either greater losses due to the less durable material of the coffin or a lower-ranking member of the community. However, the latter seems unlikely, due to the privileged position of the burial within the cathedral.

Grave 5

- Stone cist, grave robbed, fully excavated
- Silver coin (No. 2, 1307–9), bone bead (No. 35, possible prayer bead or shroud toggle?)
- Dating: *terminus post quem* early 14th century (coin)

Although encased in a stone cist, this burial yielded no finds of religious significance, except a possible prayer bead.

However, a photograph of the newly opened cist shows clear drag marks in the thin layer of soil covering the floor and provides strong evidence of robbing at the time it was accidentally broken into by later grave-diggers. The grave, therefore, may well have contained a chalice and paten, and possibly more (Dingwall, Chapter 2.3.1).

Grave 7

- Wooden coffin, few skeletal remains, possibly very disturbed from chest down, fully excavated
- Enamelled gilt crozier (No. 6), silver chalice (No. 10) and paten (No. 11), decorative vestments represented by silver-gilt spangles (Nos. 21–24), glass bead (No. 25) and threads, fragment of ?shroud cloth, possible pinnacle (No. 8)
- Dating: *terminus post quem* mid-14th century (chalice, paten, spangles, wire shroud pin)

This is an unusual and contradictory burial for several reasons (Dingwall, Chapter 2.3.1; Lowe, Chapter 9). The wealth of the grave-goods seems at odds with the manner of burial and the manner of burial seems at odds with the location. However, the crozier and silver plate clearly indicate the presence of another notable bishop.

If we accept that the most likely candidate for this bishop is Simon de Wedale (d 1355) (Lowe, Chapter 9), this would mean he was buried with an old crozier, disused because its knop had been lost or hopelessly damaged, which is not improbable, and an elaborate, almost new, chalice and paten, which is unusual. Current research into the history of chalice design indicates a date no earlier than *c* 1350 and more likely some time after. The spangled vestments also suggest a mid-14th century or later date (as would the pinnacle, if it came from this grave).

The possibly brand new and expensive items in this grave add to its strangeness. We may once again be looking at an origin in York, where fashion and taste vied with London. It may be possible that the 'mullet' chalice foot was introduced in sophisticated artistic milieux earlier than previously thought. Wedale was consecrated in York in December 1326 and at Westminster on 1 February 1327, but no Galloway bishop offered formal obedience to York after his death (Watt & Murray 2003, 168, 170–1; Oram, Chapter 8).

Grave 8

- Stone cist, grave robbed?, fully excavated
- No finds
- Dating: unknown (on basis of finds)

There was some disturbance around the chest area of this skeleton with some associated white staining seen in the excavation photograph, possibly lead remains. There is also some brown staining on the pelvis which may in fact be the remains of flesh, preserved by the presence of a bactericidal metal such as lead or silver (Dingwall, Chapter 2.3.1; Henderson, Chapter 4.1.3). As with Grave 5, grave-robbing is implied. Given the nature of the assemblages in the other stone cists, a body without grave-goods would otherwise seem a little incongruous.

Grave 21

- Wooden coffin with wrought iron ring handle, undisturbed, only lower end excavated
- Pewter chalice (No. 16), layered cloth (probably shroud remains)
- Dating: *terminus post quem* 13th century (chalice)

This interment is apparently that of a less exalted priest. However, the upper end of the grave was not excavated and further grave-goods may have been deposited with the burial.

6.10 WINDOW GLASS

JULIE FRANKLIN

There were 28 sherds of window glass, all generally small and in very poor condition, appearing black and opaque. Eight of the sherds are painted in the grisaille tradition. This uses a paste of lead and iron oxides, which on firing turns red-brown, though appearing black when seen against the light (Graves 1995, 111). It is known from as early as the late 12th century at York Minster (Graves 1995, 112) and has been found at many 13th- and 14th-century wealthy Scottish ecclesiastical sites (Graves 1995; Graves 2002; Graves 2006; Stone 1989; Dunn 2001). No sherds of coloured glass could be identified. These, being more valuable, were generally saved and reused. Twelve of the sherds are grozed, and one (No. 42) also has a distinct came shadow, indicating these, at least were definitely part of a window, rather than off-cuts from glazing. There were no accompanying finds of lead cames. There is no evidence for the production of glass in medieval Scotland. The glass was probably imported from England or Northern Europe, though conceivably painted in Scotland (Graves 1995, 112). The glass was scattered across the area, within and around the graves. The disturbance caused by grave-digging means all that can be said of their original location is that they were presumably part of the windows at the east end of the church.

The painted sherds (Figure 6.20) include one (No. 40) with curving tendrils and a cross-hatched background. The simplicity of the design finds close parallels at the abbeys of Dundrennan (Dunn 2001) and Glenluce (Cruden 1952) and early sherds from Jedburgh (Graves 1995). Cross-hatching

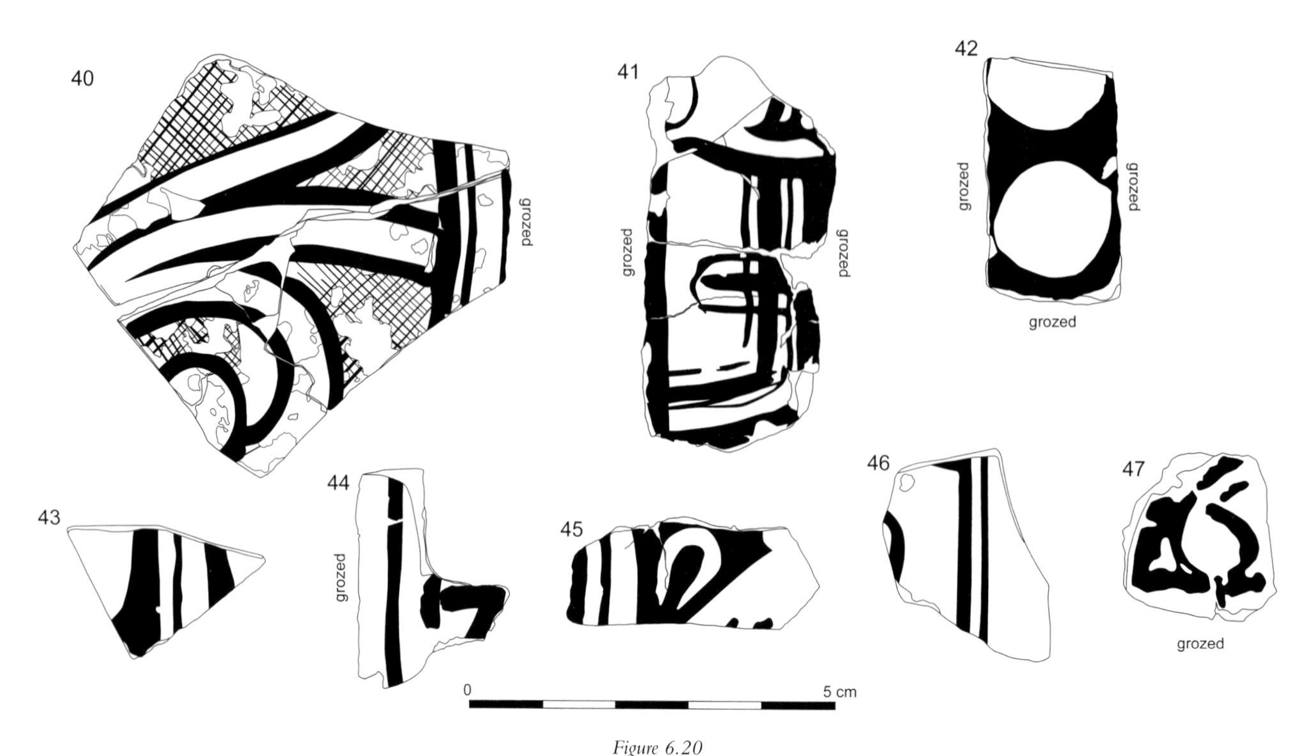

Figure 6.20
Painted window glass (Cat. nos 40–47). Some of the glass appears stylistically to relate to the expansion of the church *c* 1200, while some is likely to post-date the fire of 1286 and relate to subsequent rebuilding and repair

is found on early sherds, and is superseded by plain grounds in the second half of the 13th century (Graves 2002, 133). Unfortunately little remains of the trefoil, the shape of which would also have given a clue to its stylistic affinities and dating. Other sherds have plain grounds, but are too small to give much away as regards design. The beaded sherd (No. 42) has came shadows along both long edges indicating it was used as a narrow border. Beaded borders are commonly found in 13th- and 14th-century windows (Graves 1995, 112, illus 88:3).

The only sherds from securely stratified contexts are two undecorated fragments from Grave 7 and a painted sherd (No. 44) from Grave 11. In both cases, the sherds are grozed, indicating they were used, and their deposition must represent destruction or repair of existing windows. There must, therefore, have been decorative windows in place by at least the early 14th century, and probably some time earlier. All the other sherds of window glass are unprovenanced.

There are no historical records for the site that specifically refer to its glazing. There are, however, records that the church was badly damaged by fire in 1286 and there are suggestions that building repairs were undertaken in the late 13th and early 14th centuries. The next recorded major phase of work is not until the early 15th century (Oram, Chapter 8).

Stylistically, sherd No. 40 predates the fire of 1286. It is likely, therefore, to be part of the extended eastern arm of the church, conventionally dated to the period around 1200. As windows would have been one of the first casualties of any fire, it would seem reasonable to assume that major repairs would be needed in the late 13th century and thus the glass here probably represents at least two major phases of glazing.

6.11 FLOOR TILES

JULIE FRANKLIN

There are eight sherds of plain square green-glazed floor tile. The majority was found in 1960 in the backfill from the 1957 season. Similarities in manufacture imply they were all originally part of the same floor.

They are rather carelessly made, of a coarse sandy, slightly micaceous red fabric, reduced grey in the core. All are slightly sunken and uneven on the base, and slightly bowed on the top. Drag marks on the base indicate they have been shaped upside down. The bevel usually found on tiles, making them slightly wider on the top surface, to minimise gaps between them when laid, is either absent or slightly reversed. Compared to contemporary tiles, they are towards the smaller and thinner end of the range, at 21–5mm thick (average 22mm). The only complete tile measures 142 x 137mm. All are glazed olive green, though this often does not quite reach the edges.

Five of the eight sherds have either mortar on the base or are worn on top to the extent that the glaze has worn off almost completely, confirming that they were part of a floor, probably for some time, rather than waste from floor laying. One appears to have been laid upside down, with a broad band of glaze running across the un-mortared side, a feature sometimes seen on the base of tiles, where glaze has run during firing.

They are probably locally made, very much in the tradition of Scottish redware pottery. The nearest comparable tiled floor is from Glenluce Abbey (Cruden 1952). Excavations there in the 1950s uncovered over 100 square metres of tiled flooring, much of which was left *in situ*. Most tiles were plain, *c* 155mm square by *c* 30mm thick; a few were incised with crudely drawn designs. Norton (1994, 157) speculatively dates them to the 15th century. Cadzow Castle near Hamilton was extensively tiled, probably in the 1530s, again using mostly plain, though somewhat larger tiles (Franklin forthcoming A). A floor at Linlithgow Palace, though previously thought to date to *c* 1504 (Norton 1994, 153), now seems more likely to date to *c* 1540, from architectural evidence and connections with Cadzow (Dunbar 1999, 167–8; Franklin forthcoming A). A number of tiles of more comparable thickness at 22–3mm were found at Stirling Castle, although none was *in situ*. They were found in a 16th-century midden (Franklin forthcoming B).

There are no reports of *in situ* tiles having been found at any of the many excavations at Whithorn, so the original location of this floor must remain speculative. There are, in fact, no reports of any floor tiles found at all, though in the case of William Galloway's work in the late 19th century they would not necessarily be the type of find deemed worthy of collection or mention. It is possible Ritchie himself found more but discarded them during the original rush to rescue the first of the bishops' graves in 1957. However, the only floor surface that Ritchie observed during the course of his excavation was one of stone, albeit one that was extremely patchy and much disturbed (Dingwall, Chapter 2.3.1).

The relative rarity of tiled floors at this period and their exclusivity to high-status sites would imply they had to be specially commissioned from a local potter and it follows that the area to be paved was sizeable enough. Tile production is often linked to pottery kilns (Stopford 1993, 103). Findings of waster tiles at pottery kilns sites such as Throsk (Caldwell & Dean 1992, 22) and Hamilton (Franklin & Hall forthcoming), indicate these were occasionally produced. There is even a historical record of tiles being ordered from Throsk for Stirling Castle (Caldwell & Dean 1992, 5).

The most likely location for the Whithorn tiles is the South Chapel that was built around 1500 (Chapter 8.2.1), although there is no record of any surviving original floor. The only sherd whose find-spot can be located, though presumably not *in situ*, is recorded as having been found 'on top of wall S of Grave 9' (ie over the south choir wall). Assuming the whole of the South Chapel (roughly 20' by 45') was tiled, it would have involved over 4,000 tiles and begs the question why so little might remain. After the Reformation, however, the area was used as a graveyard. The resulting disturbance, weathering and plant growth would have wreaked considerable destruction by the time Galloway came to the site.

6.12 POTTERY

JULIE FRANKLIN

6.12.1 Prehistoric and Roman

Prehistoric

There are two large sherds and a number of smaller fragments of prehistoric pottery dark grey with buff surfaces, coarse, thick-walled and shapeless with large mica inclusions. They are of later prehistoric date (Fraser Hunter, pers comm). It is not clear, however, if these were recovered from Ritchie's excavations; or, indeed, if they come from Whithorn at all. They have no context information and they were found in a box with some Whithorn ironwork and window glass. Given the evidence for a possible Romanised settlement nearby, discussed below by Wallace, it is not impossible they could be from Whithorn.

Samian ware

COLIN WALLACE

A single piece of Roman pottery came from an early feature on the site. It is a worn body sherd originally from a red-slipped fineware (samian) bowl imported from what is now France. The vessel itself is likely to have arrived here in the 2nd century AD. The context (as recorded from the finds bag) was given as 'pit beneath Early Christian cemetery, 1962'. This presumably refers to the earliest graves lying on top of bedrock, which turned out to be no earlier than the 11th century. Nothing more is known of the 'pit', except this one reference, and no other finds are linked to it. Potentially then, it is *in situ* in an Iron Age pit, though the level of abrasion suggests it was buried rather later.

Description

A heavily worn body sherd of Central Gaulish samian (National Roman Fabric Reference Collection fabric

LEZ SA 2: Tomber & Dore 1998, 32–3), either trimmed or naturally broken to a roughly rectangular shape. Weight 15.7 grammes. The red slip is almost completely gone, just surviving in one or two areas of the outer surface (thanks to deeper parts of the original moulded decoration) and towards the bottom of the inner surface. It is from the middle part of the body of a form 37 decorated bowl and traces of the panelled decoration can be made out below the ovolo band. This is enough to suggest, tentatively, that the original vessel was of early to mid-Antonine date.

Discussion

The *terminus ante quem* for the deposition of the samian sherd in its pit is provided by the 11th- and 12th-century radiocarbon dates associated with the graves of Phase 1 (Dalland & Lowe, Chapter 7). It is certainly another useful piece of evidence to support the case for 2nd to 4th-century AD settlement in the locality (Wilson 2001, 91,107). Whithorn was the first known Christian community in Britain beyond Hadrian's Wall. The origins and character of the very earliest settlement are not yet clearly understood, there still being a gap in the sequence at Whithorn between the Bronze Age enclosure and the early medieval site. Because of the range of existing interpretations, the Roman material from the nearby 1984–91 excavations, though clearly residual, is of great interest (Hill 1997, 292–7). The Roman finds (alongside pottery, there was also glass and a coin of the House of Constantine) may result from either settlement or later collection. The Roman pottery comprised Central Gaulish samian, South Spanish amphora, Nene Valley colour-coat and unsourced fine oxidised ware body sherds (Dickinson & Millett in Hill 1997, 293–4). The absence of greywares or BB1 and the possible reuse of a Roman-period glass bangle (Price *in* Hill 1997, 294) might suggest that this was material 'collected' from a Roman site in the post-Roman centuries, were it not for the fact that all the Roman finds were quite well-dispersed across the area excavated in the 1980s and through the excavated sequence.

In south-west Scotland in the 2nd century AD and later, comparable samian ware was imported and found at sites such as Luce Bay (burial), Brighouse Bay and McCulloch's Castle. A more restricted range of wares was either available to, or chosen by, the occupants of sites north of Hadrian's Wall, when compared to excavated sites in modern Cumbria. But the differences are those of degree rather than substance. It has been suggested that it is reasonable to expect some complete 2nd-century samian vessels to have survived into the 4th century (Wallace 2006). A Scottish example comes from the eastern Borders, with the association between some plain samian and some Late Roman BB1 at Hownam Rings (Gillam, in Piggott 1948, 217). An extreme example of curation (of a chip of decorated samian some 12mm x 8mm) comes from the possible foundation grave at the otherwise largely 7th-century long-cist cemetery of Hallow Hill, at St Andrews in Fife (Proudfoot 1996, 420 & 438).

The interpretation of the occurrence of samian on non-Roman and post-Roman sites in what is now Scotland has been helpfully contested between Fraser Hunter and the Alcocks (eg Hunter 2001, 292, *contra* Alcock & Alcock 1987, 131 and Alcock & Alcock 1990, 130–6). In this author's view, the dating evidence is such that, for the Argyll sites of Kildonan Bay, Dùn Fhinn, Kintyre and Dùn an Fheurain, Lorn, the contexts of deposition of their samian can be consigned to the post-Roman period along with those at Loch na Beirgh, Lewis, Dunadd, Argyll (1929 excavations), Little Dunagoil, Bute, Mote of Mark, Dumfriesshire and Kiondroghad, Isle of Man. In the south-west, the samian sherd and the (rather later) E-ware from Buiston crannog both came from the horizon of activity dated late 6th/7th century AD (Crone 2000,32–4 & 164). Castlehill, Dalry, is another early medieval site also yielding sherds of samian (Alcock 1996, 52–5), as are Doon Hill and Dunbar Castle Park in East Lothian.

There are more specific parallels for samian sherds on later religious sites. Excavation of the site at St Ninian's Point, Bute (an early medieval chapel and earlier burials), produced a well-preserved sherd of decorated Central Gaulish samian from the floor of the chapel (Scott 1985, 30). Dorothy Marshall (1985) contrasted its condition with that of the 'small, very much rolled' sherds of samian from Little Dunagoil. Nearer to Whithorn, it is notable that other medieval ecclesiastical sites in south-west Scotland (perhaps with early medieval antecedents) have yielded Roman pottery. For example, the publication of the 1912 clearance work at the late medieval (with a possible earlier chapel) Castle Loch island, Mochrum, included some previously unrecorded Roman pottery: a worn sherd of Central Gaulish f37 bowl (Steer *in* Radford 1950, 60) and sherds from a cream-slipped flagon and a fine oxidised bowl (Gillam *in* Radford 1950, 60; fig 7). An unstratified sherd of plain samian came from a site at Chapelton, Haugh of Urr (Thomas *in* Alexander 2004, 68), that itself may be medieval or early medieval in date (Thomas, in Alexander 2004, 73–4). Other (vaguely identified) Roman(?) pottery sherds have been claimed from the medieval church sites at Brydekirk and Kirkmirran, Dalbeattie. The collection of Roman material for reuse is, of course, well-attested from sites like Hoddom (building stones: Lowe 2006, 38–47) and possibly also Barhobble (glass bangle: Cormack 1995).

Modified samian sherds have been found in Late Roman and early medieval contexts in southern Britain, ground down and shaped (eg as spindle whorls). One sherd from Worcester even bears a (?)Middle Saxon runic inscription (Page 2004) and another from London seems to have been used as a trial-piece by someone working out Late Saxon interlace patterns (Wheeler 1935, 194 & pl XXI). Closer to Whithorn, collected pieces include a roundel made from a South Gaulish, Flavian f37 bowl found in a 10th/11th-century context in Dublin (Bélier 1982). The long-running Dublin urban excavations have produced more samian (Bateson 1976, 179) and even a sherd of a successor ware (Late Roman Argonne red-slipped) in a 12th/13th-century context (Bateson 1973, 87). Plain and decorated (Central Gaulish f37, late Antonine) samian sherds are known from Carrickfergus in late medieval contexts (eg Brannon 1982). It is worth pointing out, however, that the attempt made in the 1980s to explain the finds of samian sherds in such contexts as items prized for medicinal use (Bradley 1982) relied far too much on an anachronistic reading-back of medieval and later references to medicinal red clay or *terra sigillata* rather than what we call samian ware (King 1985). The Whithorn 1962 samian sherd is only lightly modified and certainly unaccompanied; its cultural biography potentially extends from Roman-period importation as a vessel, through possible long life, fragmentation and curation to early medieval deposition in a pit.

6.12.2 Medieval and post-medieval pottery

JULIE FRANKLIN

The rest of the pottery from Ritchie's excavation spans the period from the 13th to the 17th century and is made up predominantly of locally produced redwares. Sherd size is, for the most part, small, consistent with residual sherds in graveyard soil. Very few have any kind of stratigraphically identifiable context information. Four small and unremarkable local redware sherds were from or closely associated with Graves 1, 2, 8 and 12, which date to the 13th and 14th centuries, but this helps very little. Most of the pottery comes from the 1960 season. There is none from 1957 and only a little from the later 1960s. Though large quantities of pottery would not be expected in a graveyard, there is a distinct possibility that pottery was not initially deemed worth collecting, or that some has since been thrown away or lost.

There are four sherds of pottery which appear to derive from Tabraham's excavations. As they are of some interest and have not been published before, they have been included in this report. They were found in a grocery box, stored with the rest of the Ritchie archive, labelled 'Whithorn Priory, Excavation, 1972, outside area', containing some loose human bone and some unlabelled mortar samples. The two bags of pottery were both accompanied by cardboard labels marked 'WP72, Field, Area 2, unstrat in rubble', and 'WP72, Field, Area 3, unstrat'. It is believed that these sherds came from the Glebe Field (Christopher Tabraham, pers comm; Tabraham 1979, Field I; Hill 1997, 9), where well-constructed walls and traces of human burials were found (Tabraham 1979, 33); no mention, however, is made of small finds. The sherds are unstratified, but all date to the 16th or 17th centuries. Activity in the Glebe Field seems to quieten down after the Reformation. There was a substantial stone building at the north side of the field, interpreted as the Commendator's House, which was refurbished as the Manse at the end of the 17th century. The late date of the pottery implies it is related to the occupation of this structure.

Another bag of sherds was labelled only 'Whithorn Priory 12.9.51'. This predates Ritchie's involvement at the Priory and places it squarely in one of Radford's trenches. Radford excavated at Whithorn in 1949–51 and 1953, including various trenches towards the east end of the church. The location of his finds is not known and he makes no reference to any in his report (Radford 1956). The 1951 season, he states (rather unhelpfully), 'saw the completion of various minor tasks' (Radford 1956, 131).

Local medieval redwares
(44 sherds; Figure 6.21)
This is the largest group of pottery. It is a broad group with some variation in fabric, but typically it is hard fired, red to pale red, with a reduced grey core, to a greater or lesser extent. In texture it varies from coarse quartz gritted to sparsely gritted and sandier versions. It equates with Clarke's

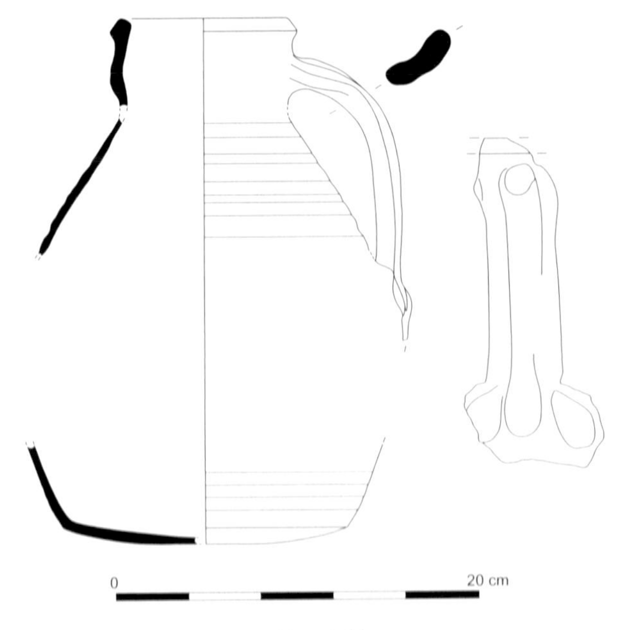

Figure 6.21
Medieval redware jug (Cat. no. 48)

Whithorn Fabrics 2 and 7, which are essentially oxidised and reduced versions of the same (Clarke 1997, 511–4).

One unglazed sherd has a faint trace of sooting and may be from a cooking pot. All other sherds represent jugs, with an olive green glaze which generally becomes patchy towards the base. There is little evidence of form: four strap handles, a rod handle. Two bases are thumbed, a common feature seen on 13th- and 14th-century jugs. Decoration is limited to four sherds, possibly from the same jug, though found in different seasons, with rows of stabbed impressions; one also with an applied strip. Another small sherd has a similar applied strip but is coloured with iron.

The most complete jug in the assemblage (No. 48) is, in fact, from Radford's 1951 excavation (see above). It is represented by ten sherds, some of which join to form the complete handle, a fragment of rim, a large piece of the shoulder and two sherds from the base. The gritty fabric and thin walls with pronounced rilling suggest a probable 13th-century date for this jug. The (relatively) intact state of this pot suggests it was not from the graveyard soil, but its context is unknown.

Post-medieval greyware
(2 sherds)
These were sherds of 16th- or 17th-century olive-glazed jugs. One is probably related to the occupation of the post-Reformation Commendator's House (see above). The other was unlabelled, though from a box of finds from the 1962 season.

French wares
(2 sherds)
The first was a body sherd from a probable Saintonge jug with characteristic mottled green glaze. These vessels were imported from south-west France between the mid-13th and mid-14th centuries and are associated with the Bordeaux wine trade (Brown 2002, 26). The fabric is relatively coarse, containing some large white quartz inclusions as well as the more usual red haematite, and thus is probably an early example of the type (George Haggarty, pers comm). A sketch section accompanying the find suggests it was from the graveyard soil under the cut for the stone cist of Grave 8 (Dingwall, Chapter 2.3.1).

Saintonge wares are common finds in medieval contexts in Ireland and there is a scattering around the south-west coast of Scotland (Haggarty 2006, Map C). It has been found at the abbeys of Glenluce (Cruden 1951, 179) and Dundrennan (Radley & Will 2001), while it made up the largest group of medieval imported wares from excavations in the burgh of Ayr (Franklin forthcoming F). Hill's Whithorn excavations produced 37 sherds, concentrated in the 14th- to 16th- century graveyard, which were thought to have been displaced from underlying 13th-century debris (Clarke 1997, 515). There were also probably sherds from Tabraham's excavations, although these have since been lost (Haggarty 2006, file 43, p.17).

The second sherd is later and is probably related to the occupation of the Commendator's House (see above). It is a small strap handle of a fine creamy buff fabric with a slightly darker surface and occasional small inclusions of red haematite and mica. It has features in common with jugs from the Loire region (Hurst *et al* 1986, 100; Haggarty 2006, File 32), which were imported in the 16th and 17th centuries, probably as containers for olive oil. Hill's excavations produced two sherds of narrow-necked Loire jugs from 16th-century debris (Clarke 1997, 516). However, it may in fact be from the Saintonge region (George Haggarty, pers comm), possibly the handle to some form of jug or a chafing dish (Hurst *et al* 1986, 78; Haggarty 2006, File 14). Chafing dish sherds have been found at nearby Cruggleton Castle (Haggarty 1985) and Glenluce Abbey (Cruden 1951).

North Devon sgraffito ware
(1 sherd; Figure 6.22)
There were four conjoining sherds from the shoulder of a small sgraffito-decorated jug. Again, it is probably related to the occupation of the Commendator's House. The fabric is fine, hard fired, reddish brown, with greying margins. The exterior is covered with a white slip, which has spilled over onto the inside of the neck. A floral design has been scratched through the slip on the exterior, comprising a series of fine lines, larger areas and comb impressions. The jug has then been lead glazed, the design appearing brown on golden-yellow.

This type of pottery was produced in the Bideford and Barnstaple area and was widely traded in the 17th century, particularly the second half of the century. In her book on the industry, Grant publishes a jug of similar form and decoration (Grant 1983, facing title page). The wares are well known in Wales and Ireland, and have been found as far afield as the New World. Trade records show occasional cargoes travelling as far north as Whitehaven in Cumbria and Belfast. There is no record of it travelling to Scotland, but, clearly, if it were to be found anywhere in the country, this coast at the north end of the Irish Sea is the most likely place. Bowls and dishes are more usual imports in Ireland (eg McCutcheon 1997, 92), jugs seem to travel more rarely. It was probably more of a souvenir or item of personal trade, a brightly coloured jug with an improving inscription for the minister's table perhaps?

To the author's knowledge, this was the first sherd of North Devon pottery identified in Scotland. However, such is its rarity here that it is possible that sherds have gone unnoticed. A recent chance discovery in an archive box from Greyfriars Church, Kirkcudbright (unpublished watching brief, Headland Archaeology) revealed three conjoining sherds from a North Devon sgraffito dish, misidentified as '19th-century pottery', which, to the untrained eye, it does resemble. The similarity between the two sites, both ecclesiastical, and within 20 miles of each other along the same stretch of coast, is striking. There is also a contemporary sherd from the Donyatt pottery in Somerset, found in Dumbarton (Hall 2004, 339), showing further links between south-west Scotland and south-west England.

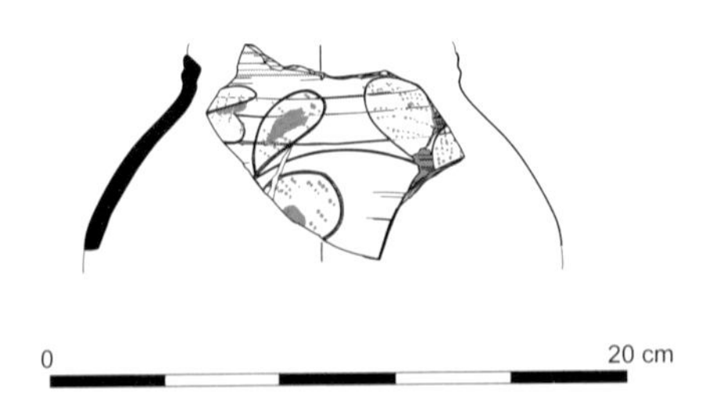

Figure 6.22
North Devon sgraffito jug sherd (Cat. no. 49)

6.13 INDENTED SLABS

KIRSTY DINGWALL

Four large stone slabs lie at the eastern end of the priory. Three stand against the north parapet wall (Whithorn 2, 3 and 4), and one (Whithorn 1) against the wall to the east. Although it is not known exactly when the stones were placed in this position, it must have occurred after Galloway's rebuilding of the eastern end of the church in the late 19th century, as they are clamped to the section of wall which he added. An extract from a Historic Scotland record file of the monuments at Whithorn, dated 1922 (PRO ref MW/1/39), records two of the stones already clamped to the parapet walls (albeit in different positions to where they are now), that another lay 'to the north of the foundation of the Lady Chapel' and that the fourth was still in use as a gravestone dedicated to William McCall, dated 1875.

A drawing of one of these stones (Whithorn 1, referred to by Ritchie as 'the Tournai stone') formed part of the Ritchie archive (Archive A2) but the circumstances of its discovery and its inclusion in the record are nowhere explained; nor does Ritchie mention the stone in any of his typescript reports (Archive D8 & D9). The subsequent discovery of Greenhill's little known paper on Whithorn's monumental brass-mounted slabs (Greenhill 1949) was to provide the answer, identifying it as the reused 1875 gravestone (whose reverse face, of course, is currently hidden). Clearly, then, this must have been one of the gravestones that was removed by Ritchie during the course of the excavation, probably in 1960 (Dingwall, Chapter 2.2). The other fragments (Whithorn 2–4) are assumed to have come to light during the course of Galloway's late 19th-century excavations in this area.

Previously overlooked, these four fragments, which go to form two large slabs which originally held monumental brasses, shed considerable light on the later medieval east end of the church. All descriptions of the slabs (unless explicitly stated otherwise) are given relative to their reconstructed form in Figures 6.23 and 6.24.

6.13.1 Whithorn 1

(Figure 6.23; Plate 6.25)
Large fragment of Tournai limestone, 1.44m x 1.12m and roughly 0.15m thick, although tapering to 0.11m around its edges. The slab is currently clamped to the east wall of Galloway's parapet and stands on its left-hand edge. The stone is broken and forms the upper part of a larger slab.

There is an extensive crack across its top right corner, and from this another smaller crack runs towards the main break at the base of the fragment. The cracked fragments have been reconstructed into a whole, although no attempt appears to have been made to repair the detail on the face of the stone. It seems likely that these cracks occurred after 1967, as the final photograph in the Ritchie archive shows Whithorn 2, 3 and 4 clamped in their existing positions, and a large slab, clearly Whithorn 1, to the right of them and intact. Ritchie's drawing of the slab (Archive A2), moreover, shows it as undamaged. The stone has also suffered some degree of weathering, and this is particularly apparent on the left side, where the carved indents are far shallower and have a smoother profile.

On the face of the slab there are effectively three 'levels' of carving: Level 1, the face of the stone which would have been visible on the completed monument; Level 2 areas showing pecking which would have held the brass plates; and Level 3, comprising further bands that have been more deeply carved and which would have accommodated joining bars holding the complete brass together. Around the exterior of the stone, framing the main section is a narrow band of Level 2 carving, which would have held the brass plates inscribed with the marginal inscription. Within this band, there are then a series of small Level 3 carved rectangular areas which measure roughly 80 x 40mm and would have held the joining bars.

The marginal inscription surrounds an area of Level 1 carving, where the stone has not been substantially altered beyond basic dressing of the slab as a whole. This defines the central image of the slab and comprises a band surrounding a rectangular area. At the top of the slab there are two inner linear elements which come to a distinct stop roughly two-thirds of the way down the fragment and frame the effigy below.

The area containing the central image is largely Level 2 carving, notable for the very obvious peck marks covering its entire area. The whole area would have been filled with brass plates, including the two linear panels down the sides which have coronet-shaped carvings at their top. Much of the definition of this carving has been lost, but the outline of the coronets can be seen. Greenhill suggests that the area between the two linear elements could have been filled with what he describes as 'tabernacle work', presumably some sort of design detail which suggests structural elements. At the very top of this part of the slab, the edge of the Level 2 carving (which is deliberately not square) gives an indication of the shape of the missing brass plate which, in turn, almost certainly will have reflected that of the structural detail present.

At the base of the fragment, below the canopy filled with structural designs, there are two further distinct elements. The first is an area of Level 1 carving, edged with a series of fleur-de-lis shapes. The curve of the features can only be seen in some cases, and many of the faces have worn or broken off. The second element is an area of Level 2 carving lying within the Level 1 work, a sub-triangular shape with rounded points on two of the ends. The full extent of these features is beyond the break at the bottom of the fragment. The Level 1 carving represents part of the underside of the canopy, effectively intended as a carved niche with fleur-de-lis detail. Below this, the sub-triangular shape is a bishop's mitre, apparently lying on a block or cushion. Greenhill describes them as the 'indents of a mitre and tasselled cushion on which the head of the effigy rested' (Greenhill 1949, 234), and the correlation between the rounded points of the sub-triangular shape and the tassels is convincing. Presumably a further two tassels would have been present further down either side of the head, with more of the outline of the cushion, but this has been lost to the break between Whithorn 1 and 2.

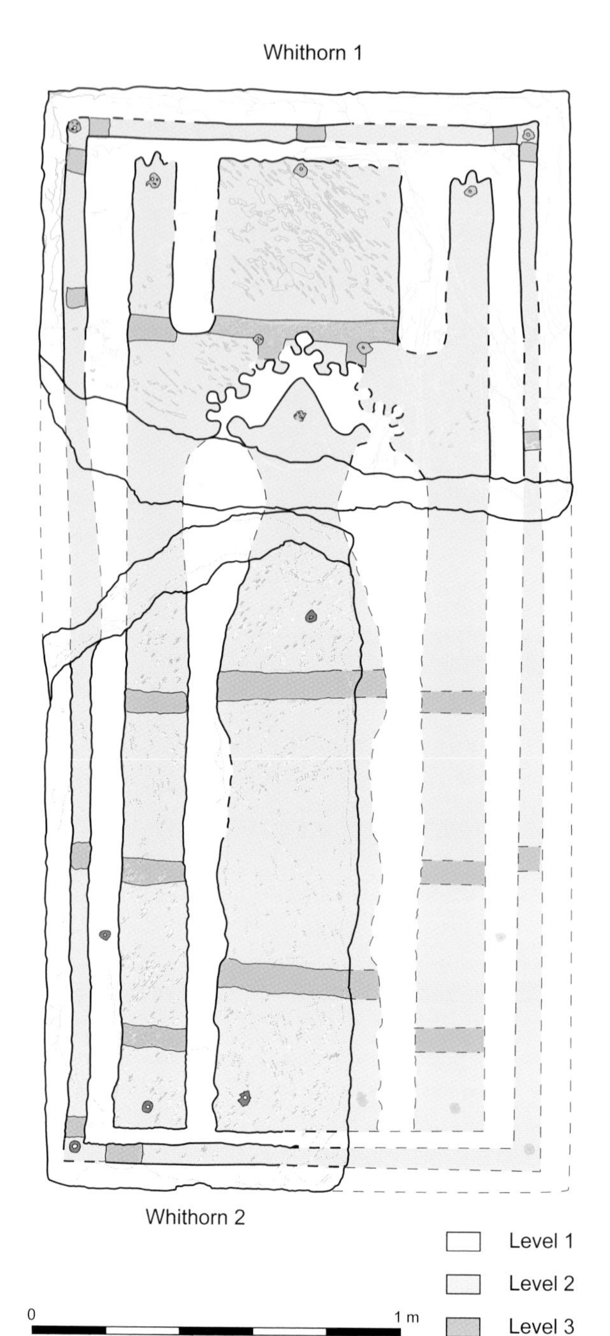

Figure 6.23
Indented slab: Whithorn 1 and 2. The reconstruction shows the three different levels of carving, and gives an impression of what the brass effigy may have looked like

6.13.2 Whithorn 2

(Figure 6.23; Plate 6.26)
Large slab of Tournai limestone, 1.76m x 0.85m and 0.15m thick. The slab is currently clamped to the north wall of Galloway's parapet and stands on what would have been its bottom edge. The top and right edges of the slab are broken and the latter, although heavily weathered, may have been retouched, indicative perhaps of later reuse. Overall, the stone forms the lower left-hand part of a larger slab.

Plate 6.25
Indented slab: Whithorn 1. The indented slabs were photographed at night using raking light to highlight the carved detail

The sequence of Level 1, 2 and 3 carvings can also be seen in this fragment. Again present around the exterior of the stone is a band of Level 2 carving designed to hold the brass marginal inscription. This is heavily weathered and only partially visible on the bottom edge, but within it, small rectangular areas of Level 3 carving can again be distinguished. These deeper areas would have held the joining bars of the marginal inscription.

The areas of Level 2 carving on the slab continue the divisions seen in Whithorn 1, with the right-hand portion forming the main part of the effigy and the left-hand area forming a frame to the main image. The left hand area (375mm wide) would presumably have been mirrored with something similar on the right hand side of the complete slab. Along the edge of the central image, there appears to be some detail to the carving, with a number of definite curved indents along the left side. This clearly indicates that the brass inlay was shaped to reflect the detail carved on the brass itself, most likely here the folds of a robe.

6.13.3 Whithorn 3

(Figure 6.24; Plate 6.27)
Large slab of Tournai limestone, 1.46m wide, up to 0.90m long and 0.14m thick. The slab is currently clamped to the north wall of Galloway's parapet and stands on its (probable) left-hand edge. The fragment is broken along its bottom edge and is likely to join (although not directly) with Whithorn 4.

Whithorn 3 is noticeably different from Whithorn 1 and 2 in that it does not appear to have an indent for a marginal inscription. Around the edge of the stone is a broad panel of Level 1 carving, present on the left, top and right edges, although it is heavily worn on the left side. While part of the face of this area has flaked off, its slightly polished nature can also be distinguished. Within the central area defined by this raised border, the majority of the slab is a rectangular area of Level 2 carving, within which are numerous horizontal and vertical linked bands of Level 3 carving. No further detail can be discerned within the central area, and the implication is that the whole was filled with a patchwork of brass plates,

Plate 6.26
Indented slab: Whithorn 2

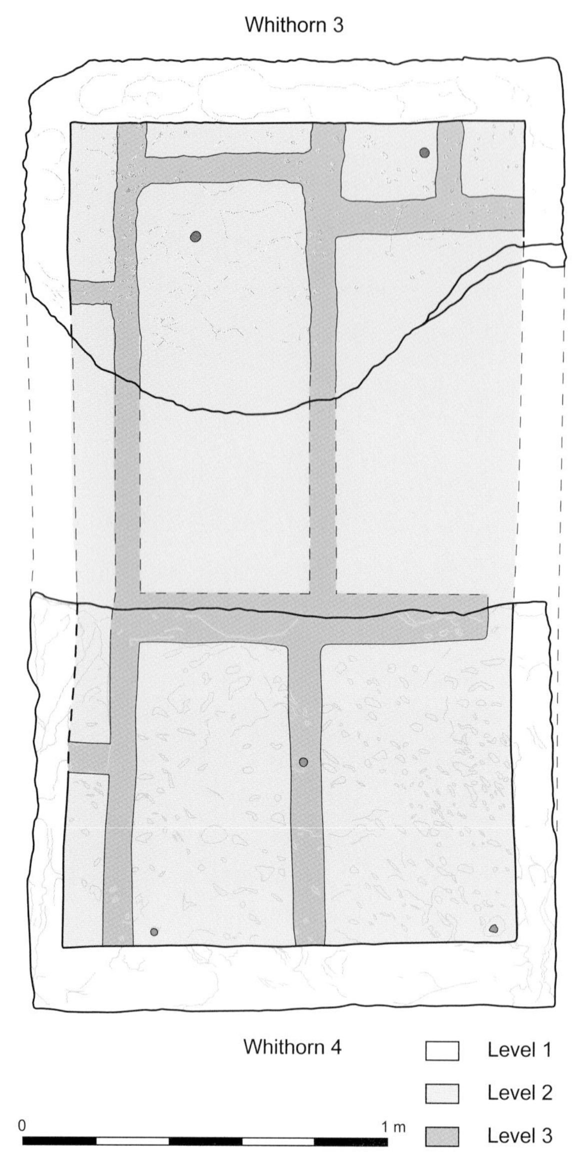

Figure 6.24
Indented slab: Whithorn 3 and 4. These fragments are reconstructed to make a slab of roughly similar size to Whithorn 1/2. It may have been shorter

effectively creating a composite panel. The Level 3 areas of carving represent a series of joining bars which held the plates together.

6.13.4 Whithorn 4

(Figure 6.24; Plate 6.27)
Large slab of Tournai limestone, 1.45m wide, up to 1.05m long and 0.16m thick. It is currently clamped to the north wall of Galloway's parapet and stands on its (probable) left hand edge. The fragment is broken on its top edge and is likely to join (although not directly) with Whithorn 3.

The border of Level 1 carving seen on Whithorn 3 continues on this fragment, with a band present on the right, bottom and left edges. Within this border is a large area of Level 2 carving, forming a well-defined rectangle, and a further series of bands of Level 3 carving. One of the horizontal bands runs along the crack at the top of the fragment and is not complete. Again, the implication is that the whole of the area of Level 2 carving would have been filled with several brass plates, creating a composite panel that was held together by joining bars.

6.13.5 Discussion

The four large fragments of Tournai limestone that survive at Whithorn are likely to represent parts of two large monumental brass indented slabs, comprising Whithorn 1/2 and Whithorn 3/4. In a broad sense both slabs are the same, in that the areas of Level 1 carving would be visible, the areas of Level 2 carving would have held the brass plates and therefore show the outline of the image, whilst the areas of Level 3 carving give an indication of the way in which the brasses were held together. With some interpretation, we can suggest a possible reconstruction for Whithorn 1/2 (Figure 6.23).

We know it is 1.44m wide, and it must be at least 2.9m in length. Existing knowledge and study of monumental brasses suggest that the maximum width of a slab used on a raised tomb would be about 3' (0.9m) (Leslie Smith, Monumental Brass Society, pers comm.). This makes it likely, therefore, that ours is a floor monument, in which case an average size might be 1.2m by 2.1m (Leslie Smith, pers comm). This is clearly a substantial example. The decoration of the slab would comprise an outer marginal inscription, acting as a memorial for the individual, and reminding all those who saw it to pray for that person's soul. Early examples are relatively generic and do not necessarily mention details of the person's life; it was only later in their use that the person's rank, status and achievements began to be included. The inscription would probably start '*Orate pro anima*' and end '*cuius anima propicietur deus amen*' (Pray for the soul of ... on whose soul God have mercy. Amen.) At the centre of the slab would be the effigy of the individual and elements that defined his/her role in society. On Whithorn 1/2, for example, there is clear evidence that the individual was wearing a mitre and we also see the outline of the kind of dress typical of a medieval ecclesiastic. Given the probable location of the slab, covering one of the burials at the east end of the church, it is more than likely that the individual would have been a bishop. On either side of him, forming part of the canopy, are tall columns, which

Plate 6.27
Indented slab: Whithorn 3 and 4

are wide enough to have contained small images of saints.

Comparanda exist for the Whithorn 1/2 slab. The brass of Thomas Cranley, Archbishop of Dublin (Figure 6.25) who died in 1417, gives an excellent idea of how the undulating edges of the carved areas of the effigy relate to the detail of the folds of the robe in which he is dressed. It is also relatively common for brasses of bishops and archbishops to show them holding a crozier, which usually extends above their left shoulder (Monumental Brass Society: www.mbs-brasses.co.uk – see, for example, Archbishop Samuel Hasnett, Chigwell Church; John of Waltham, Bishop of Salisbury and Treasurer of England, Westminster Abbey). The part of the Whithorn 1/2 slab where this would occur – the upper right part of the slab – has been subject to much surface-flaking and cracking. It may be the case that a similar layout is present here.

Whithorn 3/4 is easier to reconstruct, although as much as 0.8m might be missing between the two slabs, if it is a similar size to Whithorn 1/2. This slab was of a different style, comprising at least ten (and possibly as many as 16) individual brass plates, soldered together using joining bars which sat in the Level 3 carved bands, and forming a single large brass panel. The whole of the front would be polished and smoothed so the joints between the sections were invisible. An effigy or scene would then have been carved on the brass.

Although we cannot be certain, it seems likely that the indented slabs originally formed part of the floor in the east end of the later medieval church. There may have been others, since removed and lost. In any event, it is clear that the area containing the bishops' graves could have been adequately floored with only three or perhaps four slabs of this size. Alternatively, it could have comprised the two surviving indented slabs together with the fragments of stone paving that Ritchie occasionally noted (Chapter 3.2.3).

On the basis of a comparison with an effigy of a priest from North Mimms in Hertfordshire (which has a similarly shaped canopy), Greenhill (1949, 238) has suggested that Whithorn 1/2 dates to the mid-14th century. Whithorn 3/4 is more difficult to date as it lacks any decorative detail; a broad early 14th to mid-16th century chronology has been proposed (Greenhill 1949, 238).

Probably the most interesting aspect of the two (missing) monumental brasses is their different form. The first (Whithorn 1/2) is a typical 'English' type, where the brass inlay is shaped (at least in part) to reflect the subject matter depicted. Moreover, as at Whithorn, such brasses are often accompanied by a marginal inscription. A similar example is known in Scotland from Iona Abbey, where the remains of an indented slab dedicated to a knight lies in front of the high altar (RCAHMS 1982, 240–1). The shape of the knight is outlined in the stone, and a band that may have contained a monumental inscription runs around the edge. These types are extremely rare in Scotland and the mid-14th-century date for Whithorn 1/2 would make it probably the earliest surviving example. That such prestigious and 'exotic' slabs were present at both Whithorn and Iona, the prime ecclesiastical centres in Scotland at the time is also noteworthy.

The second type is typically 'Flemish', where the main brass is a simple composite rectangular block, where the effigy and decorative detail is carved directly onto the surface of the brass. In general, the majority of records of monumental brasses from Scotland are of Flemish type, reflecting late 14th- and early 15th-century trade in such items between Scotland and the Low Countries (Leslie Smith, pers comm).

Figure 6.25
Tentative reconstruction of the Whithorn 1/2 monumental brass. The decorative and architectural details are based on a number of known brasses of similar date, including Thomas Cranley, Archbishop of Dublin, 1417, New College Oxford; Thomas Nelond, Prior of Lewes, 1420, Cowfold, Sussex; William de Rothewell, 1361, Rothwell, Northamptonshire; Lady Cromwell, d. 1490, at Tattershall, Lincolnshire

Chapter 7

The Radiocarbon Dates

MAGNAR DALLAND

7.1 INTRODUCTION

Following the initial assessment of the material that made up the Ritchie archive along with Ritchie's notes, a total of 32 samples were radiocarbon dated. With the exception of two dates on cloth or shroud material from Graves 7 and 21, and one on a fragment of wood associated with the crozier in Grave 7, all the dated samples were on human skeletal material (Table 7.1; Figure 7.1).

Initial difficulties concerning the numbering of the skeletons (Chapter 4.1.2) were largely resolved although conflicting dates were returned for Grave 4 and this is discussed below. Given the 'long chronology' that Ritchie, Cruden, Radford and Thomas had given us to expect (Chapter 1.3), it was anticipated that the radiocarbon dates would span the period mid-1st to mid-2nd millennium, possibly earlier. In the event, however, there was a much tighter range, with extremes of 980–1430 (omitting the result of what was clearly confirmed to be a 19th-century burial). Throughout this range there was a fairly continuous spread of dates, with no specific periods of activity identifiable.

Stratigraphic evidence, along with Ritchie's observations, helped to establish a reasonably well-understood chronology and sequence (discussed in Chapter 3). This was used in conjunction with the results of the radiocarbon dating programme, which were then further analysed and calibrated using OxCal v4.0.

One of the three dates from Grave 4 has been excluded from the analysis (SUERC-12507) as it is likely to have been taken from contaminated material within the grave. The remaining two dates from the grave were in good agreement and as they were likely to come from samples taken from the same skeleton, they were combined to achieve a more precise date (Table 7.2).

7.2 BAYESIAN ANALYSIS

The Bayesian method is used in statistical analysis when relating the conditional and marginal probabilities of two random events, particularly when additional information or observations are available to the analyst. It can be used with reference to radiocarbon dating where there are known stratigraphic relationships between dated material. In this case, the presence of a known 'cut-off' around 1200 with the construction of the east end of the cathedral allows such techniques to be used. As a result, the probable dates of a number of the skeletons can be more accurately predicted. The specific date of 1200 was decided on the basis of a combination of the architectural elements (eg the style of the ribbed vault), historical records (Chapter 8.2) and the assumption that the work must have taken place during the office of Bishop John, between 1189 and 1209.

The graves that were radiocarbon dated are physically divided into two groups: those that lay under the foundations and the mass of dumped material at the east end of the church and which, therefore, must pre-date its extension; and those that were buried inside the church, above this material and which, therefore, must post-date its construction. These two groups are separated by over 1.5m of dumped material and as such the stratigraphic division is secure. It would be expected as a result that there would be two distinct groups of dates for the graves but this was not seen to be the case. Instead, there is an overlapping sequence of dates running from the late 10th century through to the 15th century with no obvious gaps. The majority of graves found lying physically below the east extension generally pre-date 1200 and the majority physically above it generally post-date 1200. However, there are five exceptions, three from below the church and two from inside it, which do not conform to this rule. Bayesian statistics would have the greatest impact on these five 'inverted' dates and it is these that were selected for Baysian analysis.

7.2.1 Method

The analysis was carried out using the OxCal Sequence procedure. Each of the five dates was analysed using the sequence function including the constraints defined by the stratigraphy. The syntax for each of the three lower dates was:

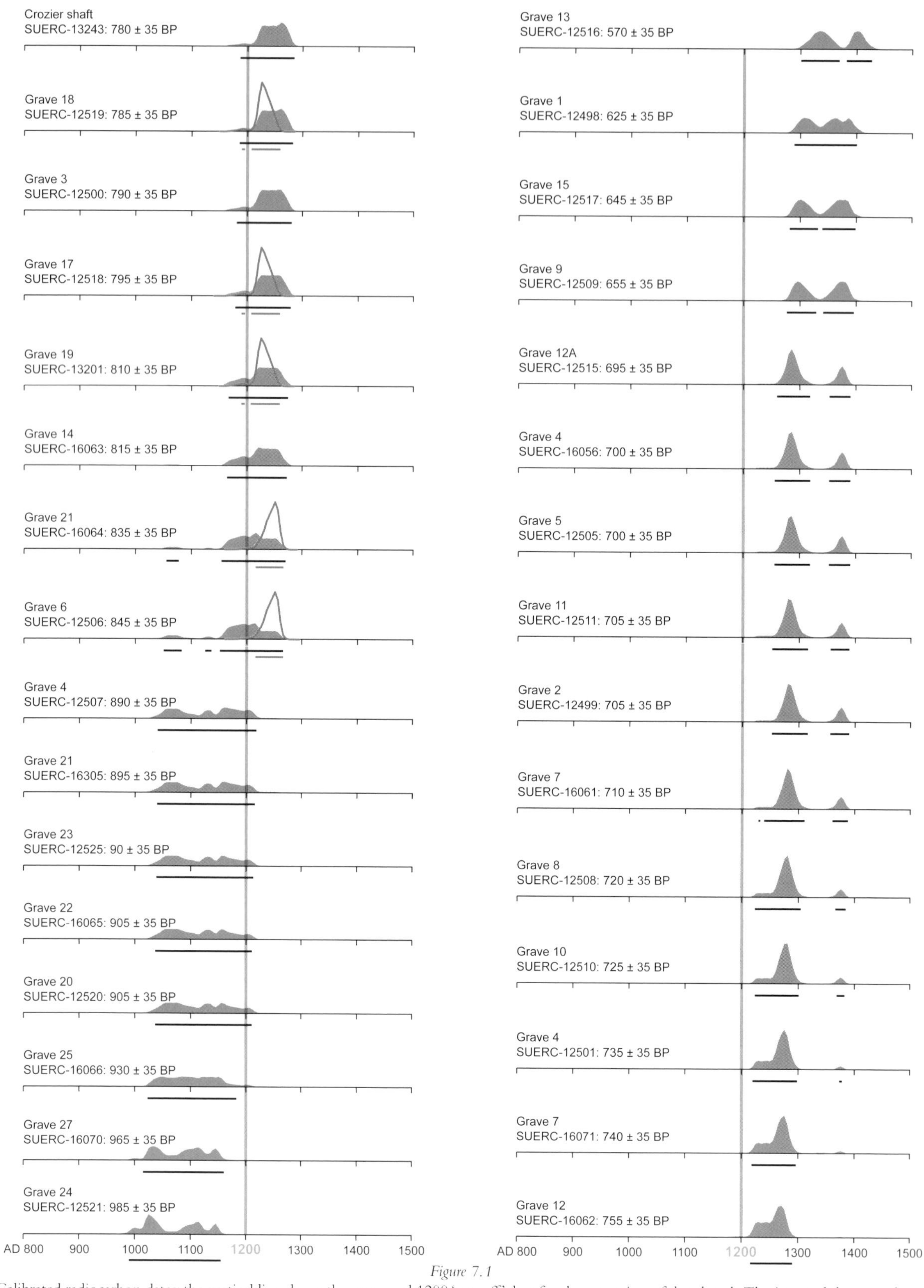

Figure 7.1

Calibrated radiocarbon dates: the vertical line shows the presumed 1200 'cut-off' date for the extension of the church. The inverted dates are shown with their original results and the adjusted results (in red) once the Bayesian analysis was undertaken

Table 7.1: The radiocarbon dates

Grave	*Dated element*	*Sample reference*	*Uncalibrated*	*Calibrated (2-sigma)*	*Laboratory code*
Grave 1	L. patella	30	625 ± 35	1280–1400 AD	SUERC-12498 (GU-14757)
Grave 2	R. fibula	31	705 ± 35	1250–1320 AD (75.6%) 1350–1390 AD (19.8%)	SUERC-12499 (GU-14758)
Grave 3	R. clavicle	32	790 ± 35	1180–1280 AD	SUERC-12500 (GU-14759)
Grave 4	L. patella	33	735 ± 35	1210–1300 AD (94.0%) 1370–1380 AD (1.4%)	SUERC-12501 (GU-14760)
Grave 4	R. scapula	52	700 ± 35	1250–1320 AD (71.8%) 1350–1390 AD (23.6%)	SUERC-16056 (GU-15864)
Grave 4	R. ulna	36	890 ± 35	1030–1220 AD	SUERC-12507 (GU-14763)
Grave 5	R. patella	34	700 ± 35	1250–1320 AD (71.8%) 1350–1390 AD (23.6%)	SUERC-12505 (GU-14761)
Grave 6	R. tibia	35	845 ± 35	1050–1090 AD (6.5%) 1120–1140 AD (1.6%) 1150–1270 AD (87.3%)	SUERC-12506 (GU-14762)
Grave 7	Crozier shaft	51	780 ± 35	1185–1285 AD	SUERC-13243 (GU-14987)
Grave 7	Cloth	60	740 ± 35	1215–1300 AD (95.4%)	SUERC-16071 (GU-15872)
Grave 7	R. 4th metacarpal	53	710 ± 35	1220–1320 AD (79.9%) 1350–1390 AD (15.5%)	SUERC-16061 (GU-15865)
Grave 8	L. patella	37	720 ± 35	1220–1310 AD (87.1%) 1360–1390 AD (8.3%)	SUERC-12508 (GU-14764)
'Grave 9' = charnel	R.tibia	38	655 ± 35	1270–1330 AD (45.7%) 1340–1400 AD (49.7%)	SUERC-12509 (GU-14765)
Grave 10	L. femur	39	725 ± 35	1220–1310 AD (89.9%) 1360–1390 AD (5.5%)	SUERC-12510 (GU-14766)
Grave 11	R. femur	40	705 ± 35	1250–1320 AD (75.6%) 1350–1390 AD (19.8%)	SUERC-12511 (GU-14767)
Grave 12	L.tibia	54	755 ± 35	1215–1290 AD (95.4%)	SUERC-16062 (GU-15866)
'Grave 12A' = charnel	R. ulna	41	695 ± 35	1250–1320 AD (68.2%) 1350–1390 AD (27.2%)	SUERC-12515 (GU-14768)
Grave 13	R. humerus	42	570 ± 35	1300–1370 AD (57.4%) 1380–1430 AD (38.0%)	SUERC-12516 (GU-14769)
Grave 14	Frontal bone	55	815 ± 35	1160–1280 AD (95.4%)	SUERC-16063 (GU-15867)
Grave 15	L. humerus	43	645 ± 35	1280–1400 AD	SUERC-12517 (GU-14770)
Grave 17	L. humerus	44	795 ± 35	1170–1280 AD	SUERC-12518 (GU-14771)
Grave 18	L. humerus	45	785 ± 35	1185–1285 AD	SUERC-12519 (GU-14772)
Grave 19	L. femur	46	810 ± 35	1160–1280 AD	SUERC-13201 (GU-14773)
'Grave 20' = charnel	Occipital bone	47	905 ± 35	1030–1210 AD	SUERC-12520 (GU-14774)

Grave	*Dated element*	*Sample reference*	*Uncalibrated*	*Calibrated (2-sigma)*	*Laboratory code*
Grave 21	Cloth	61	895 ± 35	1030–1220 AD (95.4%)	SUERC-16305 (GU-15873)
Grave 21	L. fibula	56	835 ± 35	1050–1080 AD (3.1%) 1150–1270 AD (92.3%)	SUERC-16064 (GU-15868)
Grave 22	L.tibia	57	905 ± 35	1030–1210 AD (95.4%)	SUERC-16065 (GU-15869)
Grave 23	L. humerus	49	900 ± 35	1030–1220 AD	SUERC-12525 (GU-14776)
Grave 24	L. femur	48	985 ± 35	980–1160 AD	SUERC-12521 (GU-14775)
Grave 25	L. humerus	58	930 ± 35	1020–1190 AD (95.4%)	SUERC-16066 (GU-15870)
Grave 27	R. fibula	59	965 ± 35	1010–1160 AD (95.4%)	SUERC-16070 (GU-15871)
19th-century grave	L. fibula	50	140 ± 35	1660–1950 AD	SUERC-12526 (GU-14777)

```
Sequence()
  {
  Boundary("Start");
  (R_Date("Name",age,⊠)
   <(R_Date("SUERC-16064",835,35) | R_Date("SUERC-12506
",845,35));
Boundary("End");
  };
```

For the two upper dates the following syntax was used:

```
Sequence()
  {
  Boundary("Start");
                    (R_Date("SUERC-12518",795,35) | R_
Date("SUERC-12519",785,35)
| R_Date("SUERC-13201",810,35))
  <(R_Date("Name",age,⊠);
Boundary("End");
  };
```

Where the < symbol means older than and the | between multiple dates indicate that the order between these dates are not known.

7.2.2 Results

The Bayesian analysis resulted in a clear shift in all five probability density functions (PDFs). It had greatest impact on the dates for the two upper graves, largely caused by the nature of the calibration curve. The modelling indicates that the 95.4% probability range for Grave 6 and Grave 21 lies between AD 1217 and AD 1270, a much narrower range than for the un-modelled dates.

The effect on the dates from the three lower graves is less striking although there is a clear shift from the 13th towards the 12th century. However, the modelled dates still have more than a 50% probability that they are later than AD 1200. The lower end of the 95.4% range shifted less than 20 years back during the modelling. Looking at the modelled PDFs for the three lower graves, it is likely that the dates of these graves fall within the second half of the 12th century assuming that the overlying material was deposited around AD 1200.

7.3 DISCUSSION

During the course of the excavation in the 1950s and 1960s, it is clear that Ritchie was interpreting the deepest graves as being significantly early. He considered them to be indicative of an early Christian presence on the site, something that was reasonably well-attested through documentary and artefactual evidence. In his reports to Stewart Cruden (SDD27/1582) he makes it clear that he considers the earliest graves to be earlier than the earliest medieval graves previously found, and Cruden says they must be much earlier than the 12th-century priory and makes allusions to the 'first settlement' at the site. This became the orthodoxy for the following decades and, even at the start of this study, it was expected that a range of dates from perhaps the mid-1st millennium onwards would be identified through radiocarbon dating.

In the event, a relatively narrow range of dates was present. The limits were only between 980 and 1430, and the majority lay within a few centuries of each other. While this was perhaps to be expected for the burials within the building (a limited group of individuals who would have been buried one after the other) it is more surprising for the ones predating the east end. The Bayesian analysis shifted the dates slightly and this does now form a truer representation. Despite this, the lower group of dates still continue very close to the 1200 'cut-off'. What can be inferred from this is that the burial ground where Graves 17–27 were interred continued in use right up to the construction of the extended east end. It is assumed that these graves, even if of relatively low status, would have been marked, but they clearly were not important enough to avoid or remove perhaps only decades after they had been put in the ground, almost certainly within living memory.

Following the Bayesian analysis, the three earliest graves inside the building are Graves 4, 6 and 21 based on the radiocarbon dating. This, in itself, is not problematic. However, as it is assumed that the individuals were placed there because of their high status and specific roles, the marginal positions of both Graves 6 and 21, on the fringes of the area available for burial, is perhaps surprising. It might be expected that the earliest (and presumably first) burial would have occupied a central location. This then sets up an interesting anomaly for the reasons behind the sequence of burials and the who's who of graves which is further examined in Chapter 9.

Table 7.2: Analysis of the radiocarbon dates from Grave 4

Laboratory code	*Sample Reference*	*Uncalibrated*	*Calibrated*
SUERC-12501 (GU-14760)	33	735 ± 35	1210–1300 AD (94.0%) 1370–1380 AD (1.4%)
SUERC-16056 (GU-15864)	52	700 ± 35	1250–1320 AD (71.8%) 1350–1390 AD (23.6%)
SUERC-12501 (GU-14760) SUERC-16056 (GU-15864) combined	33 and 52	717 ± 25	1258–1299 AD (92.5%) 1370–1380 AD (2.9%)

Table 7.3: Bayesian analysis – dates adjusted for stratigraphy

Laboratory code	*Grave no.*	*Sample ref.*	*Uncalibrated*	*Unmodelled*						*Modelled*					
				date	*range*	*1σ*	*date*	*range*	*2σ*	*date*	*range*	*1σ*	*date*	*range*	*2σ*
SUERC-13201 (GU-14773)	Grave 19	46	810 ± 35	1210	1265	68.2	1166	1274	95.4	1173	1227	68.2	1160	1250	95.4
SUERC-12518 (GU-14771)	Grave 17	44	795 ± 35	1219	1265	68.2	1178	1279	95.4	1180	1243	68.2	1165	1251	95.4
SUERC-12519 (GU-14772)	Grave 18	45	785 ± 35	1223	1267	68.2	1185	1282	95.4	1188	1246	68.2	1167	1255	95.4
SUERC-12506 (GU-14762)	Grave 6	35	845 ± 35	1161	1225	68.2	1050	1265	95.4	1234	1260	68.2	1217	1269	95.4
SUERC-16064 (GU-15868)	Grave 21	56	835 ± 35	1173	1252	68.2	1055	1270	95.4	1235	1260	68.2	1219	1270	95.4

Chapter 8

The Medieval Bishops of Whithorn, their Cathedral and their Tombs

RICHARD ORAM

8.1 THE PRE-REFORMATION BISHOPS OF WHITHORN OR GALLOWAY

8.1.1 Introduction: historiographical background

Although the diocese of Whithorn is amongst the more poorly documented of Scotland's medieval sees, its bishops have been the subject of considerably more historical research than their counterparts in wealthier, more influential and better documented dioceses such as Moray, Aberdeen, St Andrews or Glasgow. Much of this research has been stimulated by the successive programmes of modern excavation at the ruins of their cathedral at Whithorn, commencing in 1949 with C A Ralegh Radford's work in the nave and at the extreme east end of the choir (Radford 1956). In conjunction with that work, which formed part of a Ministry of Works project aimed at improving public access to, and interpretation of, the ruins of the cathedral-priory and the Early Christian remains at St Ninian's Cave and Kirkmadrine, the late Gordon Donaldson produced a re-analysis of the medieval bishops and priors which considerably expanded upon the pioneering study of all Scottish pre-Reformation bishops by Bishop John Dowden (1912). Donaldson's work was undertaken at the beginning of Ralegh Radford's excavations and subsequently formed the core of the historical sections of the Ministry of Works' 'Blue Guide' to Whithorn and Kirkmadrine: indeed, it still does in its current revised form (Donaldson 1949; Radford & Donaldson 1953; Radford & Donaldson 1984).

Donaldson's study was followed through the 1950s by a cluster of articles relating to Whithorn and its medieval clergy. Most of this material came as offshoots of research in the York archiepiscopal registers and focused on particular episodes and details of procedures in elections and the administration of the see of Whithorn during episcopal vacancies in the pre-1300 period. The main contributor to this work was the American scholar Robert J Brentano, who explored the Whithorn–York relationship and, especially, the vacancy following the death of Bishop Henry in 1293 (Brentano 1952, 1953a, 1953b). The equally contentious vacancy and election of 1235 was the subject of a detailed study by Anne Ashley (1959), which expanded significantly upon Donaldson's 1949 paper. After this fruitful decade, however, active research into the medieval episcopate at Whithorn appears to have ceased, with not even the exciting discovery of the series of high-status ecclesiastical burials in the east end of the cathedral ruins during Ritchie's 1957–67 excavations serving to stimulate fresh academic interest.

In the 1960s and 1970s, two major projects which focused on aspects of the medieval Scottish Church generally cast considerable fresh light on the bishops of Whithorn. The first was the second draft of the *Fasti Ecclesiae Scoticanae*, edited by the late Donald Watt and published in 1969 by the Scottish Records Society (Watt 1969). This was a major collaborative project by members of the Scottish Medievalists and involved the identification in published and unpublished primary sources of data which would allow the careers of the senior secular clergy of the kingdom to be established with greater clarity. The second contribution was also a product of Donald Watt's endeavours. The *Biographical Dictionary of Scottish Graduates to AD 1410* (Watt 1977) was a monumental exercise which charted the careers of most medieval clerical graduates down to the establishment of the first Scottish university. Watt's *Dictionary* pulled together information on several of the more obscure incumbents of the see in the 14th and 15th centuries as well as the more prominent individuals, but it presents its data from the perspective of the wider clerical community in Scotland rather than from the episcopate alone.

Renewed research commenced in 1983–8 with the present writer's PhD thesis on the *Lordship of Galloway c 1000 – c 1250*. This development coincided with the resumption of excavations at Whithorn in 1984 and then on a major scale from 1986, which led to 'spin-off' publications on the medieval diocese and its administrative institutions (eg Brooke 1987). The first new study of the pre-1250 bishops came in 1991 with publication of material extracted from the present writer's thesis (Oram 1991) and the late Donald Watt's major revision of his *Fasti* list published in the *Series Episcoporum* (Watt 1991). Commemoration of the nominal 1600th anniversary of the death of St Ninian in 1997 resulted in further examination of the medieval succession of bishops of Whithorn, published as part of the Roman Catholic diocese of Galloway's celebrations in that year (Oram 1997). While more recent analysis has concentrated on the development of the Premonstratensian priory at Whithorn and its estates, the medieval bishops have continued to be a target of largely unpublished research. The following narrative outline of the careers of the bishops is a synthesis of the last six decades of research.

8.1.2 The bishops c 1128 to 1558 (Table 8.1)

Gille-aldan c 1128–1151x54

Whithorn's succession of medieval bishops begins in *c* 1128, when, after a silence of nearly 200 years in the surviving documentary records, reference to an un-named *electus* first occurs (Watt 1991, 24). The document, a letter from Pope Honorius II (1124–30), appears to have been written in response to an enquiry from the bishop-elect of Whithorn concerning his consecration (Raine 1894, iii, 48–9). Written in the midst of the growing controversy between the bishops of the Scottish Church and the Archbishops of York over the latter's claims to metropolitan supremacy over the former, it ordered the candidate to go to 'his appropriate (or proper) metropolitan', Archbishop Thurstan of York, to receive consecration. Shortly afterwards, the oath of obedience to Thurstan of one Gille-aldan, elect of Whithorn, is preserved in the York records (Raine 1894, iii, 60). Little is known about the origins or career of this

Table 8.1: The bishops of Whithorn, *c.* 1128 – 1558

Bishops	*Dates*	*Place of burial*
Gille-aldan	*c* 1128–1151x54	Unknown (probably Whithorn)
Christian	1154–86	Holmcultram Abbey, Cumberland
John	1189–1209	Unknown (probably Whithorn)
Walter	1209–35	Unknown (probably Whithorn)
Gilbert	1235–53	Unknown (probably Whithorn)
Henry	1253–93	Unknown (probably Whithorn)
Thomas	1294–1324x26	Unknown (probably Whithorn)
Simon	1326–55	Unknown (probably Whithorn)
Michael	1355–8x59	Unknown (probably Whithorn)
Thomas	1359–62	Unknown (probably Whithorn)
Adam	1363–78	Unknown (probably Whithorn)
Thomas	1379–93x1406	Unknown (possibly in France)
Eliseus	1406–12x15	Unknown (probably in Whithorn)
Thomas	1415–20x22	Unknown (probably in Whithorn)
Alexander	1422–50	Unknown (probably in Whithorn)
Thomas	1450–8	Translated to Aberdeen in 1458, buried in Edinburgh
Ninian	1458–80x82	Unknown (probably Whithorn)
George	1482–1508	Unknown (probably Whithorn)
David	1508–26	Unknown
Henry	1526–41	Unknown (possibly Dundrennan or Whithorn)
Andrew	1541–58	Unknown (perhaps Edinburgh)

man, the circumstances of his election or the nature of the community over which he presided, other than that his name points to a probably local background and an association with the Cuthbert cult in Galloway (Oram 2000, 164–5, 170–4). It was probably during Gille-aldan's episcopate that work commenced on the new cathedral church at Whithorn and it was perhaps there that he was buried sometime between June 1151, when he is last noted as alive in a York record, and December 1154, when his successor, Christian, was consecrated. He may have been interred before the high altar of his cathedral, but as is demonstrated by the example of Bishop Jocelin of Glasgow, who was responsible for the rebuilding and consecration of his cathedral but who died at Melrose Abbey and was buried in the monks' choir there, bishops could and did choose alternative places of burial.

Christian 1154–86

As little is known of the origins of Bishop Christian as of Gille-aldan (Watt 1991, 25). Christian was consecrated as bishop at Bermondsey Abbey in Surrey on 19 December 1154 by the Archbishop of Rouen (Anderson & Anderson 1938, 127). The circumstances of his election and consecration suggest that he had strong connections with the Cistercians and may have been a Cistercian monk himself, possibly from one of the Yorkshire communities of that order (Oram 2000, 176). Christian's name may represent a latinisation of the Gaelic *Gille-crist*, but there is no hard evidence to confirm that view. The names of four of his kinsmen (a brother and three nephews), who all appear to have served in his household in the second half of his episcopate, are recorded in one of his charters (Bannatyne Club 1840, No. 25). Three of these are unremarkable and quite common English forms (Walter, Nicholas and James), but one nephew is called 'Malbet', derived apparently from Mælbeth, the name given in the *Anglo-Saxon Chronicle* in 1031 for one of the north–west British rulers who submitted to King Knútr (Garmonsway 1972, version E, s.a. 1031), itself an Anglo-Saxon scribe's effort to transliterate the Gael *Máel Bethad*. Names of this type were apparently common in the 11th and 12th centuries on both sides of the Solway and the personal links which Christian later showed with English Cumbria could point to a north–western English (Cumberland, Westmorland, Furness) origin, or to connections with the Norse-Gaelic community in Galloway. Certainly, most of the surviving evidence for his activities points to a very strong personal association with Carlisle diocese, although this perception may be distorted by the poor survival of documentation relating to his own see. The English pipe rolls for 1159 and 1160 record the payment to Bishop Christian on King Henry II's instructions of 14s 8d in each year from the noutgeld receipts (a tax levied on cattle) from the sheriffdom of Carlisle (Bain 1881, i, nos 67, 72). That Christian was in receipt of such payments could indicate that he was active in the diocese of Carlisle providing episcopal services during the long vacancy there which followed the death of Bishop Aethelwold, but on what basis is unknown. It is possible also that he was resident in Cumberland at this time on account of the civil wars in Galloway between Fergus of Galloway and his sons, Gillebrigte and Uhtred.

Despite the poverty of the surviving record sources for Christian's activities within his diocese, it appears from the fragments which have been preserved that his episcopate saw the institution of a more formalised structure of ecclesiastical government within the see. His favour to the Cistercian order, which is well-recorded later in his career, suggests that he identified himself closely with the reformist clergy of the mid-12th century who were actively undertaking a systematic restructuring of the secular (and monastic) Church in northern England, Scotland and Ireland at this date. Christian's reformist credentials can perhaps be seen in the appearance soon after 1154 of an archdeacon of Whithorn or Galloway, Robert, and *c* 1165 of two Deans of Christianity, Salmon and Macbeth (Bannatyne Club 1840, No. 52; Watt 1969, 136, 138). Together, these men would have formed the core of an administration responsible for the enforcement of ecclesiastical discipline over the other diocesan clergy, the implementation of canon law within the diocese, and the establishment of ecclesiastical courts to deal with spiritual and moral issues. A still clearer sign of his commitment to ecclesiastical reform at Whithorn can be seen in his establishment of a convent of canons regular there by *c* 1177 (Cowan & Easson 1976, 103). It has generally been assumed that the earlier 12th-century cathedral had been served by a community of secular clerks and priests, the successor clergy of the 'minster' which may have functioned on the site following the demise of the late Northumbrian monastery. Given the excavated evidence for continuity on the monastic site from the mid-9th to early 12th centuries, this is a reasonable supposition, but there is in fact no documentary evidence for the existence of such a religious community. Analogy from elsewhere in Scotland and northern England, however, supports the model of a transition from colleges of secular clerks to regular monastic communities in processes often directed or encouraged by the local diocesan (see, for example, Veitch 1999). At Whithorn, it has been argued that the community which served Gille-aldan's cathedral was converted first into Augustinian canons before subsequently adopting the more austere Premonstratensian rule (Backmund 1953). Unlike in England, where many of the older diocesan centres were served by convents of regular clergy, only Whithorn and St

Andrews in Scotland were associated with monasteries. In the case of St Andrews, an unreformed community of *céli dé* had been replaced by a priory of Augustinian canons in a process that was perhaps paralleled by developments at Whithorn. It is possible, however, given Christian's apparent personal association with north–western England and the archdiocese of York, that the example of Carlisle, where an Augustinian priory was attached to the new cathedral, provided a more direct inspiration for developments at Whithorn.

The possible north–western English links of Christian may have helped to produce a very marked attachment to the see of York from the outset of his career as bishop. The strength of that bond was underscored by his maintenance of his obedience to the archbishops throughout the extended and bitter controversy surrounding the question of metropolitan supremacy over Scotland which troubled the 1170s and 1180s. York's claim to the spiritual overlordship of the Scottish Church had been advanced regularly through the 12th century but the Scots had been generally successful in preventing the archbishops from exercising any effective authority over them. In 1174, however, following the capture of King William the Lion during a raid into northern England, Archbishop Roger of York had secured inclusion within the treaty by which the Scottish king obtained his release of a clause requiring the Scottish bishops to submit to English metropolitan supremacy. When the Scottish bishops came to Northampton in 1176 for a council of the English Church at which they would make their submission, however, a dispute broke out between the archbishops of Canterbury and York over, amongst other issues, their rival claims to metropolitan supremacy over Scotland. The council broke up in confusion and acrimony without the oaths being given, but in 1177 the pope despatched a legate to Scotland specifically to settle the issue (Barrell 1995). In July 1177, the papal legate, Cardinal Vivian, had summoned a council of the Scottish Church to assemble at Edinburgh with all the bishops being required to attend (Stubbs 1867, i, 166). Christian, however, refused to attend, claiming that he was a suffragan of York and that his own archbishop also held a legatine commission which nullified Vivian's authority over him. The bishop did not share the views of his Scottish colleagues and had already made his position abundantly clear in March 1177 when he alone of the 'Scottish' clergy had attended a council of the English Church at London. Vivian's response was to excommunicate Christian but, with Archbishop Roger's support, he continued in office (Oram 1997, 58).

Christian may have succeeded in preserving the historic link between his diocese and the Church of York but the victory for him may have been hollow. Perhaps always closer politically to Uhtred of Galloway, who had strong personal and marital ties with English Cumbria, than to his half-brother, Gillebrigte, the bishop appears to have been forced out of his diocese for much of the last nine years of his life due to the hostility of Gillebrigte and his supporters in the aftermath of their murder of Uhtred (Oram 2000, 176–8). From 1177 until his death in October 1186, Christian's presence at Whithorn cannot be established and he appears to have spent most of his time as a roving representative of the Archbishop of York in Carlisle and York dioceses. As he neared his death, he affirmed his personal association with Cumberland and the Cistercian order in a confirmation of a charter in favour of the monks of Holmcultram, in whose abbey he expressed a wish to be buried (Grainger & Collingwood 1929, no. 141). It was at Holmcultram that Christian took up residence in his last days, dying there on 7 October 1186 and being buried in the abbey (Bannatyne Club 1837b, s.a.1186). His tomb does not survive.

John 1189–1209

Christian's death was followed by a three-year vacancy at Whithorn. This prolonged gap was probably a result of Henry II of England's policy of extending episcopal vacancies to secure the maximum profit from the temporary royal control of the temporalities of bishoprics and is perhaps a reflection of the degree of influence which the English king continued to enjoy in Galloway after Roland's homage to him in 1186. It was also exacerbated by the even longer vacancy at York, where there had been no consecrated archbishop since the death of Roger of Pont-l'eveque in 1181. Following King Henry's death in July 1189, however, his successor, Richard I, acted swiftly to fill vacant bishoprics in England, and Whithorn appears to have been included in this process (Oram 2000, 179–80).

On 3 September 1189, John, bishop-elect of Whithorn, was amongst the clergy who assembled at Westminster for King Richard's coronation (Stubbs 1867, ii, 79). There is no indication of his origins but his status as 'electus' less than three months after Henry II's death could point to his being a royal clerk provided to the see by the new king. John's consecration took place at Pipewell Abbey in Northamptonshire on 17 September at the hands of the archbishops of Dublin and Trier and the bishop of Annaghdown, since his own archbishop-elect, Geoffrey Plantagenet, had not even yet been ordained as a priest (Stubbs 1867, ii, 87). The following week at Southwell, just inside the diocese of York, he ordained Geoffrey, circumventing the prohibition placed on the other English bishops by Archbishop Baldwin of Canterbury who wished to ordain Geoffrey himself to enforce his claims of primacy over York (Stubbs 1867, ii, 88). Baldwin's prohibition, however, had neglected to name John, who had not yet been consecrated at the date of its issuing. Through this act, from the very outset of his career as bishop, John proclaimed his loyalties to York, cementing the ties between Whithorn and its metropolitan.

Following Geoffrey's ordination, John, together with the bishops of Durham and Glasgow, were given a papal mandate to consecrate him as Archbishop of York, but the ceremony was delayed until 1191 and took place at Tours without any of the mandated bishops (Watt 1991, 27). There is little further evidence for John's role as a suffragan of York: in 1190–4 he witnessed one of the Archbishop's charters and in March 1194 accompanied him to a council of the English Church at Nottingham (Brown 1913, i, 227; Stubbs 1871, iii, 241). The confirmation of the separation of the Scottish Church from the metropolitan jurisdiction of York by the bull *Cum universi*, moreover, effectively excluded him from any active role in Scottish ecclesiastical affairs, although he was appointed on at least one occasion as a papal judge-delegate to settle a Scottish case (Ferguson 1997, 212, no. 11; Bannatyne Club 1843, no. 84). Despite the prominence of Roland of Galloway and his son and successor, Alan, in the political life of William the Lion's kingdom, John never occurs as a witness to any surviving Scottish royal act: his orientation was firmly directed towards York.

On stylistic grounds, the original vaulting of the undercroft of the east end of the extended cathedral has been dated to *c* 1200 (Oram, Chapter 8.2 below; Radford & Donaldson 1953, 31–2), suggesting that it may have been Bishop John who was responsible for the construction of the new eastern limb. John, moreover, was probably the first interment in the new building on his death in 1209 (Bannatyne Club 1837b, s.a. 1209). This forms the starting point of Lowe's analysis of the burial sequence in Chapter 9.

Walter 1209–35

John's successor as bishop was Walter, a clerk who served as chamberlain of the household of Alan, lord of Galloway (Bannatyne Club 1837b, s.a. 1209). By the early 13th century, the lord of Galloway was a man who held estates scattered throughout Scotland and England as well as in Galloway itself and whose kinship and marriage connections brought men into his service from throughout Britain. In earlier generations, Walter might reasonably be assumed to have been of native Galwegian stock, but by the time of Alan he could have come from anywhere with which the lords of Galloway had connections.

As with information concerning his origins, there is little evidence for his career as bishop. Like his predecessors, he does appear to have been active in northern England as a deputy for the archbishop. He apparently provided episcopal services in York diocese during the vacancy between Archbishop Geoffrey Plantagent's death in 1207 and the election of Walter de Gray in 1215. As late as January 1215 King John ordered his administrator in York diocese to pay Walter 20 merks for his expenses until the proper daily rate due to him was determined (Bain 1881, i, No. 614). Details of his administration of his own see are equally sketchy. Only one of his charters, a confirmation of the appropriation of the church of St Fillan of Sorbie to Dryburgh Abbey, appears to have survived, albeit as a 15th-century transumpt (Bannatyne Club 1847, no. 80). Likewise, there is little remaining evidence for his wider spiritual activities, but his appearance as the principal witness to two charters of Affrica, lady of Nithsdale, in favour of the Premonstratensian abbey of Dercongal or Holywood, which may have been a daughter house of Whithorn (Bannatyne Club 1837b, nos 199, 200), shows that he was active in south-west Scotland outside his own diocese. His death in late 1234 or January/February 1235 coincided with the political crisis in Galloway which followed the death of Alan, the last of its male line of rulers, and provided King Alexander II of Scotland with an opportunity to intrude his own candidate into an office which commanded considerable regional influence.

Gilbert 1235–53

For the preceding half century, Galloway had been drawn progressively into a closer relationship with the kingdom of the Scots. The death of Alan of Galloway in 1234, leaving only three legitimate daughters and one illegitimate son as his heirs, provided the Scottish king with the opening to absorb the lordship firmly into his kingdom (for discussion of the post-1234 situation in Galloway see Oram 2000, Chapter 5). The death of Bishop Walter presented King Alexander with a further mechanism for tightening his grip on the lordship for, although he could not overturn the papal settlement which had confirmed the independence of the Scottish Church and the inclusion of Whithorn within the province of York, he could ensure that the next incumbent of the see was at least favourable to the Scots. Events, however, did not proceed smoothly for another candidate quickly emerged as a rival to the king's preferred choice. The dispute which resulted dragged on for several years.

On 25 February 1235, the 'clergy and people' of the diocese had elected a certain Gilbert, at that time a monk of Melrose Abbey but formerly abbot of Glenluce Abbey in Galloway (Bannatyne Club 1837b, s.a. 1235). Election by clergy and people was the traditional practice throughout much of western Christendom down to the early 13th century, but was a formula which allowed considerable lay interference in the process. In 1235, although the leading figures in the secular clergy of the diocese, including the archdeacon, had apparently selected Gilbert, there was a strong probability that the king had exerted pressure to ensure that his candidate was chosen. The fact that Gilbert was a Melrose monk gives further support to the likelihood that he was the king's nominee, for that abbey enjoyed a particularly close relationship with Alexander II and provided him with reliable bishops for a number of politically sensitive sees in his kingdom (Oram 1998). Gilbert, however, was not just an outsider being intruded into Galloway by the crown. His name, which may represent a Latinising of the Gaelic *Gille-brigte*, and his former position as abbot of one of the Galloway Cistercian houses (which were not part of the Melrose filiation), suggest that he may have been of Galloway background and selected by the king on account of his knowledge of south-western affairs.

The speed with which Gilbert was 'elected' so soon after the death of Bishop Walter suggests the importance which King Alexander placed on securing control of the see by a reliable agent. It may have caught the Whithorn chapter off-guard, but three weeks later the prior and canons elected a certain Odo Ydonc, formerly the abbot of Holywood in Nithsdale and a fellow canon at Whithorn (Bannatyne Club 1837b, s.a. 1235). His electors regarded themselves as constituting the cathedral chapter and, since the popes had been advancing the principle that rights of election to bishoprics lay in the hands of such chapters, their stance commanded support amongst the clergy of the province of York. It has been suggested that their advancing of a rival candidate was an indication of their anti-Scottish outlook and support for the rebellion in Galloway against Alexander II's attempted partition of the lordship between the heiresses of Alan (Ashley 1959), and certainly they chose to dress it up in that fashion, but their motives were probably altogether less honourable. It was not uncommon for there to be tensions between bishops, who were nominally heads of monastic houses attached to their cathedrals but often not members of even the same order, and the members of those communities, as the relationship between successive bishops of St Andrews and the Augustinian priory there attest, and it is possible that they sought to end such problems by electing one of their own number as bishop (Donaldson 1949, note 17a).

The principal obstacle to be overcome by either candidate in securing their consecration as bishop was the need to obtain the approval of the archbishop of York. On 23 April 1235, King Alexander wrote to the archdeacon and clergy of Whithorn diocese, a copy of the letter also apparently being sent to Archbishop Walter de Gray, from what appears to have been an assembly of the Scottish royal council at Newbattle Abbey in Midlothian (Raine 1870, 173). The letter stated that Gilbert, monk of Melrose, had been elected unanimously and canonically by them, that the king approved their choice and agreed that the elect should be consecrated. Archbishop de Gray must already have known by this date that the claim of unanimous election was untrue, for Duncan, prior of Whithorn, and the canons had also written to him to inform him of the election of Odo (Raine 1870, 170, 171–2). Their letter claimed that they had sought – but, significantly, not obtained – the approval of King Alexander 'who presently holds Galloway', a turn of phrase which has been taken to suggest the canons' hostility to the recent Scottish interference in the affairs of the lordship (Ashley 1959, 66). The choice of Odo, they stressed, was unanimous and followed the current papally approved custom of capitular election. Therefore, they requested that the archbishop consecrate Odo.

On 19 May, King Alexander wrote to York countering the claims of the prior (Raine 1870, 172). The convent, he stated, had neither sought his permission for the election nor gained his assent to it, as was customary. Consequently, he demanded that the archbishop should not consecrate Odo and sent procurators to make a formal appeal against his candidature. This action appears to have prompted a counterclaim from the canons which reveals that Archbishop de Gray had called a council at York to hear the case, to which he had summoned the canons. They, however, replied that they could not come 'on account of the war of the king of Scots against Galloway', but sent one of their own number as their procurator with the power to make an appeal if it should prove necessary (Raine 1870, 170–1). Although Odo appears to have commanded significant support at York in 1235, he had been unable to secure a final settlement in his favour and Archbishop de Gray had consecrated Gilbert: the political influence of the king of Scots was too great. This result, however, did not end the matter and Odo embarked on a protracted round of litigation and appeals, leading ultimately to an appeal to Rome in 1241 and the appointment of judges-delegate by Pope Gregory IX to settle the dispute finally (Ashley 1959, 62–4). No judgement from that tribunal has survived but the fact that Gilbert continued to serve as bishop of Whithorn suggests that it had settled against Odo.

Almost immediately after his consecration at York on 2 September 1235, Gilbert was to demonstrate his worth to King Alexander. In the autumn of 1235, the men of Galloway rose in rebellion in support of Thomas, the bastard son of Alan of Galloway. A royal campaign dispersed the first rising, but Thomas and his allies had returned with Irish mercenary support. Bishop Gilbert, it is claimed, with the assistance of the Abbot of Melrose and the Earl of Dunbar, however, secured Thomas's negotiated surrender, ending the threat to Scottish control (Bannatyne Club

1837b, s.a. 1235). Apart from a second ill-fated rebellion in Galloway against the Scottish crown in 1247, these turbulent affairs at the start of Gilbert's episcopate appear to have been the only disturbances in what was otherwise a relatively uneventful career (Oram 1997, 63–4; Oram 2000, 185–6). The 1247 rising, however, demonstrated that Galloway was still not wholly reconciled to its place within the Scottish kingdom so, on the Gilbert's death in 1253 (Bannatyne Club 1837b, s.a. 1253), his successor was also drawn from a monastery associated closely with the Scottish crown.

Henry of Holyrood 1253–93

The man nominated to succeed Gilbert was Henry, abbot of Holyrood Abbey (Bannatyne Club 1837a, 59). Holyrood possessed extensive interests in Galloway, through which it is likely that Henry possessed a good knowledge of the political situation in the region (Bannatyne Club 1840, nos 23–7, 49–54, 72–4, 80 etc). This qualification may have recommended him to the council dominated by the Comyn family which was governing Scotland at that time in the name of the boy-king, Alexander III. His election, however, was challenged by John Balliol I of Barnard Castle, husband of Dervorgilla, the youngest daughter of Alan of Galloway, and one of the most powerful landowners in eastern Galloway, who claimed to have some rights in the process. Balliol protested on the grounds that the rights of the people of Galloway had been ignored, an argument which seems to hark back to the 1235 claims that the authority to elect lay with the clergy and people of the diocese (Bannatyne Club 1837a; for the hearing at York, see Raine 1870, 120–2; Raine 1873). No rival candidate appears to have been advanced by Balliol, but Henry's consecration was delayed until possibly as late as early 1256, probably due as much to the political upheavals in Scotland and the vacancy at York which followed the death of Walter de Gray as to any litigation over the validity of the election process (Watt 1969, 129).

Henry's long episcopate was largely unremarkable, characterised mainly by conscientious efforts to maintain the standards of parochial service in his diocese and loyal and active service as a suffragan of York (Oram 1997, 65). Like Walter and Gilbert before him, he took steps to ensure that suitable vicars were installed in appropriated parish churches and that adequate stipends were assigned to them (Bannatyne Club 1840, no. 83; Bannatyne Club 1847, nos. 67, 70). Down into the mid-1280s, he was regularly employed to deputise for the archbishops of York, dedicating and reconciling churches, chapels and graveyards in the western part of York diocese (Brown 1907, nos 385, 456, 690). In 1286 he was at Hexham, where on 9 September he gave his profession of obedience to the recently consecrated Archbishop John le Romeyn (Brown 1916, no. 1342). The following day, the archbishop excused Henry from his duty of an annual attendance on him at York, relaxing this obligation on account of the bishop's great age and the attendant rigours of the journey (Brown 1916, 85). It was at this time that the archbishop also issued an indulgence to all who contributed towards the repair of the cathedral at Whithorn which had been damaged during raids on Galloway by the Bruce family in the disturbances which had followed the death of King Alexander III of Scotland (Brown 1913, 8–9; see Chapter 8.2, *Later Medieval Building Work*).

The attack on Whithorn in 1286 had been part of a wider campaign in Galloway which appears to have been highly destructive of property. The exchequer accounts for 1286–7 of John Comyn, earl of Buchan, sheriff of Wigtown, refer to land lying uncultivated 'on account of the war moved by the Earl of Carrick after the king's death' (Stuart and Burnett 1878, 39). Damage inflicted on the bishop's estates and causing a general reduction in his income from spiritualities across the diocese as a consequence of this raid may have been the source of the 'adverse oppressions' of which Henry had written to Archbishop le Romeyn early in 1287 (Brown 1916, no. 1346). In reply, the archbishop asked Henry to deputise for him during his imminent absence from the archdiocese, particularly within the archdeaconry of Richmond, promising him payment for his troubles (Brown 1916, no. 1346). Henry appears to have seized the opportunity to boost his income and as early as 9 April 1287 received a commission with Bishop of Carlisle to reconcile the church of Hornby (Brown 1916, no. 1347). In August, he consecrated seven more parish churches in York diocese (Brown 1913, 166–7). Given that Henry's age had been cited as a reason for pardoning him from coming to York in 1286, it is remarkable that as late as October 1291 he was still accepting commissions to deputise for Archbishop le Romeyn within his diocese (Brown 1916, no. 1366). He died on 1 November 1293 (Bannatyne Club 1837a, 154–5).

Thomas de Dalton (or de Kirkcudbright or de Galloway) 1294–c 1324

Within a month of Bishop Henry's death, Archbishop le Romeyn had appointed an official *sede vacante*, Master Ralph de Ponthieu, to administer the see until the election and consecration of a successor (Brown 1916, no. 1386). Early in January 1294, John Balliol, king of Scots, wrote to the archbishop from his family castle at Buittle in eastern Galloway, informing him of the election of Thomas of Kirkcudbright by the prior and canons of Whithorn and un-named clergy of the diocese, but warning him that the process was tainted with simony. The king therefore requested that the archbishop should not consecrate Thomas until two royal clerks had provided him with the facts of the case (Brown 1916, 115). On examining the evidence provided, however, Romeyn decided that there was no case to answer and advised the king of his decision by letter on 22 January (Brown 1916, 115–6). No record survives of what information King John had laid before the archbishop, but the survival of a letter from Robert Bruce, lord of Annandale, to Romeyn on behalf of Master Thomas de Kirkcudbright, elect of Whithorn, describing him as 'our dear clerk and supporter', suggests that the king's objection was bound up in the competition between the Balliol and Bruce families for power in the kingdom (Brown 1916, 116). The aged Robert Bruce, grandfather of the future king, had somehow managed to secure the election of one of his own household clerks to a bishopric that could have been considered as firmly under the domination of John Balliol and his Comyn allies. The various designations by which Master Thomas was known – of Dalton, Kirkcudbright or Galloway – imply, however, that he was of local background and perhaps enjoyed wider support within the diocese than the traditional identification of him as a Bruce man intruded into Whithorn by dubious means allows. After all, even King John in his letter to Romeyn commented that he had been elected by the canons of Whithorn and other diocesan clergy.

Although he had found nothing uncanonical in the process of election in January, Romeyn had not confirmed the election. On 1 May 1294 he set a date for formal closure of the treating over the case, subject to King John raising no further objections (Brown 1916, 126–7). The king finally gave his assent on 19 May and on 30 May Romeyn confirmed Thomas's election and requested that he be given possession of the temporalities of his see (Brown 1916, 127, 128–9). His consecration was originally meant to take place at Hexham, was moved to Ripon, and finally took place at Gedling on 10 October 1294, with instructions being issued to the archdeacon of York on 14 October to enthrone him at Whithorn (Brown 1916, 129–32).

As Scotland and England slid towards war in early 1296, Thomas found himself with a conflict of interests. Although Galloway was by then well integrated into the kingdom of Scotland, he had professed obedience to the archbishop of York and his diocese was still regarded as suffragan of York. Furthermore, since the Bruce family with which he had close personal ties had mainly aligned against King John and his Comyn supporters, he may have found himself trying to reconcile divided loyalties. The swift defeat of the Scots in April 1296 may have seemed to offer the bishop a route out of these difficulties. In common with the other senior clergy of the kingdom, Thomas was at Berwick on 28 August for his fealty to Edward I to be recorded formally (Bain 1881, i, no.196). The extension of Edward's authority over Scotland, however, had one negative consequence for the bishop: on 1 September, still at Berwick, he was required to acknowledge his debts to a York merchant and agree a date for their settlement on the security of his lands and goods in Dumfriesshire (Bain 1881, i, no. 831).

There is no record of Thomas's attitudes or actions in the rising against the English occupation led initially from 1297 by William Wallace and Andrew Murray. When the Comyns threw their support behind the attempt, however, the bishop could not avoid involvement, particularly in 1300 when Edward I planned a campaign into western Galloway. It was Thomas whom the Comyns sent as an envoy to King Edward in what proved to be a futile effort to secure a truce (Riley 1865, 440). The bishop's support for the Scottish resistance, however, may have been dependent upon the stance of the young Robert Bruce, earl of Carrick, for it is clear that by 1302 he had followed the earl back into King Edward's peace. On 19 April 1302, he gave his belated profession of obedience at Burton by Beverley in Yorkshire to Romeyn's successor as archbishop of York, Thomas of Corbridge, who had been consecrated in 1300 (Brown 1928, 153).

Following his re-entry into Edward's peace, Bishop Thomas found himself still caught between a rock and a hard place. He appears to have returned to his see in 1302–3, receiving dispensation to absent himself from York for three years, probably on account of the continuing warfare in south-west Scotland where the Comyns still occupied a strong position (Brown 1928, 154). The Bruces, however, appear to have expected him to work in their interest and were disappointed that he failed to serve them well. Early in 1304, Robert Bruce, lord of Annandale, the son of the man who had secured the bishopric for him, wrote to Archbishop Thomas to complain that the property of his son, Alexander Bruce, rector of Kirkinner, had been plundered by certain 'secular men' of the diocese of Whithorn and put to their own use without the permission of either the bishop or the rector (Brown 1928, 156–7). Robert requested that the archbishop write to Bishop Thomas and order him to employ the spiritual powers of his office to force these men to make restitution, and that he should not let himself be swayed by fear of any secular person. The 'secular men' were, presumably, supporters of the Comyn and Balliol families who had seen the kirklands of the parish of Kirkinner as Bruce property and ripe for targeting, but whom the bishop, despite his personal links with the Bruces, was unwilling to challenge. On 25 February, Archbishop Thomas wrote to him directing him to order the restoration of the seized property and instructing him to bring full ecclesiastical censures to bear against the culprits (Brown 1928, 155). Fortunately for the bishop, the letter was overtaken by events, for the Scots completed a negotiated surrender to Edward I that same month.

Stability was not of long duration, however, for on 10 February 1306, Robert Bruce, earl of Carrick, murdered John Comyn, lord of Badenoch, in the church of the Dominicans at Dumfries and immediately launched a bid for the throne of Scotland. For Thomas, the sacrilege and usurpation was too great an offence to pardon and he remained firmly in the peace of the English king. On 26 June 1306, Thomas gave his profession of obedience to the new Archbishop of York, William Greenfield (Brown & Thompson 1938, v, 53–4), underscoring his separation from the Bruce family. The breach with his old patrons was confirmed in September 1306 when Greenfield instructed the appropriation of the church of Kirkinner, held by the younger brother of Robert Bruce, to the episcopal mensa, citing the poverty of the bishop caused by the ravages of warfare as a reason for the appropriation (Brown & Thompson 1938, v, 59–60). When King Robert relaunched his bid to secure control of Scotland in early 1307, operating out of bases in the hills of southern Carrick and northern Galloway, Bishop Thomas may quickly have had cause to regret his actions.

From early 1310, as King Robert and his younger brother, Edward Bruce, gained control of Galloway, Thomas appears to have been regularly resident in York diocese. On 13 February 1310, Archbishop Greenfield gave Thomas a commission of oversight of all properties of the Hospitallers in the archdiocese of York (Brown & Thompson 1938, iii, 94–5). From the summer of 1310, Thomas occurs regularly in the archiepiscopal registers providing episcopal services throughout York diocese, and from 1311 to 1314 he was regularly commissioned to act as Greenfield's deputy during the archbishop's absences from his diocese (Brown & Thompson 1938, i, 41, 223–4, 227; ii, 97; iii, 98–9, 212, 321–2, 328–33; v, 72, 73, 100, 109, 136–7, 141). After King Robert's victory at Bannockburn in June 1314, Thomas may have used the regular Anglo-Scottish truces as opportunities to visit his diocese, but, despite doubts concerning his loyalty that were circulating in England by 1319, there is no sign that he was ever formally reconciled with the Bruce regime (Watt 1969, 130). It is perhaps significant that while there is evidence that the Bruces attempted to woo the canons of Whithorn with a series of property grants and confirmations in the 1310s and 1320s, there is no evidence of similar favour being shown to Bishop Thomas.

Thomas's last years are very obscure. For long it was believed that he died in *c* 1319 (Donaldson 1949, 132). This belief was based on a misdated charter of his successor (Watt 1969, 130). In April 1323, the Archbishop of York was wrongly informed that Thomas had died and, in light of rumours that an un-named bishop-elect of Whithorn was seeking confirmation and consecration from the pope, appointed an official *sede vacante* and wrote to the curia to protest that the *electus* be sent to York as was traditional. This confusion suggests that Thomas may have been resident in his own diocese after *c* 1319 and had effectively lost contact with York. At the time of Simon of Wedale's election as bishop of Whithorn on 23 September 1326, Thomas was described as 'recently dead' (*Northern Registers*, 335). There is no record of his place of death or burial.

Simon of Wedale 1326–55

After the problems of Bishop Thomas's episcopate, it was probably inevitable that King Robert would ensure that a staunchly pro-Bruce candidate was installed at Whithorn. As an area with a strong tradition of pro-Balliol loyalties and lingering anti-Bruce sentiments, it was vital that the key secular and ecclesiastical offices of Galloway should be occupied by reliable men. The individual elected was Simon of Wedale, abbot of Holyrood, a man whose name suggests origins in the valley of the Gala Water in southern Midlothian. Like Bishop Henry in the later 13th century before him, both the close association between his monastery and the crown and also Holyrood's extensive propertied interests in Galloway probably commended him to King Robert. He was elected on 23 September 1326 and on 16 October Archbishop Melton of York instructed an examination of the process of election (Watt 1969, 130). The election occurred during a period of truce, so Simon was able to travel south to secure confirmation of his election from Melton: there was no question of attempting to sever Whithorn's ties with York despite the traumas of the previous 30 years. On 16 December, he received Melton's confirmation and possibly remained at York over the Christmas period. He perhaps travelled south with the archbishop to London early in 1327 in preparation for the coronation of King Edward III. Simon was finally consecrated at Westminster on 1 February, the same day as Edward was crowned, and gave his profession of obedience to Archbishop Melton on 8 February at Tottenham (Watt 1969, 130).

While Edward III was being crowned and Simon consecrated at Westminster, the Scots launched a major raid into northern England. On the failure of the English counter-campaign to bring the Scots to battle, Edward's mother, Queen Isabella, and her lover Roger Mortimer, who exercised real power in England in the name of the young king, opened serious negotiations for peace. The result, in 1328, was the Treaty of Edinburgh, a settlement which envisaged a return to the pre-1296 status quo in Anglo-Scottish affairs. A restoration of a stable relationship between the two kingdoms would have permitted Simon to resume an active role as a suffragan of York without the complication of divided loyalties in the midst of conflict between the Scots and the English. Unfortunately for the bishop, however, the peace lasted only four years before Edward Balliol, the son of the deposed King John Balliol, returned to Scotland with Edward III's backing and began what would prove to be a 24-year struggle first to secure, then to hold on to, his father's lost throne. Reverting to its pro-Balliol loyalties, Galloway became one of the chief centres of King Edward Balliol's power down to the mid-1350s and it is unlikely that Simon, if he maintained his loyalty to Robert I's heir, the young King David II, would have been able to function within his diocese (For discussion of the post-1332 position in Galloway, see Oram 1992, especially 43–7).

Given the turbulence of Galloway for most of this period, it is unsurprising that little record survives of Bishop Simon's activities within his diocese. The gradual slackening of the ties to York which the breakdown in Anglo-Scottish relations produced, moreover, has contributed further to the lack of sources for Simon and his successors, who figure rarely in the archiepiscopal registers which are a major source of data for their predecessors. Like many leading clerics in Scotland in the early 1330s, when it appeared that the Bruce cause was effectively lost, he may have temporarily come into the peace of the English crown. On 1 November 1335, described as being in the peace and faith of King Edward, he was given royal letters of protection for one year (Macpherson *et al* 1814, i, 385b). No further record of such protections survive, which might suggest that Simon reverted to his pro-Bruce loyalties as the cause of David II began to recover in the later 1330s.

Michael Malconhalgh or Mackenlagh 1355–8/9

After over a century of attempting to place one of their own number in the bishopric, on the death of Bishop Simon the canons of Whithorn had the satisfaction of securing the election of their prior, Michael (Watt 1969, 130). His election had occurred before 4 June 1355 and was confirmed by Archbishop John de Thoresby on 26 June, with his consecration following at the hands of commissioners on 12 July. There is, however, no record of a profession of obedience having been offered and, although Whithorn remained technically suffragan of York for a further 117 years, Malconhalgh's episcopate appears to mark a decisive watershed in Galloway's centuries-old ecclesiastical relationship with northern England. For the bishops of Whithorn, the future lay firmly in a Scottish context.

By 1355, support for Edward Balliol in western Galloway had been almost wholly extinguished and it is probable that Malconhalgh's election should be seen in the context of efforts by the Bruce regime to underpin their newly gained hold on the region through installation of an influential local figure into the bishopric. It is unfortunate that there is little evidence to indicate Michael's role in the reintegration of Galloway into the political community of the kingdom or of his relationship with the ruling regime. He is last recorded alive in January 1358 (*Foedera* iii, 387) and may have died in the course of that year. It is unknown where he was buried, but given his personal connection with Whithorn as former prior and bishop it is likely that his is one of the later burials at the east end.

Thomas 1359–62

Malconhalgh's episcopate had marked a watershed in more ways than one. Although his election seemed to mark a final triumph for the capitular formula which had been favoured by the papacy since the early 13th century, it also marked the last instance of a successful application of the principle. His successors were generally set in place through papal provision, where individuals petitioned for and, usually for payment of so-called 'common services', received appointment to benefices. Understandably, it was a system open to considerable abuse and, despite the generally high standard of the papal administration's record-keeping, also led to discord and dispute where more than one individual could produce documented evidence for their promised provision.

Following Malconhalgh's death, there appears to have been an attempt locally to elect Thomas MacDowell as his successor. His name indicates that he was a local man, connected with one of the most influential Galwegian kindreds. Although he claimed to have been elected unanimously, presumably by the canons of Whithorn, and pursued his claim actively until early 1360 (*CPP*, i, 351), he was unable to secure confirmation or consecration in the face of the papal provisee. His successful opponent was another Thomas, of unknown origins, who secured provision and consecration at Avignon by 31 December 1359 (Watt 1969, 130). Almost nothing is known of his career, which spanned little more than three years. He was still alive on 2 September 1362 (Bannatyne Club 1843, ii, 271) but was dead before mid-November 1363 when his successor was elected.

Adam of Lanark 1363–78

Thomas's successor was Adam of Lanark, a Dominican friar who claimed to have been elected but was also provided to the see by the pope on 17 November 1363 (Watt 1969, 130). Adam was a very well-connected cleric, having served as an emissary during the negotiations for the release of David II in 1356–7 and later as his confessor, and should probably be regarded as a king's man inserted into a politically sensitive see, in just the same manner as Alexander Bur was appointed to the see of Moray at around the same date (Macpherson *et al* 1814, i, 802a; *RRS* vi, no. 142; Oram 1999). His was a political appointment and he may have been involved more frequently on business in the king's service than in Galloway. He was apparently consecrated at Avignon by 2 January 1364 and on 20 February a safe conduct was issued for him, 'already overseas' presumably in France, to return through England on King David's business (Macpherson *et al* 1814, i, 808a). His closeness to the king was further emphasised in 1365 when he was one of an exclusive group of 15 men forming a 'congregation' of close advisors and leading clerics who gathered in Perth to discuss the king's policies (Penman 2004, 338).

There is frustratingly little evidence for his later career. Still alive on 16 December 1370, he effectively disappears from the record following the death of King David II in February 1371. Although it is possible that Adam himself may have died at around the same period, it is also a strong possibility that his former closeness to the late king may have made him politically undesirable at the court of the new king Robert II (Watt 1977, 325–6). Given that a first attempt to provide a successor occurred in 1378, it is more likely that he died during the vacancy which followed the death of Pope Gregory IX on 27 March 1378 (Watt 1969, 130–1). There is no record of his place of interment. On the basis of the results of the radiocarbon dating programme (Table 7.1: Lowe, Chapter 9), Bishop Adam would appear to be the latest possible contender who could be considered for inclusion as one of our bishops' graves.

Thomas Rossy 1379–93x1406

The vacancy during which Bishop Adam probably died was ended in 1378 with the election of Pope Urban VI. At some stage during this vacancy Oswald, the claustral prior of the Cistercian abbey of Glenluce, had been elected to the bishopric and an approach was made to Pope Urban for his formal provision. Oswald appears to have travelled to the Continent for consecration, which had occurred before 26 March 1379 when he was in England and about to return to his see (Watt 1969, 131; Macpherson *et al* 1814, ii, 14). However, the new bishop had already been overtaken by events beyond his control, for on 20 September 1378 the College of Cardinals, alarmed by Urban's autocratic style of government, had declared him deposed and elected in his place Robert of Geneva, who took the name of Pope Clement VII. International politics saw the escalation of the Schism in the Church as western Christendom divided into Urbanist and Clementist camps. England had declared for Urban by 5 November 1378 while France, largely on account of Urban's anti-French stance and the kinship between King Charles V and Clement, declared for the latter, who continued to base himself at Avignon. Scotland, probably chiefly on account of England's alignment with Urban, followed their French allies in backing Clement. Oswald was in an invidious position. He had been returning from his consecration carrying various bulls and letters from Pope Urban to Scottish recipients when the Schism had erupted. Protected by an English safe-conduct issued on 26 March 1379, he returned to his see only to find that he had a rival.

Sometime between 31 October 1378 and 26 February 1379, Clement VII had also provided a new bishop to Whithorn. His candidate was the secular clerk Ingram of Kettins, archdeacon of Dunkeld (*CPP*, iv, 540). Made aware of Oswald's provision by Urban VI, Clement cancelled the rival provision before the end of February 1379. Ingram, however, was unwilling to accept the provision and Clement issued a mandate to the bishops of St Andrews and Glasgow to investigate the situation. If they found that Ingram was indeed unwilling to accept the see they were to provide instead Thomas Rossy, a Franciscan friar whose surname suggests possible east Angus connections (*CPL Clement VII*, 26; Watt 1977, 471–3. For a detailed discussion of Rossy's background and career, see McEwan 1957). Although Oswald in the interim had returned to Whithorn, perhaps being enthroned in his cathedral, when Ingram's refusal was confirmed Rossy was provided and consecrated in his place (*CPL Clement VII*, 70), giving the see two formally consecrated bishops. Despite his original provision and consecration by Urban, it was to Clement that Oswald appealed, but by October 1381 the Avignon pope found in favour of Rossy. Ousted from his see, Oswald had little option but to return to Urbanist allegiance and fled to England. There, continuing to style himself 'Bishop of Whithorn', he served in York diocese until his death in 1417 (Storey 1956–70, v, 90–1, 108).

At Whithorn, his learned rival Rossy became a leading intellectual supporter of Clement VII, writing a long treatise on the controversies of the Schism, of which two manuscripts survive (Watt 1977, 472). He was, however, more than an academic warrior and was identified as a possible ecclesiastical leader of a Scottish attack on schismatic England in *c* 1382–3. Although this proposed invasion never materialised, his militant support for Pope Clement was expressed physically in a challenge to single combat made in 1384 to the English warrior-cleric, Henry Despenser, bishop of Norwich (Watt 1977, 473; Nicholson 1974, 193). Active in Scotland down into the early 1390s – he preached a sermon at the coronation of Robert III in August 1390 – he appears to have spent much of the latter stages of his life at Avignon. The last clear evidence for Rossy being alive occurs on 6 September 1397, when he was again at Avignon, but it is likely that he died shortly before the provision of his successor on 28 May 1406 (Watt 1969, 131; Watt 1977, 473; *CPP*, iv, 577). It is not known if he returned to Scotland or where he died, but the balance of evidence seems to point towards his death abroad. Whether or not his remains were returned for burial at Whithorn is unknown. The implications, however, given the date of his *obit* and the results of the radiocarbon dating programme (Table 7.1: Lowe, Chapter 9) – even if he was returned – are that he is not among the excavated graves at the east end of the church.

Eliseus Adougan 1406–12x1415

Like Oswald in 1378, Eliseus Adougan was 'elected' in his own diocese before securing his provision from the second Avignonese pope, Benedict XIII, on 28 May 1406 (*CPL Benedict XIII*, 151). Adougan appears to have been a Galloway man and had already gained prominence through attachment to the household of Archibald, 4th earl of Douglas, from whom he had received the provostry of the rich collegiate church of Lincluden. There is perhaps no greater testimony to the degree of control over the internal affairs of Galloway exercised by the Black Douglas family than the election of Adougan to the bishopric. The new bishop was a committed pluralist who used the need of both Avignonese and Roman popes to court favour to secure papal authorisation to hold several incompatible benefices simultaneously. Shortly after his formal provision, he secured letters from Benedict XIII which permitted him to hold both the parsonage of Kirkmahoe and the provostry of Lincluden conjointly with his new bishopric (*CPL Benedict XIII*, 153). There was no spiritual reason for this arrangement; Eliseus was concerned principally in maintaining possession of two lucrative benefices which would greatly augment the income he could receive from what was then one of the poorest of the Scottish bishoprics.

Given his pluralism and his use of indulgences and dispensations as money-making devices, it is difficult not to view with some cynicism his efforts in 1408 to force the canons of Whithorn to contribute towards the costs of repairs to the cathedral church. The bishop's letter to Benedict XIII has not survived, but on 11 April 1408 the pope issued a commission in response to his appeal to the archdeacon of Glasgow to compel the prior and canons to contribute from their income towards rebuilding costs. The wording of the commission probably repeats the language of Adougan's letter (*CPL Benedict* XIII, 173; for the full text, see Reid 1960, no. 1; see also Oram, Chapter 8.2 *Later Medieval Building Work*). There is no record of the result of the archdeacon's investigation. Adougan's relationship with the canons was further damaged by a second appeal which sought to force them to yield property in Whithorn to him to allow the building of a suitable residence in the burgh (*CPL Benedict XIII*, 174). It is possible that his predecessors, in fact, had no separate residence and, like the pre-13th-century bishops of St Andrews, occupied part of the monastic complex when in residence at Whithorn. Eliseus claimed that his nearest private residence, which is not named in the letter but is clearly The Clary (between Newton Stewart and Wigtown), was too remote from his cathedral to permit him to properly fulfil his spiritual functions. Again, we do not know the outcome of the appeal, but the later medieval bishops of Whithorn possessed Balnespick or Bishopton, just to the north of the cathedral-priory.

There is little evidence for his active career as bishop other than some records of his installation of priests to vacant benefices (*CPL Benedict XIII*, 291). One dispensation by him survives, arising from powers granted to him by papal bull to dispense ten persons of his choice of either sex within his diocese, to contract marriage within the prohibited degrees. This was given on 8 September 1412 to Alexander Stewart of Torbane and Elizabeth Stewart, daughter of Sir John Stewart, lord of Cally, permitting them to marry despite their relationship in the fourth degree of consanguinity (NAS GD10/348). These powers had been granted to Eliseus as far back as February 1407, when he had received two separate indults from Pope Benedict XIII, the first allowing him to dispense 12 people from 'defect of birth' to be promoted to holy orders and the second permitting the marriage of 12 individuals related in the fourth degree (*CPL Benedict XIII*, 160–1).

As with his predecessors, we have no firm evidence for his exact date of death, but papal letters concerning appointment of a successor were issued from 14 June 1415 (*CPL Benedict XIII*, 317–9). He was described as dying 'outside the curia', probably in his diocese. While there is no record of his place of burial, it is likely that he was interred at Whithorn. It is clear, however, given the date of his *obit* and the results of the radiocarbon dating programme (Table 7.1: Lowe, Chapter 9) that he cannot be among the group at the east end of the church.

Thomas of Buittle 1415–20x22

The death of Bishop Eliseus resulted in yet another disputed succession to the bishopric, this time occasioned by the reservation of provision to the see by the pope conflicting with the rights of the chapter. The canons of Whithorn had probably moved swiftly on the bishop's death to elect a man suitable to both themselves and their lay patron, Archibald, 4th earl of Douglas. Their choice was Gilbert Cavan, rector of Kirkinner, a mature and well-educated cleric with a career extending back to the early 1380s (Watt 1977, 93–4). He was connected very closely with the earl's household and secured a number of appointments to benefices through service to him. In the years immediately before his election to the bishopric, Cavan was employed in negotiations for Douglas's ransom arrangements in England, and in the early 1420s he was a member of the earl's household and tutor of the future 5th earl. These connections, however, were inadequate to secure confirmation of his election from Benedict XIII, who on 14 June 1415 provided instead Thomas of Buittle, archdeacon of Galloway and a papal chaplain and auditor of appeals (*CPL Benedict XIII*, 317–8).

Like Cavan, Thomas was a highly educated clerk who had already had a prominent career and who was linked closely to the household of the Black Douglases (Watt 1977, 70–2). He was already in possession of a substantial portfolio of benefices in Scotland when provided to the bishopric, but had recently gained papal favour through his service in the curia and consistent loyalty to Benedict XIII at a time when the 'Avignonese' cause was losing support throughout Europe. He appears to have been consecrated before 5 September 1415, when he was no longer described as 'elect' in papal letters (*CPL Benedict XIII*, 326). Shortly after securing the bishopric, however, he appears to have transferred his allegiance from Benedict to the Council of Constance, which was seeking a way of bringing a formal end to the Schism. This shift may reflect the gradual detachment of Earl Archibald from the 'Avignonese' allegiance and his growing support for the Conciliar movement which would culminate in 1418–9 with the earl's active role in formally bringing the 40-year period of Schism to an end (Brown 1998, 196–8).

Throughout his career and despite the extensive collection of church offices which he held in Scotland, Thomas appears to have been mainly an absentee incumbent. There is little evidence to show his regular presence in Scotland, let alone in his own diocese, after 1415 and his involvement in the denouement of the Schism probably ensured that he was rarely at home for long. He was present in Scotland in March 1416, possibly in conjunction with formal installation and enthronement as bishop, attending a gathering of senior clerics at Perth (Bannatyne Club 1843, no. 325). He did not attend a provincial council of the Scottish Church at Perth in July 1420, sending instead a proctor (Robertson 1866, ii, no. 166). This may be an indication of failing health but all that can be said with certainty was that he was dead before 4 December 1422 when his successor was named (Watt 1969, 131). His place of death and burial are unknown but it is likely that he died in Scotland and was buried in his cathedral.

Alexander Vaus 1422–50

The new bishop was Alexander Vaus, who had been bishop of Caithness from 1414. His translation to Whithorn represented a career advance as, though still low in the hierarchy of Scottish dioceses, the Church of Galloway was still far wealthier than the most northerly mainland see. Vaus, unlike his immediate predecessors, was apparently not university educated and may have owed his promotion to personal connections and good fortune. Gordon Donaldson suggested that he may have been a son of William Vaus, lord of Dirleton, whom he noted as dying *c* 1392 (Donaldson 1949, 141), but his earlier career seems to have been focused entirely on northern Scotland and there is no evidence for any immediate connection with the Dirleton line. This northern connection may point to a relationship with the cadet line of the Vaus family who held lands in Easter Ross in the 1400s and who were associated with Whithorn priory's daughter-house at Fearn, but their connection with the senior, Dirleton line of the family and their date of establishment in Ross is unknown. Before 1398 he was precentor of Caithness and was promoted in July that year to the archdeaconry (*CPL Benedict XIII*, 88). He was provided to the bishopric of Orkney by Pope Benedict XIII before 20 November 1407 but, despite receiving faculty permitting his consecration in Scotland in February 1408, he had still not been consecrated by 22 January 1415 several months after his translation to the bishopric of Caithness (*CPL Benedict XIII*, 166, 170, 309). In December 1422 he was at the curia, where Pope Martin V instructed his translation to Whithorn and from where he was later to seek papal absolution for his possible error in having left to take possession of his new see before having secured the requisite papal letters (Watt 1969, 131; *CSSR 1423–8*, 215).

Despite his long episcopate, Alexander Vaus has left little evidence for his tenure of the see. The earliest surviving records for his activities show him involved in settling financial disputes, possibly indicating anxiety over settlement of the common services payments which he would have been obliged to make to the curia in return for his provision. As part of this process, he reached agreement on a range of issues concerning appointment of parish priests and payment of moneys due to the bishop as ordinary of the diocese by the abbey of Holyrood, which was one of the biggest holders of appropriated parish churches in Galloway (NAS RH6/251, RH6/280, both dated 4 August 1429; Reid 1960, no. 5, 4 August 1429). He does appear, however, to have been concerned about the spiritual health of his see, sometime before February 1433 removing from post a parish priest who was unable to perform his duties and who had absented himself from his charge without making proper provision for a curate (*CSSR 1433–47*, no. 25). In 1434, he authorised the appropriation of the church of Longcastle to the chaplainry in the cathedral which Prior Thomas was setting up (Chapter 8.2.1). His last surviving act appears to be the charter of 20

September 1448 which granted lands in Kirkcolm parish to Thomas McDowell of Garthland and his wife, Margaret, daughter of Robert Vaus (Reid 1960, no. 135). The relationship between Robert Vaus and Bishop Alexander is unknown, but there seems to be some close kinship connection. Robert appears to have been the first of his family to secure a significant landholding in Wigtownshire, purchasing the properties of Barnbarroch and Barglass in Kirkinner parish from William, 8th earl of Douglas, in January 1452 (Reid 1960, nos 136, 137).

By the time that Robert Vaus was making his mark as a landholder, Bishop Alexander had resigned his see. In 1450, the bishop was probably around 80 years old, and age and infirmity, reasons which he himself had used to justify the removal of a parish priest nearly two decades earlier, seem to have prompted him to resign his position (Donaldson 1949, 141; Watt 1969, 131). On 8 January 1450, his resignation in favour of Thomas Spens was received at the Apostolic Camera (Watt 1969, 131). His exact date of death is unknown but he appears to have lived into the early 1450s. No burial place is recorded but it seems likely that he was interred in the cathedral at Whithorn.

Thomas Spens 1450–8

The man in whose favour Alexander Vaus resigned was Thomas Spens, an ambitious cleric who had started his career in the service of the Black Douglases. It is possible that he had been coadjutor to Vaus before his elevation to the bishopric (Donaldson 1949, 141), but no concrete evidence for this role has survived. Spens may have been one of many former servants of the Douglas family who had been alienated by the events of 1440 which had seen the judicial murder of William, 6th earl of Douglas, and his younger brother, David, and the succession of their great uncle, James 'the Gross', earl of Avondale, to the main Douglas titles. While he probably owed his first senior position – the provostship of Lincluden – to Douglas patronage, his later career was advanced with the support of King James II (Brown 1998, 286). The late and often unreliable account of Hector Boece suggests that he was appointed by King James to the archdeaconry of Galloway (Moir 1894, 37), which, if true, would suggest that he was a key agent in James II's policy of encroachment on the Douglases' power-base in Galloway. From 1450, he was very closely identified with the crown interest and witnessed numerous royal charters, his alignment with the crown being emphasised graphically in 1455 when he was one of two ambassadors sent to France by the king to explain his actions against the Douglases to King Charles VII (Oram 1997, 74). He was keeper of the Privy Seal before 1458 (NAS GD93/20). In 1457, James attempted to reward Spens for his services through translation to Aberdeen, with Thomas Vaus, dean of Glasgow, advanced as his successor at Whithorn (Donaldson 1949, 141–2; Watt 1969, 131). The attempted translation in 1457 was ineffective. However, in December 1458 he was again translated to Aberdeen, this time successfully. On this occasion, Thomas Vaus was not advanced as his replacement. Spens served as bishop of Aberdeen for a further 22 years and was buried in the collegiate church of the Holy Trinity in Edinburgh, which had been founded by James II's widow, Mary of Gueldres (Chapter 8.2.3).

Ninian Spot 1458–80x82

The replacement for Spens at Whithorn, Ninian Spot, was another crown servant. Prior to his provision he had been a canon of Dunkeld and served James II as Comptroller (the 'roller of accounts' who shared responsibility for management of the royal finances with the Treasurer) from 1457 to 1459. Spot was provided by Pope Pius II on 15 December 1458 as part of the arrangement which saw Thomas Spens translated to Aberdeen (Watt 1969, 132). He was consecrated between 12 March and 16 April 1459, and on 27 April King James issued instructions for his formal admission to the temporalities of the diocese (*RMS*, ii, no. 698). Spot continued to serve as a member of royal councils down to 1476 and witnessed over 20 crown charters during that period (*RMS*, ii, nos 686, 687, 706, 731, 734–7, 739, 743, 746, 748–53, 811, 990, 993, 1035, 1043, 1062, 1241, 1246, 1248, 1249), but he was apparently not a member of the inner circle of royal servants. His main service occurred in the last years of James II's reign and he fades from view during the early years of the minority of James III from 1460 to 1464. It is possible that he was out of favour with the Boyd family, who dominated Scottish government down to 1469, for he re-emerges as a witness to royal documents between 1470 and 1476. His last surviving incidence as a charter witness is in July 1476, his disappearance thereafter probably being more a consequence of advancing age than hostility towards him from James III. Ninian was still alive in June 1480 when he is mentioned in the *Exchequer Rolls*, but was dead before 9 December 1482 when his successor was provided (Watt 1969, 132). There is no record of his place of burial but the main record for the second part of his career indicates that he was most regularly resident in Galloway and the likelihood is that he was buried in his cathedral.

George Vaus 1482–1508

George Vaus, another member of the family which seems to have been established in Wigtownshire through the good offices of their kinsman, Bishop Alexander Vaus, was rector of Wigtown before his provision on 9 December 1482 (Donaldson 1949, 142; Reid 1960, 174 n. 1; Watt

1969, 132). His promotion may have been an act of James III but, coming as it did in the midst of the political crisis of 1482–3 which had perhaps seen the imprisonment and threatened deposition of the king (Macdougall 1982, Chapter 8), it is more likely that his provision as bishop was arranged by some of the men who controlled royal government at this time. Association with the political opposition in 1482 may account for his comparative invisibility for the remainder of James III's reign. George, however, cannot have been entirely out of royal favour for in July 1488 he was apparently Dean of the Chapel Royal (Macdougall 1997, 53), a position to which he was apparently appointed by the late king. The account of the events of summer 1488 offered by the 16th-century chronicler, Robert Lindsay of Pitscottie, suggests that Vaus enjoyed a close relationship with James IV as a spiritual and political advisor (Scottish Text Society 1899, i, 218–9). Indeed, in June 1488 he was named as one of the close group of nobles and clerics around the young king and who formed the core of the new regime. Certainly, Vaus was named in October 1489 in the list of complaints sent to James IV by the western nobles involved in the rising of that year against the narrow Hepburn- and Hume-dominated council which controlled the government as one of the 'parciall personis' who had sewn up the government between them against the true interests of the young James (Macdougall 1997, 71). Vaus, moreover, was one of the men who provided the king with substantial funds to raise men and equipment to counter the rising (Macdougall 1997, 75). After 1489, however, the bishop drops out of this inner circle of advisors. This change, however, does not appear to have been a consequence of disfavour, for Whithorn was subsequently to benefit significantly from James IV's patronage, not least on account of his regular visits to the shrine of St Ninian, and when the Chapel Royal was erected into a bishopric in 1501 Vaus was its first bishop. Despite that, however, he appears rarely as a witness to royal charters and seems to have focused his efforts within his diocese.

George was a very worldly man who fits easily into the rather distorted stereotype of the late medieval, pre-Reformation cleric. He had at least two illegitimate children, a son, Abraham, who was provided by his father with the lands of Portincalzie in the Rhinns (NAS GD138/1/18 and GD138/1/211), and a daughter, Margaret, who was married to Patrick Dunbar of Clugstoun (NAS GD138). He was an active nepotist, benefiting various relatives including his two children. In 1502, his daughter and son-in-law were appointed joint castellans and keepers of the episcopal 'palace and fortalice of Balnespyk', together with the 100/- lands of Balnespyk (now Bishopton on the northern side of Whithorn) and the six merklands of Balchure (now Bailiewhir; NAS GD138/1/11), while in August 1506 he directed the collation of his kinsman, John Vaus, to the rectory of Wigtown (Reid 1960, no. 93), and other relatives secured positions in the service of the priory and as tenants of episcopal and priory properties. His son Abraham also benefited from his father's patronage as assignee in land settlements arising from distraint for debts. In April 1506, Abraham was assigned various lands in the estate of Craigcaffie, belonging to Hugh Neilson, who owed £148 10s to Bishop George Vaus (*RMS*, ii, no. 2956). It is likely that George's son was the Abraham Vaus who in 1532 secured some interest in the commendatorship of Whithorn, but who proved unsuccessful in securing his title (Watt & Shead 2001, 219). By the time of George's death in late 1507 or very early 1508 (Watt 1969, 132), the Vaus family had been firmly established as a leading member of the local political and landholding community. There is no record of where the bishop was buried but, given the apparently extensive rebuilding work undertaken at Whithorn under his direction (Radford & Donaldson 1953, 28, 30) and his close personal involvement in his diocese, it seems probable that it was within his cathedral.

David Arnot 1508–26

On Vaus's death, the crown nominated James Betoun, commendator of Dunfermline, to the bishopric (Watt 1969, 132; Donaldson 1949, 142). Nominated on 1 March, formally provided by Pope Julius II on 12 May, and granted the temporalities of the see on 17 July, on 9 November 1508 Betoun was elected Archbishop of Glasgow and translated to his new diocese on 19 January 1509 without ever having been consecrated at Whithorn. The day before Betoun's election to Glasgow, James IV had nominated David Arnot, abbot of Cambuskenneth, as bishop of Whithorn, and the pope granted formal provision on 29 January 1509 (Watt 1969, 132; Donaldson 1949, 142). Arnot had been a loyal servant of King James III since the late 1470s and had remained in his service through and after the crisis of 1482–3. This identification with the old regime probably made him an acceptable figure to those who sought to purge James IV's household and administration of those closely identified with the overthrow of the late king and the apparent mismanagement of royal finances between 1488 and 1492. In August 1492, Arnot was appointed Treasurer in place of the discredited William Knollis (Macdougall 1997, 96–7), and his dutiful service to James IV saw its first reward in 1503 when he was provided to the abbacy of Cambuskenneth (Watt & Shead 2001, 27). Elevation to the bishopric in 1508/9 was fitting culmination of a distinguished career of loyal service to the crown.

Like Vaus before him, Arnot seems to have used his new authority to advance the interests of his family in the diocese. The Arnots were a minor landholding family from North-east Fife and had no previous interest in Galloway. By 1529, a Henry Arnot was in dispute over the parish clerkship of Inch, a parish annexed to the episcopal mensa since the 1290s, while a Patrick Arnot and an Andrew Arnot held the archdeaconry of Galloway in 1529–42 and 1543–75 respectively (Reid 1960, nos 123, 273, 316; Watt 1969, 138). He does not, however, appear to have intruded his illegitimate offspring into lands and offices associated with the bishopric.

Arnot's closeness to the king brought further benefits which considerably increased his power and wealth within Galloway. In 1509/10, he secured nomination and provision to the commendatorship of Tongland, which he retained down to 1529 (Watt & Shead 2001, 211). This combination of royal favour and local wealth, however, appears to have given Arnot a rather elevated view of his own authority in the diocese which, coupled with aggressive litigation against various influential local lairds, including Patrick Dunbar and Margaret Vaus over the lands of Bishopton and Bailiewhir, quickly led to friction and discord between the bishop and his flock (Reid 1960, 6–7). His relationship with the abbot and monks of Glenluce was particularly fraught, and in 1524 he procured letters of cursing directed against them (Reid 1960, 46). A forceful visitation of the abbey in July 1524, which saw extensive damage committed on the monks' property by the large retinue of laymen whom Arnot brought with him, brought matters to a head and the litigation which resulted led directly to the bishop's enforced resignation in January 1526 (Reid 1960, 7, 46–7; Watt 1969, 132). Although evidently disgraced by the events of 1524/5, Arnot succeeded in reserving a pension of half the fruits of the diocese and episcopal property plus a right to return to the office, together with the revenues of Tongland Abbey (against the king's will). He continued to draw the episcopal pension until his death sometime between 10 July 1536 and 25 August 1537 (Watt 1969, 132). It is not known where he was interred.

Henry Wemyss 1526–41

The man in whose favour Arnot was induced to resign was Henry Wemyss, archdeacon of Galloway since 1522 and previously Official of the diocese (Watt 1969, 138, 140). Another Fifer, it is possible that there was some kinship tie between the two men, but any such relationship has not been established. Wemyss emerged into political prominence in 1528 as a member of the political opposition to the Red Douglas regime headed by the Earl of Angus which had controlled the kingdom for much of the minority of King James V. In July 1528 he was a member of the party which accompanied the king from Stirling to Edinburgh in the opening round of the royal coup against the Douglases (Cameron 1998, 25). He remained thereafter a close servant of the king and probably served amongst the Lords of Council (Cameron 1998, 292). His closeness to James V probably hastened the settlement of his dispute with Arnot over the revenues of Tongland, which the former bishop was forced to yield up in 1529. At that time, James V proposed the permanent annexation of the revenues of the abbey to the see of Galloway and the Chapel Royal (Hannay & Hay 1954, 162). Wemyss, however, did not immediately secure the commendatorship for himself, which passed instead briefly to a royal kinsman, William Stewart, before finally coming to Wemyss in 1530/1 (Watt & Shead 2001, 211–2). Wemyss, however, did not suffer financially, for in October 1529 the king nominated him to the commendatorship of the far wealthier Dundrennan Abbey, whose revenues he was to hold until his death in 1541 (Hannay & Hay 1954, 160; Watt & Shead 2001, 66). Following the death of Arnot in 1537 and the return of his predecessor's reserved half of the fruits of the bishopric, Wemyss was unquestionably the wealthiest and notionally most powerful man to occupy the see of Whithorn.

Wemyss' wealth was offset by the increased financial obligations which James V imposed on the Church in Scotland in the 1530s, notionally for the establishment and maintenance of the College of Justice but mainly appropriated for his lavish expenditure on building and projection of the royal image. As a consequence, most of the records which survive of Bishop Wemyss' activities in the diocese relate to the feuing of episcopal properties to secure revenue. Beginning in 1531 but more regularly in 1536–8, for example, he issued letters of tack or assedation on several episcopal properties in Wigtownshire (Reid 1960, nos 23, 24, 24a, 26, 251, 265). Most of these property deals, however, involved families who had been tightening their hold over portions of kirklands in the diocese for some time, most notably the Kennedies, Vauses and Maxwells. The Kennedies, headed by the Earl of Cassilis, had been extending their influence south from Carrick into Wigtownshire for some time, and in 1516 had secured their position when Bishop Arnot had given the 1st earl the office of bailie of the episcopal estate in Wigtownshire, plus the offices of captain, constable and keeper of the episcopal manor on its island in Loch Inch (Reid 1960, no. 15a). The Kennedies tightened their grip on Inch thereafter and in 1546 were at litigation with Wemyss's successor, Andrew Durie, who was attempting to regain control of the castle (Reid 1960, no 296). It had been a similar infeftment by George Vaus in respect of the episcopal palace at Whithorn itself which Arnot had attempted to reverse. Despite his position, Weymss was obliged to abandon his predecessor's efforts to regain physical possession of Bishopton and Bailiewhir and in November 1539 he confirmed Margaret Dunbar, Bishop Arnot's grand-daughter, in possession (GD138/1/54).

Henry Wemyss died between 14 March and 21 May 1541. His place of burial is not recorded but is likely to have been at Whithorn or Dundrennan.

Andrew Durie 1541–58
The last of the effective pre-Reformation bishops at Whithorn, Andrew Durie, does not enjoy a good reputation. Already abbot of Melrose when he was nominated by James V in July 1541 (Hannay & Hay 1954, 425; Watt 1969, 132; Donaldson 1949, 142), his administration of that monastery was hardly an example of spiritual or moral rectitude (Fawcett & Oram 2004, 56–8, 240, 267; Oram 1997, 78–9) and would not have inspired confidence in his abilities to dispense adequately his duties as bishop. He was, however, riding high in the king's favour and was to retain for life a substantial annuity from the abbey's revenues in addition to the enlarged revenues of the bishopric. Despite his reputation as a money-seeker, Durie did also enjoy a prominent position in the official reaction to the spread of heresy in the kingdom in the 1540s and 1550s, being remembered after his death by John Knox as 'our enemy of God' (Dickinson 1949, 116, 129; Laing 1846–64, i, 242, 261–2). He was an important player in the political life of the kingdom during the early stages of the minority of Queen Mary after December 1542, and in July 1543 was one of four bishops who joined Cardinal Beaton and the earls of Huntly, Argyll, Lennox, Bothwell, Sutherland and Menteith in a bond to protest against the pro-English administration of the kingdom headed by the Regent Arran (Wormald 1991, 56; Wormald 1985, 404, no 7). Having signed up to this declaration of support for the traditional religious hierarchy and the French alliance, there is little other sign that he was engaged actively in stemming the tide of religious dissent.

Like Arnot before him, the main record for Durie's actions at Whithorn is in his disposal of kirklands at feu (Reid 1960, nos 346, 347). For the most part, however, he seems to have been obliged to accept the disposal of property instituted by his predecessor, confirming, for example, the position of the Earl of Cassilis as bailie of the episcopal estate in Wigtownshire and keeper of the manor at Inch (Reid 1960, nos 296, 243). How frequently he was resident in his see is unclear, for he appears to have been an important figure in the service of the Queen-Regent, Mary of Guise. According to Knox, he died of an apoplectic fit in Edinburgh on receiving news of a Protestant riot. His place of burial is not recorded.

Although Durie was succeeded by Alexander Gordon as bishop, Gordon quickly aligned with the Reformers in 1560 and retained control of Whithorn as a Protestant bishop (Oram 1997, 79–80; Watt 1969, 132). Durie's death can be taken to mark the end of the medieval succession of bishops and the last possible interment in the still functioning liturgical east end of the cathedral. By the time of Gordon's death in 1575, it is likely that the eastern limb of the cathedral was already in an advanced state of ruin. His place of burial, and the graves of his Protestant successors, are unidentified.

8.2 THE BUILDINGS

8.2.1 Liturgical and devotional arrangements and the position of the tombs

The 12th-century church at Whithorn
It was the view of Ralegh Radford and Donaldson, writing in 1949, that the earliest part of the visible remains of the medieval cathedral-priory at Whithorn were those of a Romanesque church, 'cruciform, with a short nave, unlike the lengthy churches of the reformed monastic orders', perhaps built in the time of Bishop Gille-aldan (Radford 1949, 102). They identified it as similar in form to churches of the mid-12th century built in the 'Celtic' monasteries of Wales. On the basis of the surviving 12th-century stonework in the south wall of the nave, they proposed that Gille-aldan's church had a western limb of perhaps less than half the length of the existing structure (plan in Radford & Donaldson 1953, 35; and revised version in Radford & Donaldson 1984, 16). Their original implication was that the east end of the building was of greater length than the nave, but in their post-excavation 1953 account of the building they commented more cautiously that the 12th-century church was 'a cruciform building the full extent of which is not known' (Radford & Donaldson 1953, 28). Given the steep fall in the ground towards the east from around midway along the length of the existing eastern limb, it is possible that the original liturgical east end may not have extended more than 20m east of the present east gable of the nave. If Gille-aldan was buried in this church, unless his tomb was moved to a new position within the later, enlarged choir, it is probable that his remains lay much further to the west. While it is most likely that his tomb lay in front of the high altar of his church, or perhaps in a grave close to the small chapel which contained the supposed burial-place of St Ninian, the 12th-century tomb recess in the base of the pulpitum at the west end of the nave suggests a high-status burial for whom there is no obvious secular candidate (Radford & Donaldson 1953, 31).

Such a compact cathedral as Ralegh Radford & Donaldson proposed may have been adequate for whatever community of clergy served Gille-aldan's cathedral, but it was probably quickly inadequate for the needs of both the swelling ranks of the episcopal household and diocesan administration which was developed at Whithorn in the later 12th and early 13th centuries, and for the convent of canons regular which was established there by his successor, Bishop Christian. There is no firm date known for when the community at Whithorn adopted regular life, but they appear to have followed a route favoured by other unreformed secular colleges and may at first have assumed the Augustinian rule before adopting the more austere rule of the Premonstratensians in 1175x1177 (Veitch 1999; Radford & Donaldson 1953, 15–6; Easson 1957, 88; Cowan & Easson 1976, 103). Whatever other political and cultural changes were involved in the process of regularisation, the adoption of a monastic rule would have required significant development of the complex of religious and domestic buildings which probably had formed the core of the community as it had evolved in the early 12th century. The most obvious change would have been the construction of an enclosed cloister to the north of the Romanesque church of Gille-Aldan, which, from the significant differences between the masonry of the north and south walls of the nave, appears to have involved the rebuilding of the north wall from foundations up. The layout of the cloister at Whithorn has never been determined satisfactorily. It may only have had ranges on its east and north quarters, with a simple screen wall at the west end – the plan employed at Prémontré itself and visible elsewhere in Britain at, for example, Alnwick and Dryburgh abbeys (Fawcett & Oram 2005, 129–30 and Figs 1 and 10; Hope 1887, 337–46). Beyond the identification of portions of the north range in trial work by C J Tabraham in the 1970s and fragments of what was probably the reredorter at the northern end of the east range during the construction of the present parish church in the 1820s, details of its layout are unknown (Tabraham 1979).

If Ralegh Radford's short nave theory is correct, then its extension was probably consequent on the adoption of the Premonstratensian rule in the later 12th century and the development of a monastic cloister. Part of this development may have been driven by the need to accommodate a growing secular population in the parish, for the nave housed the parish altar in the pre-Reformation period, but the physical requirements of the cloister layout was perhaps the primary determinant. The one surviving 13th-century lancet in the nave's south wall and the cut down bases of two more in the present 18th-century wall-head on the north suggest that the main building episode occurred after 1200 and possibly as late as *c* 1250. This later date might accord well with interpreted evidence from the 1984–91 excavations which appears to indicate a major post-1250 replanning of the outer precinct of the cathedral-priory, at least on its south and west sides (Hill 1997, 60–5). However, on the basis of the radiocarbon dates, the burial sequence and the grave assemblages, the results of the current study suggest a construction date in the first decade of the 13th century for the eastward extension of the church (Chapter 9).

The 13th-century extensions to the monastic church and rearrangement of the outer precinct were presumably also driven by a substantial growth in the size of the monastic community. By 1235, the Whithorn community was amongst the larger monastic establishments in Scotland, with 22 canons recorded in documents concerning the election of Odo Ydonc, canon of Holywood Abbey, as bishop (Raine 1870, 172). This number represents a substantial convent and, when the unrecorded numbers of potential novices, chaplains and lay servitors attached to both the monastic household and the bishops' establishments are taken into account, it emerges as a major community which would have occupied an extensive complex of domestic and ancillary buildings in addition to the church and cloister in the inner precinct.

The growth and form of shrines

Growth of the building footprint was probably also stimulated by the increasing popularity of the shrine of St Ninian. Although Ralegh Radford's excavated evidence is open to different interpretation, it appears that what was believed in the 11th and 12th centuries to be the saint's tomb was housed in a free-standing chapel down the slope from the probable east end of the first Romanesque church (Radford 1949, 106–19). An increased flow of pilgrims to this shrine may have helped to generate the revenues necessary to finance major construction work, part of which involved the eastwards extension of the choir and presbytery of the monastic church to wholly subsume the earlier shrine chapel. Such an expansion and the planning behind it is entirely in keeping with the identified trends in popular religion which developed through the course of the 12th century. These trends saw a proliferation of cult centres and new arrangements being made for popular devotion at such sites, often driven by a need to secure a stable flow of revenues to fund building projects (Morris 1972, 55–60). The location of the shrine in a purpose-built chapel behind the position of the high altar is a common manifestation of this trend, but has its origins in Early Christian traditions of the burial of relics in or under altars.

Provision of an enhanced setting for a shrine at Whithorn was part of a general development in the treatment of relics in Western Christendom which had begun in the 4th century. Around that time, the practice emerged of burying saints, especially martyred saints, beneath altars (Toynbee & Ward Perkins 1956, 195–229). By the 7th century the practice of elevating the saints' bodies in shrines rather than disposing of them in the ground had become established in the West, as the example of the disinterring and placing of Cuthbert's remains in a sarcophagus beside the altar of the church at Lindisfarne (*HE* iv, 30), or the arrangement that may have been adopted for the relics of Castantín at St Andrews. At Lindisfarne and St Andrews, provision was being made for the re-housing of complete corpses, but in most cases it seems likely that only selected pieces of the corpse (or possibly simply items associated with the saint in question) were removed from the main tomb and encased in a portable reliquary. These reliquaries were displayed on altars, placed in the crypt on or adjacent to the tomb, or kept in treasuries and placed on display or processed only on feast days (Wilson 1977, 5 and note 8). This was the probable arrangement for the display of the relics of St Columba at Dunkeld in the later medieval period (Yeoman 1999, 86–7).

While the shrines containing the complete physical remains could be very elaborate, few were located in grand settings which allowed large numbers to congregate around them. The cramped location of the shrine of St Cuthbert in the late 11th-century apse behind the high altar at Durham is a case in point. When the saint's remains were translated from their 10th-century grave into the new, elevated shrine, only a select few could be accommodated in the confined space. The development in the 11th and 12th centuries of the cult of saints with the growth in belief in their intercessory powers saw an explosion in pilgrim numbers which in turn led to a huge expansion in the provision of suitable physical settings for the more popular shrines which would allow public access while minimising the impact of their presence on the liturgical routine of the clergy. Rather than relocate the shrines from their most common positions east of the high altar, elaborate ambulatories were devised as a means of carrying the pilgrim traffic in a flowing route around and behind the choir areas. The main European manifestation of this style was for the construction of a semi-circular ambulatory aisle or chevet round an apsidal east end, with chapels radiating from the outer wall of the aisle. The form developed particularly in a series of major pilgrimage churches in southern France built in the late 11th and early 12th centuries, which derived their plan from the now destroyed great shrine church of St Martin at Tours. The surviving exemplars of the style in France are Sainte-Foy at Conques or Sainte-Sernin at Toulouse, but the largest and most influential building in this tradition was Santiago de Compostela in northern Spain, where the ambulatory and eastern chapels were constructed between 1075 and 1105 (Barral i Altet 2001, 61–9; Laule & Laule 1997, 144–9). In all of these buildings, however, the shrine remained located in a crypt chapel beneath the east end, with the shrine structure itself lying immediately below the high altar in the Early Christian tradition best represented in St Peter's at Rome. Given the traditional relationship between Tours and Whithorn, the location of the shrine *vis-à-vis* the high altar at the former may have been of influence in the planning of the extended east end at the latter. There is no way of proving this conjectured influence, but the possibility must be considered that the high altar of the post-1200 church at Whithorn lay further to the east, possibly directly over the believed location of the tomb in the crypt.

An alternative form for the public presentation of relics emerged in northern France in the mid-12th century. At the abbey of St-Denis in Paris, Abbot Suger began a major reconstruction and eastwards extension in 1140–4 of the east end of the church to allow for the large numbers of pilgrims coming to the shrine. Here, however, rather than moving the high altar into the new east end it was left in its original position and the additional space provided behind it was used to house the shrine, to which access was gained via a grand chevet with ambulatory (Panofsky 1979; Binski 1996, 78). This basic form of shrine-behind-altar is the layout which was to gain most favour in shrine churches built or rebuilt within Britain from the later 12th century onwards. The closest parallel for the use of the chevet is Canterbury, where the great Trinity Chapel or Corona at the extreme east end of the cathedral was begun in 1174 as a setting for the tomb and shrine of St Thomas Becket. Recent analysis has emphasised the influences of St-Denis on the design at Canterbury, particularly in the form of the elevated eastern chapel with ambulatory. The Trinity Chapel at Canterbury was a two-storey structure, the lower crypt stage housing the archbishop's empty tomb while the upper portion contained the feretory carried on a richly decorated base (Binski 2004, 3–23). Single-storey architectural settings were employed from 1245 for Henry III's grand new east end at Westminster Abbey, a chevet in plan and designed to house the new shrine of St Edward the Confessor, while at Hailes Abbey in Gloucestershire, founded in 1246 by Henry's younger brother, Richard of Cornwall, and to which he gave a relic of the Holy Blood, the gifts of the pilgrims paid for the construction of a great eastern chevet at the centre of which was the shrine housing his gift (Binski 2004, 144–6; Midmer 1979, 156). Despite the royal patronage of these major examples, the chevet did not gain wider popularity within Britain and, although the St-Denis arrangement of a shrine chapel east of the high altar did become widely adopted the east ends at most shrine churches in the British Isles took the form of a rectangular chapel projecting east from a rectangular choir and presbytery.

In Scotland, this rectangular arrangement was the form adopted at St Andrews, where building work on the new cathedral commenced under Bishop Arnold (1160–2). The inspiration for the plan at St Andrews has been identified as the church built by Archbishop Thomas of York at Southwell in Nottinghamshire, whose plan had already been followed in the priory church at Jedburgh, which was commenced in the 1140s. At St Andrews, however, the eastern extension may originally have been conceived of as a presbytery with the high altar placed against the east gable, but the altar was subsequently placed further to the west and the space behind it developed instead as a reliquary chapel (Fawcett 1997, 26). Unlike St-Denis or Canterbury, there was no two-tier arrangement, the eastern chapel at St Andrews having no crypt. To what extent this chapel was intended for public access is unclear, for late medieval alterations involving the at least partial blocking of part of the access into it from the north choir aisle would have severely restricted any flow of pilgrim traffic. Access would have been easier before the insertion of a tomb in the easternmost arcade of the north choir aisle, but it is possible that the relics of St Andrew (which comprised only the right arm from elbow to palm, three fingers of the right hand, the right kneecap, a tooth and portions of the skull: Baxter 1930, 120) were contained in a portable reliquary rather than displayed in a large feretory upon a monumental base such as that employed at Canterbury or Westminster, and were brought out from the chapel into the main body of the church when necessary. An alternative interpretation of the arrangements at St Andrews is explored by Yeoman (1999, 65–7). Setting aside the presence of a crypt, in its general form of a reliquary chapel behind the high altar, this may have been the plan adopted at Whithorn.

The extended east end at Whithorn

Construction of an enlarged east end may have provided both a more elaborate setting for devotions at a separate tomb and shrine of St Ninian and also accommodation for more sophisticated liturgical arrangements associated with the growing monastic community. Eastward expansion of the church could only be achieved by constructing a platform out from the falling ground to carry the presbytery (Chapter 3 Fig 3.5). This platform encased the earlier shrine chapel but also provided controlled access to it, perhaps reflecting a need to manage more carefully pilgrim traffic through what was now the ritual focus of a regular monastic community (Cruden 1986, 89–90). The exact structural layout of the 13th-century church cannot be determined from the surviving ruins, but a number of conjectural restorations have been proposed based on extrapolation from the visible fragments and other architectural elements exposed during grave-digging operations in the 19th and early 20th centuries. The earliest detailed analysis, offered by David MacGibbon and Thomas Ross but based on the architect William Galloway's plans drawn up during the course of the Marquis of Bute's excavation and consolidation of the east end of the ruins, suggested that the eastern limb was an aisleless structure with large transepts, possibly with chapels on their east walls (MacGibbon & Ross 1896, 481). Galloway, in his clearance of the crypts, had exposed the lower part of a staircase descending from the north side of the choir to the two vaulted chambers which supported the floor of the easternmost portion of the church. How these separate components joined into a functioning structure, however, was not considered by them. The Galloway/MacGibbon and Ross aisleless plan was reproduced by the Royal Commission in the Wigtownshire inventory of ancient monuments (RCAHMS 1912, Figure 101), and it remained the standard interpretation until 1934 when Henry Kerr offered a re-analysis of the standing remains which proposed that there had been a north aisle running for five bays east of the central crossing, with a further one bay unaisled extension housing the eastern chapel projecting beyond that over the vaulted crypt (Kerr 1934, 31–8). Kerr's interpretation was of a long, narrow church with shallowly projecting transepts of only one bay's depth to north and south. The shallowness of this projection was based on his identification of 'a foundation of cross form' which he interpreted as the remains of south-east angle of a south transept (Kerr 1934, 34). He adhered to the earlier suggestion of a chapterhouse immediately to the north of the north transept, which again limited the potential northern extent of the crossing. Small traces of wall foundations running east on the same alignment as the upstanding remains of the nave were interpreted as the south wall of the choir, but the position of the small sub-rectangular building to the north of the eastern crypt led him to argue that there was probably an aisle on this side from which that building, interpreted by him as a sacristy, could be entered (Kerr 1934, 34, 36). He also argued that the stair leading down into the crypt on its north side was probably accessed from an aisle rather than descending within the thickness of the wall. Despite the conjectural nature of what Kerr had proposed, by the time of the programme of excavations at the site begun in 1949 by Ralegh Radford, the aisled choir plan had become a largely accepted fact.

Ralegh Radford's main work focused on the early chapel underlying the east end of the cathedral and in the nave, but a north–south trench opened up parallel with the western side of the access path to the current parish church was intended to define the extent of the transepts. No surviving evidence for the walls of the south transept were found, but, reinterpreting the building on the north side of the choir which Galloway and Kerr had thought to be the chapterhouse as a more extensive north transept and the cross-shaped foundation which Kerr had believed to be the south-east angle of the south transept as the north–east junction of transept and choir, Ralegh Radford proposed that the north and south transepts were three bays deep and had eastern chapels in the two outer bays (Radford & Donaldson, 1953, Fig 4). More importantly, however, although no physical evidence was found to support his interpretation, he also proposed that the choir was aisled for four bays on *both* sides, with only the two easternmost bays' lengths, carried on the substructure formed by the crypt, unaisled (Radford & Donaldson 1953, 31). This interpretation was based on the view that pilgrim access to St Ninian's shrine and tomb would have to be channelled to either side of the central aisle where the canons' stalls were located, to avoid disruption of the monastic services. Ralegh Radford further argued that, to allow access to the easternmost chapel over the crypt, which he saw as containing a new shrine housing the relics of Ninian, the high altar of the cathedral was placed against a screen three bays east of the crossing (Radford & Donaldson 1953, 31). From the fourth bay of the north aisle, a straight flight of stairs descended eastwards to provide access to the crypt, and, to smooth and speed the flow of pilgrims, a second flight of stairs probably connected the crypt and the fourth bay of the south aisle, but all trace of this has been obliterated by the construction of a south-eastern chapel in the late 15th and early 16th centuries. This arrangement, it was argued, provided a means for pilgrims to circulate behind the high altar to visit the reliquary shrine, descend into the tomb by the northern stair, then re-ascend into the church and exit via the south aisle, a plan similar in design if much smaller and simpler in scale and execution than that adopted at Glasgow (Cruden 1986, 90, 160).

Ralegh Radford's interpretation was modified in the 1980s, mainly by the shortening of the transepts and the extension of the north aisle to provide a link with the upper portion of the curious detached structure which stands to the north of the eastern chapel, but his general outline was still regarded as sound (and revised version in Radford & Donaldson 1984, 16). Stewart Cruden, however, argued that the crypt stairs – a matching pair was by then accepted as fact – descended in the thickness of the wall rather than through the floor of the aisles (Cruden 1986, 90). His comparison of this plan with the scheme employed at Glasgow has been significantly elaborated upon by Peter Yeoman, whose interpretation of the devotional arrangements of the east end suggests a sophisticated and carefully managed venue for maximising the spiritual impact on the pilgrims (Yeoman 1999, 39–41).

As discussed above, there are good analogies for the location of shrine chapels east of the high altar at other pilgrimage churches in Scotland and elsewhere in Britain. The most obvious Scottish parallels for an unaisled chapel housing a feretory in this location are St Andrews, discussed above, where the unaisled presbytery is believed to have housed the apostle's reliquary, and Dunfermline, where the stepped base which supported the feretory containing St Margaret's relics can still be seen in the ruins of the eastern chapel (Yeoman 1999, 65–7, 71–4). At St Andrews, the east end of the cathedral was laid out as part of the grand new scheme commenced in *c* 1160 by Bishop Arnold, while at Dunfermline the shrine chapel was part of the new choir limb built in the mid-13th century and sufficiently complete by 1250 for the translation of St Margaret's relics to their new location (Fawcett 2005, 49). At Glasgow, the arrangements of crypt, choir and feretory chapel, constructed as part of a major rebuilding programme which commenced *c* 1240, are significantly more complex than at any other Scottish medieval pilgrimage church, but the original early 12th-century east end may have been closer in form to the plan adopted at Whithorn (Mentel 1998, 46–7; Yeoman 1999, 18–24). The developed 13th-century plan, however, provided a new feretory chapel east of the high altar while preserving the empty tomb of St Kentigern for veneration by pilgrims in the crypt. At Whithorn, no dating evidence survives for the superstructure of the choir, but the architectural details of the surviving corbels and springers for the original ribbed vault of the crypt, which are exposed in the north-east and north-west angles and mid way along the north wall, indicate that work probably commenced on this portion of the church soon after 1200 (Radford & Donaldson 1953, 32). If Scottish inspiration for its design is sought, then Glasgow offers more obvious parallels than any church in the archdiocese of York.

It must be stressed at this point that, although it is possible that the east end at Whithorn was modelled on the arrangements at Glasgow, there is actually no surviving documentary record dateable to before 1501–6 which gives any indication of the physical layout of the pilgrimage arrangements at the former. All the elaborate reconstructions of the 13th/15th-century church are based on backward projection from the records of James IV's pilgrimages to the shrine (see below) coupled with speculative analogy with other sites. Key to all of these reconstructions is the location of the high altar, which has been largely accepted on no solid grounds to have stood around two bays west of the east gable, but could equally have stood directly in front of the gable itself, over the tomb. These observations are of potentially crucial significance when the position of the bishops' tombs is discussed below. Alternative schemes of this type which may have influenced the design at Whithorn were already well developed by the 12th century, not least the arrangements derived from the forms developed at Tours where the tomb and shrine remained in a crypt directly beneath the high altar.

Clearly, the interpretations of the structural remains at Whithorn have changed several times over the centuries. As a result of this present study, the most likely arrangement is that the high altar lay right at the east end of the church, against the gable wall, with the bishops' burials immediately to the west of it.

Later medieval building work

In 1286, the enlarged 13th-century church suffered what was claimed to be significant damage from fire. An indulgence offering 40 days' remission from purgatory to all who contributed to the costs of restoration and rebuilding of the church of Whithorn, which had been destroyed by fire, was granted on 10 September 1286 by Archbishop John le Romeyn of York (Brown 1913, 8–9; Brown 1916, 83–5). While the date of the fire could be entirely coincidental, it seems likely that the damage to the cathedral-priory was inflicted in the course of the raids launched from Carrick by Robert VI Bruce, earl of Carrick, against Balliol and Comyn interests in Galloway as part of his family's manoeuvring for power in the months following the death of King Alexander III in March 1286 (Oram 1992, 30–1). A further indication of the Bruces' responsibility for this damage is perhaps to be seen in Edward Bruce's support for the convent after he was awarded the lordship of Galloway in *c* 1310, and his brother, King Robert's patronage of the canons down to his death in June 1329 (*RRS*, v, 275). The bulk of their gifts seem to have been made in recompense for damage inflicted on the priory and its interests during the campaigns in Galloway after 1306 and more especially in 1310–2, but others were more probably offerings intended to secure the canons' masses and prayers for the king. For example, in 1322 the king made provision for the maintenance of the fabric of the church during a visit to Galloway, possibly whilst on pilgrimage, when he granted the canons the teind of various crown revenues from Wigtownshire and a teind of income from the churches of the then vacant see of Whithorn (*RMS* i, appendix 1, no 21).

Despite the 1286 indulgence and the early 14th-century grants of revenue, there is no evidence for significant building work having been undertaken at Whithorn until the 1350s, probably on account of the long periods of political disturbance in the region down to 1312 and again from 1332 until the early 1350s. What may have been the final stage of an extensive programme of repair work was carried out on the eastern limb of the church in the middle of the century when Sir Fergus MacDowall, the probable head of the powerful MacDowall kin, came on a pilgrimage to the shrine and paid to have the 'quere rycht wele tyle' (the choir well roofed with tile/slate) as a thanks-offering for the miraculous aid supposedly given by St Ninian in defeating a force of English raiders in eastern Galloway (Metcalfe 1904, 68). This roofing work perhaps constituted a completion of a programme of repairs to the church that had started over half a century earlier, but could equally well have been a specific piece of maintenance work.

Architectural fragments from around the site and from within the adjoining burgh, as well as details of the upstanding remains, point to a series of building operations in the church through the 15th century. Some of this work may have been undertaken during the episcopate of Bishop Elisaeus Adougan (1406–*c* 1414), following his claim in a letter to the pope that the church was in a dilapidated state. Adougan's relations with the prior and canons were poor, however, and his appeal to the papacy may have been motivated by a desire to extract revenue from the convent to support the bishop's designs. On 11 April 1408 Pope Benedict XIII issued a commission to the archdeacon of Glasgow to force the prior and canons, of whom he says there were only 12 (marking nearly a halving of their number since 1235), to contribute from their income towards rebuilding costs. The wording of the papal letter appears to repeat the language used in the bishop's original complaint, which has not itself survived (*CPL-Benedict XIII*, 173; for the full text, see Reid 1960, no 1). It stated that the church, which was a popular place of pilgrimage, was 'unsound' (*debilem*), 'mean' (*vilem*) and 'old, more than is fitting for such a church'. The commission claimed that Adougan had wanted to contribute as much as possible from his own resources, but they were insufficient for the task in hand, while the canons, despite their small numbers but with an income in excess of 500 merks, had repeatedly refused to make any payment towards the costs. The archdeacon was instructed to investigate the situation and, if Adougan's claims were proven true, to assign half of the priory's revenues to rebuilding work for the next ten years. There is no record of the archdeacon's investigation or its findings, but there does appear to have been building work undertaken around this time.

Firm evidence for new building work on the cathedral dates from the 1420s, when the patronage of the Black Douglas family, who had secured the lordship of western Galloway in the 1370s, paid for some further extensions. The principal benefactress was Margaret Stewart, duchess of Touraine and countess of Douglas, wife of Archibald, 4th earl of Douglas, who in March 1424 granted the priory part of her demesne lands at Cruggleton to provide rental income to fund construction of a new chapel and to pay for one of the canons to celebrate mass in it daily (*RMS* ii, no 12). There is no indication of where this chapel was in the priory church, but in April 1431 there is the first surviving record of a Chapel of St Mary or Lady Chapel. Reference to it occurs in a supplication by Prior Thomas Mcgilliachnisy of Whithorn to the pope, seeking ratification of the annexation by the priory chapter of the revenues of the parish of Longcastle for the support of the chapel he had begun to build (Dunlop & Cowan 1970, 175–6). The petition includes details of the services to be offered in the chapel, beginning daily at eight o'clock with a mass of the Blessed Virgin Mary, with music provided by the canons and chantors, and with the officiating priest saying a special collect and the psalm *De Profundis* for the prior's soul, plus a collect and a sermon delivered to the public attending the service. From the details of the petition, this new building was clearly intended to be a chantry chapel for Prior Thomas, who stipulated that the canons should say mass annually on the date of his death, and that one of the canons should say mass daily in the chapel. The petition was confirmed and the process of annexation and any building was completed in January 1433 when Bishop Alexander confirmed the assignment of the revenues of the rectory of the parish church of St Nicholas of Longcastle to the priory and assigned its revenues in common to the canons. The canons, in return, were obligated to celebrate mass in the Lady Chapel, which the bishop's charter described as 'adjacent to the choir of the priory church' (Reid 1960, no 6). On the basis of this description, the more recent interpretations of the plan of the priory church have proposed that the eastern extremity of the choir limb housed this Lady Chapel (see plan in Radford & Donaldson 1984, 16). There is, however, no documentary evidence to confirm this positioning and the altar of St Mary could as easily have been located in a north or south choir aisle, as was the case at Dunfermline Abbey or Elgin Cathedral (Fawcett 1999a, 14). Bearing in mind what appears to be a strong parallel between the arrangements of the east end at Glasgow and that at Whithorn, however, it is important to note that at Glasgow the Lady Chapel lay in the crypt to the east of the site of St Kentigern's tomb (Fawcett 1998, 4). The South Chapel, erected over the barrel-vaulted undercroft that extends southwards from the fourth and fifth bays of the choir and apparently dating to *c* 1490–1500, may represent a later enlargement of an earlier 15th-century Lady Chapel, but there is also no concrete evidence for that identification (Radford & Donaldson 1953, 31–2). Further repairs or enlargements may have been undertaken in the 1460s, perhaps paid for by the indulgences which the pope in 1462 permitted to be sold to pilgrims who visited the shrine on Palm Sunday, Easter Day, the Feast of the Nativity of John the Baptist (Midsummer), Lammas (1 August) and St Ninian's Day (16 September) (*CPP* xii).

The early sixteenth-century east end and relic display

Substantial building work appears to have been underway at the end of the 15th century. When James IV paid his first visit to Whithorn in November 1491, amongst his pious disbursements he also gave 18s 'to the drink' to the masons working on the building (Dickson 1877, i, 182). On the basis of the architectural details of the doorway linking the 13th-century crypt with the undercroft of the South Chapel, it has generally been assumed that this work was focused on the building of this chapel, but there are several other architectural elements of similar date to be seen in the priory complex, including the gatehouse and the reinserted south-eastern doorway in the nave, which points to a much more general programme of work. Such work was apparently still in progress down to August 1502 when he ordered payments of 14s 'drinksilver' to the masons (Dickson 1877, ii, 104, 157), and may well have continued further. This building activity, however, needs to be borne in mind when considering the physical arrangements for display of, and devotions at, the relics of the saint in the early 1500s; we have no way of knowing whether these had been substantially altered in the course of that work.

The South Chapel, which survives only to the level of the pavement over the barrel-vaulted undercroft, is a structure whose exact relationship with the east end of the priory church has been the subject of quite elaborate conjecture in the past. Its construction was apparently part of a major operation which may have involved significant alteration to the superstructure of the 13th-century eastern chapel, for the groined vault of the original crypt, which had been carried on a single central column, was removed and replaced by two parallel barrel vaults supported on a transverse wall. Probably at the same time, a round-headed doorway with simple late 15th-century mouldings was cut through the south wall of the western of the two new chambers formed in the 13th-century crypt. The mouldings on this doorway are on its 'outer' or southern face, which suggests that the crypt under the east end of the church remained the higher status chamber rather than the new undercroft beneath the South Chapel into which it opened. While the replacement of the 13th-century groined vault and reduction of the internal space through the introduction of a transverse wall would have significantly reduced the visual impact of the original crypt chamber, it appears that it remained an important 'public' space whose status was emphasised by the positioning of the mouldings on its new south doorway: you passed from a high-status space in the crypt into a lower-status space beneath the South Chapel. These new arrangements suggest a major restructuring of access provision to what was probably still believed to be the site of St Ninian's tomb in the 13th-century crypt. As a consequence of the erection of the new South Chapel, any southern stair descending from the choir parallel to that which remains on the north side of the crypt appears to have been swept away, removing any possibility of smooth circulation of pilgrims as proposed by Peter Yeoman (1999, 39–41). From *c* 1500, the main flow of pilgrims probably descended into the 13th-century crypt via the remaining northern stair, then exited via the south door into the undercroft of the South Chapel and out by the door at its south end. Indeed, such a rearrangement is what has been demonstrated in this study (Chapter 3.2.5), along with the possibility of further crypts under the South Transept.

Such substantial alterations to the sub-structure of the east end of the church perhaps implies significant alterations to the building which they carried. The new South Chapel would alone have required the breaking through of the south wall of the choir, and the creation of access into the South Chapel from the choir, of which 'Galloway's box' is evidence (Chapter 3.2.5). Despite the various plans and conjectural reconstructions which have been offered to show how this was arranged (eg Kerr 1934; Ralegh Radford & Donaldson 1953 and 1984; or that by David Simon reproduced in Yeoman 1999, 40), the only feature of the post-1500 structure which could previously proposed with any confidence is that, on the evidence of the location of a large projecting buttress in the middle of the east wall of the south-east undercroft, the structure above was divided into two compartments. These probably both held altars beneath large windows in the sections of wall divided by the buttress.

The construction of this South Chapel should probably be seen as a manifestation of the late medieval proliferation of altars in major churches, associated in particular with the later medieval 'cult of death' and provision for the saying of *pro anima* masses. Parallels for the development of such chapels at shrine churches can be seen at both Iona and Glasgow, where enlarged southern chapels were added to the buildings. At Iona, the south transept of the cruciform early 13th-century church was massively extended in an operation perhaps intended to provide a new setting for the shrine of St Columba, but this work appears to have been abandoned uncompleted in the 14th century and was swept away in a mid-15th-century reconstruction of the eastern limb of the abbey (Yeoman 1999, 82–4 and fig 58). The southern chapel at Glasgow, although named the Blackadder Aisle and associated with that late 15th-century archbishop, appears to have been part of the scheme of work commenced by Bishop William de Bondington around 1240. It was possibly intended to house some subsidiary cult associated with St Kentigern, but was never completed. As at Whithorn, it was intended to be a two-storey structure, presumably with a chapel on its upper level, but this was never completed and appears never to have advanced much beyond the height of the lower vault (Fawcett 1998, 5). Both these examples, however, are of mid to late-13th-century date, whereas that at Whithorn was of late 15th- to early 16th-century construction. Closer functional parallels can perhaps be seen in the large chantry chapels added in the late 15th and early 16th centuries to the south side of the presbyteries at churches such as Arbuthnott in the Mearns or Guthrie in Angus. A further factor with a potential bearing on the alterations and enlargement at the east end which should be borne in mind is the possible proliferation of relics and the need for better facilities for their display to maximise access to pilgrims and, concomitantly, revenue from offerings made at each venue. Indications of such a proliferation of foci for devotions can be seen in the records of James IV's offerings in 1501 and 1506 (see below). The existence of, for example, the separate portable reliquary which contained the arm-bone of St Ninian, could point to the dispersal of the saint's physical remains around the church rather than their concentration in a single feretory.

Apart from the 15th-century references to altars and chapels of the Blessed Virgin Mary, there is no surviving record of the liturgical layout of the 13th- to late 15th-century cathedral-priory which would give a pointer to its structural form. It is only in the early 1500s that some indication can be obtained of the late medieval liturgical and devotional arrangements from records of James IV's alms-giving during his pilgrimages to Whithorn. Although most modern analyses of the building have interpreted the east end arrangements as revealing a dual focus in upper and lower chapels, the first documentary evidence to support the existence of a separate shrine and a tomb of St Ninian, possibly but not necessarily similar to the 13th-century arrangements at Glasgow, dates only from the king's visit on the night of 22 April 1501. Records of his disbursements reveal that he made separate offerings 'at the towme and at the reliques', possibly indicating that what were believed to have been Ninian's remains had been translated from his grave to a feretory. The account, however, does not make clear if the tomb and relics were at that date in separate locations within the church. On 23 April, King James made further offerings at the tomb and the relics, but the accounts record that on this occasion he also left offerings at the 'hie altar', which presumably lay in the canons' quire, and the 'Rude [rood] altar', which probably lay in front of the pulpitum at the east end of the nave, an arrangement which suggests his involvement in a series of acts of devotion and participation in masses offered at the altars (Dickson 1877, ii, 72).

The financial accounts of James IV's visit with Queen Margaret in August 1506 offer more detail. On this occasion, the king made offerings at the rood altar and high altar in the church as before, but also at 'the ferter' (feretory). This is the first documented record of the housing of the saint's remains in an elaborate shrine for public display. Further offerings were made in the 'utir [outer] kyrk' (usually meaning the nave), 'at the reliques', and at the Lady altar (Dickson 1877, iii, 280). The order in which these locations are listed perhaps reveals a defined pilgrimage route through the church, starting at the rood altar in the nave, moving through into the chancel and passing on to the feretory housing the saint's remains, perhaps in a chapel behind the high altar. From there, pilgrims may have descended into the crypt to the saint's tomb and other relics by the steps to the north of the high altar, perhaps returning to the church by the south stair (if it still existed at that date) to make an offering at the high altar, then progressing to the lady chapel, which this schedule suggests was perhaps housed in the southern chapel, before exiting the church.

Aisles or aisle-less?

A final issue which has a direct bearing on the position of the bishops' tombs within the east end of the enlarged church is how the choir was separated from the supposed feretory chapel. The plans offered by Ralegh Radford and reproduced by Historic Scotland down to the present simply suggest that the central aisle compartment of the choir carried through as an unbroken space to the east gable, with the division between the choir and feretory chapel being provided only by a screen behind the high altar at the third pier east of the crossing. There is, however, some debate as to whether the eastern chapel was carried up to the same height as the rest of the eastern limb of the church. If it was a lower structure, rising perhaps only to the height of the putative aisle walls, there would have had to have been a gable positioned probably on the line of the suggested third or fourth piers east of the crossing. This is the arrangement suggested by David Simon in his speculative reconstruction of the eastern shrine chapel and crypt and in the associated schematic floor plans of the structure (Yeoman 1999, figs 20 and 21). His reconstruction, however, suggests that there was a pier positioned midway between the north and south aisle piers, dividing the choir from the feretory chapel by a two-bay arcade and leaving an ambulatory between it and the screen behind the high altar one bay further to the west. There is, it must be stressed, no evidence for the existence of such a pier, and the arrangement seems to be based entirely on Henry Kerr's wholly speculative 1933–4 reconstruction of a soaring shrine chapel separated from the choir by a two-tiered arcade in this position (Kerr 1934, plates 1 and 5).

An important alternative to the arrangements proposed over the last 75 years by Kerr, Ralegh Radford, Cruden and Yeoman is that the eastern limb of the cathedral was entirely or largely without lateral aisles throughout its history. Only Kerr considered this possibility in the speculative plan which he published in 1934, based on William Galloway's earlier proposal of a simple, unaisled rectangle. Nevertheless, it needs to be borne in mind that only four of Scotland's medieval cathedrals had aisled eastern limbs, while the cathedrals of even comparatively wealthy sees like Aberdeen and Dunkeld seem never to have been intended to be anything other than unaisled (Fawcett 1997, 118–22). While Dornoch, Aberdeen, Brechin, Dunkeld and Dunblane had aisled naves and unaisled chancels, Fortrose and Lismore were conceived originally as extended rectangular structures with no clear structural differentiation between nave and choir space. If Whithorn had an aisled (or partly aisled) choir and unaisled nave, this would be unparalleled in Scottish cathedral architecture. Even allowing for the constraints of space for expansion imposed by the presence of the cloister to the north of the cathedral church, it is highly unusual that there was no attempt to expand the nave to provide additional space for chapels in side aisles later in the Middle Ages. This, we must allow, could account for the possible expansion at the east end, particularly the provision of the South Chapel in the late 15th or early 16th century. Without excavation, this question will perhaps never be resolved satisfactorily. There is, however, one possible analogy to consider: Whithorn's daughter-house at Fearn in Easter Ross.

Although Fearn was founded originally in the 1220s, nothing obvious survives of the first stone buildings erected on its second site. The surviving church is believed largely to be a product of the central two quarters of the 14th century, with some minor late medieval additions and a post-Reformation truncation of its nave (Fawcett 1994, 77, 134). As it stands, this is basically a simple rectangular church with no obvious external (or internal) structural differentiation between the nave and choir portions of the building. While this plain form at Fearn cannot be taken as proof positive of the plan at Whithorn, it must be considered as a possibility along with all the implications which this design would have for the speculative liturgical and devotional arrangements in the cathedral.

The above reconstructions of liturgical arrangements in and pilgrim circulation routes around the cathedral are mainly predicated upon the positioning of the post-1200 high altar and the possible existence of a shrine chapel behind that altar. While this has been since the late 1940s the preferred model for the cathedral's layout in the early 13th to late 15th centuries, bearing in mind that no solid evidence survives for the existence of the lateral aisles which would have made this arrangement possible, we must consider the possibility that the high altar stood immediately in front of the east gable of the 13th-century extended east end. This was the position occupied by the high altars at Dornoch, (probably) Fortrose, Lismore, Elgin, Aberdeen, Brechin, Dunkeld and Dunblane. Of these churches, only Elgin was provided with aisles in its eastern limb, while at the others the choir stalls were apparently positioned immediately against the side walls of the chancel without any passage behind them. At Whithorn, given the recorded size of the monastic community in 1235, the narrowness of the central compartment of even an aisled church would have made the easy flow of pilgrims through the choir area very difficult. There is no problem with allowing for the stairs to the crypt to have descended intramurally from the choir, as indeed this study has now demonstrated (Chapter 2.3.2), or for the feretory also to have been housed originally in the crypt. Indeed, the only problem with this plan is perhaps in reconciling it with modern perceptions of what a great medieval shrine church *should* have looked like. If we accept that it was a plain, unaisled rectangle throughout its history, the form taken by Scotland's one largely intact major late medieval reliquary church at Tain in Easter Ross, and that access to the crypts was via intramural stairs, this plan has significant implications for the apparent positioning of the bishops' graves within the cathedral.

Bishops' and priors' tombs?

Before considering the location of the graves, their traditional labelling requires discussion. Almost since the time of the first discovery of the group of burials which lay towards the eastern end of the ruins of the medieval cathedral-priory at Whithorn the interments have been known collectively as the 'bishops' and priors' tombs'. While some of the earliest of the graves may belong to the heads of the religious community which perhaps survived at this site between the

Table 8.2: The Priors of Whithorn, to 1516

Priors	*Dates*	*Place of burial*
Adam	-	No record survives of the places of burial of the priors of Whithorn, except for the possible record of Prior Thomas's arrangements in the 1430s for interment in the chapel of St Mary which he had endowed in the cathedral church
William	-	
Michael	-	
Malcolm	-	
Paul	-	
Duncan	-	
Gregory	-	
Duncan	-	
Dungal	-	
Thomas	-	
John	-	
Maurice	-	
Michael	-	
Gilbert	1382–1413	
Thomas	1413–31	(Possibly in Chapel of St Mary in the cathedral)
James	-	
William	1447–67x68	
Fergus	1466–1470	
Roger	-	
Patrick	1474–1503	
Henry	1503–14x16	

For outline dates of priors down to 1382, see list in Watt & Shead 2001, 216–17. After 1516, the priory was held by a series of commendators.

end of the recorded succession of Northumbrian bishops in the 830s and the emergence of the first of the medieval succession in the later 1120s, comparison with monasteries elsewhere in Scotland and more widely in the British Isles suggests that it is unlikely that any of the burials belong to the priors of the Premonstratensian community founded here in *c* 1177 (Table 8.2). The only prior for whom there is some evidence for burial on the site of the east end of the cathedral is Thomas Mcgilliachnisy, who in the early 1430s was making endowments for a chantry at the altar of St Mary in the church (discussed above). His arrangements suggest that he may have planned to be buried in St Mary's chapel, but there is no surviving evidence that this was the case.

What appears to have been the most common burial place for the heads of monastic communities was the chapter house or the cloister alley immediately outside the entrance to the chapter house. This tradition does not appear to be unique to any one monastic order, but is common to all orders present in Britain by the early 13th century, both orders of monks and also of canons regular. It was the prevailing arrangement down into the mid-14th century, when burials in the church begin to become more common, and seems to have all but ended in the 15th century, when changes in practice relating to post-mortem commemoration of the dead and increased provision of requiem masses for the individual led to construction of monumental tombs and chantry chapels by monastic heads. This shift is manifest physically in the commissioning of substantial free-standing or mural monuments, such as those of Finlay McFaid at Fearn, Bricius MacKinnon at Iona, or the unidentified late 15th-century abbot whose effigy was discovered at Lindores in the 19th century (RCAHMS 1933, 219), or richly carved slabs, like the magnificent memorial of Abbot John Schanwell (1480–1506) at Coupar Angus (Adams & McAneny 1984, 25). What is believed to be the burial chamber below the tomb of Prior James Haldenstone (1417–43) at St Andrews points to the former presence of a magnificent mural tomb, located in the north choir chapel immediately adjacent to an area of the cathedral which had been extensively remodelled under his direction (Fawcett 2002, 308, fig 4.80). It needs also to be remembered that other privileged individuals could also secure the right to be buried in the chapter house. At Melrose, for example, the royal chamberlain, Philip de Valognes, and his son William were interred in the chapter house in 1215 and 1219 respectively, as was Gervase Avenel, whose family were major benefactors of the abbey (Bannatyne Club 1837b, s.a. 1215, 129; Fawcett & Oram 2004, 25–6). Consequently, a number of the interments identified in rather crowded chapter house burials, like those at Jedburgh (see below), could belong to lay folk who had obtained burial rights there.

At Whithorn we are forced to argue from negative evidence, given that no structural remains of the chapter house survive, that not even its exact location can be fixed with absolute certainty, and no documentary record dating from before the 1430s survives to give any indication of the place of burial of the earlier priors. It is difficult, too, to make analogies with other Premonstratensian houses in Scotland, for most are even less well preserved than at Whithorn, no structural remains being visible above ground at Soulseat and Holywood and only a tiny fragment incorporating a relocated doorway surviving at Tongland. At Fearn nothing remains of the cloister and the possible burials of the 13th- and 14th-century abbots; the surviving tomb and effigy of Abbot Finlay McFaid (d 1486), however, rests in a lateral chapel said to have been built by him and attached to the south side of the 14th-century church (Fawcett 1994, 77; MacGibbon & Ross 1896, ii, 546). The absence of demonstrably earlier burials in the church at Fearn suggests that the general trend away from chapter-house towards church interments in the later Middle Ages is recorded here. Only at Dryburgh are there substantial structural remains of church and cloister, and here the chapter house again seems to have been the location for the 12th- and 13th-century abbots' graves. In Westmorland at the small Premonstratensian abbey of Shap, one coffin is still visible in the floor of the chapter house, while two plain slabs lie in the floor of the eastern alley of the cloister walk immediately outside the chapter house door (as seen by the present writer – these features are not mentioned in Colvin & Gilyard-Beer 1963). Fragmentary though this Premonstratensian evidence is, however, it does seem to indicate that the church was not a common venue for burials of the heads of the community until the later medieval period.

Comparison with other orders appears to bear this observation out. As a consequence of the major programme of excavation at Jedburgh Abbey in 1984 and documentary records relating to St Andrews cathedral-priory, perhaps more is known about the burials of Augustinian abbots and priors than of most other orders in Scotland. At St Andrews, the only other cathedral-priory in Scotland, it is known that all priors between John of Haddington (d 1304) and James Bisset (d 1416) were buried in the chapter house or its vestibule (Cruden 1950, 16; RCAHMS 1933, 237). The location of the pre-14th-century priors' graves there is less certain, but were probably also in the chapter house. Bisset's successor, James Haldenston, was the first to be buried in the cathedral church, where his monument may have been an integral part of the major programme of renovations which he oversaw during his priorship (see above). Excavations within the chapter house at Jedburgh revealed 17 burials (Lewis, Ewart *et al* 1995, 32–3, 118–26). Here, most of the interments appear to date from the 12th to 14th centuries, few evidently being inserted after a major remodelling of the chamber which involved the construction of a central pier to support a stone vault in the late 15th or early 16th century (Lewis, Ewart *et al* 1995, 145–6).

In Cistercian houses, it was also standard practice for the burials of the heads of the community to be made in the chapter house. At Melrose, the first Cistercian foundation in Scotland, the early abbots were also buried in the chapter house, where the remains of Abbot Waltheof (d 1159) were in 1171 re-entombed under a polished marble slab and where a more elaborate shrine was later constructed for the saintly abbot (Fawcett & Oram 2004, 23, 24, 184; Richardson & Wood 1949, 18–19). In 1240, the remains of the early abbots were recorded as having been moved from their original tombs next to the entrance of the chamber to new locations at the east end of the enlarged building (Bannatyne Club 1837b, s.a. 1240). One of the finest surviving groups of Cistercian abbatial burials in Scotland can be seen at Dundrennan, where five graveslabs of later 12th- and 13th-century date survive in the pavement of the chamber and a superb late 12th-century recumbent effigy of an abbot is also on display at the west end of the nave (Richardson 1981, 8 fig 4, 9, 14 figs 11–13, 15). At Sweetheart, the late 13th- or early 14th-century coffin-lid of the first head of the convent, Abbot John, and a broken portion of the coffin-lid of an unknown later medieval successor, are misleadingly displayed in the south transept of the abbey church as part of a collection of medieval sculptural fragments, but seem to have been recovered originally from the ruins of the chapter house (Richardson 1951, 13, 14–15). Comparisons outwith Scotland show the practice to have been common to all Cistercian monasteries. At Jervaulx in Yorkshire, for example, nine slabs survive in the chapter house marking the sites of abbatial interments (Breakspear 1968, 282). Further examples can be see in Yorkshire at Byland, Fountains (where 19 abbots are buried in the chapter house, the last interred in 1346), and Rievaulx, where, as at Melrose, the tomb of a saintly abbot was developed into an elaborate shrine at the entrance to the chamber (Peers 1952, 10; Peers 1967, 8–10; Gilyard-Beer 1970, 46).

There has been limited archaeological investigation of monasteries of other orders in Scotland, a problem compounded by the obliteration of the physical remains of the chapter houses or entire claustral complexes. Kelso's cloister, for example, survives only in a single element of its west range – an outer parlour – while the area of the cloister garth and east range is overlain by a post-Reformation cemetery. A similar situation occurs at Dunfermline where, although substantial sections of the south range survive, the east range has been almost entirely destroyed and its site taken over for post-Reformation burials (Bridgland 2005, 93–4; RCAHMS 1933, 115). There is, however, still potential for the recovery of information at some sites where the superstructures of the chapter houses have long vanished. At Arbroath, where only a single buttress forming the SE angle of the chapter house remains, clearance of the site in 1938 revealed the remains of ten high status interments, probably all of them abbots (Mackie & Cruden 1954, 36). Although the burials contained fragments of clothing and footwear, all, unfortunately, had been plundered for valuables in the post-Reformation period.

Considering the importance of these communities in the religious, cultural and political life of medieval Scotland, it is surprising how little is known about the men who guided and managed them. It is also surprising, given the number of monasteries whose sites are in State guardianship, how little is known about the high-status burials which occurred within them. Indeed, there seems to be no easily accessible data-base recording either known places of interment or surviving visible remains of tombs and monuments. This problem becomes even more acute when considering the burials of the medieval episcopate, considered below.

8.2.2 The location of the bishops' tombs

Given the levels of destruction at most of Scotland's pre-Reformation cathedrals, it is perhaps unsurprising that so little is known of the nature and location of Scottish bishops' tombs. A significant number of bishops' tombs, however, have survived at most of the medieval Scottish cathedrals, albeit usually in mutilated and plundered states. Most which do remain, however, date from the later Middle Ages, mainly from the 15th and early 16th centuries, but a number of 13th-century examples are known. This discussion does not include reference to Kirkwall where a number of important medieval episcopal tombs survive in what was also a major reliquary church (of SS Magnus and Rognvald). Although there are strong parallels with late 12th- and early 13th-century English forms, it was decided to concentrate on the sees which lay within the *Ecclesia Scoticana* for this present study and to explore parallels chiefly with York archdiocese, of which Whithorn was suffragan.

The existing examples follow a clearly recognisable pattern in terms of their general location and relationship with the main liturgical components of the cathedrals within which they lie. Comparison with episcopal burials in the cathedrals in the archdiocese of York (Carlisle, Durham and York) shows similar traditions there. Three distinct categories emerge. First, there are those cathedrals which do not contain any, or only a minor, shrine. Second, there are those cathedrals which do contain an important shrine but where the saint in question is not the apostolic predecessor of the medieval bishops. Finally, there are the cathedrals which contain a shrine and where the medieval bishops were considered to be the apostolic successor of the saint in question. What emerges from a survey of the surviving tombs is the potentially unique arrangement of the burials at Whithorn, not only in Scotland but also within the archdiocese of York.

Cathedrals without a major shrine

In the first category, the position of the medieval episcopal interments in the cathedrals at Brechin and Lismore are unknown (MacGibbon & Ross 1896, ii, 203–15; RCAHMS 1974, no 267). The irregular succession of bishops of Argyll in the 13th century and the appointment of Lowlanders to the see by the crown in the 15th century may have produced a situation at Lismore where few bishops chose to be buried in their cathedral. Bishop Robert Colquhoun (1475–96) is the only one for whom a burial place is known. He appears to have chosen to be buried amongst his kinsmen at Luss on Loch Lomondside (in the diocese of Glasgow), where his much restored effigy survives (Lacaille 1934), rather than on Lismore.

The best surviving group of episcopal grave monuments in Scotland is in Elgin Cathedral. These have been discussed in detail by Richard Fawcett (1999a, 67–75) and the following is offered only as a summary of his work. It is believed that 18 of the pre-Reformation bishops of Moray were buried at Elgin, seven of them apparently within the central space of the choir in the eastern limb. The earliest of these, that of Bishop Andrew de Moravia (1224–42) who relocated his cathedral from Spynie to Elgin, may be marked by a later slab of Tournai marble with a rectangular inset for a memorial brass which lies just in front of the first of the three steps which rise within the presbytery, towards the south side and in front of the opening from the south aisle into the presbytery (Fawcett 1999a, 67, 70). This is not unlikely to have been the location of Bishop Andrew's tomb, but the monument itself probably dates from after the later medieval restoration of the east end of the church, possibly replacing an earlier monument damaged in the 1390 fire. The oldest surviving tomb, believed to be that of Bishop Archibald (1253–98), comprises a gabled mural recess on the north side of the presbytery (Fawcett 1999a, 45, 67, fig 84). This was apparently a highly favoured position for tombs, especially of founders or rebuilders, as the monument was often used as an Easter Sepulchre. It was possibly the effigy from this tomb that was discovered in 1936 buried on the west side of the chapter house (Fawcett 1999a, 12, fig 9). The last surviving bishops' tomb within the choir lies in the opening from the presbytery into the north aisle. The tomb chest itself and all recognisable heraldry or inscriptions have been lost, but it is suggested to have been the burial-place of Bishop (1482–1501) (Fawcett 1999a, 67, fig 138). While the earliest tombs in the cathedral appear to have been located close to the high altar in the presbytery, in the 15th century the bishops were choosing to be buried in more visible and less cramped sites further west in the church. Further bishops' tombs do survive in the south aisle of the choir, that of Bishop John Winchester (1437–58) at its east end beside the altar of St Mary, and possibly that of Bishop William Tulloch (1477–82) midway down the north side of the aisle. In Tulloch's tomb there has been inserted an effigy from an earlier tomb, possibly belonging to either Bishop John Pilmuir (1326–62) or Bishop Alexander Bur (1362–97), but where the grave which it originally covered lay is not known (Fawcett 1999a, 70–71, figs 140–2, 144–5). Three further sites are known. In the south transept there are two recessed tombs in its south wall both of which now contain the effigy of knights. The eastern of the two is identified on the basis of its heraldry as that of Bishop James Stewart (1458–60), and the western as that of his brother and successor, Bishop David Stewart (1460–75) (Fawcett 1999a, 72, 74, fig 149). The remaining tomb identified was that of Bishop John Innes (1407–14). This stood against the north–western pier of the crossing tower and was completely swept away in the collapse of the tower in 1711. A damaged effigy of a kneeling bishop now placed in the south transept is believed to have come from Innes's tomb and indicates that it was a splendid monument similar in execution to examples from England and France (Fawcett 1999a, 6, 75, fig 153). What the surviving group at Elgin reveals is the range of forms which such high-status tombs could take. While most are mural recessed tombs which originally housed monumental effigies, others were free-standing chest tombs (again with effigies), but slab or ledger monuments were also present, some with inset memorial brasses. Changes in fashion are evident in the forms of some of the tombs, and certain styles of monument have clear chronological brackets, but it is apparent from what remains that monuments of all types could be constructed at almost any period. What does seem to occur, however, is quite a dispersed pattern of burial originally focused on the eastern limb but with a subsequent drift away from the presbytery as the chosen location for episcopal burials in the later medieval period.

All the pre-15th-century bishops' tombs at Aberdeen appear to have been lost in the post-Reformation destruction of the choir and presbytery of the cathedral. The lower levels of the transept walls have survived, however, dating from a protracted rebuilding operation which was started by Bishop Henry Lichton (1422–40) and completed by Bishop William Elphinstone (1483–1514), who completed the tower over the crossing and rebuilt the choir. Of the earlier bishops, the first for whom record of a place of burial survives is William de Deyn (1344–50), whom Hector Boece stated had been buried in the choir of the cathedral (Moir 1894, 21). Deyn's successors, John Rait (1350–4) and Alexander de Kinninmonth (1355–80) were also buried in the choir, the latter's tomb being located in front of the high altar (Moir 1894, 22, 24). The burial place of the next bishop, Adam de Tyninghame, is not recorded, but his successor, Gilbert Greenlaw (1390–1421), was also interred in the choir at Aberdeen (Moir 1894, 31). Lichton himself arranged for his own burial to take place in the chapel of St John the Evangelist in the cathedral, 'which he had built for that purpose' (Moir 1894, 34). The precise location of this chapel is uncertain but may have been in the eastern limb, where his successor, Bishop Ingram Lindsay (1441–58), was buried (Moir 1894, 37). Boece describes his monument in the choir of the cathedral as decorated 'with a stone effigy sculpted with considerable skill'. After Lindsay, there was a hiatus of 60 years before another bishop of Aberdeen was buried in his own church, when Alexander Gordon (1515–8) was interred in the newly-completed choir (Moir 1894, 114). Of Gordon's three predecessors, Thomas Spens (1458–80) had been buried in the collegiate church of the Holy Trinity in Edinburgh, and William Elphinstone before the high altar of King's College Chapel at Aberdeen, while Robert Blackadder had been translated in 1483 to the see of Glasgow (Moir 1894, 54, 109). Gordon may have been the last burial in the choir, his successor Gavin Dunbar (1518–32), being interred in the south transept, where the richly decorated arched recess of his tomb survives in the south wall. As with the bishops of Moray, the medieval bishops of Aberdeen – at least since the mid-14th century and probably since its establishment as the seat of their see – appear to have displayed a strong attachment to their cathedral church. As at Elgin, however, their tombs appear to have been dispersed throughout the eastern limb of the church rather than being clustered around an obvious cult focus.

At Dunblane, only two medieval episcopal burials are represented by still visible monuments. The probably older of the two is against the north wall of the choir and consists of the recumbent effigy of a bishop in full mass pontificals. This has been identified traditionally as the monument of Bishop Finlay Dermoch (1403–19) but its location close to the high altar in the choir as reconstructed in the second quarter of the 13th century has led to suggestions that it marks the burial place of Bishop Clement (1233–58), under whom the rebuilding of the cathedral commenced (MacGibbon & Ross 1896, ii, 110, fig 531, 112). The second monument, which is much more heavily wasted through post-Reformation exposure to the elements, lies in a mural recess in the most easterly bay of the south aisle of the nave, a favoured location for the establishment of a chantry chapel. It, too, consists of a bishop's effigy showing him in full pontificals. The monument is believed to be that of Bishop Michael Ochiltree (1429–45) (MacGibbon & Ross 1896, ii, 112), but there appears to be no hard evidence for that identification. These two monuments seem to reflect the trend recognised at Elgin, where the earlier episcopal burials were located in the eastern limb and those from the later 14th or early 15th centuries show a drift in location into the crossing and nave.

Cathedrals containing a shrine but not of an apostolic predecessor of the medieval bishops.

In the second category are the cathedrals of St Andrews and Dunkeld, the former housing relics of the Apostle Andrew, the latter relics of Columba brought to it from Iona in the 9th century. We are fortunate in the case of St Andrews to have a number of medieval sources which record the interment of medieval bishops within their cathedral, in some cases providing quite precise detail as to the location of their tombs. The reliquary chapel in the later medieval period at the cathedral occupied the four bays in the eastern half of the choir limb of the church, entered through the fifth bay of the choir arcade, while the high altar stood in front of a reredos forming a screen across the presbytery between the fourth piers of the arcade, an arrangement similar in concept to that proposed for post-1200 Whithorn (Fawcett 1994, 37–8 and fig 19).

No monuments to any of the pre-14th-century bishops of St Andrews have survived *in situ* and, of the 14th- to 16th-century bishops the only tomb to survive largely intact is that of Bishop James Kennedy (1440–65), which is located in the collegiate chapel of St Salvator which he had founded (Fawcett 2002, 314 and fig 4.88; RCAHMS 1933, no 461). Of the tombs in the cathedral which can be identified tentatively, that of Bishop Henry Wardlaw (1403–40) occupied a position similar to that of Andrew Stewart at Elgin (see above), apparently being an integral portion of a screen separating the presbytery from the north choir aisle (Fawcett 2002, 306–7 and fig 4.78). The tomb in the north wall of the second bay of the nave, in the past identified as that of Bishop William Landallis (1342–85), does not accord with chronicle references to his burial beneath the pavement of the vestibule of the west door (Cruden 1950, 13). No further tombs or monuments survive in their original positions. Two fragments of a very fine bishop's effigy (the head and the lower part of the chausuble) are preserved in the cathedral museum, pointing to the former existence of free-standing chest tombs or mural monuments with rich sculptural decoration (Cruden 1950, 18; RCAHMS 1933, fig 389). In the centre of the presbytery lies a great slab of Tournai limestone (3.18m x 2.32m), cut to receive memorial brasses. This slab, which is not in its original location, is the last vestige of an extremely expensive grave monument, perhaps that of one of the late 15th or early 16th century archbishops (RCAHMS 1933, 237).

Although Dunkeld has a long history as an episcopal see, the earliest recorded interment of one of its bishops in the cathedral is that of Bishop Geoffrey (1236–49). Of his predecessors, Bishop John the Scot (d 1203) had been buried in the choir of Newbattle Abbey, while bishops Richard de Prebenda (d 1210), John de Leicester (d 1214) and Gilbert (d 1235) were interred in Inchcolm Abbey, with which the bishops of Dunkeld had a very close relationship (Bannatyne Club 1831, 6, 8, 9; Easson & MacDonald 1938, xxii–xxiii; Wood 1950, 4–5; Paterson & McRoberts 1978, 6–7, 19; Fawcett 1999b, 99). When the church at Inchcolm was rebuilt in the later 13th century, the tombs of all three bishops were relocated, Richard and Gilbert's tombs being sited in recesses on the north side of the choir, close to the high altar and John's in a recess on the south side, part of the painted plaster decoration of which, showing a procession of clergy, has survived. Interments at Inchcolm continued through the medieval period. In 1483, for example, Bishop James Livingstone was buried in the abbey (Bannatyne Club 1831, 11, 26). At Dunkeld itself, only two bishops' tombs have survived of the various interments recorded in the cathedral. The older is that of Bishop William Sinclair (1312–37), which was decribed in the early 1500s by Alexander Myln as lying originally 'at the presbytery step in the midst of the choir, where his body is buried, covered with a marble stone' (Bannatyne Club 1831, 13). He added that a fine alabaster effigy of the bishop had lain on this slab but 'in case by any chance it should be destroyed, or should be an obstacle in front of the altar … it has now been set up close to the steps of the high altar at the western part of the north window of the choir'. It survives, although mutilated and lacking its head, in a mural recess in that location. The finer of the two surviving tombs is that of Bishop Robert de Cardeny (1398–1437), which is located in the chapel of St Ninian which occupied the two easternmost bays of the south aisle of the nave. It occupies a mural recess in the south wall but may originally have been intended to be free-standing within one of the chapel arcades (Fawcett 1997, 87 and fig 58; Wood 1950, 15). This position is very similar to that of Bishop Winchester at Elgin. Cardeny's tomb and the chapel in which it lies should probably be seen as a single component, built as a chantry for the bishop.

Cathedrals with shrines of canonised apostolic predecessors

In the third category there are four examples in medieval Scotland: Glasgow, Fortrose, Dornoch and Whithorn itself. Glasgow, as has already been observed, offers in many ways the closest Scottish parallel to Whithorn. Not only are there physical similarities in the architectural responses to the problems of a sloping site but there seems also to have been a similar approach to the location of the main pilgrimage foci within the cathedral. There is the added parallel that at both cathedrals the focus of the cult was on an individual who was regarded as the lineal predecessor of the medieval bishops, Ninian at Whithorn and Kentigern at Glasgow. Perhaps surprisingly in view of this relationship between sainted predecessor and the later bishops, very few of the medieval succession were buried within their cathedral (Stones 1969, 37–46). Indeed, what is most striking is that none of the three bishops who oversaw the major building operations at Glasgow – John (1118–47), Jocelin (1174–99) and William de Bondington (1232–58) – were buried there. Bishop John, the man responsible for the fixing of the see at Glasgow and the construction of the first 12th-century cathedral, was buried in the Augustinian priory at Jedburgh which he had founded (*Historia Regum*: Arnold 1885, 321). Bishop Jocelin, who greatly extended the cathedral in the later 12th century and probably first developed the laigh kirk housing Kentigern's tomb and the elevated east end containing the shrine, was buried on the north side of the choir at Melrose Abbey, where he had formerly been abbot (*Chron. Howden*, iv, 85). Bishop Bondington, in whose episcopate the major portion of the east end of the present building was constructed, who died at the episcopal manor house at Ancrum in Teviotdale, was also buried at Melrose 'beside the large altar' (Bannatyne Club 1837b, s.a. 1258). Six of their successors, who remained as bishops at Glasgow until death, were also apparently buried elsewhere than in the cathedral (Stones 1969, 40).

Of the five bishops of Glasgow who can be identified with some certainty to have been buried within their own cathedral, little evidence survives of their tombs (Stones 1969, 38–9). Three of these interments are said to have been in the 'lower church' or crypt, close to St Kentigern's tomb. Of these, the possible elements of only one, that identified as the tomb of Bishop Robert Wishart (1271–1316), survives albeit in a much altered condition and probably no longer contains the bishop's remains (Stones 1969, 38, 41–5, 46). This was located under the arcade between the chapel of St Peter and St Paul and the chapel of St Andrew, the two central chapels in the four which occupied the sub-vault of the ambulatory at the east end of the church (Driscoll 1998, 25–34, fig 1 for position of the altars in the lower church). The tomb of Bishop John Lindsay (1317–35) is said to have been located 'nigh to the altar of the Blessed Virgin', ie the altar of the Lady Chapel, which occupied the central compartment of the lower church between the easternmost two bays of the main body of the crypt (Stones 1969, 39). The remaining episcopal tomb in the lower church may have been that of Bishop John Laing (1474–83), but its precise location is unknown. Neither of the two recumbent slabs preserved in the laigh kirk at Glasgow and formerly identified as belonging to bishops' tombs is identifiable as a grave-marker for either of these men and they seem rather to have been the memorials of other cathedral dignitaries rather than of bishops (Stones 1969, 39, 41). Three further episcopal burials are suggested to have occurred in the cathedral, but only two of these can be attested with any certainty from a pre-Reformation source. The earlier of the three and least securely attested is said to have been that of Bishop Andrew Durisdeer (1455–73), which Alexander Nisbet in 1722 described as having been in the choir (Stones 1969, 39). The second burial, of which the tomb itself no longer survives, was that of Archbishop Robert Blackadder (1483–1508). He instructed that his tomb should be placed before the great rood in the nave of the church, between the altars of The Name of Jesus and Our Lady of Pity which he had founded (Fawcett 2002, 305; Durkan 1972). The last, which can be attested on more secure historical grounds, was that of Archbishop Gavin Dunbar (1524–47), which was located in the chancel of the cathedral. Dunbar's will sets out payments for requiem masses and arrangements at his tomb, but does not give a precise location for it in the building (Blair 1886, 110, 112). What was believed to have been Dunbar's tomb was discovered in 1804 and opened again in 1856. This, apparently, lay on the south side of the choir between the pillars of the second bay, with the burial occupying a void opened in the cavities over the vault of the lower church, although an alternative tradition reports that it was in the vicinity of the Lady Chapel (Stones 1969, 45–6; Rogers 1857, 327–9). Amongst items believed to have been removed from the grave in 1804 were part of a crozier and ring, which were displayed at the 1888 Glasgow Exhibition but whose whereabouts seem now to be unknown. There may have been other pre-Reformation bishops' burials in the cathedral but there is no surviving record to support this suggestion. What seems clear from the limited evidence available is that the medieval bishops of Glasgow did not feel it imperative to be buried in their cathedral or, indeed, to be buried close to the tomb of their saintly predecessor. The distribution of burial sites around the cathedral seems closer to the practice evident at, for example, Elgin and bears no obvious relationship to the location of Kentigern's tomb or shrine.

The original seat of the bishops of Ross appears to have been at Rosemarkie, where an early 8th-century bishop, Boniface or Curitan, is believed to have founded a monastery and later been buried. There is no record of a regular succession of bishops of the see down to the 12th century and it appears that the Bishop Macbeth on record in the early 1100s was the first of a revived succession. Bishop Macbeth's see appears to have been fixed at Rosemarkie, where it remained until the time of Bishop Robert I (1214–49) and his major re-organisation of the diocese, its chapter and location of its cathedral. Bishop Robert I, who may have been under some considerable pressure from Earl Ferchar of Ross to move his seat to the earl's new Premonstratensian abbey at Fearn, responded instead by relocating his cathedral to a new site only a mile to the west of Rosemarkie at Fortrose (Cant 1986, 54–5). It is not clear if Boniface's remains were translated from the early church at Rosemarkie or to what extent the new cathedral at Fortrose made provision for a shrine within it, and the post-Reformation destruction of the main compartment of the building has removed all evidence for the tombs of the 13th- and 14th-century bishops. A similar drift in the location of burials away from the liturgical east end of the church to more prominent locations in the western compartments as is evident at Elgin, however, may also be detected at Fortrose. The early tombs were probably located in the wholly demolished east end, but two late medieval episcopal tombs do remain in the still upstanding south aisle and south chapel of the nave. Both are chest tombs, one inserted into the western arcade of the southern chapel, the second in an arcaded opening cut into what had originally been a section of blank wall between the aisle and chapel arcades. This latter has been identified as the tomb of Bishop Fraser (1497–1507) and the former as that of Bishop Robert Cairncross (1538–45) (Fawcett 1987, 22; Fawcett 2002, 318 and fig 4.94). When what was believed to have been Bishop Fraser's tomb was opened in 1797, it was found still to contain the bishop's body and well-preserved remains of the mass vestments in which he had been buried, together with parts of a wooden crozier (Stuart 1854; for the crozier, which is now on display in the National Museum of Scotland, see Fawcett 1987, 25).

Although the 13th-century cathedral of the see of Caithness at Dornoch has survived as a functioning church in the post-Reformation period, no trace within it has survived of any shrine of St Gilbert, bishop 1223–*c* 1244, of his predecessor, 'St' Adam (1213–22), or of the tombs of their successors. The cruciform church, of which the crossing and eastern limb survive in restored condition, was largely constructed during Gilbert's lifetime and shows no sign of subsequent adaptation to accommodate a shrine. Adam's remains had been translated in 1239 from their original burial place in the church of Halkirk in Caithness, beside the site of the episcopal manor-house where he was murdered in 1222, and it seems that his successor, Gilbert, had plans to develop a saint's cult around his 'martyred' predecessor (Bannatyne Club 1837b, s.a. 1239). The translation occurred during the building of the cathedral at Dornoch but the plan of the church makes no obvious provision for a shrine chapel, and it is unlikely that there were distinct shrines of either Adam or of Gilbert himself located within it. Gilbert, presumably, was interred in the choir of the church which he had built but specific relics are on record in 1522 as being touched by John Mackay of Strathnaver as part of the process whereby he legally bound himself to do service to Alexander, Master of Sutherland (Fraser 1892, no 69, dated 6 July 1522). The act involved touching the Holy Evangels and the 'relics of the gracious Gilbert', which could be interpreted as indicating that some relic of the bishop had been removed from his tomb and was kept in a portable reliquary for just such purposes. Certainly, there is no surviving reference to a shrine or feretory of St Gilbert (nor, indeed, of St Adam), and there is no remnant of his original tomb. The only medieval monument to survive in the cathedral is a mutilated mid-13th-century effigy of a knight, believed to be from the tomb of Bishop Gilbert's brother, Richard de Moravia, which has been placed in the reconstructed nave (Gifford 1992, 566).

The position at Whithorn has been explored in more detail above. It simply needs to be reiterated here that the evidence points towards the majority of the 12th- to 16th-century bishops being buried in their cathedral and the strong likelihood that most were buried at the eastern chapel rather than further west in the choir, crossing or nave. It is unlikely that any of the burials identified are those of the medieval priors, the majority of who down to the 15th century were probably buried in the chapter house. There is no evidence for the provision of elaborate chest tombs and all evidence for mural monuments has been swept away in the destruction of the eastern limb (although three mural recesses survive in the nave). However, as Kirsty Dingwall's study of the indented stones and lost monumental brasses now shows (Chapter 6.12), one or more of Whithorn's medieval bishops provided themselves with what was clearly an expensive grave monument of foreign manufacture, set into the pavement at the east end of the church.

Archdiocese of York

Within the archdiocese of York, perhaps the closest parallels with pre-1100 Whithorn could be expected at Hexham, with which there seems to have been a close relationship in the Northumbrian period, but for the post-1100 period it is perhaps Durham, where the cathedral contained the shrine of St Cuthbert, the canonised predecessor of the medieval bishops of Durham, that is more relevant. It was also a monastic church, served from 1083 by a convent of Benedictine monks which replaced an earlier college of secular canons. As at Whithorn, the cathedral as developed in the late 11th and early 12th century contained a shrine chapel which housed Cuthbert's remains, still entombed in their late 10th-century grave, located immediately east of the high altar and later screened from the choir by the reredos. Cuthbert's relics were translated to a new shrine in 1104, comprising an ornate coffin raised on a slab carried by nine columns, set immediately behind and rising above the high altar (Wilson 1977, fig 2b). This rebuilding programme was begun under the direction of Bishop William de St Calais (1080–96), but he was not buried within his new church. Instead, his tomb lies at the western end of the chapter house. William de St Calais set something of a precedent, for his four immediate successors – Ranulf Flambard (1099–1128), Geoffrey Rufus (1133–41) and William de Ste Barbe (1143–52) and Hugh du Puiset (1153–95) – were buried alongside him, as later were Robert de Insula (1274–83) and Richard Kellaw (1311–6) (Cheetham 1968, 126). None of the late 11th- to early 14th-century bishops who were buried at Durham was buried close to the tomb of Cuthbert. Indeed, even the later bishops were entombed in various locations around their cathedral – Anthony Bek (1284–1311) and Richard of Bury (1333–45) in the Chapel of the Nine Altars at the extreme east end of the cathedral; Lewis de Beaumont (1317–33) in front of the high altar steps; Thomas Hatfield (1345–81) in his monumental tomb under his throne in the fourth bay of the south aisle arcade of the choir; and Robert Neville (1438–57) in the nave (Queckett & Cheetham 1968, 100, 107, 108, 118) - but none was interred within the somewhat cramped shrine chapel. If anything, there seems to be almost an anxiety to avoid interment anywhere close to the shrine on the part of the earlier bishops, while their 14th- and 15th-century successors appear to show the same interest in proximity to the high altar already noted for their counterparts in Scotland.

At York itself, despite the fact that five pre-10th-century archbishops had been canonised, all were buried elsewhere and the Minster acquired a major cult focus only in the 13th century when Archbishop William FitzHerbert (d 1154) was canonised in 1227 (Wilson 1977, 8 and n. 19). William's tomb lay at the east end of the nave in front of the nave altar and, despite the canonisation, received no great elaboration before the late 13th century. In 1284, Bishop Anthony Bek of Durham paid for the ceremonial translation of William's remains to a splendid new shrine located behind the medieval high altar of the Minster, which stood one bay further west than the present high altar (Wilson 1977, 8 and n. 20). This new shrine became the main focus for pilgrims, but medieval records record the existence also of a portable feretory in addition to this fixed one, plus a head shrine or reliquary containing the saint's skull. The portable feretory appears to have been kept at the otherwise empty original tomb (Wilson 1977, 8–9 and notes), an arrangement which may have been replicated at Whithorn and which may be reflected in the sequence of devotions recorded for James IV in the early 1500s.

While the lateness of the development of the cult of St William of York may be one reason for the lack of focus in the disposition of archiepiscopal burials around the Minster, it is very striking that the tomb remained isolated in the nave after 1227 and the shrine never came to form a focus for the interments of the archbishops post-1284. Walter de Gray (1215–55), in whose episcopate St William was canonised, was buried in the northern bay of the south transept, flanked by his two successors, Sewal de Bovil (1256–8) and Godfrey de Ludham (1258–65), to his north and south respectively. Of the pre-Reformation archbishops from the time of the translation onwards, only William Greenfield (1306–16), Richard le Scrope (1398–1405), Henry Bowet (1407–23), Thomas Rotherham (1480–1500) and Thomas Savage (1501–7) were buried in the eastern limb of the church, all of them except Savage in the easternmost chapels behind the shrine. Again, it is clear that there was no focus on the main shrine, or the earlier tomb, as a place of burial for William FitzHerbert's successors.

8.3. DISCUSSION AND CONCLUSIONS

The above overview raises several very interesting questions relating to the burial arrangements at Whithorn plus the planning and use of the eastern limb of the cathedral church. What is clear, however, is that the intensity of burials within a comparatively small space is unique amongst the cathedral churches of Scotland, northern England and, indeed, the wider British Isles and northern mainland Europe. This density of interment is inexplicable, given the patterns and trends which are evident elsewhere, and raises several important questions concerning the layout of the post-1200 church.

A first question is whether or not the eastern extremity of the church comprised a shrine-chapel behind the high altar, or presbytery with the high altar against the east gable. If the former were the case, then the position of the bishops' burials becomes even more unusual for they would be crowded into a narrow space of no more than one bay's length between the reredos behind the high altar and the front of the putative shrine-base supporting the feretory. At no other cathedral housing a shrine in this fashion is this clustering into such a cramped space encountered. Glasgow offers the most obvious analogy in Scotland, but there the burials were dispersed throughout both the Laigh and Upper Kirks. The situation at Durham should also be considered, where the bishops chose to be buried in the chapter house rather than in the cathedral church until after *c* 1300. If the eastern chapel at Whithorn was a presbytery with high altar, then the location of the tombs is slightly less unusual. Bishops were interred before the high altars of numerous cathedrals, such as Elgin or Dunkeld. Again, however, the density of the Whithorn bishops' burials is without parallel in a cathedral and bears closer similarity to the position in some English parish churches, like Cobham in Kent, where the floor in front of the sanctuary area is entirely composed of the tomb slabs of the local lords of the manor (Binski 1996, 89). The mentality which produced this density of interment at Whithorn is lost to us. Was it a desire for proximity to Ninian's tomb or relics, or indeed for burial within what was regarded as a particularly holy location in a church where the earlier chapel on the same site was treated as a relic in itself?

A second key issue concerns the consequences of the use of the eastern extremity as a reliquary chapel. If this chapel did contain a feretory and, in common with shrines located behind the high altars at other British and European cathedrals, was entered from north and south through the most easterly bays of the choir arcade, the proposed location of the reredos at Whithorn would have meant that the floor area occupied by the bishops' graves would have been that part of the chapel most trodden over by the pilgrims. This is not in itself a problem but, given the later medieval emphasis on the individual and the desire for personal commemoration (as evident in Prior Thomas's arrangements for requiem masses and prayers in the 1430s), the prospective interment would have had to weigh up the benefits of burial in so holy and prominent a location against the damage likely to be inflicted on his monument.

There is also a third question to consider. Most of the Phase 3 burials at Whithorn are male and the paraphernalia associated with them points to priestly, if not purely episcopal office. The radiocarbon dates (Chapter 7) indicate that these burials date to the 13th and 14th centuries and this raises the question of where Whithorn's later ecclesiastics were buried.

The later medieval trend away from burials in the presbytery of the cathedral churches towards interment in transeptal or aisle chapels is probably linked to the increasing elaboration of ritual in the so-called 'cult of death'. From the 14th century onwards, gaining pace especially after the first catastrophic outbreak of plague in 1348–50, there developed a much greater focus on preparation for death, commemoration and post mortem care of the soul. An important dimension of this development was the increased provision for *pro anima* masses, with the institution of separate altars and, for the wealthy, separate chapels and chaplains, to offer up those masses and prayers for the souls of the founder and their family. Frequently, these chapels housed the tombs of the founders, located close to the altar where their souls would derive maximum spiritual benefit from the services offered. The most sophisticated examples of such provision were the collegiate churches founded from the mid-14th century onwards, such as Lincluden in eastern Galloway, where the tomb of Archibald, 4th earl of Douglas, and his wife, Margaret Stewart, forms an integral element of the design of the chancel. In most cases, however, chapels were added to existing structures, which appears to be the case with the chapel of St Mary at Whithorn begun in 1431 by Prior Thomas Mcgilliachnisy (Chapter 8.2.1: *Later medieval building work*).

Loss of the bulk of the medieval records of Whithorn priory has possibly distorted the picture of the patterns of interments and the development of separate chaplainries or chantry chapels within the cathedral church, but the absence of any reference at any date to anything other than the Chapel of St Mary is unusual. Indeed, the records only reveal the existence of three altars – the rood altar, high altar and altar of St Mary – and, while there must have been others, if only to provide for the number of canons within the community even in the immediate pre-Reformation period, the numbers seem always to have been small.

This lack of proliferation of altars, even in the later 15th and 16th centuries, can be interpreted in two main ways, as a matter of funding or as an issue of space. It is possible, for example, that there was a lack of significant lay patronage from which the endowment of such altars or chapels most commonly arose. We know, however, that the Douglases endowed a chapel in the 1420s and that they were not alone in seeking to extend their influence within the priory in the 15th and 16th centuries. There is also clear evidence, given the presence of women among the Phase 3 burials, that lay patrons were seeking burial at Whithorn. If money was no object, then this points to our second alternative – that the lack of proliferation of altars was due to the fact that there was limited space for the physical expansion of the church to accommodate additional chapels. Here may be evidence for at worst the absence of aisles which could be partitioned by screens to form separate chapels, or at best the need to keep the aisles unencumbered by such screens to smooth the flow of pilgrims around the pressure areas in the east end of the church. Add in the unusual concentration of episcopal burials in the relatively cramped block in the east end of the church and the likelihood emerges that they were buried there because there were few other places where they could have been interred without resorting to major structural enlargement of the cathedral. The concentration of interments in the one, densely-packed space is probably the strongest argument for an absence of lateral aisles in the choir, for space for burials could have been found under the choir arcades or in the aisle walls (the solution adopted at Dunkeld, Dunblane, Aberdeen etc). The outer walls of an aisle-less choir would have been unavailable for burials, moreover, as the canons' stalls and the bishop's throne would have needed to have been placed against the wall surface, while space on the walls within the presbytery would have been occupied by the door(s?) to the stair(s?) leading to the crypt, sedilia for the officiants at the mass, piscina and, possibly, aumbries for storage of mass paraphernalia. That no attempt was made to provide a south aisle on the nave (as was adopted as a space solution at the much less cramped cathedral site at Fortrose), coupled with the conflict over finances for building operations in the early 15th century, perhaps implies that, as Bishop Eliseus claimed, his see was impoverished and the cathedral mean, old and unsound.

Chapter 9

The Ritchie Excavations: an Overview of Results and a Sequence Model for the High-Status Graves

CHRISTOPHER LOWE

9.1 THE SIGNIFICANCE OF THE ROY RITCHIE EXCAVATIONS

The significance of the Roy Ritchie excavations cannot be over-estimated. It is the first time that a large group of richly furnished graves from one of the country's principal medieval cathedrals has been scientifically investigated. We suspect, however, that the conclusions that the present study have come to are not those that Ritchie would have recognised or necessarily have agreed with. In order to fully appreciate the difference between this publication and what its 1960s equivalent might have looked like, we need to remind ourselves of the academic agenda of the time and what was being said then about Whithorn and its development. In this regard we might look to some of the things that Radford or Cruden were saying about *Candida Casa* and the dating of the foundations that William Galloway identified below and to the east of the 13th-century church (Chapter 1.2), or the conclusions regarding the presence of a cremation cemetery on the site that Cruden, Ritchie's boss, had already publicly aired in his 1963 paper in *The Scotsman Magazine* and which Charles Thomas would reiterate in *The Early Christian Archaeology of North Britain* (Thomas 1971, 55, Footnotes 1 & 2). Possibly it was these published claims, at least in part, that prevented Ritchie from completing the publication of his excavation, namely the problem of reconciling the claims of others with his findings.

The present study has been able to make considerable use of techniques such as radiocarbon dating which were only then starting to be used (although not for medieval archaeology), or isotope analyses which could then have hardly been dreamt of. Our ability to date accurately the skeletons has allowed this study to see that the primary cemetery cannot be Early Christian or Anglian in date; meanwhile, as we have seen (Chapter 4.1) analysis of the only cremated bone that we have found in the archive is sheep rather than human.

The post-excavation project that we embarked on in 2006 started out with potential cremation deposits, graves of Early Christian date and, as Cruden (1963) described in *The Scotsman Magazine*, a thousand years of history between the graves at the bottom and the 'Bishops' Graves' at the top. We have 'lost' the putative late Roman cremation cemetery, as well as any Early Christian burials. The burial chronology, from bottom to top, effectively spans, at the most, a period of 400 years and the 12 feet of soil which Cruden looked upon as a proxy record of a thousand years of history was almost certainly created within a single generation – as indicated by the overlapping chronologies between the latest burials of Phase 1 and the earliest burials of Phase 3 (Chapter 7). We are left then with our Phase 1 burials, part of the 12th-century and earlier cemetery and our Phase 3 high-status burials of the 13th and 14th centuries. Not all of these, however, are bishops.

9.2 THE BURIAL SEQUENCE: A RECONSTRUCTION

9.2.1 Introduction

Interpretation of the burial sequence is closely related to the question of who the various individuals could have been. For this exercise, we have the stratigraphic record (Chapter 3), the records of the bones themselves (Chapter 4), as well as the evidence of the artefacts and their dating (Chapter 6). We also have the historical framework (Chapter 8) which gives us the names and dates of the church's bishops. All of this, of course, was also available to Ritchie; what he did not have, however, was recourse to radiocarbon-dating of the human remains themselves and some of the statistical analyses which, by taking into account the stratigraphic evidence, can now start to give us relatively closely defined time-frames for certain individuals or events (Chapter 7). By taking all this information together it is possible to start putting names to at least some of the 'faces' that Ritchie encountered, so that we can start compiling a 'who's who' of the bishops (and possibly others) of medieval Whithorn.

Understanding the sequence also has to accommodate the observations that Ritchie himself made. Three of the

Table 9.1 Whithorn's bishops, *c* 1200–1400. (Estimated age at death = length of episcopate + 30 + 10 for any other previous senior appointments as abbot or prior. All estimates are likely to be minima.)

Bishop	*Episcopal dates*	*Length of episcopate*	*Estimated age at death (minima)*	*Place of consecration*	*Summary background*
John	1189–1209	20	50+	Pipewell Abbey, Northants.	Royal clerk to Henry II? Closely associated with York
Walter	1209–35	26	55+	York	Clerk and chamberlain of the household of Alan, lord of Galloway. Like his predecessors, active in northern England deputising for archbishop of York
Gilbert	1235–53	18	60+	York	Monk of Melrose abbey and formerly Abbot of Glenluce; royal appointee of Alexander II?
Henry	1253–93	40	80+	York	Abbot of Holyrood; regularly deputising for archbishops of York as late as 1291. Issued indulgence to all who contributed to repair of cathedral after damage of 1286 in the raids on Galloway by Bruce following death of Alexander III
Thomas de Dalton (de Kirkcudbright; de Galloway)	1294–1324x1326	30	60+	Originally planned for Hexham, then Ripon: finally, Gedling, Yorkshire	Bruce household clerk; later a supporter of Balliol? Regularly present in diocese of York 1310–14
Simon of Wedale	1326–55	29	70+	Westminster	Abbot of Holyrood, pro-Bruce faction; but 1330s–1350s Galloway reverted to its pro-Balliol loyalties, making it unlikely that Simon (if he maintained loyalty of Robert I's heir) would have been able to function within his diocese
Michael Malconhalgh / Mackenlagh	1355–58x59	4	45+	York	Prior of Whithorn; Bruce appointee
Thomas	1359–62	3	35+	Avignon	Unknown but successfully outmaneouvred rival, local appointee
Adam	1363–78	15	45+	Avignon	Adam of Lanark, Dominican friar; emissary for David II and later his confessor
Thomas Rossy	1379–97x1406	18–27	55+	Avignon	Franciscan friar; leading intellectual supporter of the Avignon pope, Clement VII. Challenged the English warrior-cleric, Henry Despenser, Bishop of Norwich, to single combat in 1384. Preached sermon at coronation of Robert III in 1390. In Avignon in September 1397

five key stratigraphic relationships that Ritchie identified (Dingwall, Chapter 3) are straightforward and need no further explanation here; two of these deal with simple super-imposition (Grave 5 over Grave 6, and Grave 12 over Grave 21), the third with Grave 8 having been cut through deposits associated with Grave 3. However, his record of the relationship between Graves 1, 2 and 3 needs carefully thinking through. As we have seen (Dingwall, Chapter 3), Ritchie's key observations in this regard were:

- that the cover stones of Grave 2 overlay the side-stones of Grave 1; and
- that the mortar lining of Grave 1 laps over the edge stones of Grave 3 and thus postdates its construction.

He interpreted this as a simple construction sequence of Grave 2 over Grave 1 over Grave 3. However, our analysis will suggest that these relationships do not represent a construction sequence or sequence of use, but rather (and crucially) a sequence of reuse. Indeed, we will argue that Grave 1, far from being one of the later graves on site (as Ritchie believed), is more likely to be the earliest grave in the extended east end of the church in Phase 3.

9.2.2 The chronological framework

The chronological framework depends in part upon the dates of the skeletons and the architectural dating of the fabric of the church itself. The conventional architectural date of *c* 1200 for the ribbed vault below the extended east end of the church provides one end of this chronological framework. The other is marked by the latest Phase 3 date which comes from Grave 1, whose remains have been radiocarbon-dated to cal ad 1280–1400 (SUERC-12498). In other words, all of the Phase 3 graves must be later than *c* 1200 and earlier than 1400.

Meanwhile, it is instructive to note that Phase 1 burials were still being interred in the graveyard, below what would become a major building site for the construction of the extended eastern arm of the church, as late as the late 12th century. The latest Phase 1 burial is Skeleton 18 (cal ad 1185–1285: SUERC-12519), although the stratigraphic constraints imply that the burial must belong to the earlier part of this date-range. By contrast, the earliest dated remains among the Phase 3 graves are Skeletons 6 and 21, which are dated to cal ad 1050–1270 (SUERC-12506 & SUERC-16064 respectively). Clearly, these must lie

Table 9.2 The Phase 3 Graves, demography and radiocarbon-dating. (Age codes: YA – 25-35 years; MA – 35-45 years; OA – 45+ years; AD = adult)

SK#	*Sex*	*Age*	*C14 dating*	*Portion present*	*Pathology*
1	Male	OA	cal AD 1280–1400	Head to thighs	-
2	Male	YA	cal AD 1250–1390	All except skull	-
3	Male	OA	cal AD 1180–1280	Head to thighs	DISH, probably obese
4	Male	OA	cal AD 1210–1380+ cal AD 1250–1390 = cal AD 1269–1289	Head to knees	Tooth abscesses, skull osteoma-
5	Male	?YA	cal AD 1250–1390	Complete	-
6	Female	OA	cal AD 1050–1270	All except skull	-
7	?Male	AD	cal AD 1220–1390	A few scraps	Arthritis of fingers
8	Male	MA	cal AD 1220–1390	Complete	Cleft palate, fractured frontal
10	?Male	AD	cal AD 1220–1390	Waist to feet	?marrow/ blood cancer
11	?Female	AD	cal AD 1250–1390	Legs	-
12	Male	MA	cal AD 1215–1290	Complete	-
14	Female	MA	cal AD 1160–1280	Head only	-
21	Male	MA	cal AD 1050–1270	Feet to elbows	?psoriatic arthritis

towards the latter part of their date-range. Indeed, the modelled Bayesian date range for these latter burials suggests that they were interred in the period 1217–70 (Dalland, Chapter 7.2.2 & Table 7.3).

9.2.3 Potential occupants: who are we looking for?

As Richard Oram's discussion of bishops and priors makes clear (Chapter 8.2.2), the community's priors, as in all other Scottish monastic orders, are more likely to have been buried in the chapter house or east cloister alley than in the church itself. In terms of bishops and their *obits*, the time frame of *c* 1200–1400 means that of Whithorn's 21 pre-Reformation bishops (Table 8.1) we can only be looking for, at most, probably nine of them. This is the group from John (1189–1209) down to Adam (1363–1378). In terms simply of historical dates, it might conceivably extend to include a tenth, Thomas Rossy (1379–1397x1406) although, as Oram (Chapter 8) points out, the balance of evidence would point to his death abroad, probably in France. This, of course, would not in itself preclude his subsequent burial at Whithorn. In terms, however, of the radiocarbon dates it seems unlikely that he could be represented here. The nine or ten possible contenders, together with a brief summary of their ecclesiastical careers and an estimate of their age at death, are set out in Table 9.1.

Although we can be fairly confident about the episcopal regnal dates for this group, none of their ages or birth-dates is known. It is important, however, that some estimate of age is made because this is one of the things that can be fairly accurately established as part of the study of the human remains (Henderson, Chapter 4). Certainly, it becomes an important criterion in our challenge of correlating the human remains with the various bishops whose *obits* can be accommodated within the radiocarbon-dating framework. Our estimate, therefore, assumes that episcopal rank is unlikely to have been achieved before the age of 30; an additional ten years has been added in those cases where a senior appointment, as abbot or prior, had previously been held. All of these estimates are likely to be minima, raising the possibility therefore that the various individuals could have well been older than the ages indicated. Meanwhile, in Table 9.2 we have the 13 graves of Phase 3, along with their basic demographic data and their calibrated radiocarbon dates.

What then is the relationship between the ten named individuals in Table 9.1 and the 13 anonymous remains in Table 9.2? Of the 13 graves under consideration here, it is clear that three are either definitely or probably female (Graves 6, 11 and 14); the extant bones of another two (Graves 2 and 5: YA or YA?) are almost certainly too young to be the remains of any of our bishops; whilst another three (Graves 8, 12 and 21: all MA) are also probably too young to be represented. For this latter group, it is clear from the radiocarbon dates that Skeletons 12 and 21 must belong to the 13th century, yet all of Whithorn's 13th-century bishops were considerably older than the remains preserved in these two graves. Meanwhile, the possibility that the middle-adult remains in Grave 8 could be one of our 14th-century bishops presents us with a different sort of challenge. On the basis simply of the radiocarbon dates, it is conceivable that the remains in Grave 8 could be the (possibly) relatively 'youthful' Bishop Thomas who died in 1362. His short tenure of office, together with the fact that very little is known about him, means that he is potentially the youngest of the bishops that we are looking for, with an estimated age, perhaps, of around 35+ years (Table 9.1). The little that we do know about Bishop Thomas (Oram, Chapter 8.1.2), however, clearly indicates that he was a man who must have been politically astute; not only did he successfully outmanoeuvre a local rival appointee but he also advocated his case before the pope in Avignon. However, it is extremely difficult to reconcile this picture with the pathology of the human remains in Grave 8 and the severe cleft palate which is displayed there. This individual, as the carbon and nitrogen isotope analyses make clear (Chapter 5), had the poorest diet of all the Phase 3 burials; and as Henderson notes (Chapter 4), he would have had a severe speech defect. It seems extremely unlikely, therefore, that Skeleton 8 can have been one of our bishops. Our 'original' Phase 3 population of 13 is thus severely diminished – both by sex and age – to a core group of just five potential candidates (Graves 1, 3, 4, 7 and 10) but, as we shall see (Chapter 9.2.4: Table 9.3), out of this group only three (the skeletons in Graves 1, 3 and 7) can be positively identified as bishops.

A missing part of the equation might be the plot of unexcavated or partially excavated ground (Dingwall, Chapter 2.2) that lies between Graves 8 and 12, to the west of the main row, yet this (at most) can have accommodated only a further four burials. Clearly, then, some of our bishops are missing; but we also have others present who are definitely not bishops (such as the three female graves). Given the prominence of female landowners in Galloway from the 13th century (Oram, Chapter 8.3), these are most likely therefore to be the graves of some of Whithorn's lay benefactors. The likely presence of lay patrons is one of the missing elements of the Whithorn story; another is to recognise that among the graves are almost certainly those of other ecclesiastical ranks besides bishops.

Before we can start to look in detail at the sequence, it would be useful to try and categorise how these different groups might be differentiated.

Table 9.3 The Phase 3 Graves by status or likely group. (Age codes: YA = 25–35 years; MA = 35–45 years; OA = 45+ years; AD = adult)

SK#	*Sex*	*Age*	*Grave type*	*Ecclesiastical artefacts*	*Comments*	*Identification*
1	Male	OA	Stone cist	Wooden crozier; episcopal ring; chalice; paten	–	Bishop (definite)
2	Male	YA	Stone cist	Chalice; small ring.	Bones are too young for recorded bishops 1200–1400	Priest (probable)
3	Male	OA	Stone-built chamber with timber lining	Wooden crozier; small ring	–	Bishop (definite)
4	Male	OA	Wooden coffin	Chalice; paten.	Statistical analysis and revised calibrated C14 date (1269–89) rules out all 13th-century bishops	Priest (probable)
5	Male	?YA	Stone cist	None (full skeleton present)	Bones are too young for recorded bishops 1200–1400; evidence of grave robbing	Priest (possible)
6	Female	OA	Wooden coffin	None	Possibly associated with adjacent Grave 12	Lay patron (probable)
7	?Male	AD	Wooden coffin	Enamel crozier; mitre?; chalice; paten	–	Bishop (definite)
8	Male	MA	Stone cist	None (full skeleton present)	Bones are probably too young for recorded bishops 1200–1400; evidence of grave robbing	Priest (possible)
10	?Male	AD	Wooden coffin	None (waist to feet only excavated)	Ecclesiastical artefacts could be present in unexcavated half; but if burial is secular, then possibly associated with adjacent Grave 11	Lay patron or priest (possible)
11	?Female	AD	Wooden coffin	None	Possibly associated with adjacent Grave 10	Lay patron (probable)
12	Male	MA	Wooden coffin	None (full skeleton present)	Possibly associated with adjacent Grave 6	Lay patron (possible)
14	Female	MA	Wooden coffin	None	–	Lay patron (probable)
21	Male	MA	Wooden coffin	Chalice (elbows to feet only excavated)	Additional ecclesiastical artefacts could be present in unexcavated half	Priest (probable)

9.2.4 Bishops, clerics of lower rank and lay patrons

As with the wider question of to whom these various graves may have belonged, our ability to differentiate between these different groups depends in part upon the nature of any associated finds assemblage, partly upon the sex of the preserved remains and partly upon the age and dating of the skeleton, given the parameters of the chronological framework under investigation (ie *c* 1200–1400) and its 'fit' with the list of Whithorn's contemporary bishops.

The presence of a crozier is the defining element for identification of remains as those of a bishop. The presence of a chalice and paten, meanwhile, need only signify the presence of an ordained priest. Female graves, we have already concluded, almost certainly indicate the presence of lay benefactors; male graves without grave-goods could also be part of the same population, and the co-occurrence of such males and females together could represent husband and wife or other types of family groups. Our interpretation of the relative status or group to which the 13 Phase 3 burials belong is set out in Table 9.3.

On the basis of these criteria, this appears to give us the remains of at least three definite bishops (Graves 1, 3 and 7); five or six priests (Graves 2, 4, 5, 8, 21 and possibly 10); and four or five lay benefactors (Graves 6, 11, 12, 14 and possibly 10), including possibly two husband-and-wife groups in peripheral areas to the north (Graves 6 and 12) and south (Graves 10 and 11). It is notable that the third female burial (Grave 14) is also located in a peripheral location.

Other potential anomalies (or at least interesting coincidences) also come into focus. For example, the 'youthful' nature of the bones in Grave 2, which *a priori* could be expected to be a clear contender as the grave of one of the cathedral's early bishops, looks decidedly anomalous; so too might the similarly young bones from another of the stone-cists, Grave 5. In any event, Grave 2 is almost certainly a candidate for reuse (and, indeed, must be if Ritchie's observation concerning its cover slabs is correct and if we are right in thinking that Grave 1 is the primary burial on the site). As we shall see, the question of the reuse of these graves by different generations of Whithorn's churchmen certainly occurs in the case of Graves 1 and 2, and possibly in other cases as well. It is less clear, however, if the use of stone cists themselves is an indication of episcopal rank; at least one of the bishops (Grave 7), for example, was clearly buried in a wooden coffin. The circumstances of this seemingly unusual burial (Dingwall, Chapter 2.3.1; Glenn & Franklin, Chapter 6.8) may, however, simply be the exception that proves the rule.

9.2.5 The burial sequence for the 13th century: an archaeological model (Figure 9.1)

The archaeological model for the burial sequence is based on the following assumptions and principles:

- that the founder or builder of the extended church will have taken for himself a prime, central position beside the altar and in proximity to any tomb to Ninian in the crypt below;
- that, generally, the construction sequence for the graves (all things being equal) will tend to work outwards from this central position; and, specifically, that the central Graves 1 and 2 were commissioned and constructed at the same time;
- and finally, that the construction sequence for the graves is not necessarily the same as their sequence of use or reuse.

If the extension of the Premonstratensian cathedral church dates to the period around 1200, then this programme of works will have been set in train by Bishop John and he is therefore likely to have reserved (or have been honoured with) the central burial plot that is represented by Grave 1. John died in 1209. It is clear, however, that the artefacts from the grave must post-date this by several decades (Glenn & Franklin, Chapter 6.8). This will have also been evident to Ritchie. Undoubtedly it was these relatively 'late' dates for the finds, together with his observation that the mortar lining of Grave 1 spilled out and overlay the stonework of Grave 3, that led him to conclude that Grave 1 was one of the latest graves on the site. On the basis of his belief that Grave 3 belonged to Bishop Henry (d 1293), he assigned Grave 1 to the period 1300x1325 (Archive D8(i), pp 7–8). The radiocarbon date from Skeleton 1 (cal ad 1280–1400: SUERC-12498), of course, also reinforces a later chronology. Our assumption, however, is that this is the primary grave in the building and that it was subsequently reused by one of Whithorn's later bishops.

The second assumption that underlies this model is that Graves 1 and 2 were commissioned and constructed at the same time. As John's successor, the responsibility for this will have lain with Bishop Walter and it is not difficult to imagine the process whereby he will have wanted to reserve for himself the next best position in the church. The suggestion, therefore, is that Graves 1 and 2 were both built and put in place in 1209. However, the problem with this is that the bones in Grave 2 are too young for any of the recorded bishops within the 1200–1400 time-frame. Clearly, Walter could have been removed at a later date, as we have already suggested was the case for Bishop John and his occupancy of Grave 1. A clue may be provided by the remains that were recovered from Grave 3, which lies

Figure 9.1
Thirteenth-century burials. Note that the graves identified as those of bishops are entirely focused on the central area

immediately to the south of Grave 1, in the next prime central position.

Grave 3 was unusual in two ways. Unlike the stone cists of Graves 1 and 2 (and others) with their carved head-niches and mortar-lined sides, Grave 3 was built as a large stone chamber, lined with wood. Incorporated into it were several reused architectural fragments and it has the appearance of a bespoke construction. The human remains also displayed an unusual pathology, Diffuse Idiopathic Skeletal Hyperostosis (DISH), a condition which leads to the overproduction of bone. As Henderson (Chapter 4.3.2) points out, this is more common in old men and is possibly linked to obesity and late onset diabetes. Moreover, the position of the skeleton, with his arms bowed out from the sides and the presence of an unusual amount of adipocere (a chalky or soapy white substance, the mineralised remains of the products of body fat decomposition) suggest that the individual may have been obese. It brings to mind the account of James the Gross, the preparation of his body for burial and the problem of its bulk (Richard Oram, pers comm):

> The zere of god 1443 the 10th day of March erll James Douglas deit at the castell of Abercorn to the takin thai said he had in him four stane of talch and maire.
>
> *(McGladdery 1990, 161)*

With over four stones (25kg) of tallow (*talch*) present, it is clear that the rendering of the corpse prior to burial cannot have been a particularly pleasant undertaking for those involved. Although there are no indications that Skeleton 3 was rendered, the problem of its bulk may have led to the construction of the somewhat 'roomier' Grave 3, instead of (as originally intended) Grave 2. Put simply, he was too fat to fit.

Bishop Walter died in 1235 and the radiocarbon date from the bones in Grave 3 (cal ad 1180–1280: SUERC-12500) is not inconsistent with this identification. Wedged onto the end of one of his fingers was a rather delicate ring of mid-13th century (or later) date (Glenn, Chapter 6.3.3), evidently a contemporary item if our identification is correct. The importance of this grave and particularly its radiocarbon date (pre-1280) is that it indirectly reinforces our view that Grave 1, adjacent, must have already been in place; and therefore that the surviving remains there relate to its later reuse.

If this model can be sustained, then it is clear that the next bishop in line, Bishop Gilbert who died in 1253, would have had a ready-made grave awaiting him; the grave, Grave 2, that Walter had commissioned in 1209 but which (we suggest) he had outgrown by 1235. As previously noted, however, the physical remains in Grave 2 are too young for any of the relevant bishops. Our interpretation, therefore, is that Grave 2 was first used by Gilbert but that he was subsequently translated elsewhere and his grave reused.

By 1253, Bishop John's new cathedral church will have witnessed his burial as well as those of his immediate successors, Walter (d 1235) and Gilbert (d 1253). Of these, only Walter (we suggest) would remain undisturbed. The next bishop to be accommodated into this sequence is the long-lived Bishop Henry who dies in 1293. It is clear, however, from the radiocarbon dates that there are several other graves that need to be slotted into the sequence before this. This group comprises two 'priestly' burials (Graves 4 and 21) and those of three 'lay benefactors' (Graves 6, 12 and 14).

The earliest of this group is probably Grave 21. Radiocarbon dates (Table 7.1) from the bone indicate a pre-1270 date whilst that from its cloth shroud indicates a date before 1220 (unless the ecclesiastical community had access to a stock of old cloth that was kept for burials). Given that Grave 21 was subsequently overlain, later in the same century, by Grave 12, we are inclined towards an earlier rather than a later date for this grave; possibly it lies chronologically between John and Walter. It is not possible to say who the priestly individual might have been, though a prominent role in the construction of the new building may, perhaps, have earned him his place (albeit a peripheral place) near the altar.

Although we cannot be certain, the rest of this non-episcopal group probably fall chronologically between Gilbert in 1253 and Henry in 1293. The female burial in Grave 6, located in our primary row but at a respectful distance from the centre, is possibly the first of this later group (pre-1270). The adjacent (and therefore similarly peripheral) grave, Grave 12 is possibly next. The extreme range of its calibrated radiocarbon date is cal ad 1215–1290 (SUERC-16062). The absence of any grave-goods and the identification of the remains as male might suggest some relationship with Grave 6 adjacent, possibly a husband-and-wife group. Conceivably, Graves 12 and 6 may be the graves, respectively, of Patrick Macscelling and his wife, Finlach, who are recorded as lay benefactors to the church at Whithorn (Oram, Appendix 3)

With these interments in place, the focus next moves to the south side of the church. Statistical analysis of the combined radiocarbon dates from Skeleton 4, at a 92% level of confidence, indicates that the priest in Grave 4 was probably buried in the period 1269x1289 (Dalland, Chapter 7). The female burial in Grave 14, set near (although not next to) the south wall of the church and radiocarbon-dated cal AD 1160–1280 (SUERC-16063) is possibly the latest of this group.

The last of our 13th-century bishops in search of a grave is Bishop Henry. When he died in 1293, he had been bishop of Whithorn for 40 years and before that abbot of Holyrood. What options were available for the positioning of Henry's grave in 1293? If our model is right, then the central area was fully taken up with Graves 1 to 3, with Bishops John, Walter and Gilbert in place. There was a 'gap site' to the north, where Grave 7 would ultimately go but its associated artefacts clearly indicate it must belong to the second half of the 14th century (Glenn & Franklin, Chapter 6.8); meanwhile, the body in Grave 4, the next best position to the south, had only predeceased Henry by a matter of a few years and would have hardly been ready for removal. Beyond this immediate ecclesiastical group, at the periphery to north and south, were the graves of some of the church's lay benefactors, hardly the most fitting position for one of Whithorn's most venerable bishops. In conclusion, therefore, our assessment suggests that the remains of Bishop John were translated from Grave 1 for entombment elsewhere, and that the founder's grave was reused by Henry. This interpretation accords (just) with the radiocarbon date from his bones (cal ad 1280–1400: SUERC-12498) but seems to be overwhelmingly endorsed by the associated artefacts from the grave. The silver chalice and paten appear to be appropriately 'old' whilst the ceremonial ring, dating to the mid-13th century, would almost certainly be the ring that he received from Archbishop Walter de Gray at his consecration in 1253. Meanwhile, in terms of the stratigraphic site sequence it is this reuse of the grave that is likely to lie behind Ritchie's observation about the mortar lining which was seen to lap over and thus post-date Grave 3, to the south. Presumably the cist was cleaned out and then relined with mortar prior to receiving the mortal remains of the cathedral priory's longest (ever) serving bishop. Interestingly, the results of the strontium and oxygen isotope analysis (Montgomery *et al*, Chapter 6.2), which imply that Skeleton 1 is not a local man, would concur with what we know of Henry's early career as abbot of Holyrood and perhaps the implication that his origins lie on the east side of the country.

If our model for the 13th century is anything like correct, then all four of its 13th-century bishops can be accommodated in Graves 1 to 3, with John and then Henry in Grave 1, Walter in Grave 3 and, from 1253 until some time in the 14th century, Gilbert in Grave 2. Also present was an 'early' priest (Grave 21) and a 'late' priest (Grave 4), as well as three lay benefactors (Graves 6, 12 and 14).

Our suggested sequence for the 13th century thus begins and ends with the original use and subsequent reuse of Grave 1. The full sequence is suggested to have been: 1, 21, 3, 2, 6, 12, 4, 14 and 1[reused].

9.2.6 The burial sequence for the 14th century: an archaeological model (Figure 9.2)

Only two of the 14th-century graves can be potentially identified as those of bishops; of these only one (Grave 7) retains positive evidence in the form of its associated grave-goods. On the basis of the sex or age of the skeletons, or in those cases where ecclesiastical plate was either recovered or its former presence can be inferred, most appear to have been set aside for ecclesiastics of other ranks or for lay benefactors.

The first of our 14th-century burials to be placed is Bishop Thomas de Dalton who died around 1325. In post for some 30 years, clearly he would have been an old man at the time of his death. It is difficult, however, to see where he was put. The stone cist, Grave 5, in the north 'gap site' might have been considered suitable and the coin, dated 1307x09, from the floor of the grave, would not be inconsistent with this. The absence of ecclesiastical plate could be explained by later grave-robbing (for which there is very clear evidence). The bones in Grave 5, however, are too young for any of Whithorn's 14th-century bishops; Thomas de Dalton, therefore, cannot be in Grave 5.

In terms simply of spatial distribution, the next best position available would have been to the north of Grave 2, the site of Grave 7. Indeed, the human remains from Grave 7 – essentially the finger bones which had been clutching the chalice – are not inappropriately dated (cal ad 1220–1390: SUERC-16061) and there is a 80% probability that the remains date to before 1320. Interestingly, the shroud cloth from the same burial has returned a date of cal ad 1215–1300: SUERC-16071). All of this might suggest that the burial dates to the early part of the 14th century and that it is conceivably, therefore, Bishop Thomas de Dalton. The dating of the associated ecclesiastical plate from Grave 7, however, indicates a *terminus post quem* of not earlier than 1350, and ideally (if the objects buried were then old), considerably later in the 14th century. Grave 7, therefore, cannot be Thomas de Dalton. This presents us with something of a dilemma. Our suggestion is that, like his predecessor, he possibly relocated Gilbert's remains from Grave 2 and took it for his own; however, if this is the case, then he too was subsequently removed and replaced by the remains of the young adult priest that Ritchie found in 1957.

The next bishop to be placed is Bishop Simon de Wedale. On the basis of the artefact dates from Grave 7, Simon would be the earliest possible contender for this grave although it would mean, as Glenn and Franklin (Chapter 6.8) point out, that he was being buried with some very contemporary pieces of ecclesiastical plate. With him in the grave, of course, was also the far from contemporary enamel crozier, dated by Virginia Glenn

Figure 9.2
Fourteenth-century burials. The focus of the bishops' burials moves slightly away from the central area

(Chapter 6.3.1) to *c* 1175. Possibly this was originally the pastoral staff of Bishop John, part of the suite of ritual objects with which he was vested at the time of his consecration at Pipewell in Northamptonshire in 1189 and which was then handed down to his successors.

Radiocarbon-dating of the remains of its wooden shaft, to cal AD 1185–1285 (SUERC-13243), indicates that the shaft was probably replaced some time in the 13th century. The crozier, however, was not the only old item in the grave; as we have seen, the shroud cloth was also several generations old. The cloth was radiocarbon dated to cal AD 1215–1300 (SUERC-16071).

Grave 7 could, of course, equally be assigned to any of Simon's later 14th-century successors with the possible exception of Thomas (d 1362) who may be 'disqualified' by virtue of his possible age. The bones from Grave 7 were clearly arthritic. The later the date in the 14th century, then the better the 'fit' with the finds' dating and the idea that only 'old' items would have been deposited in the grave. On the other hand, of course, the 'fit' with the radiocarbon dates, on the bones themselves and the associated shroud cloth, would point to a date earlier in the century. Bishop Simon, then, is very much a 'compromise' candidate. Given the political turmoil of the 1350s and his earlier support for Bruce, Oram (Chapter 8.1.2) has questioned whether he would have been able to function within his diocese at all, far less be buried within his church. Possibly this is what lies behind the 'oddness' of Grave 7; maybe it was a 'clandestine' burial by Simon's supporters.

To this latter group of bishops, if Greenhill's (1949, 238) chronology is correct, would also belong the Whithorn 1/2 indented slab (and possibly Whithorn 3/4 as well: Dingwall, Chapter 6.12). Neither, however, is easily assignable to a named individual.

Of the remaining Phase 3 graves, there are two peripheral graves (Graves 10 and 11), forming the south end of a row to the west of the primary line. Grave 10 has been identified as a possible priest or lay benefactor; Grave 11, adjacent, as possibly female. The two graves, together, might represent another husband and wife or similar family group. Their place in the 14th-century sequence is not clear but their radiocarbon dates (cal AD 1220–1390 [Grave 10] and cal AD 1250–1390 [Grave 11], SUERC-12510 & 12511) probably imply an earlier rather than a later date in the century, prior to Bishop Simon's burial in 1355.

With Grave 7 in place in the primary row and Graves 10 and 11 in place in the secondary row to the west, the final elements of the sequence are taken up with the priest burials in Graves 5 and 8 respectively. As previously noted, there is clear evidence that both these graves were robbed of their ecclesiastical plate. However, their surviving bones, like those in Grave 2, are too young to be any of our 14th-century bishops. Bishop Thomas de Dalton, who (we have suggested) removed Gilbert from Grave 2 around 1325 was finally removed, himself, some time in the late 14th century and his place taken by a young adult male, presumably one of the community's priests.

Our suggested sequence for the 14th century thus begins and ends with the reuse of Grave 2. The full sequence is suggested to have been: 2 [reused], 10, 11, 7, 5, 8 and 2 [reused again].

9.2.7 The late 14th century and later

The sequence model which attempts to identify the burial plots of Whithorn's 13th- and 14th-century bishops has taken us, with varying degrees of confidence, from Bishop John in 1209 down to, possibly, Bishop Simon in 1355 but where are the rest of the 14th-century bishops: Michael (d.1359), Thomas (d 1362), Adam (d 1378) and, if he was returned to Scotland after his death in France, Thomas Rossy (d 1397 x 1406)? Or those from the early 15th century, such as Eliseus (d 1412x1415) and Thomas (d 1420x1422)? It is just about possible that four of this group could have occupied the area between Graves 8 and 12 that was not fully excavated. Clearly, however, they would have been jostling for space.

Burial clearly shifted elsewhere after the 14th century. From the second quarter of the 15th century, it would seem that the Lady Chapel or St Mary's Chapel may have been fulfilling this role. It was constructed with a grant in 1424 from Margaret Stewart, a prominent benefactor of Whithorn in the 15th century, and is first referred to in 1431; as Oram suggests (Chapter 8.2.1, *Later medieval building work*) it possibly occupied the same site as the later South Chapel which was built *c* 1490–1500.

9.3 CONCLUSIONS

The intial focus of Ritchie's excavation – and indeed what first brought him to the site on that October day in 1957 – was with the so-called 'Bishops' Graves' and it seems only right that this is what his work there should mainly be remembered for, rather than on what we can see now to have been a suite of unsubstantiated claims relating to the origins of the site. Interesting as it might have been, we can say with some confidence that there was no late Roman cremation cemetery here. Nor was there an Early Christian cemetery in this particular part of the hillside. And this looks like an absence of evidence that could be significant, particularly given the proximity of the building that William Galloway found extending out beneath the end of the 13th century church, Radford and Cruden's *Candida Casa* or

Hill's Northumbrian chapel. Perhaps Galloway's building is even later than we could have imagined, possibly part of the 11th-century ecclesiastical layout? Indeed, the virtual absence of late first millennium material from Ritchie's excavation should lead us to reassess the nature and extent of the Northumbrian ecclesiastical settlement and its relationship with the medieval cathedral priory. That, however, would be another project.

Appendices

APPENDIX 1: COMPARABLE ITEMS FROM BISHOPS' BURIALS FOUND IN ENGLISH CATHEDRALS

VIRGINIA GLENN

(The dates of their episcopates are in brackets after the bishops' names.)

Durham
Two 12th-century gold rings set with sapphires found in the chapter house, which cannot be securely attributed (Fowler 1880, 390–2; Oman 1974, nos 13A&B; Stratford 1984, 290 nos 312, 313).

Chichester
12th-century gold ring set with intaglio, jet crozier and 13th-century silver chalice and paten, from an unidentified bishop's coffin in the cathedral, first drawn and fully described in 1829 (King 1829, 525; Waterton 1863, 234–5; Dalton, Mitchell & Couchman, 1926, 215; Henig 1978, 166, 285; Cherry 1981, no 116; Stratford, 1984, 290, no 314).

York
Gold ring set with a sapphire, silver-gilt chalice and paten and ivory crozier found, 1968, in the tomb of Archbishop Walter de Gray (1216–55). Gold ring set with a sapphire, silver-gilt chalice and paten and a wooden crozier found, 1969, in the tomb of Archbishop Godfrey de Ludham (1258–65), (Ramm 1971, 131–47; Cherry 1987, 482, no 636). Silver-gilt chalice and paten found, 1732, in the grave of Archbishop William de Melton (1317–40), (Gent 1733, 108–9; Poole & Hugall 1850, pl xxv; Hope & Fallow 1886, 208; Campbell 1987, 237, no 112).

Worcester
Silver paten found, mid-19th century(?), in the grave of Walter Cantelupe (1237–66) (Hope & Fallow 1886, 154, 375, no 4).

Lincoln
Silver chalice and paten found, 1783, in the grave of Robert Grosseteste (1235–1253). Silver-gilt chalice and paten found, 1791, in the grave of Richard de Gravesend (1258–79). Silver chalice and paten of Oliver Sutton (1280–99) (Hope & Fallow 1886, 142–3, 153–4, 364–5: Oman 1957, 300, nos 10, 11, 12; Campbell 1987, 237, no 111).

Salisbury
Silver-gilt chalice and paten found, mid-19th century, in the supposed grave of Nicholas de Longspée (1292–1297) (Nightingale 1891, 4; Hope & Fallow 1886, 143–4, 376).

Winchester
Gold ring set with a sapphire found in the 18th century in the grave of Henry Woodlock (1304–1316), (Oman 1974, 95; Keene 1985, 1051; Cherry 1987, 482, no 637).

Exeter
Small silver-gilt chalice and paten found, 1763, in the grave of Thomas de Bitton (1292–1307) (Hope & Fallow 1886, 143, 365, 377). Enamelled gold ring found, 1950s, in the grave of John de Grandisson (1327–69), (Cherry 1987, no 638, 482; Cherry 1991, 205–9).

APPENDIX 2: TEXTILE CATALOGUE

CAROL CHRISTIANSEN

Spin directions are recorded as standard S and Z; plied yarns are designated according to their singles direction, number of singles, and plied direction (S2Z = two S-twisted threads plied Z). Threading directions of tablet-woven warp threads are italicised *Z* or *S* to differentiate from spin direction (Emery 1995, 197). The term 'braid' refers to silver-gilt-wrapped threads applied as a decorative, supplemental weft. Locations relative to the body are noted, where known.

Grave 1 (Table A2.1)

No. 14/04 was unlabelled, but was from a box of bones and other finds from Grave 1 and almost certainly derives from there. There were four tablet-woven silk braids, one of which had a geometric, multiple diamond pattern

Table A2.1: Textiles from Grave 1

Lab no.	*Type*	*Description*	*Location*
01/09	Braid	6x15mm; tablet-woven braid, one selvedge; at least 16 tablets used warp: missing, except for selvedge selvedge: silk, Z/S; 2 cords, 4 threads each ground weft: silk, S, 2.5 picks/mm braid: S wrap, core missing; 20–24 threads/cm	Left shoulder
03/19	Braid	Gilt thread fragments in parallel, S wrap, core missing	Under pelvis
14/04a	Braid	Gilt thread fragments, S wrap, Ag gilt (Plate 6.13)	?
14/04b	Braid	9x12mm tablet-woven braid; geometric, multiple diamond pattern visible on surface (Plate 6.14); similar to 01/24b warp and ground weft missing braid weft: S wrap, no core	?
14/04c	Braid	7x10 tablet-woven braid; obscured by soil warp: ?silk, 2 warp cords, Z/S weft: missing braid weft: S wrap, no core	?
14/41	Braid	Two very small fragments of tablet-woven braid warp: missing ground weft: silk, S, 2.5 picks/mm braid: S wrap, core missing	On left?
01/22	Tabby	4x5mm tabby; lower remains of threads on corroded surface system 1: spin: ?; 4 threads/2mm system 2: spin: ?; 2.5 threads/2mm	?
09/03	Tabby	Small fragments of tabby adhering to ring and clasp of buckle; both systems Z on all fragments; too fragmentary to determine thread count; yarns on clasp thicker than those on ring	Right hip
09/04	Tabby	3x5mm tabby; attached to ring and clasp of buckle; layered on clasp system 1: low twist Z; 3 threads/2mm system 2: low twist Z; 3 threads/2mm	Crotch
13/40	Tabby	Small fragments of ?impressions of tabby fabrics; similar to 07/02	Finger

Table A2.2: Textiles from Grave 2

Lab no.	*Type*	*Description*	*Location*
01/12	Braid	8x12mm irregular, tablet-woven braid; at least 17 tablets used warp: silk, alternate Z/S, 2 stranded ground weft: missing braid weft: S-wrap, little Ag gilt remaining core: silk, S tie down threads: running diagonally, approx. 7-9 warp cords apart	?
01/20a	Braid	7x13mm tablet-woven braid, warp: silk, Z/S, fragmentary ground weft: missing braid weft: S wrap core: silk, S tie down threads visible, geometric pattern?	Neck
01/20b	Braid	Tablet-woven braid warp: silk, Z/S, very fragmentary ground weft: missing braid weft: S wrap core: silk, S tie down threads visible	Neck
01/24a	Braid	Irregular fragment, tablet-woven braid warp: 2-tablet ridge only, silk, Z/S ground weft: missing braid weft: S-wrap Ag gilt, core missing	Right upper arm
01/24b	Braid	Gilt threads attached to block of soil; similar to 14/04b warp and ground weft missing or obscured by soil braid weft: S-wrap, pattern?; core missing	Right upper arm
01/02	Tabby	Tabby on buckle ring; poorly preserved system 1: spin ?, 1–2 threads/mm system 2: similar to system 1 but extremely degraded	Chest
01/03	Tabby	Tabby on buckle ring; 4x10mm; poorly preserved both systems: Z, 1–2 threads/mm	Right hip

visible on the surface, and two samples of gilt thread fragments. Only two of these were located, on the left scapula and under the pelvis. There were three tabby fabrics, associated with and preserved by the copper buckles, with a further tabby textile impression associated with a finger bone. These are probably the remains of outer clothing. The fabrics are in a poor state of preservation. Some structural elements are missing or too degraded for thorough analysis.

Grave 2 (Table A2.2)

No 01/20, though not clearly labelled is probably from Grave 2. It was associated with mostly Grave 2 finds and a few from Grave 1, in a box marked 'Grave 2'. There were 16 samples in all. The majority of fragments are gilt thread wraps without cores, similar to those in Graves 1 and 7. Five pieces containing more structural elements have survived. Most were from the upper body area, head, neck, ribs, right arm and one from the pelvis. One, from the neck area, has traces of a possible geometric pattern, similar to that from Grave 1. There were two pieces of tabby, again preserved on the copper buckles and probably the remains of outer clothing.

Additional elements are recorded in fragments of gilt threads from nine samples: 01/05 (beside right upper arm), 01/06, 01/13 (behind jaw), 01/19, 01/21 (pelvis), 01/23, 01/26 (rib), 13/35 (palate), 13/37. All of the fragments were wrapped S around a core, although the cores are no longer present.

Grave 3 (Table A2.3)

Grave 3 contains a single textile: a small tabby fragment found on a buckle. It resembles similar fabrics found on buckles in Graves 1 and 2, and again probably represents outer clothing.

Grave 7 (Table A2.4)

The textiles from Grave 7 contain numerous fragments of silver-gilt threads associated with the silver-gilt spangles

Table A2.3: Textiles from Grave 3

Lab no.	*Type*	*Description*	*Location*
52/17	Tabby	Tabby, on buckle; open weave system 1: Z; too little to determine thread count system 2: Z; too little to determine thread count	Left hip

Table A2.4: Textiles from Grave 7

Lab no.	*Type*	*Description*	*Location*
03/36	Tabby	Tabby; very small fragment; threads very fine systems 1 & 2: Z2S	Chest

Table A2.5: Textiles from Grave 21

Lab no.	*Type*	*Description*	*Location*
60/34	Tabby	Tabby; balanced weave; several fragments, largest is 7x5mm; largest fragment is a stack of several layers of similar fabric; very brittle; yarns too degraded to determine fibre both systems: Z, low twist, 2 threads/mm	?Left hip

Table A2.6: Unstratified textiles

Lab no.	*Type*	*Description*	*Location*
07/02	Tabby?	Possible impression of tabby fabric on surface of white- and black-layered substance. Appears as balanced weave, 2 threads/mm in both systems. Similar to 13/40	?

and glass bead in the head and right shoulder area. A single fine tabby fragment was preserved on the chest under the silver chalice, where it is probably the remains of shroud cloth.

The surviving gilt threads from Grave 7, 03/09, 03/11 (over shoulder), 03/12 (under right shoulder), 03/20, 03/21, 03/30, 03/32, are only fragments of the outer metal wrapping, without cores. All of the threads were wrapped S. SEM examination showed the silver-gilt foil wrap measured between 225 and 325µm in width.

Grave 21 (Table A2.5)

Several fragments of tabby weave were found in the area of the pelvis, probably preserved by the antibiotic properties of the pewter plate in the area. The largest is a stack of several layers of similar fabric. The evidence suggests this is shroud cloth rather than clothing.

Unstratified (Table A2.6)

From a box of miscellaneous finds, marked as possibly recent.

APPENDIX 3: WHITHORN'S LAY PATRONS AND BENEFACTORS

RICHARD ORAM

With the exception of the family of the lords of Galloway, there is no indication of which regional noble families directed their patronage towards the priory in the late 12th century and for much of the 13th century. The first surviving indication of the identities of important donors is preserved in Robert I's confirmation of the properties of the priory, issued in May 1325 (*RRS*, v, no. 275). This lists a series of grants which appear largely to have been made in the period *c* 1300 to *c* 1320 (there is one grant by Duncan, earl of Carrick, which dates from the 1220–40 period and No. 1 below which may also be 13th-century), headed by a number of large gifts made by the king's younger brother, Edward Bruce, and by his nephew, Thomas Randolph, earl of Moray. It is possible that Edward Bruce, as lord of Galloway and earl of Carrick, may have intended to be buried at Whithorn, cementing a Bruce connection with the region, but his death in battle at Faughart in Ireland and the disposal of his body there removed that possibility. Thomas Randolph probably had no intention of securing burial at Whithorn, and was in any case buried in Dunfermline Abbey following his death in 1332. After these two major patrons comes a sequence of smaller donors.

1. Patrick Macscelling and Finlach his wife

The first benefactors of the priory were a prominent Kintyre-based couple, Patrick Macscelling and his wife, Finlach, who granted the canons the church of Kilcolmkill in the south of Kintyre. There is no firm date for their floruit – the family is otherwise invisible in the historical record after the mid-12th century – and it is possible that they are 13th-century rather than early 14th-century. Given that they are making the grant of the church of Kilcolmkill, it is perhaps likely that they intended to be buried there rather than at Whithorn, but the possible husband-and-wife interment at the priory may represent this couple.

2. Sir John Gelston

Head of an eastern Galloway family, Sir John granted the priory the patronage of the church of St Michael at Gelston. It is possible, like No. 1 above, that he was buried at his family's ancestral church of Gelston, but the scale of his grant may have been intended to secure burial rights in the cathedral-priory. John and his family were firm adherents of the Balliols and lost their lands in Galloway for their hostility to the Bruces (*Wigtownshire Charters*, xxvii). Sir John was still alive in 1296 but was dead before 1314, when his son, Dungal, was active in English service.

3. Patrick Maccuffock

The next is Patrick, son of Patrick Maccuffock, who granted three tofts in Kirkcudbright. There is little known about this family's origins, but Richard Maccuffock, a son or brother of Patrick, received a grant of the lands of Kilsture and Claunch north of Whithorn from Robert I during his last pilgrimage to the shrine on 1 April 1329 (*RRS*, v, 622). It is possible that Patrick jnr is represented in the burials in the choir at Whithorn, but there is no record of the date of his death or of his exact relationship with the Richard present at the priory in 1329.

4. Dervorguilla Marshall

The Marshall family held the lands of Toskerton in the Rhinns in the 13th and early 14th century, losing their heritage in the 1340s for their allegiance to Edward Balliol (*Wigtownshire Charters*, xxix–xxxi; Bain 1887, iii, no. 1529). The connection of Dervorguilla Marshall to that family is unclear, the property which she gave (Drumyork and Drumquhill) being in Carrick rather than in Wigtownshire. There is no evidence for her marriage or the existence of any children, nor indeed of the date at which her grant to Whithorn was made. She is, however, a strong contender for identification as one of the high-status female burials in the choir.

5. William de Soules
The de Soules lords of Liddesdale acquired an interest in Galloway following the marriage of Nicholas de Soules to a daughter of Alexander Comyn, earl of Buchan (Young 1997, 72). John de Soules, Nicholas's son, was an early supporter of the Bruces and an associate of Edward Bruce, with whom he died at Faughart in 1318. This connection with the Bruces probably ensured that the Soules family were confirmed in a portion of John Comyn, earl of Buchan's lands after 1314 (Comyn died in 1308 leaving only sisters and nieces as his heirs), John de Soules receiving the lands of Cruggleton on the coast to the east of Whithorn. John's lands passed to his younger brother, William, in October 1318 and were forfeited by him in August 1320 on account of his involvement in the conspiracy which bears his name, which planned to depose and kill Robert I and replace him with Edward Balliol (Oram 1992, 41; Penman 1999). The grant of his lands in Cruggleton – a very significant holding – to Whithorn can only have been made in that very narrow 1318–20 window and was probably made for the soul's ease of John de Soules by his younger brother. William possibly escaped Scotland in 1320 and may be identified with the Sir William Soules recorded as being killed in 1322 at the battle of Boroughbridge. The size of the gift made by William could indicate that he was looking to secure burial rights at Whithorn but he was definitely not buried there in the long run.

6. John Maclachlan
Beyond his grant of land in Sorbie to the canons there is little known of this man. There is no evidence for a family descended from him in the district.

There are two other significant candidates for burial at Whithorn whose remains may be amongst those identified in the Ritchie excavations. The first was the lord of Galloway from 1318 until his death at the battle of Halidon Hill in 1333 while the other has very strong documentary associations with repair work at Whithorn.

7. Alexander Bruce, earl of Carrick and lord of Galloway
The illegitimate son of Edward Bruce and Isabella of Atholl, Alexander Bruce is an individual who is consigned generally to the footnotes of history. Born probably around 1314/5, he was permitted to succeed to his father's lands and titles (but not to his place in the royal succession) and was confirmed in possession of a wide array of estates throughout Galloway in 1329. He was clearly intended to be the new Bruce strong man in the south-west but his career was cut short by his death in the carnage of the Scottish nobility at Halidon Hill in 1333, when he was probably no more than 19. His death ended that line of the Bruces. Unlike the slaughter at Faughart, where the bodies of the defeated were never recovered, after Halidon Hill it seems that the dead Scottish nobles were returned for burial. There is, therefore, a strong possibility that Alexander was amongst the young men whose remains have been identified at Whithorn.

8. Fergus MacDowell
This is possibly the strongest contender for interment in the choir at Whithorn in a position of honour close to the high altar. The MacDowell family appear to be a cadet of the ancient line of the lords of Galloway and emerged to prominence as the leaders of the pro-Balliol community in the lordship in the early 1300s. Recognising which way the tide was flowing, the MacDowells made their peace with David II's regime in the 1340s and quickly established a position as leaders of the Bruce interest in Galloway, for which they received due recognition (Oram 1992, 43–6: for some of their lands, see *RMS*, i, app. ii, nos 835, 1006, 1007, 1147, 1176.). A leading member of the family from the late 1340s through to at least the late 1360s was Sir Fergus MacDowell. He is explicitly stated in the late 14th-century Scots *Life of St Ninian* to have paid for the re-roofing of the choir of the priory church in thanksgiving for the saint's miraculous intervention which saved him from an English ambush (Metcalfe 1891, 330–1). His date of death is unknown but appears to have been before February 1371 on account of the confirmation of some of his lands to Dougal MacDowell, his half-brother, by David II.

Abbreviations

CDS	*Calendar of Documents relating to Scotland* (ed J Bain, 1881–7)
CLR	*Calendar of the Liberate Rolls Preserved in the Public Record Office.* [...] Henry III. Vol 1, AD 1226–40
CPL-Benedict XIII	*Calendar of Papal Letters to Scotland of Benedict XIII of Avignon, 1394–1419.* (ed F McGurk, Scottish History Society, vol 13, 1976)
CPL-Clement VII	*Calendar of Papal Letters to Scotland of Clement VII of Avignon, 1378–94* (ed C Burns, Scottish History Society, vol 12, 1976)
CPP	*Calendar of Entries in the Papal Registers relating to Great Britain and Ireland: Petitions to the Pope* (ed W H Bliss and others, London, 1896–)
CSSR 1423–28	*Calendar of Scottish Supplications to Rome 1423–28* (ed A I Dunlop, Scottish History Society, 1956)
CSSR 1428–32	*Calendar of Scottish Supplications to Rome 1428–32* (eds A I Dunlop & I B Cowan, Scottish History Society, 1970)
CSSR 1433–47	*Calendar of Scottish Supplications to Rome, iv, 1433–47* (eds A I Dunlop & D MacLauchlan, Glasgow, 1983)
HE	Bede's *Historia Ecclesiastica gentis Anglorum* (Colgrave & Mynors, 1969)
NAS	*National Archives of Scotland*
RMS	*Registrum Magni Sigilli Regum Scotorum* (Thomson *et al*, 1882–1914)
RCAHMS	Royal Commission on the Ancient and Historical Monuments of Scotland
RRS	*Regesta Regum Scotorum* (Duncan 1988: Webster 1982)
TDGNHAS	Transactions of the Dumfriesshire and Galloway Natural History and Antiquarian Society

Bibliography

PRIMARY DOCUMENTS (UNPUBLISHED)

Historic Scotland Archives	SDD27/1582: Whithorn Priory file
National Archives Scotland	GD10/348: Papers of the Murray family of Broughton, Wigtonshire, and Cally, Kircudbrightshire, 1410 –1978(GD10/348–442,documents relating to succession),
	GD138/1: Papers of the Stewart family, Earls of Galloway, 1330 –1820

OTHER SOURCES

Åberg, G 1995 *'The use of natural strontium isotopes as tracers in environmental studies', Water, Air and Soil Pollution, 79 (1–4): 309–22*

Adams, D G and McAneny, A 1984 *Celtic and Medieval Religious Houses in Angus: Abbeys, priories, hermitages, friaries, hospitals, colleges, cathedrals etc.* Brechin.

Alcock, L 1996 'The Early Historic Period', *John Smith of Dalry: Geologist, Antiquarian and Natural Historian Part 2 – Archaeology and Natural History, Ayr*, 48–56 [= Ayrshire Monograph 17].

Alcock, L and Alcock, E A 1987 'Reconnaissance excavations on Early Historic fortifications and other royal sites in Scotland, 1974–84: 2, Excavations at Dunollie Castle, Oban, Argyll, 1978', *Proc Soc Antiq Scot*, 117 (1987), 119–47.

Alcock, L and Alcock, E A 1990 'Reconnaissance excavations on Early Historic fortifications and other royal sites in Scotland, 1974–84: 4, Excavations at Alt Clut, Clyde Rock, Strathclyde, 1974–5', *Proc Soc Antiq Scot*, 120 (1990), 95–149.

Alexander, D 2004 'Early Historic and Medieval Activity at Chapelton, Haugh of Urr, Dumfries and Galloway', *TDGNHAS*, 3 ser 78 (2004), 61–77.

Alexander, J & Binski, P (eds) 1987 *Age of Chivalry: Art in Plantagenet England*. Royal Academy of Arts, London, 1987.

Ambrose, S H & Norr, L 1993 'Experimental Evidence for the Relationship of the Carbon Isotope Ratios of Whole Diet and Dietary Protein to Those of Bone Collagen and Carbonate', in Lambert, J B & Grupe, G (eds) *Prehistoric Human Bone: Archaeology at the Molecular Level. Berlin: Springer,* 1–37.

Anderson, M O & Anderson, A O (eds) 1938 *A Scottish Chronicle Known as the Chronicle of Holyrood*. Scottish History Society, 1938.

Arnold, T (ed) 1885 *Historia Regum, continuata per Joannem Hagulstadensem, in Symeonis Monachi Opera Omnia, ii*. London.

Ashley, A 1959 'Odo, Elect of Whithern, 1235', *TDGNHAS*, 3 ser 37, (1958–9), 62–9.

Aufderheide, A C and Rodriguez-Martin C, 1998 *The Cambridge Encyclopedia of Human Palaeopathology*. Cambridge University Press.

Backmund, N 1953 'The Premonstratensian Order in Scotland', *Innes Review, iv,* pt 1 (1952–3), 25–41.

Bain, J (ed) 1881–7 *Calendar of Documents Relating to Scotland*, vols i–iii Edinburgh, 1881–7.

Bannatyne Club 1831 *Vitae Dunkeldensis ecclesiae episcoporum (Alexander Myln).*

Bannatyne Club 1837a *Chronicon de Lanercost.*

Bannatyne Club 1837b *Liber S Marie de Melros (= Chron. Melrose).* 2 vols.

Bannatyne Club 1840 *Liber Cartarum Sancte Crucis (= Holyrood Liber).*

Bannatyne Club 1843 *Registrum Episcopatus Glasguensis (= Glasgow Registrum).* 2 vols.

Bannatyne Club 1847 *Liber S Marie de Dryburgh.*

Barral i Altet, X 2001 *The Romanesque. Towns, Cathedrals and Monasteries.* London.

Barrell, A D M 1995 'The background to *Cum universi*: Scoto -papal relations 1159–92', *Innes Review,* 46 (1995) 116–38.

Barrett, J H, Locker, A M & Roberts, C M 2004 'Dark Age Economics revisited: The English fish bone evidence AD 600–1600', *Antiquity* 78: 618–36.

Barrett, J H & Richards, M P 2005 'Identity, Gender, Religion and Economy: New Isotope and Radiocarbon Evidence for Marine Resource Intensification in Early Historic Orkney, Scotland, UK', *European Journal of Archaeology* 7: 249–71.

Bass, W M 1987 *Human Osteology: A Laboratory and Field Manual.* 3rd edn. Missouri Archaeological Society.

Bateson, J D 1973 'Roman material from Ireland: A reconsideration', *Proc Royal Irish Acad* 73C (1973), 29–97.

Bateson, J D 1976 'Further finds of Roman material from Ireland', *Proc Royal Irish Acad* 76C (1976), 171–80.

Battiscombe, C F 1956 'Introduction', *in* Battiscombe, C F (ed) *The Relics of Saint Cuthbert. Oxford,* 1–114.

Baxter, J H (ed) 1930 *Copiale Prioratus Sanctiandree: The Letter-book of James Haldenstone Prior of St Andrews 1418–43.* St Andrews, 1930.

Bélier, A-C 1982 'A sherd of Terra Sigillata from Wood Quay, Dublin', *Ulster J Archaeol* 44/45 (1981–2), 192–4.

Bennett, H 1987 'The Textiles', *in* Holdsworth, P (ed), *Excavations in the Medieval Burgh of Perth* 1979–81, Edinburgh, 159–74.

Bentley, R A 2006 'Strontium isotopes from the earth to the archaeological skeleton: A review', *Journal of Archaeological Method and Theory* 13(3): 135–87.

Binski, P 1996 *Medieval Death: Ritual and Representation.* London.

Binski, P 2004 *Becket's Crown. Art and the Imagination in Gothic England 1170–1300.* London.

Blair, F C H (ed) 1886 *Charters of the Abbey of Crosraguel.* Ayrshire and Galloway Archaeological Association, 1886. Edinburgh.

Blair, J & Ramsay, N (eds) 1991 *English Medieval Industries.* London.

Bocherens, H & Drucker, D 2003 'Trophic Level Isotopic Enrichment of Carbon and Nitrogen in Bone Collagen: Case Studies from Recent and Ancient Terrestrial Ecosystems', *International Journal of Osteoarchaeology* 13: 46–53.

Boyd, W E 1989 'Perth: The Wooden Coffins', *in* Stones, J A (ed), *Three Scottish Carmelite Friaries: Excavations at Aberdeen, Linlithgow & Perth* 1980–6, Soc Antiq Scot monograph 6, 117–8.

Bradley, J 1982 'Medieval' Samian ware – a medicinal suggestion', *Ulster J Archaeol* 44/45 (1981–2), 196–7.

Brannon, N P 1982 'A second sherd of Terra Sigillata from Carrickfergus', *Ulster J Archaeol* 44/45 (1981–2), 195.

Breakspear, H 1968 'Jervaulx Abbey: Architectural Description', *in* Page, W (ed), *The Victoria History of the Counties of England, A History of Yorkshire North Riding,* i (1968), London.

Brentano, R J 1952 'Re-dating a Whithorn document', *TDGNHAS,* 3 ser 30 (1951–2), 192–3.

Brentano, R J 1953a 'Whithorn and York', *Scottish Historical Review,* (1953), 144–6.

Brentano, R J 1953b 'The Whithorn vacancy', *Innes Review,* iv (1953), 71–83.

Bridgland, N 2005 'Dunfermline Abbey: Cloister and Precinct', *in* Fawcett, R (ed), *Royal Dunfermline* (2005), Edinburgh, 89–100.

British Geological Survey 1977 *Quaternary map of the United Kingdom North.* 1st edn. Southampton: Ordnance Survey/ NERC.

British Geological Survey 2001 *Geological map of the United Kingdom North Sheet.* 4th edn. Southampton: Ordnance Survey/NERC.

Brooke, D 1987 'The deanery of Desnes Cro and the church of Edingham', *TDGNHAS,* 3 ser 62 (1987), 48–65.

Brooks, S and Suchey, J M 1990 'Skeletal age determination based on the os pubis: a comparison of the Acsadi-Nemeskeri and Suchey-Brooks methods', *Human Evolution* Vol 5, No. 3: 227–38.

Brothwell, D R 1981 *Digging Up Bones.* British Museum (Natural History) and Oxford University Press.

Brown, D H 2002 *Pottery in Medieval Southampton c 1066–1510.* Southampton Archaeology Monographs 8, CBA Research Report 133.

Brown, M 1998 *The Black Douglases: War and Lordship in Late Medieval Scotland, 1300–1455.* East Linton.

Brown, T A, Nelson, D E, Vogel, J S & Southon J R 1988 'Improved Collagen Extraction by Modified Longin Method', *Radiocarbon* 30: 171–7.

Brown, W (ed) 1907 *Register of William Wichwane, Lord Archbishop of York, 1279–85.* Surtees Society (14), 1907.

Brown, W (ed) 1913 *Register of John le Romeyn, Lord Archbishop of York, 1286–96.* Vol 1. Surtees Society (123), 1913.

Brown, W (ed) 1916 *Register of John le Romeyn, Lord Archbishop of York, 1286–96.* Vol 2. Surtees Society (128), 1916.

Brown, W & Thompson, A H (eds) 1925–*8 Register of Thomas of Corbridge, Lord Archbishop of York, 1300–4.* 2 vols. Surtees Society (138 & 141), 1925–8.

Brown, W & Thompson, A H (eds) 1931–*40 Register of William Greenfield, Lord Archbishop of York, 1306–15.* 5 vols. Surtees Society (145, 149, 151–3), 1931–40.

Bryant, J D, Koch, P L, Froelich, P N, Showers, W J & Genna, B J 1996, 'Oxygen isotope partitioning between phosphate and carbonate in mammalian apatite', *Geochimica Et Cosmochimica Acta,* 60(24), 5145–8.

Buikstra, J E & Ubelaker, D H (eds)1994 *Standards for Data Collection from Human Skeletal Remains.* Vol 44. Fayetteville: Arkansas Archaeological Survey, Research Series; No 44.

Capo, R C, Stewart, B W & Chadwick, O A 1998 'Strontium isotopes as tracers of ecosystem processes: Theory and methods', *Geoderma* 82(1/3): 197–225.

Caldwell, D H & Dean, V E 1992 'The pottery industry at Throsk, Stirlingshire, in the 17th and early 18th century', *Post Med Archaeol* 26, 1–46.

Cameron, J 1998 *James V: The Personal Rule, 1528–42.* East Linton.

Campbell, M 1979 'Scribe faber lima: A crozier in Florence reconsidered', *The Burlington Magazine,* vol *CXXI,* 364–70.

Campbell, M 1987 'Metalwork in England, c 1200–1400' *in* Alexander & Binski 1987, 162–8.

Campbell, M 1991 'Gold, Silver and Precious Stones', *in* Blair & Ramsay 1991, 107–66.

Cant, R G 1986 'The Medieval Church in the North: Contrasting Influences in the Dioceses of Ross and Caithness', *in* Baldwin, J R (ed), *Firthlands of Ross and Sutherland.* (1986) Edinburgh, 47–58.

Cardy, A 1997 'The Human Bones' *in* Hill 1997, 519–62.

Cheetham, F H 1968 'The Cathedral: Monastic Buildings', *in* Page, W (ed), *The Victoria County History of the Counties of England, Durham,* iii. (1968), London, 123–36 at 126.

Cherry, J 1981 'Medieval Rings' *in* Ward, A, Cherry, J, Gere, C and Cartlidge, B, *The Ring from Antiquity to the Twentieth Century.* London, 53–86.

Cherry, J 1987 'Jewellery' *in* Alexander & Binski 1987, 176–8.

Cherry, J 1991 'The Ring of Bishop Grandison', *in Medieval Art and Architecture at Exeter, [Transactions of the British Archaeological Association,* vol XI, ed Kelly, Francis], Leeds, 205-9.

Chisholm, B S, Nelson, D E & Schwarcz, H P 1982 'Stable Carbon Isotope Ratios as a Measure of Marine Versus Terrestrial Protein in Ancient Diets', *Science* 216: 1131–2.

Christie, A G I 1938 *English Medieval Embroidery*. Oxford.

Chron. Howden, see William Stubbs 1871.

Chron. Lanercost, see Bannatyne Club 1837a.

Chron. Melrose, see Bannatyne Club 1837b.

Clarke, J 1997 'The Later Medieval Pottery', *in* Hill 1997, 510–18.

Clay, P 1981 'The small finds', *in* Mellor, J E & Pearce, T 'The Austin Friars, Leicester', (CBA Research Report 35), Leicestershire Archaeological Field Unit Report, CBA, London, 130–45.

Colgrave, B & Mynors, R A B (eds and transl) 1979 *Bede's Ecclesiastical History of the English People*. Oxford Medieval Texts.

Collingwood, P 2002 *The Techniques of Tablet Weaving*. McMinnville, Or.

Colvin, H M and Gilyard-Beer, R 1963 *Shap Abbey*. London.

Cormack, W F 1995 'Barhobble, Mochrum. Excavation of a Forgotten Church Site in Galloway', *TDGNHAS,* 3 ser 70 (1995), 5–106.

Cowan, I B & Easson, D E 1976 *Medieval Religious Houses: Scotland, 2nd edn, London, 1976.*

Cox, A 1998 'Grave consequences: A consideration of the artefact evidence from four post-medieval graveyard excavations', *Tayside & Fife Archaeol J 4*, 289–99.

Craig, D 1997 'The provenance of the Early Christian Inscriptions of Galloway' *in* Hill 1997, 614–19.

Crone, A 2000 *The History of a Scottish Lowland Crannog Excavations at Buiston, Ayrshire 1989–90.* Edinburgh [= STAR Monograph 4].

Crosraguel *Charters of the Abbey of Crosraguel* – see (ed) Blair, F C H 1886.

Cross, J F and Bruce, M F 1989 'The Skeletal Remains' *in* Stones, J A (ed) *Three Scottish Carmelite Friaries: Excavations at Aberdeen, Linlithgow and Perth* 1980–6 Soc Antiq Scot Monog 6.

Crowfoot, E and Hawkes, S C 1967. 'Early Ango-Saxon Gold Braids', *Medieval Archaeology* 11, 42–88.

Crowfoot, E et al 2001 *Textiles and Cloth c 1150–c 1450.* London. (Medieval Finds from Excavations in London, 4).

Crowfoot, G M 1956 'The Braids', *in* Battiscombe 1956, 433–63.

Cruden, S 1950 *St Andrews Cathedral.* HMSO.

Cruden, S 1951 'Glenluce Abbey: Finds Recovered During Excavations: Part I', *TDGNHAS*, 3 ser 29, 177–94.

Cruden, S 1952 'Glenluce Abbey: Finds Recovered During Excavations: Part II', *TDGNHAS*, 3 ser 30, 179–90.

Cruden, S 1963 'Excavations at Whithorn and Iona' *The Scotsman Weekend Magazine.* 4 May 1963.

Cruden, S 1986 *Scottish Medieval Churches*. Edinburgh.

Dalton, O M, Mitchell, H P & Couchman, J E 1926 'The Warden Abbey and Chichester Croziers', *Archaeologia,* LXXV, 1926, 211–5.

Dansgaard, W 1964 'Stable isotopes in precipitation', *Tellus* 16: 436–68.

Darling, W G 2004 'Hydrological factors in the interpretation of stable isotopic proxy data present and past: A European perspective', *Quaternary Science Reviews* 23(7–8): 743–70.

Darling, W G & Talbot, J C 2003 'The O and H stable isotopic composition of fresh waters in the British Isles. 1. Rainfall', *Hydrology and Earth System Sciences* 7(2): 163–81.

Darling, W. G, Bath, A H & Talbot, J C 2003 'The O & H stable isotopic composition of fresh waters in the British Isles: 2, Surface waters and groundwater', *Hydrology and Earth System Sciences* 7: 183–95.

DeNiro, M J 1985 'Postmortem preservation and alteration of in vivo bone collagen isotope ratios in relation to palaeodietary reconstruction', *Nature* 317: 806–9.

Devon, F (ed) 1836–7 *Issues of the exchequer; being payments made out of His Majesty's revenue during the reign of King James I. Extracted from the original records belonging to the ancient Pell Office.* London.

Dickinson, W C (ed) 1949 *John Knox's History of the Reformation in Scotland.* Edinburgh, 1949.

Dickson, T (ed) 1877 *Accounts of the Lord High Treasurer of Scotland.*

Dingwall, K 2008 *Proposed Cemetery Extension, Whithorn, Dumfries and Galloway.* Results of an archaeological evaluation. Unpublished client report, prepared by Headland Archaeology (UK) Ltd. October 2008.

Donaldson, G 1949 'The Bishops and Priors of Whithorn', *TDGNHAS,* 3 ser 27 (1948–9), 127–54.

Dowden, J 1899 'The inventory of Ornaments, Jewels, relicks, Vestments, Service-Books, etc belonging to the cathedral church of Glasgow in 1432, illustrated from various sources and more particularly from the inventories of the Cathedral of Aberdeen', *Proc Soc Antiq Scot,* 33 (1899), 280–329.

Dowden, J 1912 *The Bishops of Scotland.* Glasgow, 1912.

Driscoll, S T 1998 'Highlights of the Excavations at Glasgow Cathedral 1992–3' *in* Fawcett, R (ed), *Medieval Art and Architecture in the Diocese of Glasgow.* (1998), British Archaeological Association Conference Transactions, 25–34.

Dryburgh Liber – see Bannatyne Club 1847.

Dunbar, J 1999 *Scottish Royal Palaces: The Architecture of the Royal Residences During the Late Medieval and Early Renaissance Periods.* Edinburgh.

Duncan, A A M (ed) 1988 *Regesta Regum Scotorum, v, The Acts of Robert I.* Edinburgh, 1988.

Dunlop, A I and Cowan, I B (eds) 1970 *Calendar of Scottish Supplications to Rome 1428–32.* (Scottish History Society).

Dunn, A 2001 'Window glass', *in* Ewart, G 'Dundrennan Abbey: Archaeological investigation within the south range of a Cistercian house in Kirkcudbrightshire (Dumfries & Galloway), Scotland', *Scottish Archaeological Internet Report 1*, 48–9.

Durkan, J 1972 'Archbishop Robert Blackadder's will', *Innes Review*, 23 (1972), 138–48.

Dyer, C 1998a 'Did the Peasants Really Starve in Medieval England?' *in* Carlin, M & Rosenthal, J T (eds), *Food and Eating in Medieval Europe*. London & Rio Grande: The Hambledon Press, 53–71.

Dyer, C 1998b *Standards of Living in the later Middle Ages. Social change in England c 1200–1520* (revised edn). Cambridge: Cambridge University Press.

Easson, D E 1957 *Medieval Religious Houses: Scotland*. London, 1957.

Easson, D E and MacDonald, A 1938 *Charters of the Abbey of Inchcolm* (Scottish History Society). Edinburgh.

Egan, G 2005 *Material culture in London in an age of transition: Tudor and Stuart period finds c 1450–c 1700 from excavations at riverside sites in Southwark*. MoLAS Monogr.19, London.

Egan, G & Pritchard, F 1991 *Medieval Finds from Excavations in London 3: Dress Accessories c 1150–c 1450*. London.

Emery, I 1995 *The Primary Structures of Fabrics*. New York.

Ericson, J E 1993 'Ba/Ca as a diagenetic indicator for evaluating buried bone tissues: Advances in tissue selection, reducing contamination and data evaluation', *in* Lambert, J B and G Grupe (eds) *Prehistoric Human Bone: Archaeology at the Molecular Level (*1st edn): 157–71. Berlin: Springer-Verlag.

Evans, J A & Tatham, S 2004 'Defining "local signature" in terms of Sr isotope composition using a tenth–twelfth century Anglo-Saxon population living on a Jurassic clay-carbonate terrain, Rutland, UK', *in* Pye, K and Croft, D J (eds) *Forensic Geoscience: Principles, Techniques and Applications:* 237–248232. London: Geological Society of London Special Publication.

Evans, J, Stoodley, N & Chenery, C 2006 'A strontium and oxygen isotope assessment of a possible fourth century immigrant population in a Hampshire cemetery, southern England', *Journal of Archaeological Science* 33(2): 265–72.

Fawcett, R 1987 *Beauly Priory and Fortrose Cathedral*. Edinburgh.

Fawcett, R 1994 *Scottish Abbeys and Priories*. Edinburgh.

Fawcett, R 1997 *Scottish Cathedrals*. London, 1997.

Fawcett, R 1998 'Introduction', *in* Fawcett, R (ed), *Medieval Art and Architecture in the Diocese of Glasgow*. British Archaeological Association Conference Transactions, 1–8.

Fawcett, R 1999a *Elgin Cathedral*. Edinburgh.

Fawcett, R 1999b 'Inchcolm Abbey' *in* Crawford, B E (ed), *Church, Chronicle and Learning in Medieval and Early Renaissance Scotland (*1999), Edinburgh.

Fawcett, R 2002 *Scottish Medieval Churches. Architecture and Furnishings*. Stroud.

Fawcett, R 2005 'Dunfermline Abbey Church', *in* Fawcett, R (ed), *Royal Dunfermline. (*2005), Edinburgh, 27–63.

Fawcett, R and Oram, R D 2004 *Melrose Abbey*. Stroud.

Fawcett, R and Oram, R D 2005 *Dryburgh Abbey*. Stroud.

Ferguson, P C 1997 *Medieval Papal Representatives in Scotland: Legates, Nuncios and Judges-Delegate, 1125–1286*. (Stair Society, 1997).

Finlay, I 1991 *Scottish Gold and Silverwork*, revised and edited by Henry Fothringham, Stevenage.

Foedera, see Thomas Rymer

Fowler, J T 1880 'An account of excavations made on the site of the Chapter-house of Durham Cathedral in 1874', *Archaeologia,* XLV.

Franklin, J 2001 'The Finds', *in* Moloney, C 'New evidence for the origins and evolution at the Captain's Cabin, Castle Park, Dunbar, East Lothian', *Proc Soc Antiq Scot,* 131, 303–6.

Franklin & Collard 2006 'Other Finds', *in* Collard et al 'Archaeological excavations in St Giles' Cathedral, Edinburgh, 1981–93', *Scottish Archaeological Internet Report 22*, 52–62.

Franklin, J forthcoming A 'Finds Report for Excavations at Cadzow Castle, 2001–3', Kirkdale Archaeology.

Franklin, J forthcoming B 'Finds Report for Excavations at Stirling Castle, 1992–7', Kirkdale Archaeology.

Franklin, J forthcoming C 'Pottery Report for MSC Excavations in Ayr', SUAT.

Franklin, J & Hall, D forthcoming 'Pottery, from a possible kiln site in Hamilton', SUAT.

Fraser, W 1892 *The Sutherland Book*. Edinburgh.

Fricke, H C, O'Neil, J R & Lynnerup, N 1995 'Oxygen isotope composition of human tooth enamel from Medieval Greenland: Linking climate and society', *Geology* 23(10): 869–72.

Gammack, J 1883 'Notice of a sepulchral chalice and paten of pewter found in Bervie churchyard', *Proc Soc Antiq Scot* 17 (1882–3), 371–5.

Garmonsway, G N (trans) 1972 *The Anglo-Saxon Chronicle*. London, 1972.

Gauthier, M 1972 *Émaux du moyen âge*. Fribourg.

Gent, T 1733 *Antient and Modern History of Rippon, with Particular Accounts of several Archbishops*.

Gifford, J 1992 *Highland and Islands*. London.

Gilyard-Beer, R 1970 *Fountains Abbey*. London.

Glasgow Registrum (Registrum Episcopatus Glasguensis) – see Bannatyne Club 1843.

Glenn, V 2003 *Romanesque and Gothic – Decorative Metalwork and Ivory Carvings in the Museum of Scotland*. Edinburgh.

Grainger, F & Collingwood, W G (eds) 1929 *Register and Records of Holm Cultram*. (Cumberland and Westmorland Archaeological and Antiquarian Society, 1929).

Grant, A 1983 *North Devon Pottery: The Seventeenth Century*. University of Exeter, Exeter.

Graves, C P 1995 'Window Glass' *in* Lewis, J H & Ewart, G J *Jedburgh Abbey: The Archaeology and Architecture of a Border Abbey*. (Soc Antiq Scot Monog 10), Edinburgh, 110–3.

Graves, C P 2002 'Window Glass', *in* Lewis, J & Pringle, D *Spynie Palace and the Bishops of Moray: History, Architecture and Archaeology,* 132–7.

Graves, P 2006 'Window glass and lead', *in* Collard et al 'Archaeological excavations in St Giles' Cathedral, Edinburgh, 1981–93', *Scottish Archaeological Internet Report 22*, 57–61.

Greenhill, F A 1949 'Scottish Notes II', *Transactions of the Monumental Brass Society VIII*, 234–8.

Haggarty, G 1985 'The Pottery' *in* Ewart, G *'Cruggleton Castle Report of Excavations 1978–81', TDGNHAS,* Occasional Paper (1985) Dumfries.

Haggarty, G 2006 *A gazetteer and summary of French Pottery in Scotland c 1150–c 1650.* Resource Disc.

Hald, M 1980 *Ancient Danish Textiles from Bogs and Burials.* Copenhagen.

Hall, D W 2004 'Pottery from 94–102 High Street', *in* Coleman, R 'Three excavations in medieval Dumbarton: 94–102 and 101–3 High Street and 75 College Street', *Proc Soc Antiq Scot*, 134, 337–43.

Hannay, R K and Hay, D (eds) 1954 *Letters of James V.* Edinburgh, 1954.

Harvey, B 1993 *Living and Dying in England 1100–1540. The Monastic Experience.* Oxford & New York: Oxford University Press.

Hawkes, S C & Grainger G 2006 *The Anglo-Saxon Cemetery at Finglesham, Kent.* Oxford Univ School of Archaeology, monograph no.64, Oxford.

Hector Boece – see Moir, J (ed) 1894.

Henig, M 1978 *A Corpus of Roman Engraved Gemstones from British Sites.* British Archaeological Reports (British Series) 8, 2nd edn.

Hedges, R E M & Reynard, L M 2006 'Nitrogen isotopes and the trophic level of humans in archaeology', *Journal of Archaeological Science* doi 10.1016/j.jas.2006.10.015.

Hedges, R E M, Clement, J G, Thomas, C D L & O'Connell, T C 2007 'Collagen turnover in the adult femoral mid-shaft: Modeled from anthropogenic radiocarbon tracer measurements' *American Journal of Physical Anthropology* 133(2): 808–16.

Henshall, A S 1950 'Textiles and Weaving Appliances in Prehistoric Britain', *Proceedings of the Prehistoric Society* (16), 130–62.

Henshall, A S 1952 'Early Textiles Found in Scotland, Part I: Locally Made', *Proc Soc Antiq Scot*, 86, 1–29.

Henshall, A S 1965 'Five tablet-woven seal-tags', *Archaeological Journal*, 121, 154–62.

Henshall, A S et al 1956 'Early Textiles Found in Scotland, Part II: Medieval Imports', *Proc Soc Antiq Scot*, 88, 22–39.

Hill, P 1997 *Whithorn and St Ninian: The Excavation of a Monastic Town, 1984–91.* Stroud.

Hillson, S 1986 *Teeth.* (Cambridge Manuals in Archaeology) CUP.

Hillson, S 1996 *Dental Anthropology.* 1st edn. Cambridge: Cambridge University Press.

Historia Regum, continuata per Joannem Hagulstadensem, in Symeonis Monachi Opera Omnia: see Arnold 1885.

Hoke, E & Petrascheck-Heim, I 1977 'Microprobe analysis of gilded silver threads from mediaeval textiles', *Studies in Conservation*, 22, 49–62.

Holyrood Liber = Liber Cartarum Sancte Crucis, see Bannatyne Club 1840.

Homer, R F 1991 'Tin, Lead and Pewter', *in* Blair & Ramsay 1991, 57–80.

Hope, W H St J 1887 'On the Premonstratensian Abbey of St Mary, Alnwick, Northumberland', *Archaeological Journal,* 44 (1887), 337–46.

Hope, W H St J 1893 'Some remains of early vestments found in a Bishop's coffin at Worchester', *Proceedings of the Society of Antiquaries, London,* 14, 196–200.

Hope, W H St J 1907 'The Episcopal Ornaments of William of Wykeham and William of Waynfleet, sometime Bishops of Winchester, and of certain Bishops of St. Davids', *Archaeologia, LX*, 465–92.

Hope, W H St J and Fallow, M 1886 'English Medieval Chalices and Patens', *Archaeological Journal, XLIII* (1886), 137– 61, 364–402.

Hunter, F 2001 'Roman and native in Scotland: New approaches', *J Roman Archaeol* 14 (2001), 289–309.

Hurst, J G, Neal, D S, & van Beuningen, H J E 1986 *Pottery produced and traded in north-west Europe 1350–1650.* (Rotterdam Papers VI). Rotterdam.

Iacumin, P, Bocherens, H, Mariotti, A and Longinelli, A 1996 'An isotopic palaeoenvironmental study of human skeletal remains from the Nile Valley', *Palaeogeography, Palaeoclimatology, Palaeoecology,* 126(1/2), 15–30.

Iscan, M Y, Loth, S R and Wright, R K 1984 'Age estimation from the ribs by phase analysis: White males', *Journal of Forensic Sciences* 29: 1094 – 1104.

Iscan, M Y, Loth, S R and Wright, R K 1985 'Age estimation from the ribs by phase analysis: White females', *Journal of Forensic Sciences* 30: 853–63.

Issues of the Exchequer: see Devon 1837.

Jay, M & Richards, M P 2006 'Diet in the Iron Age cemetery population at Wetwang Slack, East Yorkshire, UK: Stable carbon and nitrogen isotope evidence', *Journal of Archaeological Science* 33: 653–62.

Katzenberg, M A 2000 'Stable Isotope Analysis: A tool for studying past diet, demography and life history', *in* Katzenberg, M A & Saunders, S R (eds) *Biological Anthropology of the Human Skeleton.* New York: Wiley-Liss, 305–27.

Keene, D 1985 *Survey of Medieval Winchester.* (Winchester Studies), Oxford.

Kelly, J F 2000 'Stable isotopes of carbon and nitrogen in the study of avian and mammalian trophic ecology', *Canadian Journal of Zoology* 78: 1–27.

Kemp, R L & Graves, C P 1996 *The Church and Gilbertine Priory of St Andrew, Fishergate.* The Archaeology of York. 11/2. York: Council for British Archaeology.

Kerr, H F 1934 'The priory church at Whithorn', *Transactions of the Scottish Ecclesiological Society, xi, pt* 1 (1933–4), 31–8.

Kidd, K 1979 *Glass Bead-Making from the Middle Ages to the early 19th century, (National Historic Parks and Sites Branch, Parks Canada, History & Archaeology 30).*

King, A 1985 'Medieval terra sigillata – A source of confusion?', *Ulster J Archaeol* 47 (1984), 182–3.

King, D 1963 *Opus Anglicanum – English Medieval Embroidery.* (The Arts Council exhibition, Victoria & Albert Museum).

King, D 1987 'Embroidery and textiles', *in* Alexander & Binski 1987, 157–61.

King, T 1829 *Gentleman's Magazine, part I, 545.*

Klinken, G J van 1999 'Bone Collagen Quality Indicators for Palaeodietary and Radiocarbon Measurements', *Journal of Archaeological Science* 26: 687–95.

Klinken, G J van, Richards, M P & Hedges, R E M 2000 'An Overview of Causes for Stable Isotopic Variations in Past European Human Populations: Environmental, Ecophysiological, and Cultural Effects', *in* Ambrose, S H & Katzenberg, M A (eds), *Biogeochemical Approaches to Palaeodietary Analysis.* New York: Kluwer Academic/Plenum 39–63.

Lacaille, A D 1934 'Loch Lomondside Fonts and Effigy', *Proc Soc Antiq Scot,* 68 (1933–4), 100–16.

Laing, D (ed) 1846–*64 The Works of John Knox.* Edinburgh, 1846–64.

Laule, B and Laule, U 1997 'Romanesque Architecture in France', *in* Toman, R (ed), *Romanesque: Architecture, Sculpture, Paintings. Cologne* 1997, 120–78.

Lee-Thorp, J, Sealy, J C and Van der Merwe, N J 1989 'Stable carbon isotope ratio differences between bone collagen and bone apatite, and their relationship to diet', *Journal of Archaeological Science,* 16, 585–99.

Levinson, A A, Luz, B & Kolodny, Y 1987 'Variations in Oxygen Isotope Compositions of Human Teeth and Urinary Stones', *Applied Geochemistry* 2: 367–71.

Lewis, J, Ewart, G et al 1995 *Jedburgh Abbey, the Archaeology and Architecture of a Border Abbey.* Soc Antiq Scot Monog 10. Edinburgh.

Liber S Marie de Dryburgh – see Bannatyne Club 1847.

Lightbown, R W 1992 *Mediaeval European Jewellery with a catalogue of the collection in the Victoria and Albert Museum.* London.

Longinelli, A 1984 'Oxygen isotopes in mammal bone phosphate: A new tool for paleohydrological and paleoclimatological research?', *Geochimica et Cosmochimica Acta* 48: 385–90.

Lord, P 2003 *The Visual Culture of Wales - medieval Vision.* Cardiff 2003.

Lovejoy, C O, Meindl, R S, Pryzbeck, T R and Mensforth, R P 1985 'Chronological metamorphosis of the auricular surface of the ilium: A new method for determination of adult skeletal age at death', *American. J. Phys. Anthrop.* 68: 15–28.

Lowe, C E 2006 *Excavations at Hoddom, Dumfriesshire: An Early Ecclesiastical Site in South-west Scotland.* Soc Antiq Scot Monog. Edinburgh 2006.

Luz, B, Kolodny, Y & Horowitz, M 1984 'Fractionation of Oxygen Isotopes between Mammalian Bone-phosphate and Environmental Drinking Water', *Geochimica et Cosmochimica Acta* 48: 1689–93.

McCutcheon, C 1997 'Pottery and Roof Tiles', *Excavations at the North Gate, Cork, 1994.*Cork, 75–101.

Macdougall, N A T 1982 *James III: A Political Study.* Edinburgh.

Macdougall, N A T 1997 *James IV.* East Linton.

McEwan, H 1957 '"A Theolog Solempne", Thomas de Rossy, Bishop of Galloway', *Innes Review,* viii (1957), 21–9.

MacGibbon, D & Ross, T 1896 *The Ecclesiastical Architecture of Scotland,* ii. Edinburgh, 1896.

Mackie, R L & Cruden S 1954 *Arbroath Abbey.* Edinburgh.

Macpherson, D et al (eds) 1814 *Rotuli Scotiae in Turri Londiniensi et in Domo Capitulari Westmonasteriensi Asservati.* 2 vols. London, 1814.

McRoberts, D 1959 'Material destruction caused by the Scottish Reformation', *Innes Review, X,* 126–72.

Marshall, D N 1985 'A report on early artefacts found at St Ninian's Chapel', *Trans Buteshire Nat Hist Soc* 22 (1985), 27.

Mays, S A 1997 'Carbon Stable Isotope Ratios in Mediaeval and Later Human Skeletons from Northern England', *Journal of Archaeological Science* 24: 561–7.

Mentel, R 1998 'The Twelfth-Century Predecessors of Glasgow Cathedral and their Relationship with Jedburgh Abbey', *in* Fawcett, R (ed), *Medieval Art and Architecture in the Diocese of Glasgow, British Archaeological Association Conference Transactions,* xxii (1998), 42–9.

Metcalfe, W M (ed) 1891 *Legends of the Saints,* iii. Edinburgh, 1891.

Metcalfe, W M (ed) 1904 *The Legends of SS Ninian and Machor.* Edinburgh, 1904.

Midmer, R 1979 *English Medieval Monasteries.* London.

Moir, J (ed) 1894 *Hector Boece's Murthlacensium et Aberdonensium Episcoporum Vitae.* (New Spalding Club, 1894).

Montgomery, J 2002 *Lead and Strontium Isotope Compositions of Human Dental Tissues as an Indicator of Ancient Exposure and Population Dynamics.* Ph.D. Thesis, University of Bradford, UK.

Montgomery, J, Evans, J A & Neighbour, T 2003 'Sr isotope evidence for population movement within the Hebridean Norse community of NW Scotland', *Journal of the Geological Society* 160: 649–53.

Montgomery, J & Evans, J A 2006 'Immigrants on the Isle of Lewis – combining traditional funerary and modern isotope evidence to investigate social differentiation, migration and dietary change in the Outer Hebrides of Scotland', *in* Gowland, R and Knusel, C (eds) *The Social Archaeology of Funerary Remains:* 122–42. Oxford: Oxbow Books.

Montgomery, J, Evans, J A & Cooper, R E 2007 'Resolving archaeological populations with Sr-isotope mixing models', *Applied Geochemistry* 22: 1502–14.

Montgomery, J, Evans, J A & Wildman, G 2006 '87Sr/86Sr isotope composition of bottled British mineral waters for environmental and forensic purposes', *Applied Geochemistry* 21: 1626–34.

Mooney, J 1925 'Notes on Discoveries in St Magnus Cathedral, Kirkwall', *Proc Soc Antiq Scot,* 59.

Morris, C A 1972 'A critique of popular religion: Guibert of Nogent on the relics of the saints', *in* Cumming, G J and Baker, D (eds), *Popular Belief and Practice: Studies in Church History,* 8 (1972), Guildford, 55–60.

Morrison, J 2001 *An Archaeological Evaluation at Whithorn, Dumfries and Galloway*. Unpublished client report for The Whithorn Trust, prepared by Headland Archaeology.

Morrison, J 2003 *Research and Training Excavation in the Manse Field, Whithorn, Dumfries & Galloway: Data Structure Report.* Unpublished client report for The Whithorn Trust, prepared by Headland Archaeology.

Muir Watt, J 2001 'William Galloway's excavations at Whithorn, 1886–97: Selections from unpublished correspondence in the Bute Muniments' *TDGNHAS,* 3 ser 75 (2001), 133–49.

Müldner, G & Richards, M P 2005 'Fast or Feast: Reconstructing Diet in Later Medieval England by Stable Isotope Analysis', *Journal of Archaeological Science* 32: 39–48.

Müldner, G & Richards, M P 2006 'Diet in medieval England: The evidence from stable isotopes', *in* Woolgar, C, Serjeantson, D & Waldron, T (eds), *Food in Medieval England: History and Archaeology.* Oxford: Oxford University Press, 228–38.

Müldner, G & Richards, M P 2007a 'Stable Isotope Evidence for 1500 Years of Human Diet at the City of York, U.K', *American Journal of Physical Anthropology* 133: 682–97.

Müldner, G & Richards, M P 2007b 'Diet and Diversity at Later Medieval Fishergate: The Isotopic Evidence', *American Journal of Physical Anthropology* 134: 162–74.

Myln – see *Vitae Dunkeldensis ecclesiae episcoporum* (Bannatyne Club 1831).

Nicholson, A 1997 'The Copper Alloy' & 'The Iron' *in* Hill, P, *Whithorn and St Ninian: The Excavation of a Monastic Town,* 1984–91, 360–89 & 404–33.

Nicholson, R 1974 *Scotland: The Later Middle Ages*. Edinburgh.

Nightingale, J E 1891 *Church Plate of the County of Wiltshire.* Salisbury.

Norton, C 1994 'Medieval Floor Tiles in Scotland', *in* Higgit, J (ed) *Medieval Art and Architecture in the Diocese of St Andrews.* British Archaeol Assoc Conference Trans 1986, 137–73.

O'Connell, T C, Hedges, R E M, Healey, M A, & Simpson, A H R 2001 'Isotopic comparison of hair, nail and bone: Modern analyses', *Journal of Archaeological Science* 28: 1247–55.

Oman, C C, 1957 *English Church Plate, London.*

Oman, C C, 1962 'English Medieval Base Metal Church Plate', *Archaeological Journal,* Vol CXIX, 196–207.

Oman, C C, 1971 'The ring, chalice and paten' *in* Ramm 1971, 126–7.

Oman, C C, 1974 *British Rings 800–1914.* London.

Oram, R D 1991 'In Obedience and Reverence: Whithorn and York c 1128–c 1250', *Innes Review,* 42 (1991), 83–100.

Oram, R D 1992 'Bruce, Balliol and the Lordship of Galloway', *TDGNHAS,* 3 ser 67 (1992), 29–47.

Oram, R D 1997 'Heirs to Ninian: The medieval bishops of Whithorn (c 1100–1560), *in* McCluskey, R (ed), *The See of Ninian: A History of the Medieval Diocese of Whithorn and the Diocese of Galloway in Modern Times.* Ayr, 49–80.

Oram, R D 1998 'Prayer, Property and Profit: Scottish monastic power centres in the twelfth and thirteenth centuries', *in* Foster, S, Macinnes, A I and MacInnes, R *Scottish Power Centres,* 79–99. Glasgow.

Oram, R D 1999 'Alexander Bur, Bishop of Moray (1362–97)', *in* Crawford, B E (ed), *Church, Chronicle and Learning in Medieval and Early Renaissance Scotland.* (1999), Edinburgh, 195–213.

Oram, R D 2000 *The Lordship of Galloway*. Edinburgh.

Ortner, D and Putschar, W J 1981 *Identification of Pathological Conditions in Human Skeletal Remains Smithsonian Institution Press.*

Page, R I 2004 'Runic inscription', *in* Dalwood, H and Edwards, R *Excavations at Deansway Worcester 1988–9 Romano-British small town to Late Medieval city.* York, 461–62 [= Council for British Archaeology Res Rep 139].

Panofsky, E 1979 *Abbot Suger, on the Abbey Church of St-Denis, and its Art Treasures,* revised edn. Princeton.

Paterson, J W and D McRoberts 1978 *Inchcolm Abbey,* 3rd edn. Edinburgh.

Patterson, R 1987, 'Tablet-woven braids', *in* Ingram, E (ed) *Thread of Gold: The Embroideries and Textiles in York Minster.* Andover, 20–1.

Payne, B 1965 *History of Costume: From the Ancient Egyptians to the Twentieth Century*. New York.

Peers, C 1952 *Byland Abbey,* 2nd edn. London.

Peers, C 1967 *Rievaulx Abbey*. London.

Penman, M 1999 'A fell coniuracioun again Robert ye douchty king: The Soules conspiracy of 1318–20', *Innes Review,* 50 (1999), 25–57.

Penman, M 2004 *David II 1329–71*. East Linton.

Piggott, C M 1948 'The Excavations at Hownam Rings, Roxburghshire, 1948', *Proc Soc Antiq Scot,* 82 (1947–8), 193–225.

Poole, G A & Hugall, J W 1850 *An Historical and Descriptive Guide to York Cathedral and its Antiquities.*

Pritchard, F 1988 'Silk Braids and Textiles of the Viking Age from Dublin', *in* Bender Jørgensen, L et al (eds), *Archaeological Textiles.* Copenhagen, 149–61.

Privat, K L, O'Connell, T & Richards, M P 2002 'Stable Isotope Analysis of Human and Faunal Remains from the Anglo-Saxon Cemetery at Berinsfield, Oxfordshire: Dietary and Social Implications', *Journal of Archaeological Science* 29: 779–90.

Proudfoot, E 1996 'Excavations at the long cist cemetery on the Hallow Hill, St Andrews, Fife, 1975–7', *Proc Soc Antiq Scot*, 126 (1996), 387–454 & fiche

Quekett, J and Cheetham, F H 1968 'The Cathedral: Architectural Description', *in* Page, W (ed), *The Victoria County History of the Counties of England, Durham*. iii, (1968), London, 96–123.

Radford, C A R 1949 'Excavations at Whithorn, First Season, 1949', *TDGNHAS*, 3 ser 27 (1948–9), 85–126.

Radford, C A R 1950 'Castle Loch Island, Mochrum', *TDGNHAS*, 3 ser 28 (1949–50), 41–63.

Radford, C A R 1956 'Excavations at Whithorn: (Final Report)', *TDGNHAS*, 3 ser 34, (1955–6), 131–94.

Radford, C A R 1967 'The early church in Strathclyde and Galloway', *Medieval Archaeology* 11 (1967), 105–26.

Radford, C A R and Donaldson, G 1951 'Post-Reformation Church at Whithorn', *Proc Soc Antiq Scot*, 85 (1950–1), 117–33.

Radford, C A R and Donaldson, G 1953 *Whithorn and Kirkmadrine*. HMSO.

Radford, C A R and Donaldson, G 1984 *Whithorn and the Ecclesiastical Monuments of Wigtown District*. Edinburgh.

Radley, A & Will, R 2001 'Ceramics', *in* Ewart, G 'Dundrennan Abbey: Archaeological investigation within the south range of a Cistercian house in Kirkcudbrightshire (Dumfries & Galloway), Scotland', *Scottish Archaeological Internet Report 1*, 39–41.

Ræder Knudsen, L 2004 'Written Patterns in Early Tablet Weaving', *in* Maik, J (ed) *Priceless Invention of Humanity: Textiles*. Łódź, 121–7.

Ræder Knudsen, L 2005 'Brocaded Tablet-Woven Bands: Same Appearance, Different Weaving Technique, Hørning, Hvilejoj and Mammen', *in* Pritchard, F and Wild, J P (eds), *Northern Archaeological Textiles: NESAT VII*. Oxford, 36–43.

Raine, J (ed) 1870 *Register of Walter de Gray, Lord Archbishop of York*. Surtees Society 1870.

Raine, J (ed) 1873 *Historical papers and letters from the Northern register*. Rerum Britannicarum Medii Aevi Scriptores, London.

Raine, J (ed) 1894 *Historians of the Church of York and Its Archbishops*. London, 1894.

Ramm, H G , 1971 'The Tombs of Archbishops Walter de Gray (1216–55) and Godfrey de Ludham (1258–65) in York Minster, and their Contents', *Archaeologia, Vol CIII*, 101–47.

RCAHMS 1912 *Fourth report and inventory of ancient monuments and constructions in Galloway, i, County of Wigtown*. Edinburgh, 1912.

RCAHMS 1933 *Eleventh report with inventory of monuments and constructions in the counties of Fife, Kinross and Clackmannan*. Edinburgh.

RCAHMS 1974 *Argyll: An Inventory of the Ancient Monuments, vol 2, Lorn*. Edinburgh.

RCAHMS 1982 *Argyll: An Inventory of the Monuments, vol 4, Iona*. Edinburgh.

Registrum Episcopatus Glasguensis – see Bannatyne Club 1843.

Reid, R C (ed) 1960 *Wigtownshire Charters* (Scottish History Society, 1960).

Richards, M P 2000 'Human consumption of plant foods in the British Neolithic: Direct evidence from bone stable isotopes', *in* Fairbairn, A S (ed) *Plants in Neolithic Britain and beyond. Neolithic Studies Group Seminar Papers*. Oxford: Oxbow Books, 123–35.

Richards, M P & Hedges, R E M 2003 'Variations in bone collagen d13C and d15N values of fauna from Northwest Europe over the last 40 000 years', *Palaeogeography Palaeoclimatology Palaeoecology* 193: 261–7.

Richards, M P, Hedges, R E M, Molleson, T I & Vogel, J C 1998 'Stable Isotope Analysis Reveals Variations in Human Diet at the Poundbury Camp Cemetery Site', *Journal of Archaeological Science* 25: 1247–52.

Richards, M P, Mays, S & Fuller, B T 2002 'Stable Carbon and Nitrogen Isotope Values of Bone and Teeth Reflect Weaning Age at the Medieval Wharram Percy Site, Yorkshire, UK', *American Journal of Physical Anthropology* 119: 205–10.

Richardson, J S 1951 *Sweetheart Abbey*. Edinburgh.

Richardson, J S (revised Tabraham C J) 1981 *Dundrennan Abbey*. Edinburgh.

Richardson, J S and Wood, M 1949 *Melrose Abbey*. Edinburgh.

Riley, H T (ed) 1865 *William Rishanger: Chronica et Annales*. London, 1865.

Robert Lindsay of Pitscottie: The Historie and Cronicles of Scotland – see Scottish Text Society (2 vols), 1899.

Roberts, C and Manchester, K 1995 *The Archaeology of Disease*. Alan Sutton Publishing.

Roberts, C and Cox, M 2003 *Health and Disease in Britain; From Prehistory to the Present Day*. Sutton Publishing.

Robertson, J (ed) 1866 *Concilia Scotiae: Ecclesiae Scoticanae Statuta tam Provincialia quam Synodalia quae Supersunt, 1225–1559; Statuta Ecclesiae Scoticanae*. 2 vols. Bannatyne Club, 1866.

Rogers, J C 1857 'Notice of Sculptured Fragments, Formerly in the Episcopal Palace, Glasgow; also Notice of a Sarcophagus Found Within the Choir of the Cathedral Supposed to Have Contained the Remains of Archbishop Dunbar', *Proc Soc Antiq Scot*, 2 (1854–7), 317–29.

Rogers, J and Waldron, A H 1995 *A field guide to joint disease in archaeology*. Wiley.

Rorimer, J J 1972 *Medieval Monuments at the Cloisters, As They Were and As They Are, Metropolitan Museum, New York*.

Rymer, T (ed) 1704–13 *Foedera, Conventiones, Literae, et Cujuscunque Generis Acta Publica, Foedera, Conventiones, Litterae et Cujuscunque Acta Publica*. London A & J Churchill.

Schoeninger, M J & DeNiro, M J 1984 'Nitrogen and carbon isotopic composition of bone collagen from marine and terrestrial animals', *Geochimica et Cosmochimica Acta* 48: 625–39.

Schoeninger, M J, DeNiro, M J & Tauber, H 1983 'Stable Nitrogen Isotope Ratios of Bone Collagen Reflect Marine and Terrestrial Components of Prehistoric Human Diet', *Science* 220: 1381–3.

Schwarcz, H P & Schoeninger, M J 1991 'Stable Isotope Analyses in Human Nutritional Ecology', *Yearbook of Physical Anthropology* 34: 283–321.

Scott, J G 1985 'Finds from the Chapel Site at St Ninian's Point, Isle of Bute', *Trans Buteshire Nat Hist Soc* 22 (1985), 28–31

Scottish Text Society 1899 *Robert Lindsay of Pitscottie: The Historie and Cronicles of Scotland*. 2 vols. 1899.

Sealy, J 2001 'Body Tissue Chemistry and Palaeodiet', *in* Brothwell, D R & Pollard, A S (eds) *Handbook of Archaeological Science*. Chichester: John Wiley & Sons, 269–79.

Sealy, J, Armstrong, R & Schrire, C 1995 'Beyond Lifetime Averages – Tracing Life-Histories Through Isotopic Analysis Of Different Calcified Tissues From Archaeological Human Skeletons'. *Antiquity* 69: 290–300.

Serjeantson, D & Woolgar, C M 2006 `Fish Consumption in Medieval England', *in* Woolgar, C, Serjeantson, D & Waldron, T (eds) *Food in Medieval England: History and Archaeology*. Oxford: Oxford University Press, 102–30.

Shand, P, Darbyshire, D P F, Goody, D C, Darling, W G, Neal, C, Haria, A H & Dixon, A J 2001 'The application of Sr isotopes to catchment studies: The Plynlimon upland catchment of Central Wales', *in* Cidu, R (ed) *Water-Rock Interactions:* 1577–80. Balkema: Villasimius, Italy.

Stallibrass, S 2002 'The possible use of fish and cattle bones as rosary beads', *Finds Research Group* 700–1700 Datasheet 29.

Stones, E L G 1969 'Notes on Glasgow Cathedral: The Burials of Medieval Scottish Bishops with Particular Reference to the Bishops of Glasgow', *Innes Review*, xx (1969), 37–46.

Stones, J A 1989 'The Small Finds' *in* Stones, J A (ed) *Three Scottish Carmelite Friaries: Excavations at Aberdeen, Linlithgow & Perth* 1980–6 (Soc Antiq Scot Monog 6), Edinburgh, 147–65.

Stopford, J 1993 'Modes of Production among Medieval Tilers', *Medi Archaeol* 37, 93–108.

Storey, R L (ed) 1956–70 *The Register of Thomas Langley Bishop of Durham, 1406–37*. 5 vols. Surtees Society, 1956–70.

Stratford, N 1984 'Metalwork', *in Zarnecki, G, Holt, J & Holland, T (eds) English Romanesque Art* 1066–1200. Hayward Gallery, London, 1984, 232–95.

Stroud, G and Kemp, R L 1993 *Cemeteries of the Church and Priory of St Andrew, Fishergate* (=The Archaeology of York, Vol 12 Fasc. 2) CBA.

Stuart, J 1854 'Notice of Remains Found in an Ancient Tomb Recently Opened in the Cathedral Church of Fortrose', *Proc Soc Antiq Scot*, 1 (1851–4), 281–4.

Stuart, J & Burnett, G (eds) 1878 *The Exchequer Rolls of Scotland, i, 1264–1359*. Edinburgh 1878.

Stubbs, W (ed) 1867 *The Chronicle of Benedict of Peterborough*. (Rolls Series, 1867).

Stubbs, W (ed) 1871 *Chronica Rogeri de Hovedon*. (Rolls Series, 1871).

Stuiver, M, Reimer, P J & Braziunas, T F 1998 'High-precision radiocarbon age calibration for terrestrial and marine samples', *Radiocarbon* 40: 1127–51.

Tabraham, C J 1979 'Excavations at Whithorn Priory, Wigtown District, 1972 and 1975', *TDGNHAS*, 3 ser 54, 29–38.

Taburet, E & Dhénin, M 1984 'Le trésor de Colmar', *La revue du Louvre et des musées de France*, XXXIV, 89–101.

Taburet-Delahaye, E 1989 *L'Orfèvrerie gothique – XIIIe – début XVe siècle – au Musée de Cluny*. Paris.

Tait, H 1986 *Seven Thousand Years of Jewellery*. London.

Thomas, C 1971 *The Early Christian Archaeology of North Britain*. Oxford University Press, 1971.

Thomas, C 1992 *Whithorn's Christian Beginnings*. (=1st Whithorn Lecture), Friends of the Whithorn Trust 1992.

Thoms, L M 1982 'Trial Excavation at St Ann's *Lane, Perth', Proc Soc Antiq Scot*, 112, 437–54.

Thomson, J M et al 1882 – 1914 (eds) *Registrum Magni Sigilli Regum Scotorum (Register of the Great Seal)*. Edinburgh.

Tieszen, L L & Fagre, T 1993 'Effect of diet quality and composition on the isotopic composition of respiratory CO2, bone collagen, bioapatite and soft tissues', *in* Lambert, J B & Grupe, G (eds), *Prehistoric Human Bone: Archaeology at the Molecular Level*. Berlin: Springer, 121–55.

Theiner, A (ed) 1864 *Vetera Monumenta Hibernorum et Scotorum Historiam Illustrantia*. Rome

Tomber, R and Dore, J 1998 *The National Roman Fabric Reference Collection A Handbook*. London [= MoLAS Monograph 2].

Toynbee, J C M and Ward-Perkins, J B 1956 *The Shrine of St Peter*. London.

Trickett, M A, Budd, P, Montgomery, J & Evans, J 2003 'An assessment of solubility profiling as a decontamination procedure for the Sr-87/Sr-86 analysis of archaeological human skeletal tissue', *Applied Geochemistry* 18(5): 653–8.

Veitch, K 1999 'The conversion of native religious communities to the Augustinian Rule in twelfth- and thirteenth-century Alba', *Records of the Scottish Church History Society*, xxix (1999), 1–22.

Veizer, J 1989 'Strontium isotopes in seawater through time', *Annual Review of Earth and Planetary Sciences* 17: 141–67.

Wallace, C 2006 'Long-lived Samian?', *Britannia* 37 (2006), 259–72.

Wang, Y & Cerling, T E 1994 'A model of fossil tooth and bone diagenesis: Implications for paleodiet reconstruction from stable isotopes', *Palaeogeography, Palaeoclimatology, Palaeoecology* 107(3–4): 281–9.

Ward-Perkins, J B 1940 *London Museum Medieval Catalogue*. London.

Waterton, E 1863 'On Episcopal Rings', *Archaeological Journal*, XX, 234–5.

Watt, D E R (ed) 1969 *Fasti Ecclesiae Scoticanae Medii Aevii Ad Annum 1638*. Scottish Record Society, 1969.

Watt, D E R 1977 *A Biographical Dictionary of Scottish Graduates to AD 1410*. Oxford, 1977.

Watt, D E R (ed) 1991 *Series Episcoporum Ecclesiae Catholicae Occidentalis, series VI: Britannia, Scotia et Hibernia, Scandinavia*, i, 19–28. Stuttgart, 1991.

Watt, D E R and Shead, N F 2001, *The Heads of Religious Houses in Scotland from Twelfth to Sixteenth Centuries*. (Scottish Record Society, new series, vol 24), Edinburgh.

Watt, D E R and Murray, A L 2003 *Fasti Ecclesiae Scoticanae Medii Aevi Ad Annum 1638*. (Scottish Record Society, new series, vol 25), Edinburgh.

WEA (Workshop of European Anthropologists) 1980 'Recommendations for age and sex diagnoses of skeletons', *Journal of Human Evolution* 9: 517 – 49.

Webster, B (ed) 1982 *Regesta Regum Scotorum, vi, The Acts of David II*. Edinburgh.

Wheeler, R E M 1935 *London and the Saxons*. London Museum Catalogue 6, London.

White, C D, Spence, M W, Stuart-Williams, H L Q & Schwarcz, H P 1998 'Oxygen isotopes and the identification of geographical origins: The Valley of Oaxaca versus the Valley of Mexico', *Journal of Archaeological Science* 25: 643–55.

Whitehead, R 1996 *Buckles 1250–1800*. Chelmsford.

Wigtownshire Charters – see Reid, R C (ed) 1960 (Scottish History Society, 1960).

Wilson, A 2001 'The Novantae and Romanization in Galloway', *TDGNHAS*, 3 ser 75 (2001), 73–131.

Wilson, C 1977 *The Shrines of St William of York*. Yorkshire Museum.

Wood, M 1950 *Dunkeld Cathedral*. Edinburgh.

Woolgar, C 2000 'Take This Penance Now, and Afterwards the Fare will Improve: Seafood and Late Medieval Diet, in Starkey, D J, Reid, C & Ashcroft, N (eds) *England's Sea Fisheries: The Commercial Sea Fisheries of England and Wales since 1300*. London: Chatham, 36–44.

Woolgar, C 2001 'Fast and Feast: Conspicuous Consumption and the Diet of the Nobility in the Fifteenth Century', *in* Hicks, M (ed) *Revolution and Consumption in Late Medieval England*. Woodbridge: Boydell, 7–25.

Woolgar, C 2006 'Group diets in late medieval England', *in* Woolgar, C, Serjeantson, D & Waldron, T (eds) *Food in Medieval England: History and Archaeology*. Oxford: Oxford University Press, 191–200.

Woolgar, C M (ed) 1992–3 *Household Accounts from Medieval England*. Records of Social and Economic History, New Series 17–18. London: British Academy.

Woolgar, C, Serjeantson, D & Waldron, T (eds) 2006 *Food in Medieval England: History and Archaeology*. Oxford: Oxford University Press.

Wormald, F 1971 'The Pastoral Staff', *in* Ramm 1971, 125, pls XLIX–LII.

Wormald, J 1985 *Lords and Men in Scotland: Bonds of Manrent, 1442–1603*. Edinburgh.

Wormald, J 1991 *Mary Queen of Scots: A Study in Failure*. London.

Yeoman, P 1999 *Pilgrimage in Medieval Scotland*. London.

Young, A 1997 *Robert the Bruce's Rivals: The Comyns, 1212–1314*. East Linton, 1997.

Zarnecki, G, Holt, J & Holland, T (eds) 1984 *English Romanesque Art 1066-1200*. Hayward Gallery exhibition catalogue, London.

Index

Chapter extents are shown in **bold** numbers.
Page numbers in *italics* indicate illustrations or maps.
Sub-entries are in aphabetical order.